SUSAN
SONTAG
The Making of an Icon

SUSAN SONTAG
The Making of an Icon

Carl Rollyson *and* Lisa Paddock

W. W. Norton & Company   NEW YORK • LONDON

For information about permission to reproduce selections from this book, write to
Permissions, W. W. Norton & Company, Inc., 500 Fifth Avenue, New York, NY 10110

The text of this book is composed in Bodoni Book with the display set in Shelley Andante
Composition by Gina Webster.
Manufacturing by Courier Companies, Inc.
Book design by Judith Stagnitto Abbate

Library of Congress Cataloging-in-Publication Data
Rollyson, Carl E. (Carl Edmund)
Susan Sontag : the making of an icon / Carl Rollyson and Lisa Paddock.
p. cm.
Includes bibliographical references and index.
ISBN 0-393-04928-0
1. Sontag, Susan, 1933– 2. Women and literature—United States—History—
20th century. 3. United States—Intellectual life—20th century. 4. Authors,
American—20th century—Biography. I. Paddock, Lisa Olson. II. Title.
PS3569.O6547 Z876   2000
818'.5409—dc21
[BBB]   00-020402

W. W. Norton & Company, Inc., 500 Fifth Avenue, New York, N.Y. 10110
www.wwnorton.com

W. W. Norton & Company Ltd., 10 Coptic Street, London WC1A 1PU

1 2 3 4 5 6 7 8 9 0

FOR *Carole Klein*

Marion Meade

Ann Waldron

Sed quid agas? Sic vivitur.
What would you have me do?
This is the way we live now.

—CICERO

Contents

	Introduction	*xi*
1.	My Desert Childhood [1933–1945]	*3*
2.	A World Elsewhere [1945–1948]	*15*
3.	Towards a Better Life [1949–1953]	*25*
4.	The Life and the Project [1952–1957]	*37*
5.	Quest [1957–1958]	*43*
6.	Making It [1959–1961]	*51*
7.	Made [1962–1963]	*63*
8.	Supremacy [1963–1964]	*78*
9.	Fame [1965–1966]	*88*
10.	Peter and Paul [1965–1967]	*105*
11.	Neoradicalism [1967–1969]	*119*
12.	Styles of Radical Will [1969–1971]	*130*
13.	Ms. Sontag [1971–1973]	*146*
14.	Promised Lands [1971–1974]	*158*
15.	Old Complaints Revisited [1975]	*164*
16.	Becoming a Little Posthumous [1975–1978]	*169*

17.   Recovery   [1976–1977]   175

18.   The Salonistes   [1977–1985]   182

19.   I, etcetera   [1979]   202

20.   A Wandering Jew   [1980]   210

21.   Susan the Apostate   [1982]   218

22.   Retrospection   [1982–1983]   228

23.   President Sontag   [1986–1989]   236

24.   Pitching Susan Sontag   [1986–1989]   256

25.   The Way We Live Now   [1986–1995]   264

26.   The Volcano Lover   [1990–1992]   279

27.   Sarajevo   [1993–1995]   287

28.   The End and the Beginning   [1991–1999]   297

       Appendix: A Brief Anthology of
          Quotations [Homage to S.S.]   305

       Notes and Comments   310

       Acknowledgments   344

       Index   347

Illustrations follow page 178.

Introduction

At the end of the twentieth century, Susan Sontag stands as an American—indeed an international—institution. She has appeared as one of 50 Great Living Americans in Marquis's *Who's Who*. She is number 61 on *Life*'s list of "Women Who Shook the World." She has been named a Chevalier in the Order of Arts and Letters in Paris. "Notes on 'Camp'" is ranked number 72 on American Journalism's Top 100 works, compiled by thirty-six judges working under the aegis of New York University's journalism department. She has won a MacArthur "genius" award and the Montblanc de la Culture award for her humanitarian work in Sarajevo. She has been recognized by the Women's National Book Association for having written *Illness as Metaphor*, one of seventy-five books by "women whose words have changed the world." Her books have been translated into twenty-three languages, and few writers who address the subjects of photography, science fiction, disease, or pornography can conduct their arguments without alluding to, quoting, and often taking issue with Susan Sontag. The reference to her in *Gremlins 2* sums up her unique status in American culture.

> The niceties, the fine points, diplomacy, standards, tradition—that's what we're reaching toward. We may stumble along the way but, civilization, yes, the Geneva convention, chamber music, Susan Sontag, yes, civilization.

Sontag's striking looks seem inseparable from her intellectual appeal. Certainly her publisher capitalized early on her aptitude for the dramatic pose, and reviewers described her book jacket photographs even as they discussed her ideas. Sontag has shaped herself into the very image of a writer, but she has repeatedly—often adamantly—refused to discuss how that image has been created by her and her culture. Nevertheless, she is a phenomenon, a kind of keystone of the age. A biography seems, in the end, the best—perhaps the only—way to explore Sontag's appeal. Discussions of her works alone cannot begin to capture this sense of her status as an icon or exemplary figure (the latter is the term she would prefer) or to explain how it developed.

We decided to write this biography partly because of our first encounter with Susan Sontag. We met her at an academic conference in Poland in 1980. We approached her with a proper sense of awe, yet Carl found it remarkably easy to sit next to her at a table and talk for fifteen minutes about contemporary literature. The discussion led to Norman Mailer and his ego, and while Sontag deplored the uses to which he had put it in literature, she admired the quality of his writing and spoke of him as a colleague whose work might have failed on this or that occasion, but who deserved respect. The brief conversation immediately created a sense of intimacy, of resuming a dialogue.

Lisa, meanwhile, remained caught up in a strong physical reaction to Sontag. Nothing she had read about Sontag, no photograph she had seen, prepared her for Sontag's sheer size. Not only is Sontag tall, she is substantial—meeting her was like encountering an Amazon. (Unlike the sleek self often presented in photographs, the real Susan Sontag has hips.) Some female powerhouses are celebrities trailing glamour in their wakes. But Sontag's imposing figure is a bulwark to her towering intellect. In person she is, like a goddess (Athena comes to mind), simply larger than life.

An androgenous figure equally appealing to men and women, Sontag, in fact, personified the "erotics of art" that she called for in her signature essay, "Against Interpretation." We had no idea, then, that we would ever write her biography. And it has come as no surprise that she has not welcomed our effort. Biographies all too often destroy the spell that Sontag believes originated with the first artist's craving for the magical ability to create a world, not merely to imitate one. Biography is a kind of regurgitation that she and many other writers find distasteful.

It seems to us that there are as many theories of biography as there are biographers and biographical subjects. Of course, our subject wants to conceal certain things—although to put it that way is unfair to Susan Sontag. For the issue of secrets, of concealment, does not even arise until the moment one becomes a biographical subject. Any other kind of book, any other kind of article about Susan Sontag can observe, may have to observe, certain limits; the interviewer knows, or is obliged to know, that certain boundaries cannot be transgressed.

This biography breaks those boundaries. Biography is, by our definition, the story of a life—not just a rehearsal of what made Susan Sontag a writer but an analysis of what made her Susan Sontag. Neither her own autobiography, which it seems she will not write, nor a memoir by someone who knows her can do justice to the record of her ambition and achievement. Her name has become synonymous with a set of expectations—most notably of the dream of self-creation, of self-fulfillment, of standing alone, on the cutting edge, articulate, independent, and attractive.

When critics of unauthorized biographies of living figures catalogue the failings of the genre, they do not reflect that virtually every criticism they level is true in some fashion of all biography, which is, by definition, a problematic form. How can biographers ever get inside the minds of their subjects? A distinguished group of writers—Virginia Woolf and Mark Twain, to name just two—have had their doubts about biography. Yet Woolf wrote a biography, and even writers like W. H. Auden and T. S. Eliot, who opposed biographies of themselves, relished reading biographies of others. Susan Sontag is no exception. Although she has recently declared that she has no interest in biography—that is, in biography as a genre—in fact, she once proposed a program on biography to the English Speaking Union, expressing some fascination with how the form functions and how biographers go about their work.

This is a first biography, subject to the perils involved in writing the first narrative of a person's life. To advocates of the complete life, we can only say that some lives, in the aesthetic and historical sense, are complete before the subject stops breathing. Like Marilyn Monroe, Susan Sontag is a platonic figure. The great acting teacher Lee Strasberg once said that "Marilyn Monroe was a dream of Marilyn Monroe." So Susan Sontag as the world now knows her is a dream of Susan Sontag.

Finally, biographers of living figures understand that there is no substitute for the palpable, visceral kind of evidence they can obtain simply by observing their subjects. We have been able to look Sontag directly in the eye, to stand next to her, to experience something of her magnetic aura. We have also been able to interview sources who have already died or who will almost certainly pass away over the next few years. We have recorded the testimony of witnesses who probably will not leave memoirs. Someday others will listen to those voices and draw their own conclusions.

It is characteristic of Sontag to say, "I feel in many ways self-created, self-educated." The evolution of Susan Sontag took decades and surely involved an act of will, but not every act of will successfully engages the machinery of an age. It is in the nature of biography to examine the pistons and the cylinders. Biography is the study of hydraulics; it can only hope to re-create the magic, the art of being Susan Sontag.

SUSAN
SONTAG

The Making of an Icon

My Desert Childhood 1

One of her earliest memories—she is about four—is set in a park. She listens to her Irish nanny talking to another giant in a starched white uniform: "Susan is very high-strung." Susan thinks: "That's an interesting word. Is it true?"

She is "remembering" an event that occurred circa 1937, an event she describes in her *Paris Review* interview of 1995. The park is in New York City, the nanny's name is Rose McNulty, and she is illiterate. It is Susan's impression that Rose does not know what to make of her temperamental charge. Sontag will spend her first five years in New York living with her grandparents and being cared for by relatives.

What Sontag wants to tell us is that she felt alone at a very early age, bored with her environment, and that her inner life—the only one she had control over—became paramount. Already at four, she claims, she was engaging in critical analysis, wondering about that word "high-strung." Sontag has preferred to use the word "restless" to describe her child self, one who felt that "childhood was a terrible waste of time."

Where were her parents? In China most of the time. Jack Rosenblatt had a fur-trading business, the Kung Chen Fur Corporation. When Susan was born, on January 16, 1933, in Woman's Hospital in Manhattan, her parents had a residence at 200 West Eighty-sixth Street. She was their first child. Mildred had been nervous about giving birth overseas, but not long after Susan was safely delivered, Mildred returned to China to be with her husband. Another pregnancy brought her back to Manhattan, where she gave birth to a second daughter, Judith, on February 27, 1936, in New York Hospital. By this time, the family had a home in Great Neck, Long Island.

Susan's parents had money, they were young, and they were very much involved in their business. Jack was only twenty-eight, and his wife Mildred, née Jacobson, only twenty-six, when Susan was born. On the company's books Mildred is listed as president-treasurer. Jack, or Jasky (as he was named on his birth certificate), had come a long way from 721 East Sixth Street in lower Manhattan, where his father, Samuel, and his mother, Gussie, née Kessler, both Jews from Austria, had begun a fur business and raised five children, two daughters and three sons. Mildred's family, Jews from Russian-occupied Poland, were also involved in the clothing trades. Her father, Isaac, a tailor, and his wife, Dora, née Glasskovitz, raised seven children. Mildred, born at home (139 Cook Street), was the second-youngest child and the only girl. She and Jack met at Grossinger's, a resort in the Catskills where Mildred had a waitressing job.

On October 19, 1938, just before midnight, Jack Rosenblatt died of pulmonary tuberculosis in the German American Hospital in Tientsin, China. He was not quite thirty-five. Mildred, staying at the Astor House Hotel in Tientsin, telegraphed his father and brother Aaron the next day, and she made arrangements to begin the journey back to New York a week later.

Sontag remembers that her mother waited several months to tell her that her father had died, and then was brief, saying only that he had died of pneumonia.

Then five-year-old Susan experienced her first asthma attack. Asthma is an alarming disease for anyone but is especially frightening in children. Coughing attacks usually occur at night, between the early hours of two and six; the child gasps for air and sometimes regurgitates a sticky mucus.

In 1939 Mildred decided to remove her small family from New York in search of a better climate for Susan, and a doctor recommended Miami. Recalling her family's brief residence in that city for an interviewer, Sontag presented brief vignettes: a house with coconut palms. She is in the front yard with a hammer and screwdriver trying to open the tropical fruit. An obese black cook takes her to a park and Susan notices a bench marked "For Whites Only." She turns to the cook and says, "We'll go sit over there and you can sit on my lap." It all seemed so nineteenth-century, Sontag told the interviewer. The city's humidity only made Susan's asthma worse, and after a few months the family left Miami.

Mildred was only thirty-one when she moved her family to Tucson. In interviews, Susan portrays Mildred as a vain, self-absorbed woman who did not know how to act like a mother, who worried instead about growing old and losing her looks. Mildred told Susan not to call her "Mother" in public because she did not want anyone to know she was old enough to have a child. Susan, puzzled, wondered what her mother did with her time, for even after Jack Rosenblatt's death Mildred would be absent from home for long periods, "parking" Susan and Judith with relatives.

It is likely that Mildred was depressed throughout Susan's earliest years. The massive change in lifestyle that accompanies mothering had to be especially hard on the peripatetic Mildred. Not only had she lost a husband, she had lost the income from their business, her employment, independence, and status—all of which were replaced by the insatiable demands of young children. Alcohol provided temporary relief, a cushion, perhaps even an elevation of feeling, although the image Sontag presents is of a phlegmatic mother, too drowsy or listless to read or comment on her child's all-A report cards. It is a familiar scene, repeated in the lives of many writers who begin writing as children, like the writer Anne Rice, moping at her alcoholic mother's bedside.

Sontag has said little about her upbringing in Tucson, although she remembers that as a young child she walked along the old Spanish Trail toward the Tanque Verde foothills, where she examined the "fiercest saguaros and prickly pears." She searched for arrowheads and snakes and pocketed pretty rocks. She imagined herself the last Indian, a lone ranger. Tucson in the late 1930s occupied nine square miles of broad desert valley, with rolling foothills, unusual colors, and stunning mountains with jagged peaks. The desert is no endless sea of sand dunes. There are thorny bushes and weeds, spiny saguaros, and other trees with bright red fruits and flaming orange, spiky flower buds. When it rains, the desert blooms, the sky spreads wide with double rainbows, and the landscape looks freshly scrubbed. The British writer J. B. Priestley, visiting Arizona in 1937, just two years before Mildred and Susan arrived, never forgot its haunting beauty: "Voices, faces, blue birds and scarlet birds, cactus and pine, mountains dissolving in the morning mirage or glowing like jewels in the sunset, the sweet clear air, the blaze of stars at midnight."

In 1939 these desert delights were close to home. The city had a population of less than forty thousand, although it was rapidly growing as a tourist and military site. It had only two radio stations. Walking down a street, residents heard the same radio programs coming from open windows in almost every house. There were five motion picture theaters, and a few combination book and stationery stores. There was a symphony orchestra, a little theater, music and art programs at the university, a state museum, and a Carnegie library. The pace was leisurely. The city attracted outdoor types and health seekers, with about thirty hospitals and sanitariums catering to sufferers of various respiratory illnesses. Susan's asthma improved in Tucson. She grew into a sturdily built, surprisingly sociable girl.

In September 1939 the school year began with a cloud of dust, and in this haze Susan started the first grade. In retrospect, it seemed a joke: "I was put in 1A on Monday when I was 6 years old. Then 1B on Tuesday. 2A on Wednesday. 2B on Thursday, and by the end of the week they had skipped me to third grade because I could do the work." There were no classes for gifted children then. Susan studied the same subjects as everyone else: writing, spelling, reading, music, art, arithmetic, social studies, health and physical education, and elementary science. Classmates accepted her. "I was born into a culturally democratic situation. It didn't occur to me that I could influence the way these kids were," Sontag later realized. She could always find common ground, saying things like "Gosh, your hair looks great today," or "Gee, those are nice loafers."

Even at the age of six, however, Susan felt a need to dramatize her sense of separation from the other students, telling them that she had been born in China. She wanted to make an impression and to establish her connection with faraway places, and China seemed, she later remarked, "as far as anyone can go."

Already, at seven, Sontag had established a lifelong habit of reading through an author's body of work. To begin with, there was Alfred Payson Terhune: *Caleb Conover, Railroader* (1907), *A Dog Named Chips* (1931),

The Critter and Other Dogs (1936). Perhaps his most famous series focuses on Lad and his exploits in rural New Jersey. Terhune's themes touch on right and wrong and the abuse of authority, as in *Further Adventures of Lad* (1922), in which an ignorant, overbearing sheriff threatens to shoot Lad, whose adventures usually involve redressing injustice. Anger at the unfairness and insensitivity of the adult world has often stimulated young writers and readers, and it is what drew nine-year-old Susan to more substantial novels such as Victor Hugo's *Les Misérables,* which she read in her mother's six-volume set. The chapter in which Fantine sells her hair made the young Susan a socialist, she would later declare.

Even more important, however, was Susan's discovery of the travel writer Richard Halliburton. One only needs to look at his frontispiece photographs to understand why: in *The Royal Road to Romance* (1925), he stands in front of the Taj Mahal, turbaned, arms akimbo, his legs at ease, and a broad smile on his face; in *The Flying Carpet* (1932) he sits atop his two-seater plane, poised for adventure; in *Richard Halliburton's Complete Book of Marvels* (1937), a photograph of the handsome, thirty-ish-looking author is set next to a letter to the reader explaining how as a boy his favorite book was filled with pictures of the "world's most wonderful cities and mountains and temples." He loved that book because it carried him away to "strange and romantic lands."

Asked what books had changed her life, Sontag later gave Halliburton pride of first place. He showed her how "privileged" a writer's life could be, full of "endless curiosity and energy and expressiveness, and countless enthusiasms." Halliburton described climbing Etna and Popocatépetl and Fujiyama and Olympus. He descended the Grand Canyon and crossed the Golden Gate Bridge when it was still under construction. He visited Lenin's tomb in Moscow and the Great Wall of China. "Halliburton made me lustfully aware that the world was very big and very old; that its seeable wonders and its learnable stories were innumerable; and that I might see these wonders myself and learn the stories attached to them," Sontag recalled.

This remembrance evokes something of the excitement Susan felt as a seven-year-old, realizing how much larger the world was than Tucson—and how small-minded it was of her playmates, teachers, and other adults not to yearn for that larger world. Why were adults so cautious? Susan wondered. "When I grow up I've got to be careful that they don't stop me from flying through open doors," she thought.

Reading made much of the life around Susan shrink in size. She read about the war and about modern life. She had no place in her imagination for, say, Tucson's Pima Indians: "The folklore of the Southwest was static; picturesque even to the people who lived there," she later said.

> If you were a small kid discovering George Eliot or Thackeray or Balzac or the great Russian novels, little Indian dolls with turquoise beads sure couldn't hold a candle to the nineteenth century novel—as far as being an experience which could blast you out of your narrow framework. If you're looking for something to take you somewhere, to expand your consciousness it's going to be a great world culture.

In her love of Halliburton, Sontag speaks as an enthusiast who sees a world of marvels. She longed for just that kind of companionable parent-writer—but instead, Mildred told her articulate daughter: "In China, children don't talk." Mildred might, in the right mood, reminisce, telling Susan that in China "burping at the table is a polite way of showing appreciation," but that did not mean Susan had permission to burp.

So much of Susan's early life seemed fragmented. In those early years in Tucson, before Susan reached the age of ten, Mildred moved her family several times and Susan attended several schools. What had gone before quickly disappeared.

In 1943 Mildred moved her two daughters to a neat, compact four-room stucco bungalow at 2409 East Drachman, then a dirt road. Sontag implies that her mother, pressed for money, had auctioned off many of her Chinese mementos. The house still stands, on one edge of the University of Arizona, looking exactly the same as it does in the photograph taken of it in 1943, when it was brand-new—except that now the road is paved. Susan, her sister, and her mother were its first occupants. How Mildred managed to afford the rent, support herself and her family, and pay for household help is not clear. Perhaps there was still money left from Jack Rosenblatt's business. Sontag has said her mother taught. There is no record of Mildred teaching in the Tucson public schools, though she may have been employed in one of the city's numerous private institutions.

In her backyard, Susan dug a hole with the suspiciously exact dimensions of six feet by six feet by six feet. "What are you trying to do," a maid asked, "dig all the way to China?" No, Susan replied, she only wanted "a place to sit in." She laid eight-foot-long planks over the backyard hole to keep out the intense sun. The landlord complained, saying it posed a hazard for anyone walking across the yard. Susan showed him the boards, and the entrance that she could just barely squeeze through. Inside she had dug a niche for a candle, but it was too dark to read, and she got a mouthful of dirt that came in through the cracks in her makeshift ceiling. The landlord told Mildred the hole had to be filled in within twenty-four hours, and Susan complied with the help of the maid. Three months later she dug another hole in the same spot. Taking her cue from Tom Sawyer, who got the neighborhood kids to do a chore for him—whitewash a fence—she conned three playmates into helping her, promising they could use the hole whenever she was not there.

Susan's hole was her hiding place, her miniature world. Her crude dugout also marked the border between "the scary and the safe," as she later put it in an article about grottoes. Her cave was the equivalent of the world elsewhere, of the China where her father had died. All Susan had of her father was a ring with JR on the signet, a white silk scarf with his initials embroidered in black silk, and a pigskin wallet with Jack Rosenblatt stamped in small gold letters. His record, in short, remained unwritten, an "unfinished pain" in her imagination. For this kind of pain, extroverted writers like Halliburton had no cure.

Fortunately, Sontag found her first literary father early on, before her tenth year. Sontag discovered Edgar Allan Poe. Like Halliburton, Poe conjured up a world of marvels. He wrote detective stories, hoaxes about trips to the moon and about other fantastic voyages of exploration—like *The Narrative of Arthur Gordon Pym*. But Poe also gave Susan her "first vision of inwardness, of melancholy, of obsessiveness, of the thrill of ratiocination, of morbidity, of a recklessly self-conscious temperament—another span of nascent avidities." Poe's writing is both adventurous and intellectual; his narrators are self-conscious and enclosed in their own worlds. Like the adult Sontag, his characters are devotees, metaphorically speaking, of grottoes—those caverns of the mind. As the narrator of "Berenice" confesses, "My passions *always* were of the mind."

Poe, like Sontag, is an American writer who sought his inspiration in Europe and in literature itself, and like her, he was obsessed with wasting diseases and death. It is not easy to catch your breath in Poe's Gothic tales, for the sense of doom is as unrelenting as his alliteration. "During the whole of a dull, dark, and soundless day in the autumn of the year . . ."—these sonorous, mesmerizing words in "The Fall of the House of Usher" are a literary narcotic. Poe's fiction confirmed what the therapeutic climate of Tucson tried to deny: the inescapable fact of mortality. If that seems like a morbid discovery, it was also a godsend to a child who sensed what those around her were denying.

If Richard Halliburton spoke to the extroverted pleasure of roaming the world and taking from it what you liked, Poe did the same for the introvert, demonstrating that literature could be a vehicle of transportation to other worlds, and—even better—that literature could be a destination in itself. He taught her to rely on her own sensibility, excluding whatever nonliterary environment she encountered.

What neither Poe nor Halliburton could give Sontag, though, was a sense of career—an important concept for a child who thought of herself as on her own and who had come to regard herself as her own authority, a common enough feeling in children who suffer from what has been variously called "father-thirst" and "father-hunger." She found her sense of mission in two books that have electrified many generations of young girls: *Madame Curie: A Biography* and *Little Women*.

By the age of ten, Susan had read Eve Curie's moving book about her mother. The first sentence of the biography's introduction is captivating: "The life of Marie Curie contains prodigies in such number that one would like to tell her story like a legend." Here is the complete Curie paradigm related in Eve's ecstatic version, a version that provides nearly a perfect blueprint for the arc of Sontag's life to come: Marie spends many years of poverty and solitude in the backwater of Poland. She is fired with a desire to "adore something very high and very great." Eve asks: "How is one to imagine the fervor of this girl of seventeen?" Marie becomes involved in Polish nationalism and socialism, desiring to free her country from Russian occupation and to build a better, a more just society. She aspires to an education in France, the seat of learning and liberty. She writes to her sister, "I dreamed of Paris as of redemption." When Marie's opportunity comes, Eve observes: "How young one felt in Paris, how powerful, trembling, and swelling with hope!" In Paris, Marie studied to a state of near exhaustion, living in spartan quarters, guided by her "will of iron." She attracts the attention of a great scientist, Pierre Curie. Like a novelist, Marie searches for new subjects of research. Together Marie and Pierre give birth to a "new science and a new philosophy." They become joint authors, embodying the "superior alliance of man and woman, the exchange was equal." They have children, and Marie is nearly as passionate about motherhood as she is about science. Her husband dies, and Marie dedicates herself to a "kind of perpetual giving," nursing the wounded in World War I and opening herself up to people around the world. She is excited by the world's mysteries and marvels that she must plumb. Above all, Marie has a sense of destiny. As Eve observes: "We must believe we are gifted for something, and that this thing, at whatever cost, must be attained." She persisted with a "superhuman obstinacy." As Marie matured, she saw the need for an international culture and relied upon her "innate refusal of all vulgarity."

Curie's is a noble story as well, because Marie would, in her daughter's words, treat her honors with "indifference," with an "immovable structure of a character" and the "stubborn effort of an intelligence." Eve quotes Einstein's remark that "Marie Curie is, of all celebrated beings, the only one whom fame has not corrupted."

It is not just that Sontag wanted to be like Marie Curie, or that she built a backyard chemistry laboratory, or that she decided she would try to combine careers as a writer and doctor like Chekhov. Imagining herself finding cures, discovering a new element like radium that would be used to treat diseases, was no stretch for Susan. More important is Eve's evocation of a selfless career—so selfless that Marie did not look upon it as a career but as a vocation. This Marie Curie resembled a mythic goddess, a figure of such austere purity that she seemed invulnerable, "intact, natural and very nearly unaware of her astounding destiny."

Susan strove to emulate the ideal Curie, the scientist who painstakingly stood over hot, heavy cauldrons refining ore and making her Nobel Prize–winning breakthrough. When Sontag later spoke of her writing, it would be in terms of agonizing labor, a concentration only on the work itself—not on the honors that might accrue, not on the machinery of self-promotion which she could have patented—and she reacted with hostility to any vulgar suggestion of careerism.

Susan would not entirely give up the idea of a medical/scientific career until she began college, but the idea of creating literature already beckoned to her. "What I really wanted was every kind of life, and the writer's life seemed the most inclusive," she later said. The writer is free to invent and reinvent herself in a way the scientist or doctor cannot.

Susan fell in love not just with reading and writing but with the idea, the *role* of the writer. It was part of her self-consciousness project not merely to write but to be *seen* as a writer: "I *did* think of being published. In fact, I really thought that that's what being a writer was." The impulse to write was an act of emulation and homage to the great writers she had read: "People usually say they want to become a writer to express themselves or because they have something to say. For me it was a way of being. It was like enlisting in an army of saints. . . . I didn't think I was expressing myself. I felt that I was becoming something, taking part in a noble activity."

Where would a ten-year-old girl come upon the idea of a publishing world? From two novels: *Little Women* and *Martin Eden*. She identified with Louisa May Alcott's budding writer, Jo, although Sontag is quick to add that she did not want to write anything like Jo's sentimental, melodramatic stories. Rather, it is Jo's avidity that captures Susan: "I want to do something splendid . . . something heroic or wonderful that won't be forgotten after I'm dead. I don't know what. I'm on the watch for it. I mean to astonish you all some day." Significantly, Jo's sense of greatness is connected to Europe: "Don't I wish I'd been there!" Jo cries. "Have you been to Paris?" Jo rejects Laurie, her childhood companion, for Professor Bhaer, an older European who welcomes her writing rather than seeing it as an eccentric tic. Susan surely spotted Jo's alienation from her family and community—in spite of all the talk of family togetherness. Sontag probably saw the David Selznick production of *Little Women*, in which Katharine Hepburn glamorized Jo's role. To be Jo, to be a writer, was to be a star.

There is more to *Little Women* than adolescent fantasies of becoming a writer. Jo becomes confused when she begins changing her stories to suit her family. The futility of trying to please and of expecting a consensus among readers is pointed up by reviewers' contradictory reactions to Jo's work. When Jo prostitutes her talent to produce a cheap magazine piece, her father scolds her: "You can do better than this. Aim for the highest and never mind the money." Indeed, Alcott could have been writing for all budding artists, demonstrating how the writer must find her own voice and integrity.

Even more directly, Jack London's *Martin Eden* presents a fable of the writer's life, a naturalist's grim yet exhilarating study of individual aspiration that appealed to Sontag's somber but determined sensibility. Eden forges his own identity largely through his reading of books, which are treated almost literally as the building blocks of his personality. They have a tangible, tactile, erotic appeal for him. He does not merely handle books; he caresses them.

Like Martin Eden, Susan wanted her writing to make some kind of impression on the world, no matter how indifferent that world seems to be. London's novel is still valuable as a kind of handbook for the free-lance writer; it contains pages and pages describing Martin's feverish efforts to publish, constantly sending out manuscripts in self-addressed envelopes and constantly receiving rejections, and then sending out the stories and articles over and over again until something is accepted. The ratio of rejections to acceptances is daunting: for every piece that is accepted, dozens and dozens are rejected. Yet Martin persists.

What Martin cannot control, of course, is the means of production. Sontag tried to solve this problem at the age of nine or ten, as she later told students at the University of South Carolina, by starting her own four-page monthly newspaper, produced on a hectograph:

> The cheapest way of reproducing anything: you need a stencil, a tray, and gelatin. You just put the stencil face down on the gelatin, after putting the ink on the stencil. You can then put about 20 pieces of paper onto the gelatin. It reproduces the stencil. It's wonderful to use in closets. At 10 I made a literary magazine of my own and sold it to neighbors for 5 cents.

Sontag smiled telling this story, recalling how this act of publishing emancipated her. She wrote poems, stories, and at least two plays, one inspired by Karel Čapek's *R.U.R.*, and another by Edna St. Vincent Millay's *Aria da Capo*. Throughout the war she wrote articles on battles such as Midway and Stalingrad, condensing what she read in the newspapers.

By the age of twelve, she was simply biding her time, serving out what she calls in her essay-memoir "Pilgrimage" the "prison sentence" of her childhood. It was an ordeal, but she was a good actress, a good dissembler.

Then a disturbing event intruded into Susan's world. Her mother remarried. Mildred, still morose, but also still beautiful, had attracted a new mate. Susan quietly rejected him. But he did provide a new name that fit her emerging identity as a writer; and he brought with him the prospect of travel—away from the desert of her childhood and into the land of dreams: California.

A World Elsewhere 2

1945–1948

> There is a world elsewhere.
> —*CORIOLANUS*, Act III, Scene iii

In 1945 Captain Nathan Sontag, on a "kind of furlough" in Tucson, moved into the little stucco bungalow on Drachman Avenue occupied by Mildred Rosenblatt and her two daughters. Nat Sontag was a war hero replete with military medals, an Air Force ace shot down five days after D day. Wounded by shrapnel, he had been hospitalized for a year and then sent to Tucson to convalesce. Even better, Nat was handsome and cheerful. The marriage would endure. None of this meant much to Susan.

Nat tried to parent Susan by giving well-meant advice: "Don't be too smart: you'll never get married." Susan had just turned thirteen, and she burst out laughing. "I don't want to marry anybody who wouldn't like somebody like me," she answered. Susan was not so much offended as she was amused, thinking, "This idiot doesn't know there are intelligent men out in the world. He thinks they're all like him." But what he said did not matter: "I was impervious. I was on the moon," she later commented.

Nat was not overbearing. He could see that Susan, in a class of her own, might have to lead a solitary life. He would become very proud of her fame as a writer. Susan was grateful that both parents "treated me as if my life was my own affair."

Aside from her incipient literary ambitions, Sontag was reacting to a postwar society that urged conformity, a dulling group-think that she heard in the "jovial claptrap of my classmates and teachers, the maddening bromides I heard at home." She hated the weekly radio shows with laugh tracks, the stupid sentimental songs on the hit parade, and the raucous announcers of prizefights and baseball games that invaded her home on weeknights and weekends. She gritted her teeth and twisted her hair but kept her opinions to herself.

The Sontags moved to California in 1946, settling into a pert little home, a "cozy shuttered cottage with rosebush hedges and three birch trees," perched at the approach to the San Fernando Valley. Nat Sontag, with the crisp efficiency of his military training, commandeered the patio barbecue, adopting the Southern California style in which increasingly elaborate barbecues became a monument to postwar prosperity.

Susan lived in California from 1946 to 1949. One of her first discoveries was a "real bookstore," the Pickwick, which she had "tracked down" on Hollywood Boulevard. At thirteen, she had "outgrown" periodicals like the *Saturday Review* and turned to the "fancy prose and convoluted arguments of *Partisan Review*." She read every issue, cover to cover, and "dreamed of going to New York City and writing for them."

At home, Susan had a room of her own. After being sent to bed and told to turn off the light, she would read by flashlight, choosing from her extensive library of comics, *Compton's Encyclopedia*, the Bobbsey Twins, biographies, Halliburton, and various Victorian classics. She hoarded books; she did not go to libraries. Books were her "household deities. [Her] spaceships." Susan had a fierce desire to possess literature and to be possessed by it. Her fervent memories of this period, and the sense of isolation, seem stifling. Her passion for collecting literature even evolved into criminal activity when she occasionally stole the books she could not afford to purchase with her meager allowance.

Susan wrote stories and journals, and stood and conducted the music she had collected on 78 r.p.m. records. Her high school classmate Mel Roseman remembers spending many hours at her house listening to her favorite phonograph records, especially the Mozart String Quartet in D Minor.

At the age of thirteen Susan also discovered the French writer André Gide. His journals had been published in English in 1947, although Susan may have read some Gide in French. The image of a twenty-one-year-old Gide writing his journal is compelling: "I had always felt vaguely that I communicated my zeal to others, but that they lacked the divine spark," he wrote in 1890. Or:

> *I must learn to keep silent.* . . . I must learn to take myself seriously. . . . To have more mobile eyes and a less mobile face. To keep a straight face when I make a joke. Not to applaud every joke made by others. Not to show the same colorless geniality toward everyone. To disconcert at the right moment by keeping a poker face.

One of Susan's North Hollywood High School classmates remarked: "She was so focused—even austere, if you can call a fifteen-year-old austere. Susan—no one ever called her Susie—was never frivolous. She had no time for small talk." Sontag's high school pictures give little away; she does not mimic Southern California friendliness when she poses; her face is placid, immobile, her eyes alert.

Gide was a voracious reader, the product of a "solitary and sullen childhood," high-strung and temperamental: "I am like a well-tuned harp, which sings, according to the poet's whim, a gay scherzo or a melancholy andante." He surrounded himself with a library of books, constantly picking them up and reading several of them at once. Reading and arranging these books was a sensuous, a voluptuous experience. His doctrine: "The world of art is an equilibrium outside of time, an artificial health." He was attracted to characters dominated by their fate, by Orestes, "born under the sign of Saturn." In Gide as in Sontag, journal-keeping (one keeps, one does not merely write, a journal) confirms one's sense of destiny. His devotion to theater, art, politics, and music made him the complete intellectual and artist.

Susan Sontag recalled that her main project at fourteen was to protect herself from the drivel of contemporary society threatening to drown her. She looked for friends who might share her dedication to what Gide called the cult of art.

No one quite met Susan's austere standards, but there were two boys, Peter and Merrill, who shared some of her aesthetic passions and who were loners. Peter was a refugee, part Hungarian and part French, and

Susan discovered that they could swap anecdotes about their glamorous-
ly dead fathers when they were not "rolling about, embracing, in the
weeds." They bicycled and went to movies and argued about politics—
particularly about the Henry Wallace third-party campaign for the presidency. Peter had the virtue of being tall, a prerequisite for Susan, who
towered over most boys. She needed to look up to her romantic objects.

Susan's other partner, Merrill, was blond, cute, and, in the parlance
of the day, "a dreamboat." She doted on him and "wanted to merge with
him or for him to merge with me." Alas, he was shorter than she, and the
passion was intellectual.

It was Merrill's idea to visit Thomas Mann. It is difficult to exagger-
ate Mann's stature in America during and immediately after the war. A
Nobel Prize winner, a prominent opponent of fascism, a man of regal and
austere bearing, he had been received at the White House and lionized
in the press. He spoke of literature and politics like an exiled head of
state. When Mann, a private citizen, flew from Los Angeles to San
Francisco, he was met by a squad of motorcycle police who escorted him
to his speaking engagement at Berkeley. Not just for Sontag but for millions of readers, *The Magic Mountain* was a "transforming book, a source
of discoveries and recognitions." This novel in which all the characters
are exiles—as Sontag perceived herself to be—and are wasting away
was like the "exotic elsewhere" that had claimed her father's life. *The
Magic Mountain* liberated her, Sontag implies, from her mother's inti-
mation that tuberculosis was a "shameful disease." In *The Magic
Mountain*, "ideas are passions," Sontag has said, finding a warrant for
her own essayistic novelizing that would bloom in *The Volcano Lover*.

Sontag, a recovered "asthma-disabled child," a "half-orphan," identified with Mann's "orphaned protagonist," Hans Castorp, a "hero after
my own unprotected heart." If she was not "simple" or "mediocre" like
Hans, she shared his overearnest and docile demeanor (her mother had
once called her "Goody Two-shoes"). Both know how to live politely with
others while carrying their solitude with them, and both are watched over
by guardians who believe they know what is good for them. But what
made *The Magic Mountain* most appealing was the kind of "free, passionate conversations" that were hard to come by in Southern California.

Literature was Susan's world elsewhere: "Wherever he [Mann] was,
it was where-I-was-not. Europe." This was not the world in which her
mother collected Early American furniture and enjoyed the Southern

California sunshine. One day Merrill phoned Susan to say that he had arranged a meeting with Thomas Mann. Susan thought the very act of contacting Mann an impertinence, and she cross-examined Merrill about how the Manns had reacted to his call. The exuberant Merrill declared there had been no problem at all. Mann's number had been in the telephone book. But Susan told no one about her appointment and dreaded its outcome.

The idea of meeting Mann was distressing. That her grand notion of literature should sink to the level of a meeting between two high school kids who had yet to achieve anything of note and this olympian writer humiliated her. She did not want this kind of commerce between life and art—many readers of literature do not want it. Such encounters spoil an ideal, spoil the purity of reading. It is vulgar. It reveals a low taste for biography: to some, an act of revenge on the bookish.

Mann did indeed look like a grand old man of letters. To Susan, he resembled his posed photographs (unposed photographs in Mann biographies show him smiling, almost like a regular guy). He was very grave and spoke more slowly than anyone Sontag had ever heard. The conversation was halting, though Merrill and Susan did get the opportunity to convey their enthusiasm for Mann's work. Susan worried that he would ask her about books of his that she had not read. He did not. He was courteous and correct and boring. He talked like a book review, Sontag remembers. She was more interested in his library than in him. When he turned the conversation to what they were studying, Susan could hardly bear it. What could this lofty, august man know about her dreadful high school education: driver's education classes, teachers who assigned *Reader's Digest,* condoms that littered the school lawn, the Chicano kid who sold marijuana at recess, and the classmate who stuck up gas stations?

North Hollywood High School had a handsome arcade and courtyard that gave the school a college-campus-like feel. When Susan entered in 1947, it had over two thousand students. Susan was editor of the school newspaper, *The Arcade,* for a year and was "commissioner of publications." She wrote editorials about politics and school life and reviewed movies. She argued for a bipartisan foreign policy, a dedication to the potential of the new United Nations, an institution that would avoid the "extremes of aggression and appeasement." She excoriated the mentality of those who argued, "Let's drop a bomb on them before they drop one on us." She deplored the anti-Communist hysteria that branded every dissenter a Communist. She had a good sense of her audience, recommending Olivier's *Hamlet:* "If any of you have any ideas that it is boring or academic, you'll probably change your mind. . . . There is enough melodrama and action in this picture to fill a hundred Hollywood creations." She also liked *Red River,* "a glamorized western . . . featuring [Montgomery] Clift and ten thousand head of cattle." She published one enigmatic poem, evocative of her solitary sensibility: "gazing into quietness . . . / Re-charging the breath with which I sigh the air."

But there is nothing of the aesthete or the saturnine about her other contributions. They are sober, sincere, and civic-minded. Joan Kurland, Sontag's coeditor on *The Arcade,* remembers collaborating with her on an editorial about the need for a traffic light near the school which got the attention of local authorities, who acceded to the editorial's recommendations. Robert Low remembers how after first period Susan would enter his classroom for long, intense conferences with her mentor, Miss Seda Garapedian, twenty-five, an advisor to the school newspaper. Susan and Miss Garapedian seemed to lose track of time and continue their talk into second period—to the delight of Low and some of his classmates, who did not mind at all that their English class would begin late. Editor Sue credited Garapedian in her valedictory: "Pink petunias to Miss Garapedian, our peachy-keen teacher, who has borne the brunt of our collective carelessness and fiendish senses-of-humor."

Susan was well enough known to win an election (she was one of three candidates) for the post of commissioner, which also gave her a seat on the student council. Van Hirst nominated her, noting that she had all A's in her academic subjects and had done an excellent job as an *Arcade* reporter: "She is willing to work hard for your interests and I believe Sue Sontag is the most capable person for the job." She was almost always referred to as Sue Sontag, which is also how she signed her articles.

Sue Sontag made no waves. Art Sol, president of the council during her tenure, does not remember her. Other students have a vague recollection of a very pleasant, if not terribly forthcoming, fellow student. But those who did remember her, remember her well. "She was my first, albeit unrequited, love," Mel Roseman recalled. Roseman, a senior at North Hollywood High when he knew Sontag, had no idea that she was younger than he; she seemed so mature. Fred Margolin (who has never read a word of Susan Sontag's writings beyond her contributions to the high school newspaper) remembers a "good-looking" Sontag as one of the few Jewish girls in the school and someone who was "always her own person, never one of the crowd." She used to meet with Margolin, Mel Roseman, and a few other students, including a girl Margolin remembers as an outspoken Communist. "For whatever reason," Margolin says, "my memories of Susan are crystal clear. When Susan smiled, she lit up a room." He remembers that, weather permitting, she always wore a raincoat. "She would stride, she wouldn't walk. She did not need to be around people. She was very sure of herself." She did not flirt, she did not have boyfriends, she did not go out on dates. She maintained, in Margolin's words, a "masculine kind of independence." Asked if he met anyone else in Sontag's family, Margolin said no, it was "enough to know Sue."

A violinist in the school orchestra and a participant in a world friendship society and the Harlequin Club, Sontag at fifteen was already an accomplished public speaker. She delivered a speech about Abraham Lincoln and joined in a debate on the need for a third party. She represented the school in the semifinals of the World Friendship Oratorical Contest, addressing the theme "Who is my neighbor?" For all her brilliance, students did not treat her as eccentric. Most of them hardly noticed her at all. Did she seem arrogant? No one remembers a Susan Sontag who was in the slightest way offensive, except for physical education instructor Jane Sullivan. She recalled a "supercilious" Susan, who spent most of her time avoiding exercise.

Kurland, Low, and others remember a vibrant, largely young faculty in a progressive school. Students had extraordinary freedom to pursue their course of study and pick their teachers. They remember the lack of prejudice—testified to by one Mexican-American student at a recent class reunion.

Mel Roseman, however, recalled a "world for teenagers in the 1940s entirely remote from today's world," one that encouraged solitude:

> There was no teen culture. Each of us lived in his/her private hell. We talked about many things that moved us deeply; we talked about many of our concerns and fears and hopes; but we didn't talk about our relationships with our families. Those, along with sex, were entirely private matters which we'd never have considered discussing even with our most intimate friends. Those topics were simply taboo, often even from our own thoughts. Perhaps that's why we

were so passionate about the books we were reading and the music we were listening to.

Occasionally a teacher broke into this private world. For Roseman and Sontag, that teacher was Sophia Leshing. Susan took Leshing's English class, and Leshing invited Susan to her home. Years later Leshing introduced herself to Sontag at a book signing. "I can't tell you what she had meant to me," Sontag reminisced. "We talked a long while and we both cried. I can still remember her living room. There was a Paul Klee reproduction over the fireplace."

Frances Garner, a popular teacher of English and French, drama coach, and well-traveled, sophisticated reader of avant-garde literature, was another important intellectual mentor, one who became a "second mother to Susan. She and Susan just clicked," says daughter Joan Garner Taylor. "I heard about this after I was at UCLA. My mother just raved about her. They spent a lot of time together." Susan visited the Garner home, finding a welcoming older woman attracted to the "offbeat." Frances Garner told her daughter about a Sontag who was a sort of rebel who did not have many friends, a girl who did not sit in class with hands folded following assignments mechanically. The usually guarded Sontag opened up, and Mrs. Garner learned that she had problems with her mother and was not close to her family. Mrs. Garner had no doubt that Susan Sontag would be a great success. "They corresponded when Susan was in Chicago," recalls Joan Garner Taylor. "My mother had graduated from the University of Chicago, and that was a tie between them."

Sue did not look anything like her other classmates. She was not childishly cute or conventionally pretty. No, she was "marvelously handsome: intensely dark and solemn, her eyes filled with exceptional intelligence, her thick black hair shorter and curlier than it is today, and her delicately shaped lips always poised to let loose a spectacular flood of articulate ideas that both fascinated and infuriated me," remembers writer Jamake Highwater, who was two grades behind Sontag. Sue's eyes showed enormous empathy, a trait he found missing in his tense but fleeting and conflicted later encounters with the writer Susan Sontag. Highwater served on PEN's executive board with SS and found her unfriendly. As Karen Kennerly, PEN's executive director, told Highwater, Susan often got annoyed with friends and "slammed the great gate of her life in their faces."

Jack (he was then called Jack Marks by the family who adopted him) had in common with Sue a love of argument and ideas. Even then, "she was tough," a supreme believer in reason. Jack was the romantic, the defender of the irrational. "Sue wanted to drag me back into the naïveté of the world of realists. She preferred Lionel Trilling's masculine, straightforward style." She was a few years older and better read. She challenged him to support his ideas, to come up with better arguments— but she usually won anyway, ending debate with a phrase like "as T. S. Eliot says." She infuriated Jack, but she intrigued him, too, insisting that he read "an endless list of novels and essays." She educated him, making him into a better adversary. In turn, he introduced her to a few authors, notably Federico García Lorca and Djuna Barnes, both of whom, he thought, might cure Sue of her excessive reliance on logic. He won a few arguments, and when he showed her a letter he had received from T. S. Eliot (who agreed to let Jack dedicate a book to him), she was beside herself. He had really one-upped her.

Highwater remembers that Harry Shepro, chair of the social studies department, engaged Sue in political discussions. Shepro scared Jack. The cerebral teacher intimidated many students, who circulated a rumor that he had been a German U-boat commander. The characterization suited the fierce Mr. Shepro. Shepro boldly discussed the basics of Marxism, and Sue, Highwater remembers, "seemed to thrive on these discussions."

In 1983 Patricia Rogart-Roth wrote a letter to the *Los Angeles Times* honoring Shepro and his eleventh grade civics class: "He would present you with a problem and require that you arrive at an appropriate constitutional defense. Woe betide the student who did not understand that the Constitution was the greatest document ever devised by man." When a student turned in an essay on Henry Ford in fulfillment of Shepro's assignment to write about an outstanding American, Shepro, a Russian Jew, told him he had not done his homework; otherwise he would have discovered that there were some "distinctly un-American sides to Ford." Shepro was later called before the House Committee on Un-American Activities, where he invoked the First and Fifth amendments, with the result that he lost his tenure and his position as a teacher.

One young and attractive teacher was dating another teacher in the school. They appeared to be the "quintessential heterosexual couple." Yet one day "Miss T." casually mentioned to Jack and Sue that she was a lesbian. "She recognized that we were outsiders who would not be dismayed and would not breach her confidence. Perhaps she knew something that we did not know," Highwater, an openly gay man, recalls. Jack and Sue did not discuss their own sexuality or speculate about that of others. But they were not terribly shocked by Miss T.'s revelation; after all, this kind of thing was commonplace in an environment dominated by the movie industry. Miss T. explained that pretending to be romantically involved with heterosexuals was their way of dealing with the world's bigotry. Her confidence in these two students exhilarated Jack. He took it as an acknowledgment of their maturity, "the same way our social studies teacher had discussed his radical political ideas."

Susan Sontag graduated from North Hollywood High School at the end of the fall term of 1948. She had entered in the tenth grade. At the end of her third semester, the principal told her that there was nothing else the school could teach her. In January 1949 a column in the North Hollywood High newspaper announced what the seniors would do after graduation. Some would be attending UCLA, some Southern Cal, some Occidental. Sue, just turned sixteen, planned to enroll at the University of Chicago.

Towards a Better Life 3

1 9 4 9 – 1 9 5 3

Susan Sontag had read an article about the University of Chicago in a national magazine. The school's president was Robert Hutchins, a handsome, articulate, and dynamic figure. He was a "star," an educator who caught the public imagination like no other university president of his day. In the 1930s and 1940s he gave over eight hundred public addresses, arguing for the centrality of great books in the university curriculum and for the key role of philosophy, which had been eroded in an age of specialization, academic discipline-building, and departmentalization. Hutchins held out the idea of a university as a home for great thinkers, broadly trained in the liberal arts. To a young woman who had steadily read her way through the list of Modern Library giants, it must have sounded like that world "elsewhere" peopled by kindred spirits. Sontag later said she picked Chicago because it did not have a football team and all people did there was study. As one of her favorite professors, Ned Rosenheim, said, if Chicago had had a football team in the high Hutchins era, it would have had to be coached by Aristotle.

Chicago would have been a striking choice for any North Hollywood

High student. To many Southern Californians, Chicago represented the mean Midwest—a violent city, a campus sinking into a slum, dominated by radicals. To send young Susan from North Hollywood High to the harsh midwinter climate of Chicago was painful for Mildred, and at the last minute she balked. "Chicago? The South Side? All you'll find there are Communists and Negroes." The University of Chicago had a legacy of student activism and political involvement that only the City College of New York, Columbia, and Harvard could rival.

In fact, the University of Chicago had trouble attracting and retaining students because of concerns like Mildred's. By the time Susan applied, Chicago had experienced a severe enrollment decline, and surveys showed that prospective students were worried about its deteriorating neighborhood. The city itself, of course, has never lost its rugged image, and the university's champions embrace it: "This is the city for us," said Ned Rosenheim; "there's a tough-mindedness in this town that's shared at the university. This is a great city that gets things done, and is characterized by energy of all kinds . . . and it has transferred a great deal of moxie to this university."

Students balked at this harsh urban competitiveness, and at what they considered to be Hutchins's narrow, elitist great books approach. Hutchins hardly cared about these gripes, for, like Sontag, he was an enemy of the very idea of adolescence. Only in America did institutions of higher learning profess to develop the character and social skills of its students, he pointed out. Americans were far too sentimental about education, which should not coddle students or pretend to offer them family values. Indeed, he had been attracted to Chicago as the only first-rate university in the country that had a European ambience.

The demanding curriculum forced on wunderkinds—some even younger than Susan—generated a good deal of anxiety. As Earl Shorris, who attended Chicago at the age of thirteen, says, "there was a high level of neurosis." Suicide attempts were not unusual. Any university campus—even one in a major city—can seem a world unto itself and can generate a level of intensity upsetting to earnest young students, but David Riesman, Chicago's eminent sociologist, acknowledged the "hegemony academic matters held" in the "enclave of the University of Chicago."

Riesman's words suggest what Chicago meant to Sontag. She wanted a world in which ideas dominated. That she was so young and might have to struggle with those ideas did not engender fear; instead such a challenge stimulated passion. She readily admitted that she had not understood all those Modern Library giants, but the idea of intellectual giantism motivated her. The notion of an enclave—one that many students regarded as claustrophobic—appealed to a child who had excavated her own cave and wanted a self-contained enclosure.

To please Mildred, Susan agreed to attend Berkeley for the spring semester of 1949 and then to apply to Chicago for the fall. Mildred hoped the Berkeley campus, then a vision of "gleaming granite and marble splendor," would eclipse her daughter's infatuation with the corrupt and dangerous world of Chicago.

Mildred's faith in Berkeley was not misplaced. In 1937 the American Council of Education reported that the university had twenty-one distinguished departments and was second only to Harvard, which had two more. Surveys in national periodicals placed Berkeley in the top five. Sontag liked it. She studied with distinguished critics like Mark Schorer and audited graduate courses. But then Chicago accepted her and she thought, "It's going to be even better at Chicago."

In the spring of 1949, Harriet Sohmers, then a junior at Berkeley working in a bookstore, watched as a stunning Susan Sontag walked in. The male staff, including the poet Robert Duncan, were gay. They looked at the gorgeous Susan, then they looked at Harriet and said: "Go get her." Harriet walked over to Susan, picked up a copy of *Nightwood*, and said: "Have you read this?" It was a classic lesbian pickup line that had been worked on Harriet earlier at Black Mountain College in North Carolina.

Of course, Susan had read it and had already imagined herself as part of the Parisian bisexual world Djuna Barnes so famously evokes with her portrait of the elusive Robin Vote, whom both men and women love but cannot fathom. The novel's narrator is an anatomist of sex by epigram, a connoisseur of style. So is the campy Dr. O'Connor, who is constantly throwing out intriguing aperçus on an impressive array of subjects, such as lesbianism: "Love of woman for woman, what insane passion for unmitigated anguish and motherhood brought that into the mind?"

Surely one reason *Nightwood* has had such a devoted following and made such an impression on young literary minds is its insistence that "one's life is peculiarly one's own when one has invented it." The book is one of the few narratives of that era in which female readers can observe women having to find themselves. The novel is liberating for an adolescent because it explodes neat categories and rigid distinctions. "I'm the other woman that God forgot," Dr. O'Connor asserts. *Nightwood* is such a fine book precisely because it is so expansive.

Harriet had a commanding presence: to her friend Edward Field, she was "a dead ringer for Prince Valiant with her boyish, regular features and shoulder-length, straight brown hair and bangs." Six feet tall, Harriet strode confidently, with none of that stooped, round-shouldered quality that certain women acquire trying to meet people's low expectations. Harriet enjoyed the "theatricality of her appearance." Like Susan, she knew she was dramatic-looking and that she attracted attention. Unlike Susan, there was nothing tentative about her: "Her voice, too, had a rich, thrilling timbre that filled every room."

If Jamake Highwater remembers Sue as stoical, Harriet remembers a lonely, vulnerable, emotional Susan. Susan's intellect struck Harriet immediately; still Susan was a "kid, a baby." For all her intelligence, she was insecure. She would hold back, waiting to see what Harriet or other, mostly older friends thought of the movie they had just seen. Susan could carry her weight in any intellectual conversation, but she was trying so hard to be an adult that the strain would sometimes show. She was young but also brave.

Susan was sweet and accommodating, and though this agreeableness touched Harriet and made her very fond of Susan, Susan's hesitancy irritated her. If Harriet was hard on Susan, she also encouraged her: "I knew Susan would be something special." Harriet recalls a train trip together when the company of this amazing, brilliant young woman and the momentum of going somewhere compelled her to turn to Susan and say: "You have a great destiny." It was not clear to Harriet what Susan would be. She knew, of course, of Susan's interest in literature—they talked of Thomas Mann, and of Susan's friendship with a boy in high school who had a similar literary sensibility—but it was not apparent then that Sontag would be a writer. Like Jamake Highwater, Harriet saw a Susan largely preoccupied with her academic studies.

Susan had a photographic memory. She seemed to lock in whatever she read. Harriet thought of her as carrying around whole libraries in her head. Susan could exude a surface calm coupled with intellectual brilliance and beauty—it was just overwhelming to see that combination in a woman so young. Harriet was close enough to Susan, however, to see that image occasionally fall apart, for Susan had not yet had enough experience to defend herself in a sophisticated adult world. It did not take any great event to overwhelm Susan, who cried easily. Harriet in a nasty mood was enough to upset her.

After that Berkeley semester, Harriet and Susan parted; they remained friends but lost touch until Susan made her break for Europe in the late 1950s. They would resume in Paris what they had started in Berkeley, but not before Susan had exhausted her love affair with Chicago and her marriage to Philip Rieff.

In the fall of 1949, Susan Sontag arrived at the University of Chicago. She took placement exams and placed out of all but six of the fourteen yearlong courses required of undergraduates. This meant she would take graduate courses, usually reserved for the student's fourth year.

Hutchins had been president of the university since 1929. For all his prestige and popularity with the public, he was a contentious presence on campus. The faculty had battled his flouting of departmental prerogatives and his championing of the great books enthusiast Mortimer Adler. Yet Hutchins's own personality infected the brightest and most ambitious students, remembers critic George Steiner:

> The university was immensely liberating for those who wanted to work very hard, depressing for those who didn't. It was not a place in which you could just have a good time. First, the climate was too harsh. Second, you were encouraged to go fast. Hutchins despised holidays, despised breaks. He was a workaholic, and no one was ashamed of trying to be one after him. He hated sloppiness, mediocrity, cowardice; he made no secret of his standards. He made bitter enemies because of this. If you weren't up to it, get out. No bluffing. And he was very, very demanding of himself, he didn't see why he shouldn't be demanding of others. Hutchins was a high Platonic elitist, through and through.

So Sontag too would become. "Platonic" is the key word. Devotion to ideas came first—Hutchins never did commit the university to improving the neighborhood. He was above that, above environment, detached from it.

Hutchins was at odds with the institutionalization of higher learning, with what one had to do to become a registered intellectual. He disliked the idea of grades and the division of subjects into disciplines. He believed in mastery—not in the grind of writing papers and fulfilling class assignments. End-of-year comprehensive exams would demonstrate what students had learned. The emphasis on a single proof of mastery drove some students away from the university and others such as George Steiner and Susan Sontag to it. Steiner got his degree in a year; Sontag took less than two. Chicago was a place where you could put your accelerator to the floor.

Sontag liked what other students dreaded: the fixed curriculum. Chicago had a prescription for learning, and Sontag has taken it with her; her course syllabi have accompanied her through the twenty moves she has made since graduation.

She immersed herself in the curriculum, learning how to read texts closely, reveling in a class that might spend three hours on a couple of sentences. She described the Hutchins regime as a "benevolent dictatorship." She had never been happier, attending classes, concerts, the opera, and film screenings.

Sontag acquired poise, no doubt, from her experience onstage in school plays—and from her theater experience at Chicago, where she was directed by Mike Nichols. In the classroom, one did not simply answer questions but conducted arguments—intellectual arias that would "go on for several minutes"—like a Platonic dialogue, Sontag later told interviewer Molly McQuade.

Sontag learned the Socratic method from Joseph Schwab, whom she regarded as Chicago's greatest teacher. She took his philosophy course for credit her first year and then audited the same course her second year. He was a great showman, a kind of Bogart of the classroom, one of his colleagues remembers: "He could pull a cigarette out of the package while he was talking, and he'd have the class absolutely hypnotized."

Sontag studied the classical philosophical and literary texts with Chicago's other renowned professors, including Elder Olson, Leo Strauss, and Richard McKeon—the last of this troika a revered but also much feared figure. McKeon expected brilliance. Anything less might provoke a withering "That is a very stupid answer." Like Hutchins,

McKeon believed in mind over matter. In a cold classroom he could cut himself off in mid-sentence and say to a student: "I'll wait until you take off your coat." Sontag audited his course and never said a word, she told McQuade.

Students never addressed professors by their first names and professors called students "Mr." or "Miss." The school did not permit disrespect for academic authority. McKeon might have intimidated even Susan Sontag, but she never challenged his right to behave like a god— her word for the professors she revered. The point was to learn.

Another of Sontag's gods was Leo Strauss, a European Jew who left Germany in 1932 to escape the impending Holocaust and who settled in Chicago in 1938 after stopovers in France and England. He exemplified the manner and the mystique of a master which she would later employ so dramatically in the cause of her own career. "Ladies and gentlemen, good morning. In this classroom, the name of [Martin Heidegger] who is, of course, strictly incomparable, will not be mentioned. We can now proceed to Plato's *Republic*." A cult formed around the esoteric Strauss. He gave Hutchins's great books curriculum the deepest philosophical underpinning it was ever to get, and he thus gave students a profound reason to keep reading—not merely to master ideas but to become a master.

Although Sontag had placed out of Humanities I and II, she audited them anyway. At the same time, she took Humanities III with a professor who would put an indelible stamp on her literary sensibility. The first day of class he wrote his name, "Mr. Burke," on the blackboard and began talking about his approach to literary texts. He sounded familiar to Susan. After class, the shy sixteen-year-old Susan Sontag, who rarely approached her professors, asked him gingerly if he would tell her his first name. He wondered why she had to know. Because she thought he might be Kenneth Burke. The startled professor wanted to know how she could know who he was. Well, she had read his books: *Permanence and Change, The Philosophy of Literary Form,* and *A Grammar of Motives*. "You *have?*" was apparently all he said. Burke was hardly a household name, even for the precocious students at the University of Chicago, and that she should have read him was simply, for both of them, "a miracle."

Burke saw a genius in the making, as he explained years later to literary critic Stanley Edgar Hyman. His pride in Sontag went well beyond the recognition of his own influence on the "best student I ever had." Susan would subsequently revel in having spent in his class nearly a whole year devoted to the exegesis of a single Joseph Conrad novel, *Victory*, "word by word, image by image." Burke gave her a copy of his novel, *Towards a Better Life*, which presented an idea of fiction as self-referential—that is, fiction that is about the making of fiction and the consciousness of its author.

But Burke did more than teach Sontag; he fathered her conception of the literary life. He told her about "sharing an apartment in Greenwich Village in the 1920s with Hart Crane and Djuna Barnes—you can imagine what that did for me," Sontag later said. Unlike her meeting with Thomas Mann, her association with Burke made that library of literature in her head palpable and immediate. Although Burke functioned as an academic, he was really a visitor to Chicago without the requisite academic degrees, the kind of freelance intellectual she would, a decade later, aspire to be. He was one of those writers who created the "idea of New York as a city of lyrical modernity, a running metropolitan romance." What is more, he straddled the same divide that Sontag would later attempt to master: "He was political, but not too political, and he was immersed in the latest aesthetic discussion from Europe." He was the first male in Sontag's life to have lived and worked with women on equal terms, communicating to her his easy commerce with the militant feminism that pervaded the Village art scene in the years just before World War I. To be a socialist, a feminist, an artist—this could all be combined.

Yet the combination was not without conflict, and like Burke, Sontag would seek a synthesis—what critic Christine Stansell calls a "third path between art for art's sake and art for politics' sake, between the aestheticism that was seeking the high ground of the Modernist movement and the didactic and ideological imperatives which increasingly dominated writers who remained on the left."

Burke presented, then, an awesome image of the exhilarating but also daunting career of a public literary intellectual. It would be a good while yet before Sontag the writer could put to use what professors like Strauss and Burke taught, let alone conceive of herself as an autonomous literary engine. Like Steiner, she found Chicago all-consuming. There was no time for her own writing, and there were no papers to hand in. Exams were multiple-choice, but each choice presented an intellectual challenge of the highest order. Ned Rosenheim, a thirty-two-year-old professor and a war vet who taught Sontag Humanities III, provides an example: "Of the following statements about Austen's *Emma,* the one most characteristic of the Platonic position would be . . ."

Ned Rosenheim took a personal interest in Susan. He asked her about the army jacket she wore to his class. It was her father's, she told him, not bothering to explain that she meant her stepfather. Susan did not expect her professors to be warm or to take an interest in her, but Rosenheim's solicitousness moved her. He did not cultivate a professorial air, and she regarded him with great fondness. What did she see in Ned Rosenheim? His own modest response is, "Let's be honest, I think it was the books that she read with me while we were talking about all kinds of other stuff."

Like her other professors, Rosenheim was influential because he taught Sontag how to value great texts—particularly those of Hume, Pater, and Croce, who helped to hone her own aesthetic sensibility. Rosenheim, an engaging talker, appealed to Sontag's desire to admire what she read and to feel saved by it. As Rosenheim says with typical self-deprecation: "We were probably all a little self-righteous."

Sontag was responsive in class, but by no means a show-off. She was striking with her long dark hair and beautiful face, but she did not seem pretentious. She excited no particular notice—as far as Rosenheim can recall. Rather, it was her after-class discussions with him that demonstrated her impressiveness, for she continued to think beyond her assignments.

Susan Sontag was nonetheless a phenomenon. Men outnumbered women two to one at Chicago, and one of Sontag's contemporaries recalls that most Chicago women, like the men, were not physically attractive. Sontag stood out. A Sontag watcher of that epoch pictures her long dark hair framing an oval face and a figure gliding along quietly, rarely speaking, and exuding an air of mystery. Another Sontag contemporary at Chicago describes her as lithe with hair long, dark, and lovely. On a more mundane level, a fellow student remembers a commanding girl wearing exactly the same outfit to every class: blue jeans and a plaid shirt.

Sontag could appear and disappear at will, since Chicago put no emphasis on class attendance, and she could audit and pick and choose classes, sometimes sitting in on two different sections of Humanities III, for example, one with Rosenheim and one with Burke. In that sense, the seemingly rigid and prescribed curriculum was nevertheless consumer-oriented. Rosenheim remembers he had "drifters," students who would appear in class even though they were not officially enrolled. If Sontag heard about a class or a professor who sounded interesting, she would show up. That is how she first came to see Philip Rieff, an instructor of sociology. It was December of her second year, 1950, and she turned up in his class, Social Science II, at the urging of a friend. She had reached the point in the syllabus which dealt with *Civilization and Its Discontents* and *Moses and Monotheism,* and Rieff, Sontag had been assured, was good on Freud.

Philip Rieff was a Chicago product, born in the city in 1922 and attending its public schools. Graduating with a B.A. from the university in 1946, he became a graduate student and instructor the next year. He looked older than his age and acted the part. He was not an imposing man physically, but he had a formidable, superior air.

Rieff was descended from a famous rabbi and conducted classes that required close readings resembling Talmudic commentaries on texts. The formidable Rieff could be as recondite as Burke and as withering as McKeon. Graduate students who could take the pressure to perform became disciples; the rest—cowered and resentful—saw him as an arbitrary authoritarian. He would sometimes corner a student to find out exactly how much he or she really knew. He expected students to perform extemporaneously. One student—we will call her Miss Smith— once tried to mask her reading of notes as a spontaneous answer. Rieff, in a sotto voce aside to the class, remarked: "Miss Smith will now read to us from her marginalia."

Rieff was formal. Going to lunch at his house meant being greeted by a maid in uniform. He was not religious. One of his colleagues said of him, he was the type of Jew who could discourse about Jewishness "while eating Westphalian ham." Steeped in literature, Rieff taught a semester course on social theory concentrating on Kafka—one of Sontag's gods. One student later called him "intellectually paternal." To earn his approbation was to be enlisted in an esoteric discipline: Rieff would later claim that there were only seventeen people in the world who could read his jargon-dense, abstruse work.

That day in December 1950, Sontag was late for Rieff's class. She had to walk across the room to the only empty seat—a dramatic entrance for a dramatic-looking person. At the end of class, she was the last to leave. Rieff had positioned himself by the door. As she exited, he grabbed her arm and asked her name. She began to apologize, saying she had only come to audit the course. "No, what's your name?" he pressed her. "Will you have lunch with me?" She did, and they were married ten days after meeting. He was twenty-eight; she was seventeen.

In Rieff's class, Sontag rarely spoke, which only enhanced her air of mystery. Rieff dominated that class of fifteen students with flashy teaching, and with his own air of mystery. But of course there had to be some gossip, Sontag was aware of that: "Oh, have you heard? Rieff married a 14-year-old Indian!" whispered one student in class. With her long dark hair, imposing carriage, and Western temperament, she seemed a noble savage.

Rieff wanted sole possession of this beautiful woman. He wanted much more, however, than just a lover and wife. When he proposed, he outlined a program for marriage: "When I proposed to Susan, it was in the name of our children." With her penchant for the "earnest, the strenuous," Sontag found his proposal appealing.

After Sontag married Rieff, the two lived off campus at 6227 Ingleside Avenue. They were like operatic lovers. They talked nonstop. Even when her bladder ached and she had to relieve herself, Rieff followed her into the bathroom, still talking. Sontag felt that Rieff was the first person who had ever really talked to her. And she thought she would have a family that she could shape according to her desires. In the heady atmosphere of Chicago, the implications of Rieff's traditional proposal, and his expectations of a conventional 1950s family setup, eluded Sontag—she did not even take his name. As she later admitted in a rather oblique fashion: "I was too young to have noticed and become confused by the peculiarly loose, ambivalent way in which this society demands that one stop thinking of oneself as a girl and start thinking of oneself as a woman."

A year later, just after she turned eighteen, she "burst into sobs." She was reading *Middlemarch* for the first time and "realized not only that *I* was Dorothea but that, a few months earlier, I had married Mr. Casaubon." Dorothea mistook Casaubon, that dogged laborer on a "Key to All Mythologies," for a genius; instead she got a reactionary pedant. As in many marriages in which one or both partners realize a mistake has been made, it took Sontag years to come to terms with her painful blunder.

In the spring of 1951, Sontag got her B.A. Rieff, still writing his dissertation, accepted an assistant professorship at Brandeis University for the 1952–53 academic year. By January 1952, Sontag was pregnant.

1952–1957

David Rieff was born in Boston on September 28, 1952. Rose McNulty, Sontag's own Irish nanny, helped take care of him. The family lived in a tiny house near Harvard Yard. David, named after Michelangelo's sculpture, was meant to be a masterpiece. Sontag liked to fuss over him. She did not want to "miss out on this great experience of being a mother," she later said.

Mildred visited the couple when David was about eighteen months old. She told her daughter, "Oh, he's charming. And you know I don't like children, Susan." Her mother's words recalled for Sontag her own childhood alienation, and she set herself to providing a warmer and more stimulating environment for David. Reading Simone de Beauvoir's *The Second Sex* during her pregnancy, Sontag certainly took to heart the book's words that "every child is born a god . . . every mother entertains the idea that her child will be a hero." "The baby, how's the baby?" David's anxious parents would inquire of each other.

Sontag would later tell a story that summed up David's reaction to the heady, demanding atmosphere of his household:

It was a long time ago in Cambridge. . . . We had Herbert Marcuse staying with us. His wife had just died. We used to talk constantly about
philosophy, sometimes late into the night and continuing into the morning. I guess David heard us talking about Hegel because when he came
down for breakfast he just sort of marched around the table saying,
"Hegel, bagel. Hegel, bagel." He must have been two or three.

In the autumn of 1953, Sontag enrolled in the graduate English program at the University of Connecticut at Storrs. Why she chose this particular school is not clear, especially since it meant an awkward commute from
Cambridge (where the couple settled) to Storrs, Connecticut. Harvard,
where Sontag later earned a master's degree, would have been a better
choice. But some Chicago students who obtained their B.A.'s in two years
had trouble getting accepted into the best graduate schools. Connecticut,
with a less prestigious program than Harvard's, offered Sontag a teaching
assistantship as well. A woman of quiet self-confidence, she was the best
mind in her department. Like other graduate students, she taught English
composition. Dressed conventionally in skirts, blouses, and flats, she wore
little makeup. She gave an impression of slight disarray; it seemed she seldom combed her long hair. During the week she lived in a dormitory; on the
weekends she returned to Philip and David in Cambridge.

Sontag did not find the program at Connecticut stimulating; the professors seemed mediocre, and she departed after a year without a degree.
Observers of Susan Sontag in the next few years provide pleasant, fleeting images of her auditing classes at Brandeis and walking in Harvard
Yard, radiating irresistible sexuality, intelligence, and openness.

In the fall of 1954, Sontag began taking English classes at Harvard,
and the following year she enrolled in the graduate program in philosophy. Although for years reference books would list her as having two master's degrees, in fact she earned only one, in philosophy. She studied
under such eminences as theologian Paul Tillich, and in 1956 (at the time
of her preliminary examinations) her department ranked her "first among
nineteen Harvard and Radcliffe doctoral candidates." Harvard offered
nothing like the guidance she received at Chicago. "Harvard was a
superb university, but still, an ordinary university, with a big menu and
no 'right way,'" she later told an interviewer. It did introduce her to a

"whole new dimension of teaching . . . doing a long paper and having your professor give you a close and careful reading with comments."

Friends recall "a brilliant player with ideas, original and fearless, her comprehension so quick it was a joy to play with her." Dressed in a brown suede jacket, wearing her glossy black hair long, Sontag would drift into class late, sitting in a front seat saved by a friend, Henny Wenkart. One time Sontag glanced at the notes on Wenkart's clipboard: "You're always making out marketing lists on the edge of your paper," she complained. This intrusion of the mundane into the intellectual seemed to irritate Sontag.

Sontag gravitated to that most charismatic of professors, Jacob Taubes. This professor of religion, in his rumpled suits and with his lousy posture, was not a great-looking physical specimen. Perhaps no taller than five feet six, he had a weak chin and a small, elfin face. But he had the most expressive hands, an impeccable vocal delivery, and a mesmerizing manner. He could speak without notes, and he seemed to enter directly into the lives of the classic writers he discussed. An expert on St. Paul, on the Gnostics, and on the development of early Christianity and its cults, this learned man could startle by suddenly switching to a discussion of a contemporary writer like Jean Genet, making the connection between the ancient and the modern worlds seamless. Students felt he had the power to possess other lives. He would fasten on a student, telling him which Baudelaire poem he would like, which he would not. He could buy a student a present that suited him better than any present he could buy for himself. If a student disagreed with Taubes, he would acknowledge the merits of the student's position and then use it as a way to expound on his own views. As one student put it, "Talking to Taubes about the weather was like a page from *The Magic Mountain.* Everything was so metaphysically fraught. For you were *there* for him in ways that you were not for any other professor. Even if you wanted to, you could not rid Jacob Taubes from your consciousness." Outsiders envied his acolytes, but they were also relieved not to be sucked into his vortex.

Born in Vienna in 1924 and the scion of its chief rabbi, Taubes was a rabbi himself, educated in philosophy and history in Basel and Zurich, where he obtained his doctorate. He had been a fellow at the Jewish Theological Seminary of New York and the Hebrew University in Jerusalem before becoming a Rockefeller fellow at Harvard. A brilliant lecturer, Taubes was also a reckless sensualist. He believed in making love to many women. He could meet a woman and after his first four words touch her in a commanding way that amazed observers.

In the front row of his class sat three women: they all had long hair, they all wore long skirts, and they all looked wonderful—like they had just emerged from the Negev Desert. They were Susan Sontag; Elsa First, who would become a prominent New York psychiatrist; and Susan Taubes, Jacob's wife. Susan Taubes was an enchanting beauty. "What dark woman in what film noir?" said one Taubes student when asked to describe her. The two Susans were especially close. They had both grown up as solitaries, neither much interested in boys nor caught up in the adolescent girl's obsession with her own looks. They wanted to "remain apart, to be left alone." Both rejected society's idea of what a woman should be. Both sought their own idea of themselves.

For each Susan, Jacob Taubes addressed the problem of what to believe, infusing the search for knowledge with a religious and a rational intensity. He explored the phenomenon of gnosis—the intuitive apprehension of spiritual truths which led to an esoteric form of knowledge sought by the Gnostics. Early Christianity, with its conception of the fall from Eden, elaborated on the Gnostic idea that humankind had separated itself from nature and from the unity of the cosmos that the Greeks prized. Man discovered himself during the Roman Empire, Taubes said, by experiencing himself as an exile. Gnosis revealed man's alienation from the cosmos.

Taubes could trenchantly see through and denounce the Gnostics while still evoking the romance and the thrill of Gnosticism. He was fascinated with St. Paul's arguments against the Gnostics and also with the remnants of Gnostic thinking in Paul's teachings. His was a case of a religious charismatic warning others against charismatics.

From Taubes Sontag would absorb an imaginative sympathy for opposing ideas and the ability to enter simultaneously into conflicting mind-sets. Taubes presides, for example, over the dialectic of her essay "Against Interpretation," in which she maintains a tension between the ideas of content and style.

Sontag also devoted herself to *Freud: The Mind of the Moralist* (1959), the book that would establish Philip Rieff's reputation. Although Susan was not officially a coauthor, the work had become their baby every bit as much as little David. Husband and wife blended the aesthetic and the intellectual, throwing in references to Nietzsche and Hawthorne, Marx and Matthew Arnold. They rejected Freud's view of women, suggesting that his misogyny was not merely a foible but a major flaw shared by other great critical figures in modern philosophy, literature, and psychology, such as Nietzsche and D. H. Lawrence. Like them, Freud divided the sensual from the intellectual, perpetuating a view that thinking women were less feminine and had masculine minds.

Rieff was at heart a conservative. In his acknowledgments for *Freud* in its first edition, he thanked Susan in conventionally feminine terms, giving her the marital surname she says she never used herself: "My wife, Susan Rieff, devoted herself unstintingly to this book. . . . " And in *Esquire*, years later, he said:

> I was a traditional man. I thought marriage was for having children, a traditional family. I just couldn't adjust to the kind of family life she wanted. You see, there are families and anti-families. Ours was the latter, I suppose.

For all his doubts about Freud, Rieff held a rather romantic, even worshipful image of him. He defended Freud both as man and as thinker: "Freud needed a standard Jewish marriage, in which the wife is queen and keeper of a standard Jewish household. From the bridgehead of tradition, Freud the theoretician invaded the whole rotten empire of the family, without running the ultimate risk of cutting himself off from the devout practice of its creed." Must Freud have anchored himself in the traditional in order to subvert it? Surely this is wishful thinking that says more about Rieff than about Freud.

Sontag wanted to pick up and go when she liked (the Mildred Sontag school of motherhood). She wanted to be free to leave David with Rose or Philip or his family—as she had been left:

> I did have the idea that I'd like to have several lives, and it's very hard to have several lives and then have a husband—at least the kind of marriage that I had, which was incredibly intense; we were together all the time. And you can't live with someone on a twenty-four-hour-a-day basis, never be separated for years and years and have the same freedom to grow and change and fly off to Hong Kong if you feel like it . . . it's irresponsible. That's why I say that somewhere along the line, one has to choose between the Life and the Project.

She seems to have had in mind poet William Butler Yeats's famous line about the writer's need to choose between perfection of the life and that of the work.

Sontag did not regret her marriage, but marriage was only one of her models, and Sontag found it too confining: "I was lucky enough to have a child and be married when I was very young. I did it and now I don't have to do it anymore." She told one interviewer that she remained faithful to Rieff during their marriage. Gossip in Cambridge had it that Rieff had not made a satisfying sexual partner. It was a "complicated marriage," said one of Sontag's tactful fellow students.

In 1957 Susan Sontag, twenty-four, received her master's degree in philosophy from Harvard. With the powerful recommendation of Paul Tillich, she was awarded a fellowship from the American Association of University Women to spend the 1957–58 academic year at St. Anne's College, Oxford, in preparation for writing her dissertation on the "metaphysical presuppositions of ethics." Philip Rieff was awarded a fellowship for the same period at the Center for Advanced Study in Behavioral Sciences at Stanford. David would be cared for by Philip's family.

There was no talk of divorce. This was not even a trial separation. Rieff and Sontag do not seem to have permitted themselves the thought that their marriage might be ending. Like the husband and wife in Sontag's story "Baby," the very intensity that had brought the couple together also drove them apart. The story's couple agree: "It's good for people to get away from each other once in a while."

Quest

1957 – 1958

At Oxford, Sontag studied with such luminaries as philosopher A. J. Ayer and writer Iris Murdoch. Sontag was preparing to write her dissertation on values and ethics. But it soon became clear that she had little interest in her program of study. Neither the teaching nor the British ambience had a lasting impact on her. Oxford was best known then for its contributions to analytic linguistic philosophy. But for a student of the French and of continental literature, Oxford could not have seemed more alien.

At the end of the decade, women were just beginning to breach the ramparts of male preserves. American women like Sontag and Sylvia Plath who found themselves among English academics were greeted with contempt or condescending curiosity. An intelligent woman was advised: "The main thing is to think like a man."

In this suffocatingly male milieu, Sontag was a towering and exotic presence. She makes a cameo appearance in fellow student Judith Grossman's novel *Her Own Terms* (1988): a "tall, slim, androgynous figure, dressed all in black, with dark hair, olive skin, and a classically handsome face." She seemed to Grossman like some kind of cross between a dark lady and a dark prince of Denmark. She never wore the simple black dress, and she did not fit the conventional idea of a female. Her fellow students knew they had never encountered anyone like her before.

A female undergraduate watched Sontag stride past her in straight black trousers and wondered where she got her clothes and her face. "Was it South America? The Hindu Kush?" She seemed very tall and very dark, dressed in her American version of guerrilla clothing, accentuated with thick scarves. What was she? German? Jewish?

The men speculated: Was she layable? She was the brightest woman they had ever met, and she held her liquor as well as they did. Sontag appeared alone and unattached, and they immediately started to vie for her. The only one to really claim her attention was Harold Solomon, a graduate student. He seemed a surprising choice. Solomon was a loner, difficult to engage. But like Sontag he was studying philosophy.

With everyone else Sontag kept an ironic distance. She listened more than she talked, creating an atmosphere of "pronounced skepticism." Everyone tried to impress her, because even when she did not say anything, her presence was so powerfully alert. You did not want to make a fool of yourself. This poised American was never rough around the edges; you would not catch her at a disadvantage. She had tremendous control.

During the early winter of 1957–58, Sontag invited Grossman to her lodgings. Grossman went, feeling honored but also puzzled, since she was then a budding poet of twenty, and no philosopher. She found conversation difficult, as she had not read most of the books Sontag had with her. Sontag complained about the cold, saying she always wore pajamas under her clothes to keep warm—and then she turned up the hem of her black trousers to prove as much. Grossman could tell that Sontag was already disenchanted with England, with its "sadly arrogant provincialism, and sexism heavy all over."

Sitting on the couch, Grossman seemed to discern a note of romantic warmth in the situation, until Sontag showed her a photograph of little David back in America—"the shock absolutely flipped things for me," Grossman recalls. "I assumed that I was mistaken, that she must be heterosexual. But in any case a mother, to my understanding then, was sexually out of the question—not to mention the disturbance I felt at seeing the child in the photo, still so young." Grossman gathered that Sontag felt very attached to David and missed him. About her husband, she said nothing at all. He was not in the picture.

Part of what made Sontag so American and so fascinating to her English acquaintances was that she seemed so much her own woman. To leave your husband, to go off to do your own thing, seemed quintessentially American—but almost unthinkable in England. To Grossman, Sontag in black, from shirt to skirt, strode in a kind of "action uniform." She was on a quest, "intensely directed, as if she knew what she wanted before she had met it."

Soon after, Grossman heard that Sontag had left after the Christmas holidays to study in Paris. She left a vacuum. Her English cohort felt put down, although there had been nothing dismissive about her manner. She just vanished. Harold Solomon committed suicide in the spring. To Grossman, the event seemed something like the thunder following Sontag's passage—a final confirmation of the force she embodied.

Grossman's friend Elaine Scarry (author of *The Body in Pain*) asked Sontag if she minded her fictionalization in Grossman's novel. No, she told Scarry, it rather amused her. To journalist Zoë Heller, Sontag described her brief British interlude as a lark, in which she "gadded about on a bike in a gown" and met "interesting young chaps." She called it "being young in a way that I had never allowed myself to be before—it was the first proper student life I'd ever had, even though I was married and a mother by then. In fact that year [it was actually only about four months] in Oxford was the end of the marriage."

Paris, of course, meant landing in *Nightwood*, the Paris of "abject carnival, a kind of human menagerie. Those who wander this city want, impossibly, to *be* what they desire." Sontag did what one would have expected: she struggled with the language, stared at the city's grand architecture, pursued sensual adventure, and browsed in bookstores. She found a room in the Latin Quarter on the rue Jacob, not far from the Sorbonne, where she was supposed to continue her Ph.D. project on ethics. The urban Sorbonne suited her far better than the sedate, almost bucolic Oxford. The solemn Parisian students appealed to her. They lived in shabby hotels on tight allowances from their families (there were very few state scholarships). They did not work—"waiting on tables or washing dishes would have been beneath their dignity." They had plenty of time to argue at café tables, finding complexity in the simplest matters. Known as *l'esprit de contradiction,* the mantra of the period was "Oui, mais c'est beaucoup plus compliqué que ça."

Irv Jaffe, a journalist in Paris since 1949, met Sontag at a party on New Year's Eve, 1958. He gathered that she had separated from her husband because of temperamental incompatibility, that she had a five-year-old boy living with Rieff and his family, and that she still seemed to be on good terms with them but had found Rieff a bit too academic for her, old-fashioned, too conventional. Jaffe knew they had been working on a book together—in fact, he remembers Sontag picking up the galleys of *Freud: The Mind of the Moralist* at the American Express office in Paris.

Sontag and Jaffe went to restaurants, never anything fancy, and sat through many movies. He remembers her wanting to watch Westerns. "Let's go, it will be a lot of fun," she would urge him. Films were her primary way of relaxing. She was never funnier than when she went to old Hollywood movies. Indeed, anyone who accompanied her as a moviegoer remembers an easygoing, fun-loving Susan.

Jaffe realized many years later that her pleasure in watching those movies grew out of Sontag's interest in the camp sensibility—the concept that would later make her name. He liked Susan because she was so lighthearted, alert, and observant. She spoke passable, American-accented French. They went to hear Simone de Beauvoir lecture at the Sorbonne. They were impressed. They were critical. At the end of her Paris year, she and Jaffe parted amicably.

In 1958 Sontag contacted Harriet Sohmers, her closest companion at Berkeley, then working for the *Herald Tribune* in Paris. They became a couple again and traveled through Europe.

Everyone, regardless of sex, fell in love with her, Harriet remembers. In Germany, one man thought she seemed like an exotic cat. Men followed her. The two women traveled cheaply, sometimes hitchhiking, sometimes taking trains. They stayed in cheap hotels—the one in Greece seemed especially cheap, and it was a few days before they realized they were staying in a whorehouse. They took a third-class carriage on their way back from Greece to Paris and found (as they scratched their heads) that they had brought back nits and had to go to bed with towel-wrapped hair.

In Paris, Harriet introduced Susan to all her friends. Susan was charming. She was shy. She missed David. But she was also enjoying her holiday. Harriet thought she relished this time away from the responsibilities of motherhood; she had had her boy so young. She helped Harriet with a new job, translating for a technical magazine. She was sweet about it. To Harriet, Susan still seemed very young and vulnerable, emotionally not much different from the Susan she had known nine years earlier. Harriet remembers Susan saying, "I have to learn to be more angry."

Europe represented a kind of unregulated curriculum for Susan Sontag. She had had literary and intellectual mentors like Burke and Taubes, but she had known no writer near her age who could help her immerse herself in the contemporary cultural scene. Then Harriet introduced her to the thirty-year-old Alfred Chester. Sontag sat at his feet.

Chester had published a volume of short stories, *Here Be Dragons* (1955), and a novel, *Jamie Is My Heart's Desire* (1957), as well as a pornographic novel under the pseudonym of Malcolm Nesbit for Olympia Press. He was ascending into the "hanging gardens of literary celebrity," to use Cynthia Ozick's evocative phrase. He had been in Paris since 1951 and could introduce Sontag to writers who published in *Commentary, Partisan Review,* and *Paris Review.* Indeed, he knew George Plimpton and Robert Silvers, founding editors of the *Paris Review* and the *New York Review of Books.* Silvers, another University of Chicago prodigy, had championed Chester's first book for publication in France.

Chester had the face of an infant, hairless, rosy, doll-like. He had lost all of his body hair during a childhood illness, and as a result looked fattish. Painfully self-conscious about his baldness, he wore a wig variously described as yellowish orange and ginger-colored. He seems to have fostered an outrageous gay-Jewish flamboyance to go along with—to counter?—his bizarre appearance. His ambition stood out.

Coming from Brooklyn, he talked like a gatling gun, "the toe of the next sentence stumbling over the heel of the last." A bohemian, he organized his life around being a writer. He never worked at anything but writing. He thought of ingenious schemes to get his mother to support him (announcing a fictitious marriage just so that she would send a wedding present), and to bilk landlords (securing a hard-to-get rent-controlled apartment by showing up in evening clothes pretending to be a millionaire with an architect who was going to renovate the place). Chester did whatever he deemed necessary to avoid nonliterary employment, and his escapades gave writers and editors sensational material to dine out on for years. To Sontag, who had never thought it conceivable that one could write without holding a teaching job or without having some connection to some kind of institution, Chester was a revelation.

To many Chester seemed destined for greatness, but he would never become a great literary light. Instead he would enjoy a four-year meteoric rise and fall in New York. The fame he sought disgusted him. He got more disgusted when he saw Sontag achieve fame and power and treasure her victory.

Poet Edward Field, who wrote an unpublished essay on Chester called "The Man Who Would Marry Susan Sontag," has done more than anyone else to revive Chester's reputation. He has tried to engage Sontag, asking her for letters from Chester and for reminiscences. She has remained silent, replying only once to say she could not cooperate. In the absence of Sontag's testimony, we have Cynthia Ozick's brilliant memoir, "Alfred Chester's Wig." In 1946 Ozick and Chester attended the same composition class at New York University. He was eighteen, and already consumed by "literary passion." She begins her reminiscence with the conceit that Chester—really the idea of Chester—is eternal. He "stands firm" as if on one of her mind's "impermeable platonic islands." He represents, in other words, the pure idea of literary striving: "He wrote energetically snotty reviews that swaggered and intimidated—the kind of reviews that many young men (and very few young women) in the Fifties and Sixties wrote, in order to found a reputation." Here is a sample sentence from Chester's demolition of John Rechy's *City of Night* in the *New York Review of Books:* "The episodes are so gracelessly, clumsily written, so stickily, thickly literary; in his determination to boil every last drop of poetry out of pederasty, Rechy ends up with nothing but a pot of blackberry prose." After reading this review, Gore Vidal called Chester a monster—but also a master, a practitioner of the "black art." As Ozick realizes: "Every new half-decade sprouts a fresh harvesting of literary writers, equally soaked in the lust of ambition, equally sickened (or galvanized) by envy."

Writing to a friend after his relationship with Sontag had soured, Chester spit out: "How dare you say 'your friend S. Sontag'? You rat, she is my enemy. She is everybody's enemy. She is The Enemy."

An allusion to Sontag slips into Ozick's essay when she mentions the published portion of Chester's unfinished novel, "The Foot." This fragment contains fictionalizations of his writer friends. Paul Bowles, for example, becomes Peter Plate. Ozick also mentions Mary Monday but does not identify the real-life model, who is clearly Sontag, whose last name in German means Sunday. Ozick points out that in "The Foot" Mary Monday has a double, also named Mary Monday. Chester's letters describe Sontag as having a two-track personality (the noble literary figure and the "cynical whore"). Sontag later wrote a short story, "The Dummy," with precisely the same conceit: the idea of having a second self who can be seen to be living one life while that self's original is free to live quite another.

Chester died in Israel in 1970. His memory remains vivid for those who knew him personally because he never lost his edge or his anger. He never mellowed. He remained, Ozick observes, "single-mindedly literary."

In 1958 Susan Sontag seemed to Alfred Chester, and to Harriet Sohmers, still something of an ingenue. But Sontag was studying André Breton and his surrealist confreres, who were interested in the figure of the artist, of the creator behind the work. They provided a link for Sontag with Walter Pater and Oscar Wilde—writers she had studied with Ned Rosenheim at Chicago—who created a style inseparable from the idea of the aesthetic personality. For Breton, the "creator and the work were inextricably bound. . . . The artist's first and most important creation . . . was himself."

Sontag immersed herself far more deeply in the French intellectual and cinematic world than other Americans living in Paris in the early postwar years. Novelists like Norman Mailer and James Jones befriended French writers, to be sure, and learned much from Sartre's existentialism. But Sontag stood virtually alone in her efforts to speak the language of French philosophers, novelists, and film critics. She absorbed the French intellectual interest in American popular culture and was already beginning to form her ideas of an aesthetic that cut across the categories of high and low culture set forth by such American critics as Dwight Macdonald and Clement Greenberg. When she began to write her landmark essays in the 1960s, she brought a continental sophistication to American criticism which changed the terms of intellectual and cultural debate. Whereas her predecessors such as Lionel Trilling and Edmund Wilson limited themselves to literature, history, and to general cultural discussions, Sontag would demonstrate an understanding of all the arts, informed by a trained philosophical mind, which argued for what she would call the "new sensibility." She brought to the discussion of the contemporary scene the same seriousness she devoted to classic works of literature.

But it was not merely on the level of ideas that the French manner captivated Sontag. On the contrary, she observed how writers such as Louis Aragon and André Malraux meticulously polished their images and created a mystique. With writers like Aragon and Breton, she saw how artists of the avant garde absorbed left-wing politics, making everything about the artist's image seem progressive and daring, even though fitful alliances between the Communist Party and the surrealists, for example, were absurd and bound to fall apart. No matter. The idea, the platonic conception of the artist *engagé*, thrilled Sontag. It excused any amount of contradictory and self-defeating behavior.

In France in 1958, Sontag witnessed a small close-knit group of writers, intellectuals, and filmmakers making a major impact on the society. They were an elite caste, and served as an examplar of the status to which she aspired. Even though she wrote to her husband constantly and still could imagine sharing her year abroad with him, her married life now seemed, as she later put it, too safe. As 1958 drew to a close, she decided to return home and tell her solid and reliable husband that the marriage was over.

Rieff met Sontag at the airport when she returned to the States. They embraced. They walked to the car. Before he could put the key in the ignition, she asked him for a divorce. They sat; they wept. It was over.

The blow to Rieff was devastating. An intense man, Rieff behaved like Coleridge's ancient mariner telling the wedding guest of his woe. He seemed to be hemorrhaging internally. Professor Daniel Aaron of Harvard spent a day trying to console his colleague. And at some point Rieff would delete Susan's name from the acknowledgements of further editions of his book on Freud.

Sontag, at twenty-six, reclaimed six-year-old David from Rieff's parents and arrived with him in New York on January 1, 1959. She remembers having only two suitcases and seventy dollars. "I was thrilled. I was like Irena in *The Three Sisters* longing for Moscow. All I could think was New York! New York!"

Sontag had done little work on her dissertation in Europe. She reported to the American Association of University Women, her fellowship sponsor, thanking the organization for supporting her research year, "a most valuable one for me, perhaps the most valuable single year of my academic life," and for supporting women scholars in general. Her dissertation was a "dropped stitch that you just have to go back and pick up." She said she wanted to complete it soon. But she never did.

On her own, Sontag had to find a place to live (she settled for a small two-room apartment at 350 West End Avenue) and a job quickly. She made do for the first six months with an editorial position at *Commentary*. Her intelligence and striking looks impressed Martin Greenberg, an editor there, but he realized that the magazine meant no more than a temporary job to Sontag, who wanted to write and would begin working on her first novel soon. Greenberg pointed her out to art critic Hilton Kramer on a visit to the *Commentary* offices. Kramer saw a very attractive young woman wearing a cotton housedress, the kind his mother put on to wash the dishes. It was almost provocatively drab. While the *Commentary* staff hardly embodied the height of fashion, they had a certain sophistication, and here was this arresting woman in plain dress—"It almost seemed an affectation," Kramer observes.

Right from the start, Sontag did what many aspiring writers do in New York. She cruised "all parties, bad parties," looking for new faces. On occasion Richard Howard accompanied her. He is a devotee of French literature, a translator, poet, critic, and literary politician extraordinaire. Howard is also gay, with a Truman Capote-like capacity for sizing up the competition. Indeed, Robert Girard photographed him in a languorous Capote-like pose: stretched out, a New York literary cat, but with a harder look than Capote, Howard appears less seductive but more wily, more in *control*.

The first eighteen months in New York were invigorating and frightening for Sontag. She made rapid progress on a novel with the working title "Dreams of Hippolyte." She got to know many of the city's literati, exploring the capital very much as her novel's main character does. Sontag had to make a home for David, and she had to work hard to support him. She would not accept any child support or alimony from Rieff, even though she was entitled to both under the community property laws of California, where she had sued Rieff (then at Stanford) for divorce. Her attorney told her he had never had a client who rejected what the law entitled her to, but Sontag was declaring her independence, determined to make it on her own.

For the academic year 1959–60, she found teaching positions in philosophy at Sarah Lawrence College (in Bronxville) and City College.

This harried life left her looking haggard at times, as Seymour Kleinberg, a friend from graduate school at Connecticut, noticed. But she might have quoted a line from Alfred Chester: "It's delicious this agony of trying to find one's way, one's own way."

For guidance, Sontag looked to Alfred Chester, who had returned from Paris to New York in February 1959, and to Harriet Sohmers when she stayed at Sontag's West End Avenue apartment that summer. Sontag threw a welcome home party for Harriet, who remembers getting "insanely drunk," slipping on the parquet floor while dancing, and falling flat on her face, breaking her nose. The party ended with Susan taking Harriet to the emergency room at St. Luke's Hospital.

The party for Harriet marked the dramatic beginning of an affair Sontag would cherish ever after. Harriet introduced Susan to María Irene Fornés, who had been Harriet's lover in Paris and a fond friend of Alfred Chester's. (Fornés had returned to New York from Paris in early 1958.) "Fair-skinned against a frame of short dark hair, slightly freckled, with big brown eyes that might be described as frank," the petite Fornés kept her own counsel. Born in Cuba in 1930, she immigrated to the United States with her mother in 1945. At nineteen, she thought of herself as a painter, and by 1954 she was in Europe pursuing her art and, like Sontag, immersing herself in the movies. Then, in Paris, she saw *Waiting for Godot* and became an aspiring playwright, saying she would rather talk than read. Sontag naturally liked what she called the "autodidact" in Fornés, as well as her surprising style, which was at once "delicate and visceral." She "could use four-letter words at a tea party . . . without ever being accused of not being a lady." This vivacious, even cuddly-looking woman could be mistaken for an easy mark—until (as it apparently happened at a Greenwich Village party in the early 1960s) a masher screamed, "holding up a bloody hand tattooed with teeth marks, Irene's teeth marks."

Like Sontag, Fornés was "dramatically beautiful," to borrow poet Edward Field's words. "She had the large soulful eyes of a madonna." She and Harriet had lived together at the Hôtel de Poitou on the rue de Seine before Sontag arrived in Paris. Alfred became, in Harriet's words, the "essential go-between" when she and Irene had their "many passionate battles." Alfred was openly gay, and though his tone could be bitchy, he loved these three bright, ambitious women. Indeed, he became obsessed with Sontag and thought he should marry her. He doted on

Irene, quoting her wisdom. Edward Field remembers Alfred punctuating conversations with "Irene says . . ." For a time in New York, the three women adored him, forming a circle around him not so different from the one that formed around Jacob Taubes.

But there was tension among the three women. Sontag and Fornés did not tell Sohmers about their love affair. Even after she learned of the affair, Harriet retained her deep feeling for Irene, and she got angry at Susan, who for some time had been shuttling between her and Irene. By all accounts, Irene was a wonderful companion, with extraordinary feelings for women. Irene liked to dress up and look beautiful, and she made other women feel just as desirable.

Harriet was also angry at Alfred Chester, who knew about Susan and Irene, for he had hosted them often at his Sullivan Street flat. Harriet felt deceived all round. She had been attending a women's writing group started by Susan and Irene. Alfred called them "la Société Anonyme des Lesbiennes." Harriet remembers showing up at Susan's West End Avenue apartment for a confrontation, but both Susan and David were gone. Then she got a call from Irene, who said: "Susan is here. She would like you to leave the apartment." Harriet started to shake, and she remembers shaking for the next two weeks. She took tranquilizers; she moved in with a friend. Susan started phoning and saying it was all a big mistake: "I love you darling." Harriet did not believe her, and she left New York for Provincetown. Harriet and Susan were never really close again.

Alfred Chester meant no harm to Harriet, as she eventually realized. He found the Sontag-Fornés duo fascinating, although he could sound peevish about the way they picked his brains. He wrote to his friend Edward Field:

> Susan is getting on my tits & Irene is probing as always. Women are such pests.

Yet he thought them better company than most of the men he met in gay bars. By August, Chester was reporting to Field: "The marriage of Susan & Irene is beginning to have the look of most marriages. Susan is unloving. Irene loves & suffers."

For her part, Sontag had her own troubles. Philip Rieff, teaching at Stanford, had custody of David for the summer, but he planned to take his son with him for a Fulbright year in Germany. She suspected, in Chester's words, that Rieff was "running away" with the child. Sontag went to court in San Francisco and won the right to keep David with her.

David got physically ill boarding planes to see his father in California. He resented his father's efforts to turn him away from his mother. "We had a sort of symbiotic relationship," David told journalist Zoë Heller. "A lot of that was because there was only nineteen years between us. I was aware that it was very different from the relationships most kids had with their mothers. In the end, separation was difficult and probably took too long."

Sontag could be an aloof mother, involved in her career and her affairs. Friends watched as a succession of lovers (mostly women) walked into and out of her life and wondered about the impact on David. She barely provided a domestic life, confessing that she did not cook for David, she "warmed" for him. They lived in what David later deemed "amiable squalor." High-strung and moody like his mother, David acted out far more than she had in her childhood. Harriet Sohmers remembers that Sontag could be stern with him. But he was always by her side. She had him on her lap, she claims, when she typed her first novel. She took him to neurology lectures, concerts, parties. Susan and David were "passionately wrapped up in each other," friend Jonathan Miller remembers. A New York editor visited Sontag at her apartment and saw young David joining in conversations with the adults.

Of course, most parents think of their children, in some sense, as their protégés, but Sontag and son were unusual. Children noticed it too. David wore what might best be called Little Lord Fauntleroy clothing. He walked about like a miniature Oscar Wilde in a world that most children have never inhabited—it was a literary world Susan Sontag had dreamed of in her childhood. Even in New York City, where children can tend toward the precocious, David was a phenomenon. Walking down the street one day, an editor friend of Sontag's spotted her and her sartorially distinctive son. Out with his two young sons, the editor greeted Susan and David in passing. A moment later one of his boys turned to the other and said, "Well, you don't see that every day."

Sontag filled David's room with toys, but she conceded that pouring all her need for "family connection" into him made it difficult to be a child and to grow up. David has said that he did not enjoy my childhood. I tended more to think of it as a sentence and puberty as parole. . . . A writer friend once said of me that I come from an intellectual somewhere but a geographic and ethnic nowhere. And I guess I agree with that. I don't feel any deep loyalty to the place where I live.

Like his mother, Rieff, now a journalist, is constantly on the move. He wants to be out there, on the cutting edge; perhaps he writes about refugees because, like his mother, he is one.

Indeed, Sontag's and her son's interest in Cuba, its revolution, and its leftist, anti-Batista refugees grew out of the precarious circumstances of their own early existence in New York. They lived in a Hispanic neighborhood with Irene Fornés, and befriended Cuban poet Heberto Padilla. Cubans baby-sat David. He fondly remembers "two natty queens from next door who used to appear almost magically and whisk me away to a Cuban restaurant [Victor's] on Amsterdam Avenue for those thick tropical milkshakes called *batidos*." Mother and son would spend June through September 1960 in the new Castro-converted Cuba, where David cut a little sugarcane and Sontag inspected revolutionary culture.

In the fall of 1960, the twenty-eight-year-old Sontag began teaching in Columbia's religion department. Jacob Taubes had just begun teaching there. At Columbia, Taubes was a towering but isolated figure—practically a department unto himself, with junior faculty members like Susan Sontag who sometimes graded for him and sometimes taught their own sections of his large lecture classes. Susan Taubes also taught religion, but like Sontag, she had aspirations to be a writer, and she participated in the writing group Sontag and Fornés had formed.

Fornés remembers how Sontag came to her to talk over ideas, needing a responsive mate. Sontag would have written without her help, Fornés is certain, but they stimulated one another's writing. But much of it was talk, talk, talk. Fornés finally said: "How silly! If we want to write, why not sit down and write?" That had been the start of their writers' group, which in an intense six-month period confirmed their dedication to the writer's life.

Indeed, Sontag lived for her art, making others feel unworthy—so bourgeois with their homes and families. Sontag mentored Richard

Tristman, praising his early fiction and admitting him to her writing group while he was still an undergraduate. He was overwhelmed by these beautiful, intelligent women, and he felt privileged—but almost unworthy—to share their aspirations. He believed he had done nothing yet to deserve Sontag's confidence. But she had seen enough of his writing to believe in his potential, and she loved discovering new talent. At City College she would help to nurture the talent of Oscar Hijuelos, whose novel of Cuban-American life, *The Mambo Kings Play Songs of Love*, won the Pulitzer Prize.

Other students found Sontag cordial and perhaps more informal than most professors. In a comparative religion course, she talked about her experience at the Sorbonne and discussed Sartre. Most of Taubes's students saw Susan Sontag only as the master's shadow. She was the mystery woman. What exactly was her connection to Taubes? No one really knew.

Taubes was obsessed with the messianic expectations of both Judaism and Christianity. Taubes scholars refer to his "apocalyptic political attitude." The world was awaiting, in other words, just the kinds of interruptions of history signified by the story of Jesus and the proselytizing of Paul. Theology provided metaphors that had an explosive political potential amounting to the injunction to make "no spiritual investment in the world as it is." Taubes's Gnostic power resided in the impression he conveyed of knowing what eluded others, of anticipating a changing world. He had perfect timing, since his era was about to erupt in what is now simply called "the sixties." The world was—to borrow a phrase from a highly praised book by one of Taubes's students—at the gates of Eden. True changes made a break with history; they were, as St. Paul argued, apocalyptic. There could be a new people of God (Christians); or, in secular terms, a new political world. This might well mean violence and revolution. "As an apocalyptist I can imagine that the world will be destroyed," Taubes wrote. He later told his former student Richard Tristman that he had become a Maoist.

Indeed, Taubes argued for what he considered the Pauline way: to establish the legitimacy of a new order, the legitimacy of the old one had to be destroyed. Hence Mao/Castro. But on what authority does the revolutionary destroy? The Pauline experience, Taubes argued, involved the paradoxical circle of the "self-authorizing authority." Paul anoints himself; he "opens anew the messianic possibility of the 'exception,'" the intervening personality or force transfiguring history. Sontag and son would try to live this truth in Castro's Cuba, identifying with the oppressed whose struggle against tyranny "leads to the undermining of worldly powers." The quotation is from Marin Terpstra's discussion of Taubes's book on St. Paul, a book that links messianism and liberation—as did Walter Benjamin, who informed both Taubes's and Sontag's leftism.

Working full-time at Columbia, Sontag spent her weekends and a summer writing "Dreams of Hippolyte," later retitled *The Benefactor*. By the spring of 1961, she was ready to show a section of her unfinished novel to a publisher. Somehow, she managed to arrange an interview with Jason Epstein, the powerful Random House editor. He turned the book down, suggesting that perhaps Robert Giroux at Farrar, Straus might take it.

Giroux, soon to be made Roger Straus's partner (in 1964), had edited T. S. Eliot, George Orwell, Flannery O'Connor, Edmund Wilson, and Robert Lowell—some of the greatest figures in modern literature. Many thought him chiefly responsible for building FSG's prestigious list. What is more, he carried on a tradition of belles lettres publishing dating back to 1939, when he began as a junior editor at Harcourt, Brace & World. Epstein thought of Giroux because of his legendary efforts to promote difficult works. Giroux was also known to be willing to take chances on first novels, having published William Gaddis's lengthy and abstruse *The Recognitions* (1955). And Giroux, a fine Shakespeare scholar, was a man of letters whom other writers respected. Giroux had moved to FSG in 1955 after fifteen years at Harcourt, citing, among other reasons, Roger Straus's "publishing flair." Straus, who came from a wealthy family, could afford to look upon publishing as a long-term investment. He sought to build a portfolio of renowned foreign authors and promising American newcomers.

Sontag, on the strength of Epstein's suggestion, went to see Giroux. Her first words to him were, "Jason Epstein told me you're the only editor in New York who will understand my novel." Giroux found her gambit irresistible. She had simultaneously flattered him and degraded Epstein, who apparently had not understood the book. Epstein, who had established the Anchor paperback line of distinguished authors, was sending Giroux an intriguing prospect who was not going to be easy to take to market. Would he dare handle her? Giroux saw only the first section of the novel, but on the basis of its brilliant beginning he offered Sontag a Farrar, Straus contract, which she signed on May 24, 1961.

Sontag has told many versions of how her first novel was accepted for publication. None of them square with this account, based on a detailed letter dated July 1, 1981, from Giroux to Sontag, a letter for which there is no reply in the FSG files. To Miriam Berkley in *Publishers Weekly* (October 22, 1982), Sontag explained how she came to FSG:

> That's a fairy tale. When I wrote *The Benefactor*, I looked at my own library and thought, "Who would I like to be published by?" I made a list of publishers in the order of preference. FSG was first. And I remember thinking, the publishing house that publishes Djuna Barnes and Nathanael West, my two favorite American writers of the '30s, must have somebody who would like what I do.

She claimed she addressed her manuscript "To the Fiction Editor" and left it with the receptionist. She recalled that a week or two later she was invited to lunch and offered a contract. In the summer of 1981, Sontag told another version at a PEN gathering to honor Straus and Giroux's contributions to publishing. She delivered an encomium to her publishers, citing her own first experience with them: entering their "wonderful shabby offices" on Union Square West, leaving her first novel in a Sphinx box (used then as a package for typing paper) with a note to the fiction editor. Sontag remarked that in her naïveté she supposed that each publishing house had only one fiction editor. She counted herself very fortunate indeed that her manuscript somehow got taken up by Robert Giroux, "*the* Fiction Editor," who a few weeks later offered her a contract.

It was this version of events that prompted Giroux to write to Sontag on July 1. His is a gentle, if sly, letter. He says he is thinking of writing his memoirs, and that as a start, he is going to write an article on authors' first books he has edited. He observes that her memory is so at odds with his that he thought he should check with her. He adds, for good measure, that her story does not tally with "another witness's remembrance." Giroux then describes the setup at FSG. Since he was not a fiction editor but the editor in chief, an unsolicited manuscript would have been logged in by Hal Vursell. Giroux then gives the account of Sontag's contacting him which appears in this narrative.

To journalist Philip Nobile, Roger Straus told a version of how Sontag's first novel got accepted that confims Giroux's letter. When Nobile included Straus's story (without naming Straus) in an article on *NYRB* for *Esquire,* Jason Epstein wrote to the magazine denying Nobile's version of events. Sontag also wrote to *Esquire* protesting Nobile's inaccuracies. The magazine went to considerable trouble to verify their author's sources, and it stood by the story. Sontag backed down when she heard from *Esquire* editor Harold Hayes that Nobile's chief source was none other than Roger Straus. At one point an *Esquire* editor asked Straus for Sontag's telephone number in Paris. He gave it—but with the request that she not be told that the editor had gotten the number from Straus.

Sontag's self-mythologizing is not so different from the fantasies writers often purvey about their careers. Most beginning writers dream of being "discovered," of dispensing with the need for self-promotion, and of a publisher who will accept them immediately as promising prospects. And after all, Sontag did earn almost immediate recognition from Giroux and Straus, the latter having become almost instantly convinced of her budding greatness. Her career did begin swiftly, if not in exactly fairy-tale fashion, since Sontag as princess was hardly naïve. Yet the story preserves, for her, a kind of innocence, a purity she has always wanted to believe in, a purity that has functioned as a kind of bulwark against her cunning, ambitious side. While some interpreters would undoubtedly call her self-mythologizing hypocritical, others may see it as an endearing effort to maintain a vision of herself and of the writer's career which is not infected with cynicism.

Moreover, portraying her "discovery" as a fairy tale contributes to her iconic status. Her story becomes exemplary, the wish fulfillment of every aspirant to literary fame. Through this myth she becomes an embodiment of her readers' fantasies. For some readers, she is our Erasmus. For others, she is a beautiful ambitious woman—one of the first women who has managed to scale the heights of Parnassus, achieving a goal to which others have aspired without any real hope of success.

Roger Straus realized her uniqueness, which revealed itself not only in her work but in her regal sense of entitlement—indeed he encouraged her to regard herself as a special case. At FSG, there has always been much speculation about exactly how Sontag got her start there. The party line was that Roger Straus had discovered her. Giroux kept his own counsel, ceding to Straus his need to shine. After all, Giroux had come to a firm whose head had "flair."

Yet Straus's claim to having discovered Sontag should not be dismissed. For he saw in her not merely a talented novelist but a woman of letters who would rival and perhaps surpass figures such as Mary McCarthy, the only woman in the circle of New York intellectuals clustered around the *Partisan Review* in the 1930s and 1940s. By 1961 Sontag was writing her first provocative essays. She would write with authority not only about film, philosophy, literature, and history but about the avant-garde in New York and in Europe. Sontag had the serious European flavor of a Hannah Arendt but also the good looks, confidence, and energy of an American bringing news of the contemporary scene to an audience avid for a change from the stultifying cultural atmosphere of the Eisenhower 1950s, which Norman Mailer had attacked in *Advertisements for Myself* (1959).

The flamboyant Straus sensed that Sontag's appeal to men and women would be extraordinary. She would much later acknowledge that she had benefited from her role as token in a man's world—at the same time observing that she had not let that tokenism devalue her confidence in herself. What made her so appealing is that she simply assumed equality with men. She did not demand it. Rather, she entered the competition, so to speak, without worrying about her qualifications or about whether others would suspect her physical attractiveness contributed to her success. As with Robert Giroux, Sontag was direct with men and women, unapologetic, and engaging.

In 1961, before the publication of Betty Friedan's *The Feminine Mystique* (1963) and the advent of the feminist movement, Susan Sontag with her ambition and confidence was a singular figure. She came of age at a time when the phrase "role model" was not yet in vogue. But her poise bespoke a woman seeking her place in history. She had a sense of destiny. Straus was signing up a cultural force, not just an individual writer. Of course, he was not immediately aware of every facet of Sontag's appeal, but the careful way he nurtured her career right from the beginning demonstrates his faith in her tremendous promise.

Robert Giroux could play only a minor role in Sontag's career, since his first love was literature and not so much the process by which an author becomes a symbol and the cynosure of a literary community. But while Straus wanted to cultivate good writing, he also wanted to play a larger role in literary New York, to exert an influence over how public taste was formed. And Sontag's early essays are all about taste, about why she is enthusiastic about art as form, as an experience in itself, and she seemed as self-contained as the works of art she extolled.

Made

1962–1963

Exactly when Roger Straus met Sontag is not clear, but by the end of April 1962 he was telling her of his enthusiasm for the first eighty pages of what then was titled "The Shrinking Man: Dreams of Hippolyte." He had plans to show this "wonderfully inventive" book to publisher Fred Warburg in London. She became a show item at his parties. The distinguished American critic Edmund Wilson first met her on March 20, 1963, at a Straus affair. Either he did not catch her name or could not be bothered to remember it, for he noted in his journal "a handsome girl from California who is one of Roger's new writers." Wilson never warmed up to Sontag. In 1968, long after she had established her niche, Wilson confided to his journal: "I never have much conversation with Susan Sontag. Roger can't quite forgive me because I am not impressed by her." Wilson, once married to Mary McCarthy, may have seen Sontag as a pushy upstart; certainly he disliked her brand of criticism, which he found far-fetched, pretentious, and esoteric.

It is not an exaggeration to say that Straus engineered Sontag's career, making certain that the novels, for example, were always in print, that even the most insignificant Sontag piece was translated and marketed abroad. No detail was too trivial. The tale of this all-encompassing care is taken not just from interviews with FSG employees and authors; it also comes from the FSG files housed at The New York Public Library.

In certain respects, of course, Sontag was treated no differently from other first novelists. Her advance for *The Benefactor* was $500, a modest sum not out of line with FSG terms with other authors. But few first novelists could expect a publisher then or now also to act as an agent for magazine pieces, stories, and indeed virtually everything that came from the writer's pen. The way Roger Straus commandeered her career excited gossip linking the publisher and his author in an erotic fashion. Alfred Chester put out the word to Paul Bowles with his characteristic candor: "Susan is going to be terribly famous soon because Roger Strauss [*sic*], her publisher, is mad about her (he is very hot for lesbians) and is going to make a big thing of her very boring novel."

The dapper Straus—with the muscle of a Hollywood producer but also the savoir faire of the dandy, was Sontag's perfect match. He was not a litterateur, but he had good taste. He liked to brag about his discoveries and brand them. Sontag had arrived with a novel that spoke of French sophistication and of European culture. It was sure to attract Straus, who had been able to build an impressive literary list by acquiring European authors on the cheap and gaining for them small but dedicated audiences in the United States. That her first books would not make much, if any, profit for FSG really did not matter. She was a long-term investment.

In return, Sontag was a loyal author, offering Straus an exclusive; she would never publish with anyone else. Whether they did or did not have a physical romance is immaterial. Straus has never gotten over his infatuation with the idea of Susan Sontag, the queen of the New York literary scene.

At the same time, Straus, a shrewd judge of quality, fervently believed in Sontag's genius. He would have the courage to remain committed to her work even during her dry spells, relishing her provocative, controversial style and willing to rewrite book contracts as her interests changed and she delayed delivery of her books. Every author dreams of having a publisher as devoted as Straus, and Sontag has never wavered in her appreciation of his efforts on her behalf. To her, it was a great compliment that he included her on his list of distinguished authors. In just the last fifteen years, FSG has had six Nobel Prize winners: Wole Soyinka (1986), Joseph Brodsky (1987), Camilo José Cela (1989),

Nadine Gordimer (1991), Derek Walcott (1992), and Seamus Heaney (1995). He maintains living quarters in Stockholm and lobbies strenuously for his authors. When a million copies of Scott Turow's best-selling first novel were in print, Straus worried, according to one of his colleagues, that FSG would be seen as too commercial.

A publisher celebrated for his sartorial splendor, Straus has always been intensely concerned with appearances, with image, and he realized that Sontag would present well and always set the right tone. The silver-maned Straus, now over eighty, suits the stereotype of the literary lion, sporting (as one profile of Straus puts it) "natty ascots and salty language." Or as Sontag prefers to see him: "He's a showman, but also a man of principle." While many profiles of Straus emphasize his belief that a book's literary quality should "stand on its own," the FSG files show that the firm supported Sontag with patronage letters, publicity releases, and personal appearances—the whole panoply of modern promotion.

That a publisher should champion a valued author in this way is not unusual, except that most authors who receive the kind of intense marketing that Sontag enjoyed are best-sellers or well established and renowned. In 1963, when *The Benefactor* was published, Susan Sontag was neither. Her difficult novel might attract the attention of the literati, but other publishers surely would not have taken it upon themselves to single out Sontag. *The Benefactor* was not what is called one of those "breakout novels" that seem destined to attract a big audience. Had Sontag approached James Laughlin, the owner of New Directions famous for his advocacy of difficult modernist work, she would not have received the promotion or the image-making treatment that FSG accorded her.

Straus impresses many as exuding a sense of entitlement, born of his inherited money and position. His grandfather, Oscar Straus, was Theodore Roosevelt's secretary of commerce. His father, president of American Smelting & Refining, married a Guggenheim. Straus himself married Dorothea Liebmann, granddaughter of Rheingold Beer's founder. She has become a respected author of memoirs and a discreet supporter of her husband's literary aspirations. When she met him, she liked his paradoxical combination of all-American vigor and rather refined tastes. In *Thresholds*, she describes an enticing figure: "I examined his hands, aristocratic and delicate for such a tall athletic boy, and his small-boned wrists sprinkled with dark hair, as though they held all the secrets of his being."

Straus started prospecting for European authors shortly after World War II, when he decided to become a publisher, founding his firm with Guggenheim capital. He could not compete with established publishers who offered American authors advances that would have been ruinous to Straus's small start-up operation. Instead he made use of the contacts he had made during his war work in naval intelligence. He wisely teamed up with publisher John Farrar, who was a New York institution. A president of PEN, Farrar was a professional whose endorsement immediately sent the message that Straus was serious.

When he met Sontag, Straus had had more than a decade of experience dealing directly with authors—often counseling them to do without agents and accept advances lower than other houses were offering. The trade-off was that Straus would offer "a writer-oriented publishing house," as Scott Turow puts it. A writer could walk into the FSG offices—once described as having the look of a failing insurance company—and clearly see that the money was not going into fixtures. The message was that Straus had a program for his authors. For Susan Sontag, it meant that FSG was her house.

At an FSG party in the spring of 1962, Sontag made good her dream of writing for *Partisan Review* (*PR*), the journal in which her intellectual idols had published. Lionel Trilling, Hannah Arendt, Elizabeth Hardwick, Clement Greenberg, Dwight Macdonald and many others placed their landmark essays in *PR*. Although the magazine's influence was waning by the early 1960s, it still represented to Sontag the world of intellectual endeavor that she had been preparing to enter since discovering the magazine in a Los Angeles bookstore. Editors of mass-circulation magazines like *Time* still looked to *PR* to provide advance word on new cultural fashions and on political and social issues.

Sontag walked up to one of PR's editors, William Phillips, and said, "How do you write a review for *Partisan Review*?" Phillips said, "You ask." She said, "I'm asking." He said, "OK." A disarmed Phillips responded immediately to this "immensely attractive and impressive" young woman. He had never heard of her but she emanated intelligence. He could see it in her eyes, in her face. He had also been drinking and wondered if she had caught him at a weak moment. But he preferred to think that he had spotted a new talent.

Alfred Chester's friends—wary of a Sontag whom they think robbed Chester of his ideas and traded on his influence—tell a different version of how she came to be published in *PR*. They remember Chester, disgusted with the New York literary hothouse, handing off his *PR* assignments to Sontag, or rather recommending that she become a reviewer for the journal. Phillips had asked him to do a theater chronicle of the kind McCarthy had done for *PR*, but Chester did not feel like squeezing into her "old girdle." Sontag's recollection is that Phillips wanted her to continue Mary McCarthy's theater chronicle, which Sontag did, although only halfheartedly, quitting the venture after publishing a few reviews. Instead, she went on to write "Notes on 'Camp,'" "On Style," and other important essays.

It is indisputable that both Jason Epstein and Phillips cultivated Chester. He was also seeing a good deal of Robert Silvers, then about to launch the *New York Review of Books (NYRB)*, and Chester took Sontag along with him. For brief periods Sontag stayed with Chester in his Sullivan Street apartment. She got on Chester's lowercase nerves: "susan became excruciatingly demanding and i gave her up. stopped phoning her. what a pill." Chester and Sontag were waging terrific battles and later reconciling. He felt used, suspecting Sontag of climbing over him to get to his connections. "I had a gigantic fight with Susan over a piece of chicken the other day and all the TRUTH came out. I have hated her for four years and only endured her because of Irene," he wrote to Paul Bowles.

The four years Chester is counting date from 1959, when Sontag set off to conquer literary New York. He feared that she would be able to take anything she wanted from him. When she visited him in Mexico in February 1963, he feared she would tempt his male lover, Extro, who took to calling her "la Susanetta." Even when Sontag complimented Chester, he was suspicious. To Edward Field, Chester confided: "Susan said she was at the National Book Award dinner the other night and everyone talked about me. She goes everywhere."

Sontag's first review in *PR*, of Isaac Bashevis Singer's *The Slave*, revealed her impressive grasp of modern thought and literature, and her ability to focus quickly on important questions. It provides an inroad both to her conception of the novel she was writing and to the ground she would stake out as a literary polemicist.

Her debut sentence was: "The typical modern novel is 'psychological' in that the world it presents is really a projection, a bodying forth of the self (or selves) whose analysis constitutes the subject of the novel." In such novels the world, as an objective reality, hardly exists at all. Indeed, in Kafka, in Borges, in the French new novelists, not even the characters are "there"—that is, they have no objective existence—but rather stand for "disembodied emotional and intellectual struggles." No wonder such "post-classical" novels of psychologizing and verbal inventiveness yield a narrative that reads like a nightmare, Sontag concludes.

In a single paragraph, Sontag establishes a compelling tone of authority, based on wide reading and an incisive ability to synthesize diverse material. She is also working out the problem she posed for herself in *The Benefactor*—the novel that had in its first eighty pages intrigued Giroux and Straus. Her narrator, Hippolyte, attempts to live through his dreams, which are often nightmares in which he is dominated and tortured. His dreams are the art he makes of his life, and his desire is to make his life conform to the immediacy and sensuousness of dreams. Like Sontag's idea of art, Hippolyte's dreams are self-contained, which is to say that like Sontag he fancies himself to be self-invented. He does not want to explain away the pleasure and pain of his dreams, but to make himself more conscious of them.

Sontag seemed to offer a provocative introduction to a mental, intellectual adventure. Where could she possibly take a man who seriously, and with great sophistication, wanted to turn his entire life into dreams? The sixty-one-year-old narrator recalls self-absorbing adventures reminiscent of Poe's grotesquerie. This was not at all the kind of first novel one would expect an alluring twenty-eight-year-old woman to write.

Sontag worked on her novel over weekends and the summers of 1961 and 1962. After years of struggling with unpublishable stories, she found that her novel just seemed to flow—as if she were taking dictation. Richard Tristman remembered that Sontag gave him her work for a critical reading. Overwhelmed by its brilliance, he did not know what to say. When she asked him about it, he could offer only praise. She seemed disappointed. Tristman felt he had let her down. In Tristman's experience, most people who asked for criticism rarely could take it. Sontag's utter seriousness about the enterprise of writing impressed him.

Ever her mentor Kenneth Burke wrote to congratulate Sontag after receiving an advance copy of *The Benefactor:* "Fantasies of any sort are rare. Good fantasies are necessarily much more rare. And this is an exceptionally good fantasy." He complimented her intelligence, her ingenuity, her inviting mix of narrative and aphorisms, and he corrected her grammar, citing page numbers where he had spotted errors. He also wrote to critic Stanley Edgar Hyman begging him to give the novel a second look if he had passed it over: "She is the best student I ever had. . . . I'm sure you will find it an ingenious book."

But at least one prospective publisher deemed *The Benefactor* a failure. Milton Walman, an editor at the British publishing house Collins, turned down the novel, conceding that Sontag's erudition and originality impressed him but complaining that her novel lacked character and plot development; its strange people and bizarre incidents were not harnessed to a story. Collins rejected the idea of a three-book contract since Walman doubted that Sontag would "evolve into a novelist whose art can fully and properly absorb her ideas."

Sontag's novel requires, in fact, precisely those qualities she praises in her review of Singer: sensuousness, an evocation of a real, palpable environment. As Sontag rightly notes, unlike other modern writers, Singer does not struggle to "improvise a milieu." His Poland, his people, are *there* on the page; there is no distance between them and their creator. By contrast, *The Benefactor* simply lacks life.

Sontag uses the word "sensuous" three times in her review. It is one of her favorite terms for art that works. Hippolyte lives for the sensuous and the erotic, but *The Benefactor* tells of his quest for the sensuous without showing or dramatizing it. The novel seems perverse in its withholding of precisely the pleasures that readers derive from novels. Why? Because Sontag has already determined that modern novelists—with few exceptions, such as Singer—can only contrive contexts, approximate settings. She envies Singer's grasp of the European scene and the depth he can create by dealing with Cabalistic mysticism and magic, Hasidism, Cossack persecution and massacre, the Enlightenment, the Sabbatian heresy, and the complex history of Jews and Christians. Even better, given Singer's setting, he can indulge his "pre-modern account of motivation." He need never invoke Freud; he does not need to psychologize his demons and other supernatural forces. They are a natural aspect of his world.

Another explanation for Sontag's rejection of a palpable setting is that, as Poe did earlier, she turned her imagination away from her own surroundings. Like Hippolyte, she is not interested in naming her habitat, in giving it color and depth, because it has no substance for her. Having rejected both Arizona and California, and having traveled to Europe like Henry James, looking for history, for meaning, for the literary life, she has, *au fond*, nothing to reckon with but her state of mind.

Hippolyte, for example, never names the city he lives in. He simply calls it "the capital." It is obviously Paris, but he turns it into a generic place. Similarly, the Spanish Civil War becomes the "civil war which was raging at the time in the country to the south." The awkward phrasing is deadening. The well-read will have no trouble playing intellectual parlor games with the novel. Its first readers wondered, for example, whether the homosexual cruiser/writer Jean-Jacques was based on Jean Genet. Critic Sohnya Sayres has also made a suggestive case for seeing Jean-Jacques as a variation on Antonin Artaud. But any resemblance hardly matters. Hippolyte systematically deprives everything of specificity. What he learns from Jean-Jacques is that he can be whatever he likes, he can take himself to extremes.

If Jean-Jacques—Hippolyte's mentor and tormentor—resembles anyone, it is Alfred Chester, who did indeed adore Genet, and who did go mad, like Artaud. As Michael Feingold noted in the *Village Voice*, "Chester carried in himself two of the great polar elements on which most 20th century art is based: He was an intelligent homosexual—that is, a man perpetually conscious of life as a series of roles or poses to be taken on; and he was a madman—a visionary. . . ." He and Hippolyte argue about both the trivial and the profound—though there is no chicken fight. Like Chester confronting Sontag, Jean-Jacques challenges Hippolyte: "You are a self-made *objet-trouvé*. You are your own idea, thought up by yourself." Jean-Jacques acknowledges, ruefully, that Hippolyte has been, in a sense, his invention, but now Hippolyte declares his independence— as Sontag would from Chester. Jean-Jacques demands of Hippolyte: "My *objet-trouvé* is climbing down off my shelf?" When Hippolyte expresses regret over Jean-Jacques's attitude, Jean-Jacques echoes Alfred Chester's conclusion: "You don't need me anymore."

Jean-Jacques goes to bed with Hippolyte once—as Alfred Chester says he did with Susan Sontag. Chester would write a long story, "The

Foot," that might almost be viewed as a reply to *The Benefactor*. "The Foot" concerns what Chester called the "situational I," an identity that could not be fixed but only captured in a surreal novel, "I, Etc.," which he planned to write. When Sontag published *I, etcetera*, she had appropriated more than a title. Like *The Benefactor*, her short story collection would become an unacknowledged homage to Alfred Chester, and perhaps an exorcism of his influence as well.

Like a Poe narrator, like Susan Sontag, Hippolyte spends his childhood in solitude and melancholy. He is "inspired by the prospect of becoming learned." He has a university education, but his most serious learning comes from his own voracious reading. For him as for Sontag, the real revolutions are "revolutions of feeling and seeing." His first philosophical article ("important ideas on a topic of no great importance") is prophetic of Sontag's "Notes on 'Camp'" and of its reception. Hippolyte's work provokes "controversial and excited" discussion in the "general literary world." It provides him with an entrée into the intellectual salons. He aspires, like many of Poe's narrators, to the unutterable—that is, to silence; indeed he is a devotee of the aesthetics of silence, which will shortly become one of Sontag's key terms and, later, the cynosure of her first two films. He is bisexual and "dreams of love and domination, in both the masculine and feminine style." He contributes a few ideas on camp—although he does not use the term—when he observes the "comedy of roles which is the homosexual encounter." Jean-Jacques tells him: "Everything you do is you. You are incapable of doing otherwise." Or as Hippolyte admits, he is an "utterly self-elected man."

That last phrase is reminiscent of an observation by a Sontag friend from the early 1960s who saw the same kind of self-attachment in her, whether she was at home committed to her writing or at center stage promoting her work. Indeed, Hippolyte, though a recluse, also becomes attracted to film acting because it affords an experience comparable to being a spectator of one's own dreams. Sontag would go him one better by directing her own dreams. Prophetically, Hippolyte's film director is a Scandinavian called Larsen; it must have seemed like destiny at work when Sontag was invited to make her first two films in Sweden. Hippolyte even seems to foreshadow Sontag's book on photography, pronouncing: "Life is a movie. Death is a photograph."

The Benefactor founders on its solemnity. The language is not baroque enough or campy in a way that might befit a latter-day Poe.

Alfred Chester, who had a well-developed sense of humor, said Sontag had none. Peter Hujar, a great photographer who would take Sontag's stunning jacket photograph for *Against Interpretation,* also remarked on her humorlessness. When Sigrid Bauschinger, interviewing Sontag for a German newspaper, tried to compliment her on her wit, Sontag protested vehemently. She did not take it as a compliment; she could not abide the idea of it—it was as if she had been accused of frivolity and superficiality. The honest Hippolyte confesses: "It may be said that I lack a sense of humor."

As critic Robert Adams puts it (*NYRB,* October 17, 1963), Hippolyte is a "connoisseur of himself." He is the first of many such characters, culminating in the Cavaliere in *The Volcano Lover.* Hippolyte is acquisitive; he collects things and people for his dreams because, as Sontag vouchsafed to an interviewer, consciousness is a "form of acquisition," a devouring of the world for one's own dreams. Like Sontag, Hippolyte speaks of his family only in the vaguest fashion. He never even reveals his surname. He is reticent because he does not want family or history to hamper his dreams, to stymie his illusion that he is autonomous. And yet, like Sontag, he cannot resist seeking out father figures.

Sontag would protest this comparison of author and character. To one interviewer she asserted: "I am *nothing* like Hippolyte: at least I certainly *hope* I'm not. He fascinates me, but I dislike him intensely. He's purposeless and wasteful and evil." The absolutism of her response invites skepticism. Or as critic Sohnya Sayres observes: "For such a protracted, intense study in a youthful first novel that disclaimer calls attention to itself," and it suggests Sontag may be "hiding from a complex set of feelings" as much as she is exploring them.

Critical opinion has so hardened against *The Benefactor* that it has become nearly impossible for people to imagine why FSG published it. But the FSG files show that the firm thought it had a winner. After all, the novel came with the backing of several powerful novelists and critics. As FSG readied the book for publication in September 1963, it began to amass tributes:

THE BENEFACTOR is certainly a talented, alarming, nightmare—C. G. Jung out of Voltaire. Clearly it was not composed by any Miss Susan Sontag, whose existence I doubt in any case. It is a damned disquieting, queer, un-American piece of good work. —John Barth

This is a considerable achievement for a first novel, and a particularly refreshing one by contrast to the breast-beating and exhibitionism to which most beginning novelists, in this country at least, are prone. —Frederick Morgan, *The Hudson Review*

I just finished Miss Sonntag's [*sic*] novel and I think it is extraordinarily good. My sincere congratulations: you may have discovered there a major writer. Of course, she is quite original and she has learnt to use her originality in the French school. Which is fine. I especially admired her strict consistency, she never lets her fancy go wild, and how she can make a real story out of dreams and thoughts. . . . I really was delighted! And I shall be glad to come to the publication party. —Hannah Arendt

For the all-purpose blurb, though, Elizabeth Hardwick wins the prize. Her air of stately superiority strikes a mandarin tone uncomfortably like the wooden prose of the novel: "Susan Sontag is the new writer who most interests me. She is intelligent, rather grave, and strikingly able to write about serious subjects in a felicitous manner."

Writing to Catharine Meyer at *Harper's* just days before the novel's U.S. publication date, Lila Karpf of FSG cited Arendt's judgment and added: "We have discovered a major writer. . . . We think Susan Sontag will quickly be ranked with such writer-critics as Mary McCarthy and Elizabeth Hardwick."

With the wonderful blurbs, it is noteworthy that FSG decided to use none of them for *The Benefactor* book jacket. Instead it offered the mystique of Susan Sontag herself. Harry Hess's photograph of her is spread across the back cover. It is one of the most perfectly composed shots ever to adorn a first novel. And shot is the appropriate word, for the photograph resembles a film still from a late 1940s French film noir. She is wearing makeup, which accentuates her full lips, her deep dark eyes and brows. In close-up, her eyes are fully open and concentrated. Her erect posture suggests alertness. She is sensual but not sultry.

The photograph half exposes and half conceals her in layers of hard and soft material. Her dark hair—parted low on the left side—is cut just above her turned-up coat collar and frames and clings to the side of her oval face, creating a self-contained aura. Her turned-up collar looks almost as though it were part of a flight jacket. Carolyn Heilbrun suggested that Sontag's dust jacket picture on *The Benefactor* made her look like the "woman aviator who parachutes through the greenhouse roof in Shaw's 'Misalliance.'" This is an author ready for action, with every component of her image in order and at her command.

Sontag, a student of theater, cinema, and photography, had mastered the form. Kenneth Burke thought it "quite an idealization." To Sontag, Burke wrote on July 25, 1963: "The good, scientifically accurate photograph should contribute greatly" to the novel's success.

John Bright Holmes of Eyre & Spottiswoode, the firm that had decided to bring out *The Benefactor* in Britain, wrote to Roger Straus: "I can well understand your enthusiasm for the novel. . . . [I]t is one of the most remarkable I have come across, and not least because of its sheer peculiarity, given the French NRF [*Nouvelle Revue Française*] tone, the German surname of the author, and, to judge from her jacket picture simply, her slightly Mexican cast of features." Sontag would be an author who would travel well. Her FSG author's questionnaire, dated April 21, 1963, contained a customary question: "Will you be available for newspaper interviews, radio appearances, speeches before clubs, a short piece or two on a special subject connected with your current book?" Sontag's response was far from customary. In the middle of an otherwise blank page she wrote a single word: "Anything."

The front jacket cover with an illustration of an ornate grillwork, peacock-feathered fan and the back tour-de-force author photograph, say everything about the dignified yet erotic style that Sontag and FSG cultivated. Sontag brought glamour to the idea of being an intellectual, making it easier for men to accept her as a beauty with brains. For women, she evoked an ambitiousness that could be both sexy and serious. In the early 1960s, it was still rather common to call women babes and chicks. Here was a young woman who sacrificed none of her intellectual attributes, none of her assertiveness, to appeal to the male chauvinist desire to see women as dolls, as somehow not quite as capable mentally as men—and yet she remained desirable. One index of Sontag's wide-ranging appeal is that her image would soon begin to appear in the glossy magazines, and later she would write for *Vogue*. A whole generation of women would get to know Sontag from her photographs, from mentions of her as an authority on the contemporary scene, as well as from her writing. Arguably, more women and men knew Sontag as a "name" than as an author they had read.

Sontag was also able to profit from a change under way at magazines such as *Ladies' Home Journal, McCall's,* and *Vogue*—all of which were "reimagining themselves," as Judith Hennessee, Betty Friedan's biographer, puts it. Women were beginning to seek work outside the home, to think in terms of careers, and editors at these magazines became more hospitable to writers with controversial ideas.

Roger Straus wrote personal letters to important intellectuals like historian Arthur Schlesinger, Jr., then at the White House as a Kennedy advisor, averring, "I can't remember when in the last fifteen years I have sent you a novel which I hold in such high esteem." Schlesinger was an apt choice. He served a president who Norman Mailer said had the personality of a great box-office actor. And the Kennedy administration did much to promote intellectuals not merely as policy makers but as fashionable actors in a new, swinging style that could include, on the one hand, the presence of poet Robert Frost at Kennedy's inaugural and, on the other hand, Marilyn Monroe at his last public birthday celebration in Madison Square Garden.

Two months before *The Benefactor*'s autumn publication, FSG had tried to jump-start public reception by submitting an excerpt to *The New Yorker*. Calling Sontag "wildly talented," Paula Diamond of FSG commended the "most original and unusual first novel we've ever done." Of course, its very "off-beat, highly literary nature, and extreme stylization, would not please everyone." Sontag revised a section specifically for the magazine, but *New Yorker* editor Robert Hemenway replied that the novel was "pretty far from anything that might work for us."

Roger Straus called the novel's reception "mixed," and he put a good face on the "heavy review space" it was getting. In *Partisan Review,* a rather opaque Richard Howard spoke of a prose as "varnished and desiccated as that of Constant, say, or of Stendhal in *Armance,* though here the shellac crystallizes much too often (for those writers) into aphorisms, one of the author's irresistible inconsistencies." Granville Hicks, stationed for many years at the *Saturday Review,* seemed baffled, but he lauded Sontag's "unmistakable talents, her great care, her thoughtfulness." He ended his assessment by giving her the "benefit of every doubt." Robert Adams in the *New York Review of Books,* which would become a publication venue for much of Sontag's writing, deemed *The Benefactor* a "bold, flawed, impressive piece of work." An accolade came from James B. Frakes in the *New York Herald Tribune:* "This is a very special book, written with care, polish, daring, and certainty. Very sure. Very tough."

The novel needed more reviews like that, confident and commanding. If John Wain in *The New Republic* praised Sontag's "adroitness" and "delighted skill," he also coined a condemning phrase that stuck. Wondering what it was about her formal and colorless style that bothered him, he suddenly got it: "Of course! It is translator's English—the sort of composite idiom one gets from great Continental novels one first meets in translation during adolescence." It was a judgment echoed by Roger Sale in the *Hudson Review,* which the adolescent Sontag had read back in Southern California in the days when she aspired to appear in its pages in rather different circumstances.

The reviews were a disappointment to an FSG hoping for greater enthusiasm. By the end of 1967, the novel had sold only 1,800 copies in hardcover, although an Avon paperback, published in January 1965, sold 33,750 copies in the next three years. Less than two weeks after issuing the first hardcover edition of *The Benefactor,* Straus was advising Sontag to make her next book a collection of essays.

Straus sensed that Sontag's gift for literary polemics would win her a larger audience. In the early sixties she sounded oppositional. In the fall of 1963, at a panel on "Literary Criticism Today," she challenged critic Dwight Macdonald, saying he did not understand writers of her generation, and went on to suggest that critics such as Lionel Trilling and Edmund Wilson—the latter she called "overrated"—were through. Publicly, a disgusted Philip Rahv (coeditor of *Partisan Review*) remarked: "Middleclassism a la Trilling is out, perversion is in." To Mary McCarthy, he added: "Susan Sontag. Who is she . . . ? Above the girdle, the girl is a square."

To an older generation of critics, such as Lionel Trilling and Philip Rahv, it seemed that Sontag favored writers like Simone Weil and Jean Genet, who sought extreme states of subjectivity. As critic Liam Kennedy reminds us, Trilling warned against identifying with writer/heroes whose conception of freedom included a separation from society itself. Sequestering the self, Trilling worried, would lead to self-destruction.

Even though Sontag has sometimes been classed as the last of the New York intellectuals and has frequently cited Lionel Trilling as an early model of hers, she had an ambivalent relationship with Trilling, his wife Diana, and others of their generation. Just as many of these thinkers represented the Old Left, Sontag came to stand for much of what came to be called the New Left. Her brand of literary criticism abandoned the New Criticism that had dominated the two decades before her advent. Unlike the New Critics, she seldom spent whole essays on great works of literature, preferring a rather sweeping overview of literary and cultural trends, giving the impression of being a harbinger of things to come rather than merely the conservator of literary tradition.

Sontag was willing to engage mass society in a way that an earlier generation of intellectuals would have found unthinkable. In their era, there would have been no place for a Susan Sontag who was a trained philosopher, a commentator on contemporary culture, and a product of it. Sontag, as both emblem and exponent of her times, became the prime topic of reviewers' responses to her books. Her task was made easier in the climate of postwar America, which saw an expansion of a college-age generation brought up on both popular culture and the university curriculum. Susan Sontag's books themselves, in trade paperback, would take a prominent place on college bookstore shelves. A college student in, say, 1969 was more likely to have known about Susan Sontag than a college student in 1949 was to have known about Kenneth Burke.

Already Sontag was making great friends and great enemies. One aggrieved editor deplored her "highbrow-lowbrow swanking, and her JAP [Jewish American Princess] diabolism. She intimidated people by a thuggishness of personal style (the boots & blackness . . .) and apodictic pronouncements." She had an entourage, "a feminist gang, and middle-class women in general loved (the right word is 'adored') her gangster style, now perhaps passé." At one party in the early 1960s, Sontag showed up with two "lieutenants" and made her appearance memorable by grinding a cigarette out on the living room carpet.

Supremacy

1 9 6 3 – 1 9 6 4

The Benefactor is dedicated to María Irene Fornés, but by January 1963, when Sontag delivered the novel to FSG, Fornés was feeling abandoned. Read against the backdrop of Sontag's life, the novel seems an exploration of the relationships she had savored and renounced.

Alfred Chester watched in dismay as his beloved Irene suffered, swinging from joy to a disturbing calm. By February 1963 she was no longer living with Sontag but spending extended periods with Chester. He felt for Sontag too, observing that both women seemed miserable. In March 1963 both took to confiding their troubles to Chester, and not surprisingly, he was getting different stories. He tended to side with Irene, but he also doubted some of what she said, feeling that her anger at Susan distorted her account. Susan got angry at Alfred and Irene for excluding her from their tête-à-têtes, but Alfred and Irene only seemed more secure in their alliance, with Irene taking comfort in Alfred's harsh characterizations of Susan's duplicity. "She (Irene) had thought all these years that she was the only one who could see through Susan and that everyone else was taken in." The Sontag/Fornés relationship continued to play itself out: "They're still lovers but seldom," Chester wrote to Field in early April 1963. But by the end of the month he announced: "Susan and Irene ne sont plus. It officially ended yesterday, and Irene is holding up courageously."

Chester, as ambivalent about Sontag as always, had a sort of reconciliation with her in late May, when he finally decided to accept Paul Bowles's invitation to join him in Morocco. By then Sontag had become for Chester an embodiment of what he thought of as "New York's literary jungle"—to use the words of Chester's friend Norman Glass. Chester despised the "vulgar publicity tricks and the sordid struggle for power. He described a world in which one had to be a gangster or a film star in order to become a successful writer."

In 1959 Chester had arrived in New York feeling like "King Shit," he said, but he had departed disgruntled over the efforts of editors like William Phillips to make him the next Mary McCarthy. He cast a very cold eye on what he thought was Sontag's scheming, and watched keenly to see how her first novel would be received. He found 1963 to be a year of big changes for all of them.

Chester later said that Irene Fornés blamed him for breaking up her and Susan. He denied the charge, but even if it were true, he said, he could not have done a better thing for Irene. His suspicions about Sontag could well have had a corrosive effect on Fornés. Chester was a man with a gift for making and destroying friendships. As Cynthia Ozick said, "He is the first, most wound-bearing layer of my emotions." Norman Glass, quoting La Rochefoucauld's *Maximes*, said Chester committed the "unpardonable sin: he wounded other people's *amour-propre*." Yet Sontag stood by her relationship with Chester—whatever her misgivings—for another year (well into 1964) and would make a public defense of his work. It was a debt he felt she owed him, but it was also a generous gesture she would come to regret.

Writing to Harriet Sohmers from Morocco, Chester asked: "Is Susan famous? Jane and Paul [Bowles] couldn't read her book, it seems." Susan Sontag was not yet famous, although she was getting there. One sign of her emergence was her appearance in February 1963 in the inaugural issue of the *New York Review of Books*, later called the "country's most successful intellectual journal." As Sontag has said, "American intellectual life—poor, fragmented thing that it is—would be vastly poorer had it not been for the *Review* and the model that it gives for how to write for a generally educated audience." The country had never seen the likes of a popular intellectual forum, looking more like a newspaper than a little magazine, with intellectual headliners doing a lot more—it turned out—than reviewing books. With its first issue, it became a kind of exhibition catalogue for American intellectuals, with the reviewer as the star.

NYRB issued from that entrepreneurial book genius who invented the packaging of classics in Vintage and Anchor paperbacks, Jason Epstein. Epstein was a Columbia classmate of poets Allen Ginsberg and John Hollander. Epstein and his wife Barbara fomented the notion of a *NYRB* over dinner on the Upper West Side of Manhattan with writer Elizabeth Hardwick and her husband, poet Robert Lowell.

In writing for *NYRB*, Sontag entered the magic circle endorsed by Elizabeth Hardwick, matriarch of New York intellectuals. Hardwick became the model for Sontag of how an outsider becomes an insider. Like Sontag, Hardwick has always been besotted with literature, and from her "earliest youth determined to come to New York." Born in Lexington and educated at the University of Kentucky, Hardwick is the Sontag avatar of the "provincial in Balzac, yearning for Paris," as Hardwick herself put it to Hilton Als when he interviewed her for his loving profile in *The New Yorker*. She too had a troubled, complex relationship with her rootless mother, who had "been in too many places, had lived in too many houses"—to borrow a phrase from Hardwick's first novel, *The Ghostly Lover*. Born in 1916, Hardwick received a master's degree from the University of Kentucky, then enrolled in a doctoral program at Columbia and ultimately dropped out, afterward writing for *PR* and marrying Robert Lowell.

The couple reminded poet Derek Walcott of such Victorian pairs as the Brownings and the Carlyles. Lowell and Hardwick established a salon at their Sixty-seventh Street apartment where Walcott observed the "friendly malice with which the work of colleagues was dismissed by the guests. Whole reputations crunched out like butts." When Hardwick made the move from *PR* to *NYRB*, her writing, Als observes, had a "freer, unbridled quality, and one senses that Epstein and Silvers encouraged the particularities of her voice." Hardwick found a home at *NYRB*—and she also cleared a path for Sontag to follow later on.

Hardwick, an esteemed novelist and critic and New York chauvinist, had published in 1959 an often quoted *Harper's* article deploring the state of American book reviewing: "Sweet, bland commendations fall everywhere upon the scene; a universal if somewhat lobotomized accommodation reigns. A book is born into a puddle of treacle, the brine of hostile criticism is only a memory." With its lament for an intellectual's paradise lost, Hardwick's elegiac tone called out for a renaissance.

But years of yearning had passed without the emergence of a new organ of intellectual transformation. Even Epstein's group might not have discovered their intellectual lever without the ministrations of the perfect editor, Robert Silvers. Only three years older than Sontag, he had gone to the University of Chicago at fifteen and graduated in two and a half years. A "fantastic, fanatical, brilliant" editor, Sontag has said, he has an ascetic side similar to hers. "He is fascinated by people of distinction and power, and they all enjoy him," George Plimpton adds.

Silvers, according to his brother, was an avid reader at five. He rivals Sontag in having a virtually photographic memory. He shares her Our Crowd mentality, associating with "a pretty tight circle of New York intellectuals, Oxbridge worthies, and a select group of outriders," editor Gerald Howard observes.

Silvers returned from Paris to the United States in 1959 to become an editor at *Harper's*. It was Silvers, in fact, who commissioned Hardwick to write her excoriation of contemporary book reviewing, especially of the *New York Times*, which then had the make-nice manners that resulted in an undiscriminating attitude toward books which Hardwick despised.

Before Silvers found his niche at *NYRB*, Roger Straus wanted to help both Silvers, who coveted a new, more challenging job, and William Phillips, who needed financial support for *Partisan Review* and an infusion of new talent. Phillips describes Straus as the "first friend of the magazine outside its inner circle of writers and professional intellectuals." Phillips and his coeditor, Philip Rahv, had kept a tight rein while fighting each other for supreme power over their prestigious periodical since the mid-1930s. Rahv was always looking for ways to diminish Phillips, who doggedly held on. Straus and Rahv approached Phillips about bringing in Silvers. A taciturn Phillips says that he liked Silvers, but that "this did not seem his métier." He could not see a *Harper's* editor heading *PR*, which was not a mass publication. The entity that became *NYRB* confirmed his opinion that Silvers was not quite right for *PR*. Phillips thought *NYRB* too fashionable, too trendy.

PR had always had a small circulation and survived on modest means. Sontag has said that she grew up regarding its small but dedicated audience of 5,000 to 10,000 readers as the ideal target of her work, for it—the journal and its audience—had an influence way out of proportion to its numbers. But *PR*'s heyday was over at the time Sontag and Silvers arrived in New York. *PR* had competition from journals that appeared with university support, and the Old Left and the battles of the thirties, forties, and fifties had given way to a new era—fragmented, but also ripe with opportunities.

Phillips, an old-school intellectual, refused to take *PR* to Broadway. Jason Epstein and his cohort, on the other hand, seized their moment during a New York newspaper strike that put the *Times*'s book review out of action. They collected advertising dollars from book publishers that normally went to the *Times*. The first *NYRB* issue has been hailed as "an extraordinary performance." Including Mary McCarthy, W. H. Auden, Gore Vidal, Alfred Kazin, and Elizabeth Hardwick, the magazine had a marquee of over forty big names. *NYRB* was an overnight success.

As Philip Nobile, the first historian of *NYRB* found out, that magazine's inner circle has taken a blood oath not to discuss its initiation ceremonies. The contrast between the closed-in nature of this corps and its putative belief in open intellectual discussion is remarkable. It was this sort of cliquishness that caused Chester to flee Manhattan for Morocco in 1963.

Sometime in 1964, Sontag did a screen test for Andy Warhol, presumably as a candidate for one of his underground movies. The brief test—no more than two minutes—was recently shown in the "Fame After Photography" exhibition at the Museum of Modern Art. Sontag struggles to compose herself, taking at least three large sighs. Her pageboy haircut makes her look very young—twenty, not thirty-one. She fidgets. She does not know where to put her eyes. She wears no makeup, and there is no hint of the glamour evoked in her jacket photographs, or of the poise she would exhibit in later television and public appearances. There is only one gesture that links her to the later Sontag: it is her characteristic way of looking downward as she smiles. On camera it looks as though she is shying away from her own emotions.

That same year Sontag received a *Mademoiselle* merit award and was photographed (again looking closer to twenty than to thirty-one) in full makeup, all in black, leaning against a blank wall. She is captioned the "Writer" in a space all her own—just as another merit-award winner is the "Movie Actress," and another the "Athlete." She was about to embark on a course that would catapult her almost overnight to literary stardom. Perhaps it was Alfred Chester who showed her the way. On March 9, 1963, W. H. Auden published a review of Oscar Wilde's letters in *The New Yorker*. An excited Alfred Chester wrote to Paul Bowles, alerting him to the piece and calling it "very daring," and also to Sontag.

Chester recognized the importance of role-playing and the advent of a public style that Wilde brought to the artist's life. The circumspect Auden treated the nexus between sexuality and art obliquely, never referring to his own experiences. Instead he focused on a Wilde who was both artist and *artiste*, writer and performer, in order to come to this generalization near the end of his essay-review: "The artist and the homosexual are both characterized by a greater-than-normal element of narcissism, though neither has as much as the performing *artiste;* it is only likely that among artists and *artistes* as a class a higher-than-average percent will also be homosexual, compared with many other professions."

The word for Wilde's style was camp. He had found a way to write and to be seen performing as a writer with a gay flamboyance. Whatever else the vexed and much discussed term means, camp is an act that calls attention to itself, that plays with public perceptions of roles. This is why Sontag prefaced "Notes on 'Camp'" (published in *PR*'s fall 1964 issue) with the dedication "These notes are for Oscar Wilde"—as if she might be explaining to Wilde the complex of factors out of which he arose and in which he flourished and fashioned a powerful idea of the modern artist as star.

Auden's essay portrayed a Wilde who made himself an immense social success while dispensing daring opinions by the sentence. As Auden put it, "a performer is truly himself only when he is in a sympathetic relation to an audience." His downfall came when he decided to make an issue of his integrity, to risk exposure of his homosexuality. It was one thing to be suspected of such behavior, to be gossiped about, but quite another to challenge the public to accept his denial of that behavior. Wilde was camp so long as he seemed to masquerade, so that a certain ambiguity could remain. In camp, it is never clear whether a put-on is just a put-on or meant to be something more serious. The performer has it both ways: Mae West is a woman; she is also a woman pretending to be a woman. She remains a constant tease. In court—as Wilde learned to his everlasting sorrow—camp cannot survive: a verdict has to be rendered, whereas camp is an endlessly postponed verdict.

Alfred Chester with his dirty wig, openly gay, could not play the half-revealed/half-concealed game that is camp. But the beautifully beguiling Susan Sontag could—particularly since she was willing to pursue what Chester loathed: social acceptance. Wilde could play the bohemian all he liked, but he also fashioned a public persona that brought in as much as a $1,000 a lecture during his American tour—a sum that in today's terms would place him among the top celebrity draws. Similarly, Susan Sontag could pursue the sexual life she liked in the world's capitals, associate herself with the avant-garde, but she also crafted a role acceptable enough for *Mademoiselle*.

Susan Sontag had found her first great subject: herself taking "notes" on camp. She originally intended the essay to appear in a glossy magazine, presumably to give her ideas maximum exposure. In December 1963 she discussed the idea of the essay over lunch with Arnold Ehrlich, a senior editor at *Show*. He said he wanted to publish the essay, but he did not. Instead she published the essay in *PR* with its under-10,000 circulation; yet her work proved provocative enough to earn her "overnight" fame—as William Phillips and scores of other commentators have called it.

The opening sentence of "Notes on 'Camp'" is a wonderful come-on: "Many things in the world have not been named; and many things, even if they have been named, have never been described." This gambit is quintessential Sontag: the definer of phenomena, the philosopher who will explain that curious term she has put in quotation marks. It has never been discussed, she announces. Never? Well, Christopher Isherwood did spend a "lazy two-page sketch" on it in his novel *The World in the Evening*, she admits. The bold statement, and then its almost immediate qualification, is vintage Sontag. Scholars of camp, of course, can trace its beginnings back to the eighteenth or nineteenth century. A less provocative writer would have spent more than a few sentences trying to pin down the term's origins. Indeed, in a letter to *PR* (Winter 1965), critic John Simon did precisely that: "Miss Sontag might have profitably begun her lengthy tribute to 'camp' by quoting a lexicographer. Thus Eric Partridge's *Dictionary of Slang* defines the noun as 'effeminate, esp. homosexual mannerisms of speech and gesture,' and the adjective as 'homosexual, Lesbian.'" But of course, this is precisely what Sontag wanted to avoid: any hint of pedantry, any introduction of homosexuality before she had completely immersed her audience in the fascinations of camp.

Second paragraph, and another sentence prophetic of the full-blown Sontag: "I am strongly drawn to Camp, and almost as strongly offended by it." Sontag uses the first person, but her self-references are fugitive, a tease, just like the camp performer is. Her divided attitude pervades nearly all her writing, which is marked by what she calls in her camp essay "deep sympathy modified by revulsion." Such statements slyly sustain a tension between being caught up in her material and transcending it. She also wants it made clear that she is doing something terribly difficult: snaring a sensibility that is not governed by reason but operates by a "logic of taste." Straining to express the ineffable, she has to remain "tentative and nimble." Hence notes—not a sustained, fully developed essay.

The notes are like theses nailed to the door of contemporary culture. Sontag lists examples of the canon of camp from Tiffany lamps to *Swan Lake* to *King Kong*. Composer Ned Rorem reports that Sontag had help assembling her list of camp artifacts from observing writer Elliott Stein's one-room fifth-floor walk-up in Paris. Stein had plastered his walls with portraits of starlets and comic-strip characters. He had a Tiffany lampshade, a font for holy water, and photographs of muscle men. Rorem, a painstaking chronicler of the intersection of life and art, concludes: "Susan Sontag told me, circa 1966, that Elliott's room, no less than his *pince-sans-rire* rhetoric, was her chief source. . . . Since there is no record of Susan telling this to anyone else, I'll give Elliott credit where it's due." This vision of Stein, smiling and ironical, suggests he may have contributed to her portrayal of Hippolyte as well.

Camp becomes a Sontag vehicle for advancing her notions of style and artifice—that art itself is not mimetic, a copy of the world, but an emanation of the artist, a kind of magic. Camp is about appreciation of texture, sensuous surface, not content, not subject matter. Camp is drawn to the androgynous and to the strongly exaggerated or corny because they are constructs suggesting that life is a stage, a theater, a construction of the self. Camp is, in short, the aesthetic view of the world, especially appealing to coteries and urban cliques, Sontag points out, who spy

"behind the 'straight' public sense in which something can be taken . . .
a private zany experience of the thing."

Camp also appeals to Sontag because it is a form of control and
assimilation. Camp, she suggests, promotes the integration of homosexuals into society by making them appealing in their playful interpretations. Until his trials, Wilde did well because he offered social criticism
as entertainment. Auden argues that when Wilde no longer found himself socially acceptable, his creativity waned. He needed the largest possible audience, one that cut across classes and could take in the British
aristocracy and American miners—whom he had no trouble entertaining
during his American lecture tour. This socially acceptable avant-
gardism is Oscar Wilde's legacy to Susan Sontag, and she would not
make the mistake of forcing her public to witness a trial or risk exposure
of her private life.

On December 11, 1964, a two-column five-paragraph sum-
mary of "Notes on 'Camp'" appeared in *Time*. One word in bold, **TASTE**,
followed by a word in quotation marks, "Camp," made Sontag an instant
intellectual celebrity, conferring a status she has managed to maintain
through decades of social change.

Time, calling Sontag "one of Manhattan's brightest young intellectuals," reprised the history of dandyism, quoting Sontag lavishly. The constant references to her as well as to the term suggested that she owned
it—or, better yet, that she dared to own it. For as *Time* put it: "And if this
somehow suggests homosexuality, Miss Sontag is not one to deny it." To
a mainstream mass-circulation newsmagazine in 1964, even aligning
oneself so closely to the camp sensibility seemed rather bold. Certain
sentences in "Notes on 'Camp,'" clearly caught *Time*'s attention: "Camp
is the answer to the problem: how to be a dandy in the age of mass culture." Sontag was not merely describing camp; she became the definition
of how to be distinctive, a thinker who knew how to snare the contemporary sensibility. But John Simon, in a letter to *PR*, slyly noted that
Sontag's "catalogue reads very much like *Harper's Bazaar*'s 'Chic is . . .'
or *Vogue*'s 'People are talking about . . .' or any of numerous similar tab-
ulations of what is 'in' and what is 'out.'"

For her colleagues at *PR*, for the audience of literary quarterlies, and
for the college-educated, Sontag had done something wonderful. As

William Phillips observes in *A Partisan View*, she had come to terms, "if only obliquely and somewhat playfully, with a world of popular taste and entertainment." To be sure, there had been others, like Clement Greenberg and Dwight Macdonald, who had published provocative essays on kitsch and mass culture, but they took an aloof approach. Sontag seemed absorbed in what she described, thus ending, Phillips notes, the "adversary attitude to the products of popular and commercial culture." Sontag's style transcended the terms of the old arguments and heralded a "new way of looking at the objects of our culture." Phillips's most telling phrase captured the role Sontag would continue to perform throughout the 1960s and 1970s: she had a "capacity for surmounting the ordinary terms of the arguments." Phillips himself had doubts about her position, but he realized that nothing like Susan Sontag or her way of presenting an argument had ever appeared on the American scene. The camp essay, Phillips concluded, seemed the "result of an immaculate conception."

Sontag, then thirty-one, had become a star. She looked and behaved like one. "She was so full of herself," remembers a couple—we will call them the Wildes—who saw her shortly after her instant fame caught up with her on a lecture tour. She was sitting behind a desk in a Berkeley professor's office, a group of students clustered around her. The Wildes entered and sat down. But they could never really converse with her. Someone would be just about to say something and the phone would ring. Sontag would pick it up and say, "Yes, this is she." She would have a conversation and hang up. Then someone would lean over and begin to speak. Sontag proved difficult to engage, treating the Wildes (one of them was a novelist about her age) kindly but offhandedly. Then the phone would ring again. "I remember thinking this is what it is like when you get to be famous," one of the Wildes remembers. Indeed, Sontag's new stature suited her well. "She was like Elizabeth I. She did not have a ruff, but she had everything else."

9

Fame

1965–1966

In 1965 and 1966, Susan Sontag seemed to be everywhere. She was "almost as famous now in Britain as in America—and it seems impossible to pick up any literary weekly or little magazine there without coming upon an article by her or, at least glancingly, about her," wrote Alan Brien in *The Spectator*. He was taken with her "pixie face under a Rolling-Stone pompadour." In person she seemed "neither the beatnik Boadicea of her writing nor the precocious girl-scout of her television appearances." This tall, tough-looking woman was a cheerful, forthright, and "rapid-fire talker" who "denied any intention of patenting her own individual, clotted, pedagogic, polymathic, parodiable style of criticism."

Sontag's London success was followed by a "People Are Talking About . . ." column in *Vogue* (June 1966): "Sontag & Son." Then nearly fourteen and attending a French lycée in Manhattan, David appeared in a John Lennon cap—that vaguely nautical look Lennon sported at the time—and a herringbone tweed jacket, with arms folded, sitting hunched over a table. Mother Sontag has her right arm around his shoulder and her hand gripping his right arm. He is, in fact, her right-hand man. He too is a thinker and has an "acute sense of his times." *Vogue* calls him an avid reader of books on the Boxer Rebellion and the Albigensian Crusade who also discourses (that is the word) on movies of the thirties and actresses like Kay Francis.

Irving Penn's photograph pictures a Sontag who appears to have borrowed Natalie Wood's hairdresser and makeup artist. The short hair of her book jacket photograph has grown into a glamorous shoulder-length softness. Penn shoots this pair as fashion idols, with a head-on look that accentuates their very dark, large-eyed, wide-open Sumerian stares.

This image of the intellectual as mother suited the times—still a good six years away from the flourishing of a new feminist movement. Sontag could appear to be titillating, yet at the same time she had a nurturing role that reassured women—certainly women who read *Vogue*. And Sontag was very proud of her son, and like any mother liked to show him off. What is more, she was a single mother who had relied on her own ambition and shrewdness to support herself and her son. If Sontag exuded glamour, it was glamour with guts.

Penn's composition makes striking viewing when aligned next to Diane Arbus's classic shot of Sontag and son taken for *Esquire* (July 1965). There Sontag—a worried, almost tortured expression on her face—clings to David, her body and her head resting against him as he—an effeminate-looking twelve- to thirteen-year-old with long bangs—leans into her. They seem a single unit. Sontag's hair is barely combed, and her clothing is casual: a turtleneck sweater and jeans, half covered by a long overcoat. David is definitely the sportier item, in his Carnaby Street clothing.

David, "mascot of the trendy left wing," consorted with Warren Beatty, Jasper Johns, Tom Hayden, and Jane Fonda. He later called himself a "child born in Harvard Yard and brought up in Andy Warhol's factory." Arbus seemed to capture his disgruntled sense of himself as a child pressured to excel, reading *War and Peace* at eleven and weeping because "he knew he would never write so well." If Sontag looks unhappy in the Arbus photograph, she has a right to: her ex-husband was suing her for custody, alleging she was an unfit mother. (She told Richard Tristman that she had been forced to take a Rorschach test. But she managed to keep custody of David.) Although Sontag and son seem inseparable in both photographs, David remembers that by the age of fourteen he was spending much of his time alone. Like his mother, he was out the door at an early age—traveling through Europe and the Middle East on his own at fifteen.

The custody battle between David's parents seems only to have strengthened his identification with his mother; he remained estranged from his father for more than twenty years. Often out at New York events or embarking on a European travel itinerary that would have exhausted all but the hardiest of travelers, Sontag maintained a mystique even for her son. If she was not a caring mother in terms of domestic arrangements and day-to-day routines, she was supremely caring when it came to sharing access to her own quest for greatness with her son. If he felt intimidated by her expectations of him, he also felt gratified to travel in her company. Being in her orbit gave him an extraordinary sense of entitlement.

No sooner had Susan Sontag achieved fame than she wished to escape it, to back away from articles like Mary Ellmann's "The Sensational Susan Sontag" in the *Atlantic Monthly* (September 1966), which began: "In the land of *Vogue*, People are Talking About Susan Sontag." In the spring of 1966, Sontag wrote to William Gass expressing her embarrassment that her blurb for his novel *Omensetter's Luck* had been featured prominently on the front of the book jacket. It looked like she was setting herself up as "someone's patron," when in fact she had assumed her name would appear on the back as one of many writers who praised the book.

In 1966 Sontag turned down an offer from *Esquire* to do a monthly film column, calling the magazine "pretty loathsome." Writing on August 11 to Roger Straus, she noted: "I don't want to be the new Dwight Macdonald any more than I want to be the new Mary McCarthy, estimable as these worthy people are." She declared her intention to run from any kind of "pop-celebrity fame." Her letter to Straus crossed with his dated the same day. Straus thought better of *Esquire*, observing that while Sontag might not want to steal time from writing her novel, there was no problem with, "you should pardon the expression, your image."

Straus's use of the word "image" touched a sore point. Sontag simply could not accept that she now had a public persona, that to certain women and men she was a kind of heroine whose own example had expanded the range of cultural discussion and behavior. Her readers (including those who only read about her or saw photographs of her) delighted in precisely the image of a woman who could be seen to be doing, in that sixties cliché, "her own thing."

Sontag disliked becoming the latest hot tip in *Time*. She told her readers in the preface to the paperback edition of *Against Interpretation,* "I was not trying to lead anyone into the Promised Land except myself." Such statements bespeak what Leo Braudy calls, in *The Frenzy of Renown,* the "Lindbergh syndrome," the desire of the famous to "relinquish their fame only partially,"

> to achieve fame because you fulfill the desires of an audience for a hero and then to deny that the audience or the times have anything to do with your fame. You deserve it only for your pure self, which you will dispense in increasingly tiny droplets to the faithful.

Sontag did not campaign for camp—she never wrote about it again. Of course she wanted her ideas to be influential, but as a person she wanted to be left alone:

> As long as I have solitude and a place to work . . . as long as I'm published and have enough money for books and movies and the opera, I'm perfectly content. . . . I don't see why anyone would look for . . . publicity. I know quite a few movie stars and most of them are confused and unhappy.

Sontag did not say why her movie-star friends were "confused and unhappy." Is it because of too much publicity, or too little? For the famous, what is enough and not enough is constantly shifting in a dynamic that Sontag did not acknowledge.

To recognize the fluctuations of fame is to admit, as Braudy shrewdly observes, the element of theatricality. Sontag would have had to say that she enjoyed the perks of fame, which include, in Braudy's words, the "glow of being observed and appreciated by others." But to admit that one craves adulation puts one in the audience's debt. As long as Sontag remained silent about her relationship to her audience, it was free to admire her, and she was free to savor its applause.

Critic Marcie Frank points out that Sontag is one of the great withholders of literature: "She wants to limit the performance of sensibility even though her own writing is the performance of her sensibility." She rejects the autobiographical mode as exhibitionism: "Sontag does not identify the characteristics that allow her to know camp. Instead, she produces her revulsion as a badge of the average, which offers the reader grounds for identifying with her."

The complaint often voiced in reviews of Sontag's critical works is that she is so elliptical. She takes provocative positions, but she does not really sustain her arguments. Frank suggests that to fully embrace critical practice instead of performance, Sontag would have had to embrace autobiography. That way lies Norman Mailer, of course, whom she derides in *Against Interpretation* for his egoism. But at the other extreme, Sontag is hiding, dispensing morsels of wisdom to the faithful in bad faith, Frank implies, since Sontag never really comes clean about the personal sources of her authority.

A few years after the appearance of "Notes on 'Camp,'" Sontag suspected that Jill Johnston, an art and dance critic—and by 1959 a carte blanche columnist for the *Village Voice*—was about to publish an article about Sontag's sexuality. Sontag phoned Johnston, hurling all manner of insults and managing to convey her horror that Johnston might out her. Sontag had become agitated, Johnston remembers, because Roger Straus had warned her of the dire consequences of such an article.

Actually, Johnston has never had an objection to Sontag "remaining a closet lesbian." Johnston herself did not come out as a prominent lesbian activist until 1971. She realizes that politicized lesbians and gays have wanted "those of any influence and renown" to come out, but Johnston believes that the "still precarious, even dangerous position, both legally and socially, of lesbians and gay men" makes the desire to remain hidden understandable. She asserts that the literary and art community is well aware of Sontag's sexual orientation, but this is a "family" type of knowledge. "Everyone in the family 'knows,' but no one is supposed to mention it (except in the context of a rumor mill), much less go abroad with it." She documents this world of "privileged information" in her book on Jasper Johns.

Johnston notes that Sontag has much in common with the closeted gay men covered in her book:

Successful before Stonewall [1969], they could only have had reason to think, subconsciously at least, that they had much to lose by coming out after Stonewall provided a consensus for doing so. Another way of putting it: Any controversial (sexual) political identity was liable to threaten their publicly affirmed identity as artists and writers. Susan, of course, became politically identified with liberal left causes that were acceptable.

The fear of marginalization had its intellectual roots in figures like Leo Strauss. He argued that the great philosophers concealed as much as they revealed, and that certain truths, spoken too boldly or openly, as Socrates and Spinoza demonstrated, led to death or at least to ostracism.

In the pre-Stonewall world, very few women discussed lesbianism openly. The word itself was not spoken in Lillian Hellman's controversial play *The Children's Hour* (1934), and the homosexual drama at the heart of the play had to be transformed into a heterosexual triangle for the Hollywood film version, *These Three* (1936). A child of the 1930s and 1940s, Sontag could see that not much in the culture had changed, although William Wyler, the director of *These Three*, was finally able to introduce the lesbian theme in his remake of *The Children's Hour* in 1962. But what does Martha do in the play when she acknowledges her sexual attraction to Karen? She kills herself. Lesbianism is a moral and physical affront to normality. It is treated with revulsion. In fact, Martha and Karen are guilty of nothing; it is the very idea of homosexual congress that isolates them, destroying their lives as teachers and their reputations in the community. Nineteen sixty-four was not 1934, but could Susan Sontag take a chance on finding out how much had changed? And who could she put such a question to? As Johnston explains, "In our world of the 60's, Susan was the only other lesbian I knew of."

At a turning point, Johnston and Sontag took entirely separate paths—Johnston toward explicitly dealing with her sexuality and its political implications in *Lesbian Nation* (1973). To Johnston, Sontag's writing was "too abstracted from the human interpersonal concerns that have preoccupied me." Yet their paths would continue to cross, with Johnston observing Sontag as a "celebrity buff; we were all influenced by media selections for star status," Johnston admits, "but I believe Susan, like, say, Jasper Johns, was particularly smitten by celebritydom. I have had my doubts that she is a people person at all, i.e. that persons per se are interesting to her. Anyhow it was her brand of fame and my onrushing credentials along that line that brought us together."

In July 1964 artist Joseph Cornell watched Susan Sontag on television excoriating the educational system. Riveted to her image, he confided to his journal that she made him "momentarily inspired." A shy, retiring man cooped up with his invalid brother and domineering mother in a home on Utopia Parkway in Queens, Cornell found an outlet in visits to theaters and opera houses, lurking outside stage doors, first observing female performers and then turning them, literally, into icons in his work. A devotee of divas, Cornell selected Sontag as one of his obsessions. His elaborate and exquisite boxes were themselves frames or stages in which he situated his dancers, singers, movie stars, and, now, Susan Sontag.

Like Sontag, Cornell enjoyed the act of admiring. An enthusiast, he lived to acquire, though unlike Sontag, he found it difficult to disburden himself of his obsessions. In this sense, he was a collector and she was not. Whereas he could wallow in the paraphernalia of the past, constantly reconfiguring his collectibles into the ingenious boxes and settings that were his world, Sontag had to go out into the world and slough off history, championing what she would call in her final essay in *Against Interpretation* the "new sensibility."

The "new sensibility," however, had its origins in surrealism, in the art of radical juxtapositions, an art that combined so-called elite and popular cultures, an art Cornell treasured as much as Sontag did. He sensed a kindred spirit. Indeed, when he read *Against Interpretation,* he realized she adored the avant-garde filmmaking that he himself had indulged in and that would be rediscovered in the 1960s and 1970s. They were alike in their desire to take visual possession of things, although Cornell realized that Sontag as an icon also knew how to stimulate an audience's visual possession of her.

When Cornell read Sontag's review of Maurice Nadeau's *The History of Surrealism* in the New York *Herald Tribune* (November 1, 1965), he began to study her avidly. Cornell's biographer, Deborah Solomon, reports that inside his edition of *Against Interpretation* is a "proof sheet with nine different head shots of Sontag, handsome in a turtleneck and jacket, her short hair framing a face devoid of makeup." Solomon speculates that Sontag herself gave Cornell the photographs. Why Solomon should have had to speculate is puzzling, since she acknowledges Sontag's help in writing her biography.

A contact sheet with nine different head shots is in effect a strip of film that Cornell, as avant-garde filmmaker, deeply prized. Cornell assembled for Sontag what Solomon calls a "fan package," which included a copy of *Monsieur Phot*, his surrealist film scenario of 1933. Solomon says Sontag was "charmed." Her letter to Cornell sounds straightforward enough: "Dear Mr. Cornell," she wrote on December 12, 1965, "Thank you very much for your letter, and your gift of the film script. I was very moved and delighted by both."

Five weeks later, on January 19, 1966, Cornell visited Sontag, then living on Washington Street in Greenwich Village. Recording the details in his diary, he mentioned a Jeanne Moreau photograph on the wall, as if, Solomon cannot resist adding, he were "getting two stars for the price of one." A week after the visit, he again mentioned meeting Sontag in his diary, as if commemorating a historic event. Three days later he called her and had a "decent talk."

Solomon does not comment on this last diary entry. Decent does not sound very exciting, not exactly what Cornell might have wanted from his icon. Or is it the business of the icon to remain at least slightly aloof? Cornell does not say he was disappointed. Solomon says that "for all his affection for her, Sontag could not take Cornell quite seriously as a suitor." Sontag told Solomon that the sixty-year-old Cornell seemed frail and had the transparency common among the aged. She assumed he did not have a sex life, and she was right. Solomon comments only that "Cornell's feelings for Sontag were genuine." He continued to write about her in his diaries, to telephone her, to write her letters (some of which remained unsent). He talked her up to friends, extolling *Against Interpretation*. Many of the camp items she listed in her essay—*Swan Lake* and Greta Garbo, for example—had already been subjects of Cornell boxes. He reveled in the world of artifice, of theatricality. But Sontag would greet her appearances in his art with mixed emotions. Her camp essay positions her outside, looking in; Cornell's boxes reverse this image.

Sontag admits that on her visits to Utopia Parkway she was uncomfortable. She called it a "great privilege" to be asked to this artist/recluse's home, but the implication that she was a part of his world might have increased her unease. Yet she returned again and again, and Cornell gave her parts of his collections, photographs and film stills and other mementos.

Cornell assembled several collages in homage to Sontag. One focused on Henriette Sontag, a nineteenth-century diva. These two Sontags are not literally related, but Cornell reveled in the idea of the pair as doubles, which accentuated, Solomon observes, the "dreamy feelings of identification that made him their double as well." Only one collage has Sontag center stage. *The Ellipsian,* as Cornell brilliantly titled it, is based on the book jacket photograph for *The Benefactor.* Solomon's description of the collage reveals that Cornell anticipated the goddess or priestess-like quality that reviewers of *Against Interpretation* would soon be remarking on, although Cornell's evocation of the icon is more reverential: the "photo of Sontag—torn at the edges to suggest the passage of time—occupies the upper right corner of the page, from whose heights she stares into space with cool self-possession. A scrap from a chart of the solar system and penciled circles endow her with an otherworldly dimension." Publicity, theater, religion, myth—they all make up Cornell's version of the "new sensibility," one that Sontag would say delights in the sensuous, in surfaces, in—although she would never admit as much—the stylish photographs of Sontag herself.

But enchantment can easily give way to disenchantment. Solomon concludes with the report that Sontag was amazed when a young man introducing himself as Cornell's assistant requested that she return the two boxes Cornell had given her.

Cornell's enthrallment with Sontag was typical of the public infatuation with her already under way by the time her second book, the collection of essays called *Against Interpretation,* appeared in early 1966. She was titled "Lady on the Scene" (*New York Times Book Review,* January 23, 1964), and her work became symbolic of "Swingtime" (*New York Review of Books,* June 9, 1966)—to cite just two of the book's more influential reviews. In the former, Benjamin DeMott, who had plenty of qualms about Sontag's arguments, nevertheless deemed her "a genuine discovery." The book contains twenty-six essays, culled from the several dozen she published between 1961 and 1965. Section I presents her critical credo in "Against Interpretation" and "On Style"; II concerns her studies of artists, critics, philosophers, and anthropologists; III, her take on modern drama; IV, her dissection of film (science fiction, the avant-garde, and the European New Wave); V, her evocation of the new sensibility as exemplified in camp and Happenings. This encyclopedic performance was graced once again by a stunning back-of-the-jacket photograph, this time by friend Peter Hujar, who built on the iconography of Harry Hess's *Benefactor* photograph. But Hujar has added his characteristic brilliance to this effigy. He shoots her with eyes cast down but with her lips wearing an almost enigmatic Mona Lisa–like expression. He compresses this image into a close-up tighter than Hess used, so that the photograph is cropped well above Sontag's waist. The neutral light gray background and the lighter-colored jacket have an effect of lightening Sontag's image while preserving the air of intrigue. Another pose that FSG distributed with the press materials for the first edition shows a Hujar take of Sontag against a stark white background, looking older (with circles under the eyes and laugh lines). DeMott in his *Times* review shows how jacket and text were meant to be conflated:

> The haunting image is that of a lady of intelligence and apparent beauty hastening along city streets at the violet hour, nervous, knowing, strained, excruciated (as she says) by self-consciousness, bound for the incomprehensible cinema, or for the concert hall, where non-music is non-played, or for the loft, where cherry bombs explode in her face and flour sacks are flapped close to her, where her ears are filled with mumbling, senseless sound, and she is teased, abused, enveloped, deliberately frustrated until—

What is revealed, DeMott suggests, is the solemn Sontag, the "self-lacerating Puritan" radically juxtaposing herself against the phenomena of culture in a "vivacious, beautifully living and quite astonishingly American book."

With press like that, it hardly mattered that Eliot Freemont-Smith of the *New York Times* complained that

> she did not creep modestly and hesitantly into the intellectual scene. . . . Instead, she burst from nowhere amid something like a ticker-tape parade . . . throwers being her publisher (Roger Straus, Jr.) and the somewhat brassy, assertive and valuable junior members of the

Partisan Review–New York Review of Books cultural coterie. . . . Instead of being announced, she had been proclaimed.

That Sontag was sensational and controversial is what mattered. Tom Nairn in the *New Statesman* (March 24, 1967) only made her seem more formidable when he deplored her image as "a cult leader one wants to be in with . . . a prophet of the contemporary ineffable." Similarly, Robert Phelps in *Life* worried about Sontag's "peculiar ambition to be regarded as an emblem, to present her trials, tastes, committals as themselves expressing a truth greater than any even she can yet know—her generation's truth which others will have to perceive." Like all great mythic figures, Sontag combined what Robert Mazzocco in his *NYRB* review called "contrary components, austerity and voluptuousness." (This is best seen, perhaps, in her sober, almost anthropological description of the Happening, a kind of rehearsed chaos that follows the "alogic of dreams rather than the logic of most art.") She brought an impressive intellect to bear on works like Jack Smith's underground film *Flaming Creatures,* in which the "shaken breast and the shaken penis" became interchangeable, "flaming out in intersexual, polymorphous joy." Smith's films were of value because they were sensuous and immediate, an antidote to the staid, complacent art that critics and philistines (often one and the same to Sontag) praised.

Reviewers pointed to the influence of Edmund Husserl, the great European phenomenologist who believed that significance grew out of the description of phenomena, not out of converting phenomena into the terms of some other kind of analysis, such as Freudianism or Marxism. Thus Sontag counsels, again and again, an immersion in art, in the experience of art, and not in the intellect, which tries to make something out of art. The trouble with her position, as many reviews took satisfaction in pointing out, is that she was herself an enthusiastic interpreter of the art she liked, not just a devotee of it.

Sontag was not insensitive to that objection. Critic Ihab Hassan has called "Against Interpretation" and "On Style" essays that "refuse dating, refuse obsolescence, because they address a timeless human impulse: to interpret and appropriate the world." She is right to be wary of interpretation, what she calls "open aggressiveness, an overt contempt for appearances" that subverts art for selfish purposes. At her finest, Sontag's writing has a wonderful tension, a self-correcting rhythm that keeps in check her own polemical/interpretative inclinations.

"Against Interpretation" argues that contemporary critics concentrate on content, ignoring style and form, which are the signature of the artist. Yet Sontag knows quite well that Western criticism and philosophy since Plato and Aristotle has not been able to abandon the content/form distinction even as it has argued that the two are inseparable and are only treated as distinct for purposes of criticism. Indeed, she argues (in a passage often overlooked by her critics) that there have been periods in criticism when an analysis of content was not only useful but essential. It is just that in her age, critics have gone content-mad. She produces a polemic to redress the imbalance between form and content, to tug the discussion closer to style, to call a moratorium on the eager hunting for hidden meanings, for symbolic patterns—to declare, as Gertrude Stein did, "a rose is a rose is a rose."

Sontag, then, was promulgating a kind of therapy, an antidote to the psychologizing that had infected both the academic and journalistic discussion of art for more than twenty years. Reviewers, thinking of themselves as a sophisticated gendarmerie of literature, bridled at her prescriptions. Alicia Ostriker in *Commentary* (June 1966) complained about Sontag's "refusal to carry any line of reasoning through to the end." Peter Brooks in *PR* (Summer 1966) lamented her "failures of logic, language and historical understanding." These are the typical failings of polemics, which are not measured, academic considerations of a subject. As Irving Howe noted in his attack (also a polemic) on Sontag in "The New York Intellectuals," she was the product of a generation of provocateurs who had contempt for transitions. Leaps of logic were prized, not punished.

Jack Behar in the *Hudson Review* (Summer 1966) identified the historical moment that was so receptive to Sontag. She came on the scene when the great figures of modernism like Joyce and Eliot had been absorbed into the universities and cultural life of the country. Irving Howe announced in "The New York Intellectuals" that philistinism had been conquered; the vulgarity of mass culture had been put in its place by the likes of Clement Greenberg and Dwight Macdonald. Most of the 1930s radicals still around had moved away from Marxism and toward anti-Communism and bourgeois culture—even if, like Howe, a few tried to keep the hope of socialism alive.

Sontag saw herself as emerging out of that *PR* world and transcending it. It would have been unthinkable for Greenberg or Macdonald to train their intellects on science fiction the way Sontag did in "The Imagination of Disaster," which is still one of the key critical guides to science fiction film. But to Sontag the new sensibility was about precisely that ability to move between high and low, the so-called elite and popular or mass cultures of the day. She did not see herself as undiscriminating, although Howe and others saw her positions as ruinous to the precious distinctions between high and low art they had worked for decades to establish. For her to call the criticism of the day philistine was a deliberate provocation—and, to some minds, a gross distortion. As Jack Behar observed, nowhere did she actually name the philistines she had in mind. Who were these critics who wallowed in content? They were straw men. To name names would inevitably have led to qualifications in her argument, to those dull transitions she wished to avoid, to the plodding, if truthful, claims of history.

Yet Howe himself acknowledges that by the mid-1940s both Greenberg and Macdonald had exhausted what they had to say about popular culture. Their arguments, their categories, were static. What made Sontag exciting is that she saw a dynamic between Beckett and the Beatles. As she argued in the last essay of *Against Interpretation*, there was one culture, one sensibility—not two, as C. P. Snow argued in contrasting art and science, or as in high and low, as the *PR* critics had maintained. But Howe mistook Sontag when he judged that her argument obliterated distinctions between good and bad art. Sontag, as she reiterated in countless interviews and in a retrospective essay on *Against Interpretation*, never thought of herself as advocating an abrogation of aesthetic standards. True, when she lapsed into the mantra about the appeal of sensuality, spontaneity, surfaces and textures, the language she used made her sound to Howe and others as if she were recommending superficiality and anti-intellectualism, a "do your own thing" mindlessness. She caricatured Matthew Arnold's belief in literature as moral uplift, and set it aside for a new sensibility that valued new "modes of vivacity." This was the kind of vague phrase that riled Howe. Thirty years later Sontag would gloss her program as a brief for a "more alert, less complacent seriousness." But without some definition of content, Howe had trouble taking her seriously. What exactly was there to be serious about? If almost anything could be turned into an object of serious study, then what did the term "serious" really mean? To Howe, Sontag had to be rejected as "a publicist able to make brilliant quilts from grandmother's patches."

Howe attacked Sontag's eclecticism, sarcastically lamenting, "If only one could learn to look upon intellectual life as a variety of play." He deeply distrusted Sontag's and *NYRB*'s deference to intellectual and political fashions. A writer who had gone through a painful journey from Marxist true believer to a stoic believer in the worth of bourgeois democracy, Howe was appalled that Sontag and her patrons seemed ready to "abandon traditional precepts for a moment of excitement." Sontag was now writing for periodicals like *Vogue* and *Mademoiselle*, unimaginable acts for an intellectual of the 1930s, one who would even have had qualms about publication in *The New Yorker*. She seemed to have thrown herself into what Howe called the "absorptiveness of modern society." She was part of a new generation that Howe deeply distrusted because it was "attracted to the idea of power." That Sontag had been published in *PR* only demonstrated Howe's concern about the journal's conflict between upholding standards and embracing the moment. According to William Phillips, Philip Rahv wanted to reject Sontag. Phillips—no matter his qualms about some of Sontag's ideas—became her staunch advocate.

Sontag became a heroine for a new generation with intellectual ambitions precisely because she extended the range of what it meant to be serious. She did not compartmentalize culture: to be able to appear in both *Vogue* and *Partisan Review* was not hypocritical; rather, it reflected an energetic, bold woman who could appear in any venue she chose. Susan Sontag's great gift to American culture was to show that the world of the intellect could be found everywhere. To be sure, her behavior was taken by some as self-promoting, and as a freelance writer she needed the income from glossy magazines. Nevertheless, her desire to speak to an audience far larger than Lionel Trilling or Irving Howe ever imagined addressing seemed laudable to many. Susan Sontag helped to change both what *Vogue* and *Partisan Review* found it possible to publish.

In *A Partisan View*, Phillips reports that he tried to bring the generations together, inviting elements of the old and the new sensibilities to meetings that finally only exacerbated the differences between them. But Phillips remembers that at one *PR* soiree "Irving Howe said he was so charmed by Susan that he forgot she was his political adversary." Indeed, Howe's attack on her in "The New York Intellectuals" turns him into a kind of Ulysses striving mightily to resist Sontag's siren song.

What bothered Sontag's intellectual "fathers"—to borrow Liam Kennedy's term—was her vanguard role in a new generation for whom the "world seemed to be opening up." By the fall of 1965, Subsidiary Rights at FSG had also sold 1,000 copies of *Against Interpretation* to the Mid-Century Book Society. In February 1966 FSG sold mass-market and trade paperback rights to *Against Interpretation* to Dell. As of the end of 1967, the book had sold over 10,000 copies in hardcover, a very respectable showing for a work of criticism. The Delta trade edition paperback had sold 21,994 copies by May 1969.

FSG was following a path that publishers of other literary figures such as Norman Mailer, William Styron, and James Baldwin had pursued. Trade paperbacks would often be adopted for college courses; the cheaper mass-market editions were aimed at general readers. The author became a personality available for appearances on television and in other forms of the mass media. Of course, the author as celebrity was nothing new, but the older means of promotion—the lecture tour and advertisements—were augmented by an author's tour during which he or she was interviewed in media outlets every time a new book or controversial essay appeared. Sontag preferred newspaper and periodical interviews. She made no effort to become a television personality, a media debater in the mold of Norman Mailer and Gore Vidal.

Indeed, Sontag charted a more precarious course than these two writers. Not only had she rejected the idea of becoming a columnist for *Esquire,* she refused, in most instances, to work on commission or have editors dictate her subjects. After her initial bout of reviewing in the early 1960s, she by and large eschewed the steady income she could easily have earned from reviewing. When she had to, she did piecework to pay the bills, but she was remarkably courageous in pursuing ideas that had no immediate economic payoff. Similarly, she could easily have become a pundit. When she did appear on television, she was forthright, well spoken, and charming, with the delivery of a professional speaker.

Sontag had another option open to her. She could teach. Although she would occasionally teach a course, give a lecture, or take a brief writer-in-residence position, she refused most jobs that would have hampered her independence as a writer. In 1964 she quit teaching at Columbia. Teaching, she would say, had been a pleasure, but it was different from writing: more explicit, and not as exciting and daring. "I would pitch my tent outside the seductive, stony safety of the university world," she reminisced in her 1996 preface to *Against Interpretation*.

Sontag did not relinquish a tenured position at Columbia. Indeed, Robert Giroux (still involved in editing some of her work) sought financial support from the Merrill Foundation for Sontag, pointing out that Columbia did not value her highly. She was then a sensation but certainly not the kind of revered writer a university would seek out in order to have bragging rights. She was a lowly instructor without a Ph.D. and would have had to submit to the grind of completing one. She would have had to write academic articles spelling out what she preferred to have remain elliptical in her polemics. Even brilliant scholars have lost their bids for tenure. Academia is a great risk, a huge investment of time that pays off only for a very small percentage of professorial aspirants. And then there is the petty world of institutional politics, where arguments become all the more vicious because the stakes are so small. The old-boy atmosphere of Columbia and elsewhere was not favorable for a brilliant woman. Nevertheless, Sontag could probably have conquered this academic world.

But with the stalwart Roger Straus committed to publishing her, Sontag had no reason to continue an academic career. In early 1966, when Paul Flamand of Editions du Seuil considered dropping Sontag from his list because of *The Benefactor*'s poor sales, Straus made a "special plea," pointing out that she was devoting full time to completing a new novel and that *Against Interpretation* had already sold 3,800 copies with a mass-market paperback offer and "great review space." Straus advised: "Hang on to her, if you can," since she was "one of the most interesting writers we have in the U.S."

Sontag repaid Straus's efforts by informing him about authors like Walter Benjamin, whom she recommended that FSG publish under its Noonday Press imprint. When Straus heard of other authors he thought were likely publishing projects, he often sought out Sontag's opinion. She did not confine herself to literary interpretation, but rather sized up market conditions, so to speak, so that Straus had some idea of what kind of sales he could expect among the intelligentsia.

It was an extraordinary collaboration between author and publisher that resulted in the publication of much fine work that might otherwise have entered American culture more slowly, if at all. In this respect, Sontag used her fame to further the careers of other writers such as Elias Canetti, Danilo Kiš, Robert Walser, and Roland Barthes. She did so realizing that the times provided her with a unique opportunity to shift American culture toward a more international perspective. As Sontag herself put it in her 1996 preface to *Against Interpretation,* the sixties were a delightful decade for opportunists: "There were new permissions in the air, and old hierarchies had softened, had become ripe for toppling."

$\mathscr{P}eter\ and\ \mathscr{P}aul$

1 9 6 5 – 1 9 6 7

Susan Sontag wrote Alfred Chester in Morocco in April 1965, saying she
wanted to see him. Would he like to see her? Chester called it a "very
strange twisted letter that makes you wonder why she wants to come
here. Really to see me? Is she doing an article? Is she afraid I will
become famous and powerful and be her enemy? I will try to fathom her
black sinister depths." Yet Sontag had proven herself a friend to
Chester's work. At his urging, she had written a letter to the *New York
Times Book Review* (May 31, 1964) taking issue with Saul Maloff's review
of Chester's short story collection, *Behold Goliath*. Besides attacking
Maloff's literary judgment, Sontag accused him of homophobia, and
ended with an encomium: "There is a great range in 'Behold Goliath,'
and at least half of the stories (above all the remarkable title story) seem
to me beautiful achievements."

In Tangier, Chester had found some solace outside New York's literary precincts: "The whole literary thing including Susan makes me want
to vomit and I haven't even any kif to make me feel amused about it,"
Chester wrote Edward Field. Sontag's imminent appearance set off a
train of musings in Chester:

Do you think great fame and power will always be just out of our reach? I don't think Susan's celebrity is so strange. Remember, there is a millionaire behind her, she is beautiful, she says things or thinks things that really couldn't upset the establishment, and that whole dead New York liberal literary crowd was dying for a new face. Or voice. Remember what they were offering me? I am glad now I rejected that world. Oh, a letter for Susan came from Straus, and holding up the envelope to the light I could read some of it. (I am too lazy to steam it open.) Her book Against Interpretation, which I assume is essays, is apparently coming out in the fall. She will be here next week. I have had two letters and so has Paul and we compared them and roared with laughter as they go together so interestingly. A woman, Paul kept saying, she's a woman. Naturally. I think she is trying to make us compete for her. I still wonder why she is coming.

As soon as Sontag arrived, Chester felt spied upon: "I feel as though Susan was taping my hysterical babblings," he confided to Field. In his calmer moments, Chester reflected: "I don't know if Susan is really a rat. I think she is just very much at home in the world."

Paul Bowles, an aloof but commanding figure, took great pleasure in Chester's company, finding him wonderfully entertaining in conversation. Chester believed Bowles to be the only one in Tangier on his level. And Bowles received many of the literary greats, members of an avant-garde drawn by the exotic life he evoked in his fiction. Sontag set herself up in the Minzah Hotel, Tangier's most elegant, for several weeks. As Edward Field reports, her stay stimulated "irony mixed with admiration. Where else would Susan Sontag stay?"

Confronted with Sontag the successful, Chester girded himself, fearing that she would lure away his bisexual Moroccan boyfriend, Dris, although there is no evidence that she did. Bowles told Field that Sontag came to tea and announced that Chester was crazy. "Of course," the unflappable Bowles replied. "We're all crazy here in Tangier." "No, Paul," Sontag insisted, "I mean Alfred's *really* crazy." One of Chester's friends describes him as "snappish . . . almost as if he were slightly rabid." His sense of specialness eroded as Sontag dined chez Bowles and sans Chester. Sontag told one of Chester's friends, Ira Cohen, that Chester had proposed to her and that she was afraid of him, perhaps even fearing a physical attack.

Right after Sontag's visit, in the fall of 1965, Chester admitted to Field: "Susan's visit was catastrophic. I didn't entertain her at all because I was nuts, out of myself or induced, I don't know. . . . Her visit is impossible to describe." She had read his new novel, *The Exquisite Corpse,* and said she liked it, but a bitter Chester doubted her word since FSG had turned it down. By November, a couple of months after Sontag's visit, Chester wrote to Harriet Sohmers: "By this time you've probably seen Susan. I don't know for sure if she was here. Paul says she was and others do too. There was a dark lady, much less lovely than our Sue, and dressed like you, and with your belly, who hung around a lot in early September. I don't believe this was Susan." Chester seemed to be losing his grip on reality.

Gore Vidal, who never met Chester, calls him a "monster" whose life was a "fascinating black comedy." But Vidal also considers Chester a "master," a "Genet with a brain." What Ozick terms ventriloquism—Chester's ability to ape other literary styles—Vidal deems his "leaking into other people," which was coupled with an inability to "pin down his own personality." Perhaps this shifting sense of self, Vidal speculates, along with drugs and drink, made Chester mad. Yet, Vidal concludes, "Chester's voices (among them not the least his very own) command our attention, make us laugh even as we make the sign to ward off the evil eye."

Sontag put up with a lot before excommunicating Chester, perhaps because, like his other friends, she had also experienced a sweet, endearing, and helpful side of him rarely on display in his correspondence. He liked to be catty in his letters. A severe critic of himself, he detested Sontag's unwillingness to examine her motivations, even to concede the complex psychological forces behind her conduct. Indeed, *Against Interpretation* is replete with jibes at the psychological. There are no hidden depths, Sontag asserts in her title essay: "The mask is the face." She hates the idea that an individual can be an instance of a psychological type; such notions alienate the self from its own humanity, she argues in "On Style." Psychological explanations deprive Susan Sontag, in other words, of her uniqueness. She wishes to be as autonomous as a work of art, and as resistant to interpretation. She extols Robert Bresson's films because he does not try to understand his characters. They are opaque. "Why persons behave as they do is, ultimately, not to be understood," she asserts. Bresson is an artist precisely because he preserves human mystery; his films develop not the psychology of souls but their physics. Bresson is a great describer, an anthropologist, Sontag argues.

The trouble in Tangier paid down any further debt Susan Sontag might have owed to Alfred Chester, but he did not realize—or he refused to acknowledge—the extent of her disaffection. Returning to New York in early 1966, he had difficulty finding a publisher for *The Exquisite Corpse*. Then Richard Kluger, a new editor at Simon & Schuster, decided that this surrealistic novel deserved a chance. Kluger had been the editor of the New York *Herald Tribune*'s *Book Week*, where Chester had published what Gore Vidal praises as "sharp and mordant" reviews. Chester was a tough sell, but Kluger's skeptical boss, Robert Gottlieb, gave him the go-ahead anyway. Kluger, who had published Sontag in *Book Week* and had met her at Roger Straus's soirees, knew of her defense of Chester in the *New York Times Book Review* and wanted her to supply an endorsement. Kluger had no idea of the fracas in Tangier. Over drinks at the Plaza in January 1966, he shared his enthusiasm for Chester's new book with Sontag, who said she liked it too. Indeed, Kluger thought she rated it more highly than he did. Several months later he called her to solicit a blurb and was surprised at both her reluctance and the form it took: "I am tired of playing den mother to America's homosexuals."

A baffled Kluger knew nothing about Sontag's reputation as a "fag hag." Sontag—like a number of other women, especially those in the art world—had become integral to the lives and careers of male artists, although unlike Sontag, most of them did not emerge as artists with their own following. Sontag, having served a kind of apprenticeship under Chester in Paris and in her early years in New York, now reversed the roles—attracting gay artists like Paul Thek (1933–1988) and Peter Hujar (1934–1987), with whom she would go through the same cycle of "acquisition and disburdenment" (one of her favorite phrases) that had miffed Chester. Kluger, not wanting to hear a final rejection in Sontag's voice, said he hoped she would reconsider when he sent her the galleys for the book in the fall of 1966. She replied that she did not want to have anything to do with the book. Kluger persisted in thinking "the door was still open, at least a little."

In the fall, Kluger put together a collection of quotations under the heading "What the Critics said" about Chester's previous book and included the final sentence from Sontag's letter to the *Times Book Review*. Kluger then wrote to Sontag, still hoping she would write a fresh blurb for the new book. She responded saying her feelings about Chester caused her acute distress. She had loved him very much, but since he had returned to New York, she had found him impossible and her patience with him had run out. She regretted not being able to do Kluger this favor because she respected his integrity.

With no new Sontag blurb, and knowing there was precious little support at Simon & Schuster for Chester's avant-garde novel, Kluger decided to go with an enthusiastic endorsement from critic Seymour Krim (which appears on the back of the jacket), and then wrote flap copy noting that Chester's work had been praised by several important writers, including Susan Sontag. When Sontag saw an advance copy of the jacket, given to her by Richard Howard, she exploded and called Roger Straus. He in turn called Peter Schwed, Robert Gottlieb's boss, demanding that the jacket be changed. Schwed complied, and he called Kluger to account for his actions, telling him about Straus's complaint. It was a bad moment for Kluger, who knew Schwed had no liking for Chester's novel. Straus had put the situation in the worst possible light, complaining to Schwed that Kluger had invoked Sontag's name even though she had told him she did not like *The Exquisite Corpse*. The editor searched his memory of his contacts with Sontag and could not remember her ever expressing a reservation about the book, although she had made it clear that her personal relationship with Chester had soured. Kluger was made to feel that he had done something "dishonorable." He wrote to Sontag relating his understanding of what had happened. He concluded: "For my part, I think you are being more than a little willful and I am not grateful to you for having helped me launch my publishing career with this undeserved rebuke." Kluger copied his letter to Roger Straus, Candida Donadio (Sontag's sometime agent), and Richard Howard.

Sontag's rebuttal, dated February 1, 1967, referred to the "record" Kluger had established by copying his letter to others. She now felt obliged to defend her position. It was simple and Kluger knew it: she did not want to be associated with Alfred Chester. She did not deny that she had liked the novel. But she objected to his using her name as an endorsement of all Chester's work. She resented his saying that she was emotional about Alfred. It was only the book jacket that had angered her. She found his remarks about her irrationality offensive. And to repeat her casual comment about homosexuals was spiteful—presumably because the letter had been copied to Richard Howard, a force among gay writers. As to why she did not call Kluger directly but instead brought in "daddy" (as Kluger later referred to Straus), she said she wanted the problem resolved quickly. Books were being shipped out. For her this was not a psychological issue, and not a quarrel or "misunderstanding." There was nothing to clear up. She simply wanted her name off the jacket. She was sorry that Kluger took her action to heart. She was not angry with him, only surprised at his poor handling of the matter.

Kluger regarded Sontag's action as a rewriting of history. After all, her letter about Chester had been a part of the public record. Certainly she had a right to sever her connection with Chester. But if there was nothing "personal" in her reaction to Kluger's use of her name, then why object to its use on behalf of a writer she had admired and whose work she still respected? Curiously, she does not deal with Kluger's remark to her that he knew "you were tired of having your name batted around by so many people for so many shallow reasons." He had approached her because of her avowed respect for Chester and because she was a "big name." But Sontag would not deal with that aspect of their non-"misunderstanding": that she was a big name and that she wanted to pick and choose—why not?—how her big name was used. In other words, she could act like a big name, she could sit at the Plaza and be treated like a big name, but she could not acknowledge, in so many words, that as a big name she could extend and withdraw her favors. Sontag preferred to think that she was dealing only with the physics of how one gets one's name off a book jacket.

The Sontag whom Chester could never pin down becomes in his novella, "The Foot," Mary Monday, dogged by her double (also named Mary Monday). Sontag/Monday is startled to see herself. It is as if Chester is saying: If she would only stop for a moment and look at herself! If she could only watch what she is doing! But then the sly but candid narrator turns on himself: what was he doing sitting at a table with

Mary Monday? Chester was disgusted by his own complicity in a world that created Mary Mondays.

Mary Monday is a "gorgon-headed beauty." Chester's allusion to the Gorgon, or Medusa, is oxymoronic: a beautiful monster, one that fascinates the spectator even as it forms part of the "imagination of disaster." To gaze upon her turns one cold as stone. She is at once desire and the death of desire. Nowhere in Chester is Sontag's attraction/repulsion for him made more vivid or more crude. The narrator goes on to report that Mary Monday lives in the "city of New York where she sticks combs up her ass to induce her intellectual activity. As always she lives with her son Joseph."

In "The Foot," Mary Monday remains in Morocco, walking hand in hand with her double, forsaking Manhattan, forsaking glamour. "No returning to the world of mirrors" where the two Mary Mondays "led separate identical lives." In Morocco, the image and the woman will fuse, as they do in Chester's sentence: "They were a woman who had suffered only in the spirit and were unprepared for the torments of a dirty, bug-ridden hotel." The two Mary Mondays, in other words, are the person and her image of herself. They can be discussed separately, but they are one.

The coming together of the two Mary Mondays makes them think that perhaps they are free—that is, that they have transcended the person/image dichotomy: "They discuss the possibilities of this line of reasoning, for Mary Monday is nothing if not an intellectual, a theorist." For his part, the narrator is frightened of the doubling in his own life, confessing, "I am afraid of who I am behind my own impersonations." But the incorrigible Mary Monday forsakes her double and fucks, rather indifferently, a man who she then discovers has apparently been fucked at the same time in her hotel room by her double. Thus the "separate identical lives" remain intact. The mnemonic Mary Monday is Chester's brilliant Platonic conception of Susan Sontag's nemesis, who is relentlessly attracted to the pursuit of the perfect idea/image of herself.

Susan Sontag is attracted to image-makers, especially to photographers. In her introduction to her friend Peter Hujar's *Portraits in Life and Death* (1976), she contends that photographs "instigate, confirm, seal legends. Seen through photographs, people become icons of themselves." The idea of instigation—what are her polemical essays except instigations and icons of Susan Sontag as thinker?—led to her engagement with photographers like Hujar and later Robert Mapplethorpe, who have provided exquisite images of her articulating her way of becoming strikingly visible to the world. In *Portraits in Life and Death*, there is a shot of Sontag "supine, from the diaphragm up, seemingly captured in a dream-like gesture, not by the lens, but by amber or mummification; half Mary Tyler Moore, half Nefertiti." This description is taken from a Web site titled "Why I Hate Susan Sontag"—only one example of the fascination of readers who find Sontag pretentious and yet difficult to dismiss. Another reader of the same Hujar photograph meditates on Sontag "wearing a simple ribbed turtleneck sweater," reclining on her back, "relaxed, clear-eyed, clear-sighted." The two descriptions convey an Egyptian equivalent, the repose of a goddess. In her stillness, she resembles—as do Hujar's other living subjects—his portraits of the preserved corpses in the cat-acombs near Palermo. Hujar seems to be searching for just that point in life where we can glimpse death, that final stillness. His photograph of Sontag recalls a query in *Death Kit:* "When does death become percep-tible?" Hujar uses Sontag to illustrate the question; Sontag would use Hujar's perception to elucidate her novel. Indeed, one of Hujar's pho-tographs of the catacombs graces the cover of the Anchor Books edition of *Death Kit*.

Hujar should be better known, say his friends and devotees of his photography. That he is not has to do with his rejection of fame, of the maneuvers that must be performed to attain celebrity. Like Alfred Chester, Hujar wanted recognition, perhaps even stardom, and he liked to consort with stars. "He loved divas, gossip, drama, scandal," his friend Nan Goldin remembers. Like Sontag, he wanted a command of his persona and of his art which would rivet an audience's attention. Gallery and coffee-house owner Helen Gee remembers a very young Peter Hujar slipping his prints under the nose of the famous photographer Imogen Cunningham, who was seated at a table eating.

But Hujar deeply disliked politicking on behalf of his photography, or even taking advantage of opportunities held out to him by those who had already arrived. Felicity Mason, a movie publicist and an influential force in the art and literary worlds, introduced Hujar to renowned photographer Cecil Beaton. "I understand that you are a very fine photographer," Beaton said to Hujar. Hujar replied, "I hear the same about you," and walked away. It was a funny story Hujar liked to tell his friends; it was also a huge bridge he had detonated, blocking his way to fame. Alfred Chester would have appreciated the gesture, but Cecil Beaton was no one to shrug off—especially when he was being nice to you.

Stephen Koch, a Sontag intimate, met Peter Hujar in her living room in 1965. Koch, now Hujar's executor, remembered a "tall, handsome, polite, remote, exact"—the description could almost be of Sontag— young man. Hujar had just spent a day photographing Jayne Mansfield, and he treated everyone to an intricate, dramatic account of the scene, of her body, of her movements, of the way she dressed. Hujar was a sexually charged man, and he could talk about sex brilliantly. In his up moods he would include listeners in his world. "There was something about him that invited a personal intimacy. He was very allowing," recalls his friend the writer Vince Aletti. Men and women easily fell in love with him, confessing their most intimate secrets. "He allowed people to be themselves." He had, in other words, the transparency that Sontag has always admired in great works of art. Called a "human tranquilizer" who "hypnotized his subjects," Hujar made everyone feel he was their best friend, or at least that he wanted to be.

But for all his sociability, Hujar was, like Sontag, a "profoundly alienated person." Abandoned by his parents, he was brought up by grandparents, and by sixteen he was on his own. Like Sontag, he made his career by becoming "unusually articulate." Although he could be "slightly ironic, a bit sweet and witty," his photographs portray a melancholy sensibility that suited Sontag's. He had pet theories about fame— for instance, that a disproportionate number of famous people had first and last names beginning with the same initial.

Like Sontag, Hujar had developed an aesthetic that encompassed a huge range of Western art. One Hujar friend said:

Style and self-assurance show up in his work early on. He understood what he was doing in ways that only first-rate artists do. He understood what the problems and challenges were. He wanted photographical portraiture to have the same qualities he admired in painted portraits. He avoided humanizing emotions, the smile, the frown, the deep look of brooding, the intellectual look. He said he wanted none of those. He liked the art when the subject simply gazed calmly back at the painter. That often revealed the most. He wanted their faces at rest, with the same kind of unaffected, unacted expression as paintings gave.

Hujar's aesthetic might almost be called "against interpretation." Certainly he was against forcing any kind of content on his subjects, or the "humanizing" that Sontag would later deplore in *On Photography* when she faulted the famous "Family of Man" show and touted Diane Arbus, who shared with Hujar a frank, straight-on style of portraiture.

Absent from Hujar's aesthetic, however, is an appreciation of artifice—a key term in *Against Interpretation,* a book that attacks faith in reality, in pure classicism, in the notion that the artist imitates what is *there.* What troubles Sontag about the mimetic is that it puts the artist in a secondary position as a recorder, not an originator. Photography is especially suspect—she can never quite bring herself to call it an art—because it is a mechanism of reflection. Artifice, on the other hand, is the essential ingredient of art because it is by definition made up; it cannot be confused with nature. Art as artifice is not a slice of life.

Art, in fact, is its own environment. This was the idea that brought Sontag to artist Paul Thek (once Peter Hujar's lover), or that brought Thek to her. In July 1979, on a notebook list of the most important things in his life, Thek listed Sontag as number 2, just after "my painting." A few months later he wrote in a notebook:

> Hujar—dreary, morbid, show-off
> Sontag—bright, lively, active; ill at ease
> etc etc etc etc etc

A friend of both Hujar and Thek believes Hujar never got over his breakup with Thek, whereas Thek seemed to go on happily from affair to affair, gay in every sense of the word, yet attracting a horde of women whom he was always promising to marry. Thek seemed to identify Sontag with the persona of her short story collection, *I, etcetera,* a protean, topsy-turvy self engaged in seeking and shedding, acquiring and disburdening. Thek loved her ambition, her European savoir faire. His greatest successes as an artist would come in Europe, and they would meet in Paris often. Partisans of Peter Hujar see Thek and Sontag as two of a kind, cold and ruthless, on determined quests for greatness and recognition, and Hujar as cozy and warm.

The trouble began when Thek broke Hujar's "triangle rule": "If you're A, never repeat to C what B has told you about C." Paul did exactly that when Peter complained about Susan. Peter said that Susan was cold, completely lacking in a sense of humor, pretentious. He went through a catalogue of Susan's character defects. Paul told her everything. She then called Peter and said, "I understand that you think I am . . ." Peter later admitted to a friend: "I was stunned. I couldn't deny any of it. They were my exact words. What could I do? But she is humorless."

After The Benefactor, Sontag's attention turned toward her essays, which quickly established her reputation. But it was always her intention to write another novel and to be the kind of writer devoted more to fiction than to nonfiction. In fact, she abandoned more than one long work of fiction in the four years between the appearances of her first and second novels, and some of this aborted work would be refashioned into the stories of *I, etcetera* (1978). Not until she could conceive of another novel that extended the themes of *The Benefactor* could she complete the work. Indeed, *Death Kit* reads like a resumption of her first published novel.

Diddy in *Death Kit* is a kind of Alfred Chester narrator, looking at a double of himself. He narrates his life in the third person—the tip-off comes when he lapses occasionally into references to "we," meaning Diddy and his view of himself. The book is his artifice. He inhabits his dreams as much as Hippolyte lives in his. It is clear that the "events" of *Death Kit* are actually Diddy's hallucinations in the final minutes of his life (he has committed suicide). Sontag makes him a failed novelist who loses the manuscript of his fiction about the Wolf-Boy, a first-person narration about a hirsute creature who shuns but yearns for human society after he learns that he is the offspring of apes. Diddy recovers the Wolf-Boy story in his dreams (which, remember, are dreams within the dream he is having in his dying moments). The story is obviously a commentary on Diddy's own estrangement from society and from his animal nature, his instinct for survival. Diddy's death dream is an attempt to repeat his life and to get it right the second time. His tragedy, like ours, is that there are no second chances. So when he speaks of "we," he also means all of us.

Writing as a willed activity intrigues Sontag; the writer as a self-made construct thrills her. Critics who like her second novel praise its form—its ingenious dream-within-a-dream properties—while admitting that Diddy is deadly dull (see Theodore Solotaroff's insightful review in *The Red Hot Vacuum*). Not only is Diddy dreaming, making the whole novel unreal, Sontag implies that he is unreal, merely a confection of literature. Diddy, or Didi—as Tony Tanner points out in *City of Words*—is the character Vladimir's nickname in Samuel Beckett's *Waiting for Godot*. Like Didi, Diddy seems paralyzed. He wishes to move, but he stands still—or his life does, at any rate. He is a man of action only in his dream, which is itself, ironically, brought on by his suicide. Diddy is also another double for Sontag. He remembers a childhood spent on Drachman Avenue in Tucson, the site of the Sontag home. Diddy has a plainspoken nurse, Mary, who is reminiscent of Sontag's Irish Rose. He is lonely and isolated, sharing his imaginative world with a doll, Andy. But when Diddy feels injured, he wounds his doll, who is called a "familiar, diminished double." To alleviate his own depression, he invents a cousin, Ann, transferring ownership of Andy to her, thus allowing her to express the tears and the grief for Andy that the stoic Diddy will not shed for himself, any more than Sontag will shed them for herself.

And there are other autobiographical echoes. Sontag creates a brother for Diddy, just as she had a sister, Judith. But it is Diddy's brother, Paul, who is the Sontag genius, a musician who becomes famous overnight. Diddy dies at thirty-three, Sontag's age when she completed the novel in 1966. With its ending in a charnel house/catacomb, *Death Kit* reflects Sontag's lifelong fascination with tunnels and caves (her natural homes). She even pictures Paul reading by flashlight under the covers just as she did when young. Diddy can only imitate his more famous brother and feel inauthentic, "not being in his life." He cries out: "I want to be seen." Like Diddy, Sontag tries to watch herself: in an episode set in Tucson, she depicts herself, a black-haired, skinny twelve- or thirteen-year-old girl, climbing a mountain toward the Wolf-Boy, Diddy's fictional creation. This is Sontag's fictional effort to come to terms with her own desire to be seen as well as with her estrangement from society and family. The girl has a dog with her called Lassie. He is the companion of that lonely little girl who read all those dog books written by Alfred Payson Terhune. The girl stops her climb just before reaching the Wolf-Boy in his cave. She is a curious, ambiguous figure in her "sneakers, blue jeans, a red checked shirt, and a fringed leather jacket probably bought at the tourist store on the Pima Indians reservation south of Tucson." Part tomboy, part Indian, part tourist, she pauses at the precipice as her parents, suddenly aware that she is climbing the cliff, call her back. Will she obey? the narrator (Wolf-Boy, Diddy, Sontag) asks in this triple-screened autobiographical passage. Will she "place her own self-esteem over the parents' self-pitying anxiety for her safety?" Yes and no. She does climb down, but only after muttering "Oh, hell!" and "Okay! Okay!" It is Sontag in situ, compliant and resistant, a Diddy herself, dreaming of release from her bondage, making up the story that will set her free. It is to her great glory that she will be able to write the story of her own life, but it is also an extraordinary burden. As Diddy says to himself about his story of the Wolf-Boy, "No one should be burdened with inventing his own nature from scratch."

When Diddy visits the charnel house/catacomb at the end of the novel, which presents a vision of the world as a repository of death, he finds that no corpse dates after 1933, the year of Sontag's birth. She suggests that an awareness of death is a form of knowledge that is redundant—it is everywhere visible to us—yet it is precisely the knowledge that we seek to avoid.

A dream is a splitting off of the self—as is a novel. As Hippolyte says in *The Benefactor*, "I am crawling through the tunnel of myself," which is his dreams, which is his novel, which is his death. The structure of *Death Kit*, in other words, is a House of Usher, its final charnel house evocative of Hujar's photographs of the Palermo catacombs. As Tony Tanner suggests, "environment proves to be intractable, closing in on Diddy like the walls on Edgar Allan Poe's prisoner." Ultimately, Tanner concludes, the "centre of consciousness is the house of death."

Gore Vidal was impressed with the novel's ending, but as Solotaroff says, Diddy is never quite believable as an "experiencing subject."

Critic Elizabeth Holdsworth calls Diddy and his predecessor Hippolyte "existential abstractions of modern man." We do not care enough about them. And even in formal terms, Sontag's structure does not hold up. "It is more figure than carpet," Solotaroff concludes. The gestalt (the whole, figure and pattern) does not cohere. *Death Kit* is merely tautological: it is what happens inside of one head and denies us, in critic Cary Nelson's words, "any sense of historical or social context."

Sontag has never called her second novel a failure, but she has conceded that after *Death Kit* she lost confidence in herself as a novelist. She tried several times to complete a novel, but it would take her another twenty-five years to publish one. Her *Death Kit* material is more suitable to a short story; pure formalism thrives in small spaces. Diddy is a good match for the enervated Roderick Usher, who is less a character and more a manifestation of the story's form.

How could Sontag have done better? It is a mystery as to how a writer converts his or her experience into living fiction. In *Mystery and Manners*, Flannery O'Connor quotes Joseph Conrad's formulation that the artist "descends within himself, and in that region of stress and strife, if he be deserving and fortunate, he finds the terms of his appeal." Like Diddy, Sontag "tries to force [her] way through the terrible questions to some endurable, stoical vantage point. Expunge the glittering agony. Find a cool quiet place where [she] can sit in safety." The cave.

Neoradicalism

11

1967–1969

Death Kit, published in late August 1967, received, in Roger Straus's words, "very very mixed" reviews. Some he thought malicious, for they took aim not at the book but at Sontag herself. Upset over Denis Donoghue's treatment of the novel in the *New York Review of Books*, Straus wrote to Robert Adams, an *NYRB* regular, suggesting that since he liked the novel he might write a letter to *NYRB* taking issue with Donoghue. Adams evidently declined the invitation. Straus never hesitated to call reviewers and their employers to account. Thus he wrote to an editor at *The New Republic* protesting "that ridiculous review perpetrated by Elizabeth Stevens."

But Straus liked the extensive review space given to *Death Kit*. FSG's heavy advertising campaign had paid off. It had been his strategy to publish early in the fall season, "ahead of the mob," as he put it. Even discount stores like Korvettes carried the book, and were running out of stock before the official publication date. The Literary Guild made the novel an alternate selection and had generated its own large print run. The book went into a third printing. By September 19 it had sold 14,000 copies with 20,000 in print—a very respectable showing for a literary novel. It was not a financial bonanza for the publisher, or the break-through book that FSG hoped for, but then Sontag constituted a long-term investment and a prestige item—as Straus and his staff kept reminding foreign publishers and agents. Lila Karpf, who negotiated many of the foreign sales and transactions, wrote: "We handle all of Susan's book transactions very closely from New York at her special wish. When I say 'we' I mean particularly Roger Straus, for his and my relationship with Susan is close, and that is the way she wants it." Karpf worked hard not merely to get Sontag published by reluctant houses but to increase her advances. When English publisher Eyre & Spottiswoode failed to do well with *Against Interpretation,* Straus used agent Candida Donadio to broker a new, more lucrative contract with Secker & Warburg for *Death Kit.* Similar deals were made in Spain, Holland, Sweden, and Germany. Straus's letter to an Italian publisher in late March 1967 is typical: "I have exceedingly good news. Susan Sontag has completed a new novel entitled DEATH KIT. . . . In a word, it is superb. I must go fur-ther than that and say to you that this truly is an important and original novel that I feel confident will be a success not only in the United States but throughout the world." He made sure that only the most intelligent and well-read editors, such as Maurice Temple Smith and John Bright Holmes in England, dealt with Sontag's work.

Sontag had reached the point that Norman Mailer identifies in *Marilyn,* when a personality seems to crash through a publicity barrier; there can be no return to an unacknowledged life. As English agent Laurence Pollinger put it now to Roger Straus: "Susan is always news." Sontag would complain about her reputation as the "'with it' girl," but then she expressed her disappointment that her author photograph appeared inside the back flap, reduced in size, rather than spread across the back of the jacket as it had been for *The Benefactor* and *Against Interpretation.* What a pity, since she had benefited from the services of famed photographer Philippe Halsman, who can be credited with one of the quintessential Marilyn Monroe portraits, taken in 1952 just as she was about to achieve stardom.

Here Halsman portrayed a sultry sixties Sontag. She seems clothed in her dark hair (no garment is defined). The geometrically composed photograph is a perfect counterpart to the stark front cover featuring Sontag's name in black block letters outlined in white, and the novel's title in white letters enveloped by the black background—Sontag in chiaroscuro. Sontag noted to Straus that putting the photograph on the back jacket flap instead of the back cover made the photograph look "awfully black." The black-and-white balance she wanted had been diminished.

Next to Benjamin DeMott's review of *Death Kit* in the *New York Times,* Columbia University professor Carolyn Heilbrun had an article, "Speaking of Susan Sontag," which analyzed the woman portrayed on her book jackets. Heilbrun surveyed the publicity—the *Mademoiselle* award and notice, the Irving Penn *Vogue* photographic layout of Sontag and son—and noted that jokes à la Marilyn Monroe were being made about Sontag's alliterative name. Sontag had participated in the "great American sport: have it and eat it too." She was already adept at "reaping the establishment's rewards with the right hand, damning the establishment with the left." Sontag gave an interview to the *Washington Post* (January 8, 1967), for example, in which she declared that from now on she would not appear on television and there would be no more interviews (she has easily granted over a hundred interviews since then). Sontag had become an inescapable brand name, Heilbrun concluded: "When I first began reading about Susan Sontag I thought: 'My God, she *is* Marilyn Monroe, beautiful, successful, doomed. . . .'"

Theodore Solotaroff, in his review of *Death Kit,* pinned down Sontag's mythic status and contradictory appeal:

> . . . cultural hero or villain, the lovely brave Minerva of a genuine new underground/*avant-garde* or the glib bootlegger of the latest wave of French modernism, East Village Pop, and other modes of the higher unseriousness. Like the celebrity that Miss Sontag appears to court with her left hand and disclaim with her right, her critical stance somehow managed to be both matter-of-fact and outrageous: a tone that gets under the skin in much the same way that those dust-jacket photographs of her—poised, striking, vaguely sinister—either seduce or repel.

Stories about Sontag were already legion in literary circles, for she had become a figure of envy, admiration, and fantasies of all sorts. Poet James Dickey, universally acknowledged as a world-class mythomane and womanizer, liked to claim that he had coupled with Sontag and thereby inspired a few pages of *Death Kit.* There was that scene in the tunnel—you remember, Dickey would tell his listeners—when Diddy fucks Hester. "It was me! One hell of a long night that was, boy, lemmee tell you," Dickey chortled. Preposterous. But then maybe . . . thought one writer.

Until 1966 Sontag had confined herself largely to aesthetic matters, but in February of that year she emerged, alongside Norman Mailer, Bernard Malamud, William Styron, Robert Lowell, and other figures of the arts, as a political activist, adding her voice to a "Read-in for Peace in Vietnam" at Manhattan's Town Hall. She spoke of writers who were "choking with shame and anger" because "a small nation of handsome people" were being "brutally and self-righteously slaughtered" by a "grotesquely over-armed" superpower claiming to uphold liberty while really only indulging in its self-interest.

What if the North Vietnamese had struck Sontag as ugly, venal, and militaristic? In *Trip to Hanoi,* her treatment of their physical beauty and grace, their simple lives and slogans, constitute what Leo Marx calls a "New Left pastoral," a rebuke to American corruption.

By the end of 1967, Sontag had been arrested at a three-day antiwar protest, briefly jailed, and then released for a court appearance in January 1968. The protest had been part of "Stop the Draft Week" in New York City. Sontag had been one of 264 people arrested, including Dr. Benjamin Spock and writers Allen Ginsberg, Grace Paley, and Jane Jacobs, at the Whitehall Street induction center. They had blocked the entrance and ended up in a crowded jail cell. Although this demonstration had been peaceful, the process of arrest and incarceration—however brief—was frightening. Yet Dot Lane, one of the protestors, remembers a perfectly composed Sontag, looking "beautiful and interesting," engaged in a friendly conversation with Jacobs.

In *Trip to Hanoi,* Sontag calls herself a "neo-radical," in other words, a radical reborn in a new age. There had been a huge gap in her political consciousness that lasted from 1947 to 1967. In her "precocious political childhood," she had read leftist newspapers like *PM,* and writers like Corliss Lamont and the Webbs (both apologists for Russia). Besides campaigning for Henry Wallace, she had watched Eisenstein films at the American-Soviet Friendship Society. But then there had been the Cold War years when the American Communist

Party had seemed moribund to her, a "philistine fraud" repeating hackneyed phrases about capitalism and imperialism. Embarrassed and bored by the stale rhetoric, the very antithesis of the aesthete's vaunted new sensibility, her political imagination had shut down. Then the antiwar protests, and the examples of the Cuban and North Vietnamese revolutions, stimulated her to recover her "historical memory." Once again, she felt comfortable employing words like "capitalist" and "imperialist"; she had come home, in other words, to her first set of radical convictions.

In 1966 Sontag had responded to a *PR* questionnaire that queried writers about "What's Happening in America." Sontag included her response in *Styles of Radical Will* (1969) as a preface to *Trip to Hanoi*. Sontag's *PR* piece attacked America as the "arch-imperium of the planet." Its spoiled environment and frenzied consumerism had made thinking Americans neurotic or mystics, seeking to somehow transcend the mire of materialism. Whites had simply wiped out the Indians and taken the land. Hence, "The white race *is* the cancer of human history."

Sontag deplored the "tawdry fantasy of the good life that culturally deprived, uprooted people" have imposed on the country's landscape. Cross the Hudson, she wrote, and one would find that most people simply wanted to obliterate anything that stood in the American way. America had not merely taken a wrong turn, Sontag concluded. No, it was doomed. The only hope was its protesting youth, who were "alienated *as* Americans"—apparently the only patriotic attitude that Sontag found acceptable.

At the invitation of North Vietnam, Sontag, the journalist Andrew Kopkind, and Cornell professor Robert Greenblatt—all prominent antiwar protestors—made a two-week visit to Hanoi in May 1968. They had a stopover in Vientiane, Laos. "Try not to idealize that place," a United States Information Service official cautioned the group, remembered Kopkind. In *Trip to Hanoi*, Sontag mentions meeting a USIS official but provides no details. He was Perry Stieglitz, recommended to Sontag by his friend Mary McCarthy, who had visited Hanoi in March. Stieglitz had first come to Laos in 1959 on a Fulbright Fellowship, and he had married the daughter of Souvanna Phouma, premier of Laos during the years when the Viet Minh from North Vietnam invaded Laos in support of the Communist Pathet Lao. In Laos, Stieglitz could only regard North Vietnam as an aggressive power, although he also recognized that America was making "enormous mistakes in our international policies, particularly in Vietnam." Stieglitz remembers that Sontag found it hard to be civil to a man who could not engage in an "outright condemnation of America itself."

McCarthy—hardly less outspoken against the war than Sontag—nevertheless had a friend in Stieglitz, whom she respected even though he did not share her views. Indeed, McCarthy was married to an American diplomat, James West. Stieglitz, having read some of Sontag's writing and enjoyed it, looked forward to their meeting. He hoped they could discuss North Vietnamese imperialism, but he realized as soon as she walked into his house with a "condescending attitude" that an exchange of views would be impossible. He found a Sontag so angry at her own country that she would not listen to his account of how the North Vietnamese were pursuing their own century-long desire to dominate Southeast Asia.

For Stieglitz, Sontag's visit was summed up by her appraisal of his record collection of Baroque music. She turned to Kopkind and asked him if he remembered when this period music was "'our' music." What a shame, she seemed to be telling Stieglitz, that he did not know that Baroque was now "out." Asked to recall her visit of thirty years ago, Stieglitz can think of only one word to add to his published account: "phony."

Trip to Hanoi is less shrill and more observant than Sontag's contribution to "What's Happening in America." It troubles Sontag, for example, that every North Vietnamese she meets speaks in the same style with the same jargon. The role-playing and stage-managed aspects of her two-week tour also bother her. The idea that she is a showperson, paraded as an example of the antiwar movement, makes her uncomfortable. The process is infantilizing, for she has no opportunity to exercise her intellect. The North Vietnamese seem like children, parroting a line, speaking in Marxist simples. Everyone is moralistic, pietistic—exactly the kind of content-driven fanatic she denounces in her essays. They have no style; they lack irony. Worse, North Vietnam is sexless. There is no kissing, no public display of affection. Starved of her sumptuous vocabulary, her craving for the sensuous, Sontag is depressed. After five days she regards her failure to adjust as just that: *her failure,* an inability to transcend her complex Western consciousness.

Even here, though, when she seems most humble, she makes a presumption that commentators—pro and con Sontag—seem to overlook. She contends that her consciousness includes the world of the Vietnamese, but that their consciousness cannot comprehend hers, for their concerns are elemental—having to do with survival, not with the choices available in a bourgeois society. To accept this formulation is to embrace Sontag's notion that she understands why the North Vietnamese are as simple, uniform, programmed, infantilized, and sexless as she says they are. She attributes much of their rigid and austere mentality to the war. They need to pull together, to think of society first, to modify their actions to ensure the country's survival. Their collective sameness she takes not as an example of regimentation in an authoritarian society but as a mark of the democratization of society, bringing together people from the country and the city in a "people's war." In contrast with fat Americans, the slim North Vietnamese are frugal and fastidious, making every item count—turning everything, including the parts of shot-down American planes, into salvageable goods. Sontag's North Vietnamese are reminiscent of those Indians (noble savages) who found a use for every part of the buffalo they hunted: "It was my impression that the Vietnamese, as a culture, genuinely believe that life is simple." They are joyful—no glum existential agonists in North Vietnam. And once Sontag realizes that her hosts have "virtues that thoughtful people in this part of the world simply don't believe in any more," she relaxes and is happy. She lauds the way the North Vietnamese "genuinely care" about downed American pilots, providing more meat for them because they are "bigger than we are." Not a word about torture. Not an inkling that the simplicity, the lack of irony and of style, is the hallmark of Sparta, a culture of martial discipline that made Athens, no less than America, seem bloated and wasteful.

Sensing that she has been carried away by her own rhetoric, Sontag pauses to consider whether she has succumbed to the "ideology of primitivism" and the pastoral ideal, which drives twentieth-century intellectuals who have embraced agrarian revolutions. No, she counters, the "truth is truth." She witnessed it. Through her direct experience she has earned the right to say that North Vietnam *"deserves* to be idealized."

To arrive at this conclusion, Sontag sets up a false dichotomy. She contrasts her formerly "abstract" idea of North Vietnam with what she "actually saw." Is a stage-managed two-week trip even roughly equivalent to what might be learned from reading history? Did the intellectuals who visited the Soviet Union in the 1930s for a few weeks or even months get it right?

Sontag extols North Vietnam as a "truly remarkable country" and the North Vietnamese as an "extraordinary human being." These people are "'whole'" human beings, not 'split' as we are." Sontag's quotation marks around "whole" and "split" signal the weakness of her polemic, as if on some level she suspects that she has broken faith with her own intelligence. She equates simple with being whole. She takes refuge in constructions like "It is my impression that . . ." But no mollifying phrases about her "brief, amateurish foray into Vietnamese reality" can ameliorate the arrogance of *Trip to Hanoi*.

Near the end of her essay, Sontag describes her reentry into what she considers American-dominated Laos, and she draws a picture of Vientiane meant to revolt the reader after her cleansing visit to North Vietnam. Perry Stieglitz comments:

> She observed "servile, aggressive pedicab drivers," although the Lao pedicab drivers are known to be unusually pleasant and gentle. She saw many "Cadillacs driven by American businessmen and Laotian government officials," but there were at most two Cadillacs in the city, and no more than a half-dozen American businessmen. She "passed the movie theaters showing skin flicks to the GIs"— which is the most remarkable of all because the Lao culture would never permit such films to be shown, and the American soldiers, the GIs of whom she writes, had left Vientiane fully five years before Sontag arrived.

In a final irony, in 1975, when North Vietnam finally conquered the South, among the books banned by the new regime were those of Susan Sontag.

Sontag's next political commentary, an article called "Some Thoughts on the Right Way (for us) to Love the Cuban Revolution," appeared in the April 1969 issue of *Ramparts,* then the leading New Left publication. More than just a paean to Cuba, the essay analyzed America and American radicalism. Sontag judged the country to be a prerevolutionary state and made much of distinctions between the Old and New

Left, the latter having forsaken the former's rather stodgy psychology and unimaginative adaptation to American mores, if not to the political status quo. Sixties radicals, in contrast, were groovy rockers, grass smokers, sexual liberators, freaky dressers, and all-around misfits who made a virtue of maladjustment to American life. In brief, the New Left was "more intelligent and more sensitive and more creative than the so-called Old Left." Sontag admired the new style but also cautioned that it could hardly change American society in fundamental ways. The New Left was too anarchic, too divided, and too willing to adopt Cubans as fellow revolutionaries without understanding their uniqueness.

Sontag conceded that "many of their freedoms [in Cuba] seem constricting to us." For example, pornography and private business were outlawed. So much for the pornographic imagination that Sontag would explore in her next collection of essays, *Styles of Radical Will*. If American radicals tended to think of society as the enemy, in Cuba it was just the opposite: society's strict enforcement of a group ethic was good. It had liberated the energies of the Cuban people—not to be like the insurgents of the New Left, but faithful party members. She saw a spontaneity and sensuality in its people absent in "our own white, death-ridden culture." She explained that Cubans are not "linear, desiccated creatures of print-culture."

In *Trip to Hanoi*, Sontag catalogued a couple of North Vietnam's atrocities: forced collectivization and purges of dissidents. In *Ramparts*, she mentions "one bad moment" two years earlier when several thousand homosexuals in Havana were sent to rehabilitation farms. Compared to America, a "cancerous society," Cuba had developed a convincing patriotic rhetoric. She is at pains to show that the very things American radicals rejected, militarism and traditional schooling, were positives in revolutionary Cuba, a country just beginning to develop itself. In other words, it was wrong to apply the same standards to a nascent socialist society as would be applied to America. In *Political Pilgrims*, Paul Hollander notes that the flaws in Communist systems like Cuba's are always justified on "programmatic grounds as problems of growth, transient aberrations, measures of self-defense, or trivial blemishes rendered insignificant by the overall context and to be vindicated by the future." Hence, Sontag acknowledges the public attack on Heberto Padilla, an apolitical writer, but she thinks there is probably no reason to worry since no Cuban writers had been imprisoned or prevented from publishing.

Two years later Sontag would join a chorus of protest over Padilla's treatment, discovering that Castro did persecute and jail writers along with thousands of other political prisoners. In 1968–69, however, she did not merely temporize about Cuban Communism, she shilled for it. In a collection of tributes to Che Guevara, martyred in his attempt to foment revolution in Bolivia, she expressed not only her "personal grief" but her approval for the cultivation of his "romantic image" as an antidote to the "life-style of American imperialism." It was good for American and European radical youth to idealize Che. The new, "still imperfect and emerging socialist society" of Cuba offered "revolutionary options," she declared, endorsing Che's program of exporting revolution to other countries. True, Cuba had neither a free press nor an independent judiciary, yet it stood as "in some respects the most genuinely democratic country in the world today." Sontag's article in *Ramparts* continues the clash of absolute statements and their qualifiers which makes a muddle of *Trip to Hanoi*.

Historian Alan M. Wald reports that "during the 1960s Sontag had supported the election campaigns of the Socialist Workers Party (SWP) and had even met with party representatives to discuss the possibility of joining the party." The meeting was set up by radical activist Ralph Schoenman, who was seeing a good deal of Sontag at the time, also befriending her son, David. He had been Bertrand Russell's secretary, calling himself "Secretary General of the International War Crimes Tribunal" that Russell sponsored to condemn U.S. actions in Vietnam. Schoenman, himself a candidate for SWP membership, was sent on a mission by the SWP, along with Leslie Evans and George Novack, who had played a major role in the Dewey Commission hearings that cleared Trotsky of the charges made at Stalin's Moscow Purge Trials. At Sontag's apartment, Schoenman performed the introductions and then Novack pitched the SWP as the party of Lenin and Trotsky. He added that the SWP was also prominent in the National Mobilization Committee to End the War in Vietnam, which had called the November 1969 march on Washington. The SWP "virtually controlled the Student Mobilization Committee," Novack told Sontag. Skeptical, she asked her recruiters how they could be so influential if she had heard so little about them. Novack replied that the Young Socialist Alliance (YSA) had made important gains on American campuses, recently expanding into the South, establishing new chapters in Atlanta, Birmingham, Austin,

Houston, and other cities. Sontag then called David into the room and
questioned him about the YSA. Had he ever heard of it? No, he said.
That ended the recruitment drive.

En route to Cuba in late December 1968, Sontag gave a talk about
her trip to Hanoi at the National University of Mexico City. She had been
preceded by a series of Marxist lecturers who had radicalized students
in the aftermath of the massacre of October 2, 1968, when some two
thousand demonstrators in Mexico City, protesting the army's occupation
of the university, had been beaten, shot, and jailed. "Scores of bodies
were trucked away and firehoses washed the blood from the cobble-
stones," according to a *New York Times* account (September 14, 1998).
The killings enraged the younger generation and shocked Mexico, which
experienced an event comparable to that in Tiananmen Square in China
in 1989. Sontag spoke to a militant, anti-American student audience,
perhaps a thousand bodies crammed into a room with seating for four
hundred. No matter what she said, it did not seem radical enough. Under
a ruthless fusillade of questions about the war and American foreign policy and attacks on her arguments, she broke down and wept. She recovered quickly, but when it came to the Vietnam War, the writer who was
admired for her control, who commanded the speaking platform with
such aplomb and serenity, lost her composure.

Styles of Radical Will

12

1 9 6 9 – 1 9 7 1

By 1969 Susan Sontag had gained extraordinary visibility, appearing in Paris, Prague, London, Berlin, Helsinki, Mexico City, Hanoi, Havana, Stockholm—not to mention her many lecture dates at American universities. She met with her foreign publishers, agents, and writers, establishing an intricate network of international contacts.

In the fall of 1969, Sontag published her second collection of essays, *Styles of Radical Will*. It contained her landmark essays "The Aesthetics of Silence" and "The Pornographic Imagination." She also included her best work on film, "Bergman's *Persona*," which is tied closely to the style and content of her first two films, *Duet for Cannibals* and *Brother Carl*. Her decision to include her political essays, "What's Happening in America (1966)" and *Trip to Hanoi* provoked harsh reviews that treated her not just as a writer but as a public figure. Even John Leonard, a critic usually sympathetic to Sontag, pointed out in *Life* how facile, how unproven Sontag's premises about "modern capitalist society" were. Even granting her argument that America was founded on genocide, it was hardly the first empire to act so violently. Why did she repeat Marxist jargon? What about what the North Vietnamese had done to the Thai, Meo, and Mung ethnic minorities? "She may have gone to Vietnam, but she never really left the solipsistic thicket of her questions, nor stopped singing the same song," Leonard concludes. Jonathan Raban, in *The Spectator* (December 12, 1969), called Sontag's essays "symptoms rather than critiques of the society they purport to describe." Peter Berek in *Commonweal* (October 10, 1969) said she combined the "enthusiasms of the huckster with the zeal for novelty of a garment manufacturer," echoing Gore Vidal's feeling that Sontag's quest for the new novel reflected "not so much the spirit of art as it does that of Detroit."

Nevertheless, *Styles of Radical Will* secured Sontag's place as one of the great contemporary essayists. Her second collection was more probing and less programmatic than *Against Interpretation*. Her best essays stake out a view of certain subjects (especially film, pornography, and art) which continues to stimulate discussion among critics, in the classroom, and among general readers. Available in Anchor paperbacks, her essays sell modestly (well under 10,000 copies a year), but they have always remained in print.

In early 1969 Sontag moved from a Greenwich Village apartment to a Riverside Drive penthouse. In the Village, she had rented a typical cramped affair, with a narrow entrance hall, and a small living room jammed with bookcases. The walls were hung with film stills. She had a bare minimum of furniture. On Riverside Drive her penthouse was in a large, dark prewar apartment building. The atmosphere was austere: dark wood floors, little furniture, and a few photographs (Garbo, Dylan, W. C. Fields), but mostly bare white walls. Even with a fine view of the Hudson River, the scene was like a monastery. The ascetic Sontag did not crave luxury—not that she could have afforded it, anyway. Money was always a concern. FSG advanced her modest sums against future earnings. She could command lecture fees of $1,000 or $1,500 plus expenses (her asking price would escalate to over $3,000 in the 1970s and 1980s). Roger Straus negotiated and made the arrangements, something customarily handled by publicists or lecture agents. But working the lecture circuit was tiresome, and it took Sontag away from writing. So she reduced the frequency of her appearances, inevitably shrinking her income.

Unlike disciplined writers who wrote every day no matter what, Sontag liked to go out and could be easily distracted. Activity-filled schedules blocked her from doing serious writing, as did her tendency to read many hours at a stretch. She would pick up small grants from private and public agencies, but they did not add up to a comfortable existence. She had no health insurance. But she still managed to pursue the life of an independent writer with admirable determination—and often with a lack of grace, for she hated to be beholden to the universities that paid her lecture fees and demanded her time.

When Sontag visited Brown University in the late 1960s, for example, she made it clear to her escort, Laurence Goldstein (now editor of the *Michigan Quarterly Review*), that she did not like making personal appearances. "Then why do it?" Goldstein asked. "Why else, for the money," she explained—"as if to a simpleton," Goldstein adds. She wanted to see an early Picasso at the Rhode Island School of Design and then hurry off for her early evening flight back to New York. She was polite, if not gracious, toward the organizers of the panel on which she was to appear, and she signed a few copies of *Against Interpretation*. After the panel discussion, Sontag sprang from the stage and said to Goldstein, "Let's get going." Her surprised hosts caught up with her and asked whether she would be attending the reception—so many people wanted to meet her. No, Sontag said, she had read her contract carefully and it said nothing about a reception. One of the exasperated organizers responded that surely Sontag would greet at least briefly members of the audience who had come specifically to see her? No, she would not, Sontag replied, and urged Goldstein and her driver on. Goldstein realizes that Sontag's behavior at Brown was hardly unique:

> She was the first, but certainly not the last, New York celebrity I would meet, in Providence and afterward in Ann Arbor, who would perform the minimum possible work on their visit, then take the money and run. She clearly considered her behavior a brave act of self-preservation in a philistine environment. In this view she was, as she often liked to be, a minority of one.

What seemed rude or ungracious was also a form of self-protection. Susan Sontag was not Marilyn Monroe. She did not want to give all of herself to her fans. She did not want to think that she had fans. She did not want to consider that she owed anyone a performance, except the performance of being a writer. To say that she was appearing for the money, that she was not beholden to anyone, may seem arrogant and ungrateful, but it created a separate space for her, a way to express her authentic self. She had become a writer precisely so that she could explore life as she chose, and she did not want to submit herself to the conventions of the lecture circuit.

Sontag was not happy. The years between 1963 and 1969 were heady but also disheartening. She longed to do better work, to write better fiction. She regarded her public persona as a hindrance, although she could not stop feeding the media that perpetuated it. In the intensely competitive atmosphere of New York City, she was amassing her literary capital even as she labored to hide the process of becoming the public Susan Sontag. She had to be her own sort of writer. Yet she found no way to check her own posturing by calling upon a sense of irony about herself. Some stars handle stardom with self-deprecating humor. Sontag never saw the point of that. Why pretend to be less than she was? Instead she got angry, exercised her power, or withdrew into melancholy.

Sontag seemed to have an overwhelming need to assert her moral authority in a culture she deemed corrupted by the values of the marketplace. For example, there was her hostile reaction to a telegram from Gladys Carr, an editor at Prentice-Hall. Carr inquired whether Sontag might be available to write a book on the avant-garde. Carr considered this a special project Sontag might be willing to take on, even though FSG was her regular publisher. Sontag replied by reaffirming her exclusive tie to FSG, and for good measure told off Carr, observing that the telegram and its wording reminded her of the offensive tactics of the "world of business and journalism," tactics that were inappropriate in the "realm of serious books and ideas." Sontag sent a copy of her reply to Roger Straus with the comment: "This may amuse you. I've probably scared the shit out of poor Miss Carr." In fact, Miss Carr got angry, replying that the telegram was meant only as an inquiry, not an offer. "And were I not so young and relatively unschooled in the ways of the 'world of business and journalism,' I suppose I would have been better prepared for your cynical and ungracious reply."

Sontag's expressions of petulance hide a personal sorrow she could not share outside a very small circle. She had never gotten over her love for María Irene Fornés. In retrospect, she realized that her years with Irene were as close to a "marriage" as she was ever likely to get. She was lonely. A private person, Sontag found it difficult to share her grief.

Sontag wanted to give to her friendships what she often lacked in her love life: a true sense of reciprocation, of what H. G. Wells yearningly called a "lover-shadow," a double that would help to make her whole. Since breaking up with Irene Fornés in 1963, Sontag had had lovers and suitors, male and female. There was L in New York and C in Milan, Rome, and Naples—and others in New York whose full names and lives can be documented and analyzed by future biographers. To Sontag, her lovers seemed to lack something essential that she had experienced only in her "marriage" to Irene.

To actor-director Joseph Chaikin, who became, for a time, Sontag's soul mate, she wrote about her "nightmare-ridden, stubborn, melancholy Jewish character." The legendary Chaikin, a member of the Living Theater and a stalwart in New York's avant-garde since the mid-1950s, was, in Sontag's view, a melancholic like herself. She sent him loving letters from her destinations all over the world, confiding to him the details of her own quest for love, honestly recording her failures and frustrations. She is open and vulnerable in this correspondence (much of it dating from the late 1960s and early 1970s), and passionately concerned about Chaikin's moods. She wants him to be good to himself. She is newsy, telling him about her experiences with Polish director Jerzy Grotowski and British director Peter Brook. She wants him to call her, she misses him, she wants to see him, to have him stay with her, to embrace him with all her heart. They are so alike, she says, "frenzied, restless doers." The letters to Chaikin open a vein and release feelings otherwise carefully concealed, even from the lovers she had had since Fornés.

From the vantage point of 1969, Sontag looked back and wrote to Chaikin that it seemed to her that since her split from Fornés she had lived in a perpetual state of "mourning and anxiety and petrification." She was fearful, immobilized by states of apprehension, and maintaining her air of command was the only way she knew to overcome an increasing sense of discomfort with what she had become. Sontag felt she needed a conjugal relationship such as she had had with Irene, and yet she had kept her distance, never actually living with her lovers, never believing she would find another lover as marriageable as Irene with whom she could enjoy a steady, secure life. Indeed, her incredible travel schedule seemed to express her conviction that there was no one to stay home for.

Fourteen-year-old David became the intense focus of her affections— too intense, she realized, and she welcomed male friends who acted as a kind of buffer. David often stopped by the FSG offices to visit Roger Straus, who gave him money and sent news of him to Sontag, who was often somewhere else. David, when he was not traveling on his own to Canada, or Mexico, or Peru, accompanied his mother on her forays as public figure and world traveler. The consequence for David was a failure of focus; he could not settle down. He had literary aspirations (FSG would place some of his early stories in magazines), but he was also daunted by his mother's example and found her too seductive to rebel against.

Then Sontag met renowned actress-producer Nicole Stéphane. With Stéphane, she was "very attentive, affectionate, not at all her usual assertive, almost aggressive self," observed James Lord, another American writing in Paris. Sontag had to humbly accept second place in a love triangle, since Stéphane was still involved in a sixteen-year relationship with a very possessive lover when Sontag fell in love with her.

Stéphane was a glorious actress hailed for her brilliant performance in *Les Enfants Terribles* (1950). In that legendary film, directed by one of Sontag's favorites, Jean-Pierre Melville and based on Jean Cocteau's celebrated novel, Stéphane plays Elisabeth, a girl who nurses her injured brother Paul in an aggressive-passive relationship that is as intimate and suggestive as Elizabeth and Alma's in *Persona,* an Ingmar Bergman film that is the subject of one of Sontag's best essays. Indeed, critics have called this brother-sister love incestuous, and as in *Persona,* the couple in *Les Enfants* can be seen as the shifting superior/inferior aspects of a single self, and of male and female. One critic of Melville's film puts it succinctly: Elisabeth, "although lovely, has a determined strength of body and spirit that gives her an almost masculine air in contrast to the soft, passive quality of the otherwise virile Paul."

Stéphane seemed to walk off the screen and into Sontag's life.

That Stéphane was also a Rothschild and a Jew who had been in danger of being deported during the war made her the kind of exile Sontag sought. For Susan Sontag, meeting Nicole Stéphane was the equivalent of Marilyn Monroe meeting Clark Gable, her childhood idol. Stéphane had appeared in an earlier Melville film, *Le Silence de la Mer* (1949), looking, as one critic described her, "rather like an abstract force, a living piece of sculpture in the French mold, like some personified image of feminine virtue—nobility and courage— seen in the Louvre or the Académie: sturdy with short hair that looks blown back, a strong, short nose, intense eyes, a firm, small mouth, strong and shapely legs."

Stéphane became not only Sontag's lover but her film producer. Stéphane was, in fact, one of only two female producers in France, Sontag proudly pointed out in a 1972 interview.

When Sontag first met Stéphane in the late 1960s, the younger woman seemed completely immersed in the world of cinema. She was writing long, probing essays about Bergman and Godard, praising both of them for employing multiple points of view, for "overlaying narrative voices" and conflating the first and third person just as she had done in *Death Kit*. These directors resisted interpreting the present in terms of the characters' pasts, and collapsed such distinctions into a filmic present, the "now" that Sontag kept repeating in her second novel. It was not the depth or "innerness" of the individual that fascinated these filmmakers, but rather the dynamic forms of life and of art—what she called in her Godard essay a "provisional network of emotional and intellectual impasses." At the end of *Persona*, Sontag concluded, "mask and person, speech and silence, actor and 'soul' remain divided—however parasitically, even vampiristically, they are shown to be intertwined." This theme of a bifurcated self, so apparent in Alfred Chester's fiction, would figure in Sontag's short stories and in her two films.

Sontag advanced such ideas in an international arena. In 1967, for example, she served on the juries of both the Venice and New York film festivals. She was looking for a filmmaking venue, she told interviewer Edwin Newman in 1969. She got her opportunity on a visit to Sweden, where Goran Lindgren, managing director of Sandrews, offered to fund her first film. She signed a Sandrews contract on May 29, 1968.

In Sweden as in so many other European countries, FSG had made Sontag a name to reckon with. Sweden is a small country, and it is relatively easy to make connections there. And then it was the sixties—in Sweden as elsewhere, a time of great experimentation and permissiveness. In 1963 the Swedish Film Institute had been established to promote high quality in the country's cinema, and Lindgren had had several international successes.

Lindgren soon realized that Sontag had "very definite ideas about which people she wanted in her film." Of course, Sandrews helped her with casting, and Peter Hald, then in his mid-twenties, was assigned as her production manager. What Lindgren—then turning forty—and Hald found attractive in Sontag was her grasp of the contemporary and her seemingly encyclopedic command of world cinema. The opportunity presented to Sontag seems "quite extraordinary," Hald observes, but "given the time, the political movements, it was not so strange." Sontag was a radical at a time when you had to be a radical to be accepted as an American in Sweden, he stresses. *Trip to Hanoi* would be published in book form in Sweden in early 1969, as Sontag was editing *Duet for Cannibals*. Sandrews realized that her work would not attract huge audiences or turn a profit—but the firm was committed to making both mass-market and art-house films.

Sontag told interviewer Mel Gussow that she had been on the sets of many films, had worked as an extra, had acted in school, and had learned a good deal from her friend director Mike Nichols. As knowledgeable as Sontag seemed in her talks about film—she handled press conferences deftly, Hald remembers—she knew very little about how to make a film, and there was little give-and-take among cast and crew, little opportunity for Sontag to learn her craft. She had written a script beforehand, and it was Sandrews's obligation to help her fulfill her vision. Not that Sontag was overbearing; it was more a matter of the Swedes wanting to support her. There was no improvisation to speak of, none of the kinds of happy accidents that she admired in Godard's films. Sontag explained little about her characters, but then she was not asked to justify her writing. Hald enjoyed her energy and focus, but he did not find her an especially articulate director. She was at a loss, in one instance, to convey why a certain actress's performance disappointed her. At the time, Sontag gave interviews in Sweden and in the United States in which she expressed great happiness about working in

film as a collective enterprise. She hoped to do many more cinema projects.

The film was received well at Cannes, and Mel Gussow called it one
of the hits of the New York Film Festival, where it played to sold-out
audiences. It had a limited theatrical release in New York, London, and
other major cities. But as with her early fiction, there seems something
willed about Sontag's films. In part, that is because they are about the
will and the way it functions in life and in art. She takes her cue from
Romanian philosopher E. M. Cioran, the subject of an essay in *Styles of
Radical Will.* Cioran advocated a spiritual strenuousness that requires us
to "sever our roots" and become "metaphysically foreigners." Sontag's
essay on Cioran perfectly captures her own willed existence. She
embraces a thinker who counsels extrication from the world, from
domestic commitments, in order to experience life as "a series of situations" that leaves the consciousness free to explore its own labyrinth.
What Sontag loves most about him is his elevation of the "*will* and its
capacity to transform the world."

Duet for Cannibals explores a brief moment in the political career
of Arthur Bauer, a German radical who has been associated with
Brecht and who seems to be on the run, fearing both surveillance and
attempts to poison him. His convictions are vague. At the beginning of
the film, one of the four main characters, Ingrid, is tacking up his
poster on walls that include a picture of Hugo Blanco, a Peruvian
Trotskyist, an NLF flag, and photographs of the black athletes who
gave the black power salute at the Olympics in Mexico City in 1968.
The newspapers in her apartment remind us that the film is set in the
period of the Kennedy assassination and the Soviet invasion of
Czechoslovakia. During this time of paranoia, Bauer travels incessant-
ly, alluding to important meetings, exchanges of information, and the
need to compose his memoirs—to establish a record of his career—
since his life is in danger. Indeed, he fears that if he is not murdered,
a fatal disease will overtake him. Ingrid and her lover Tomas regard
Bauer as a great man, and they welcome the opportunity for Tomas to
serve as his secretary.

This basic information is revealed situation by situation. Every
scene is a new story, a shifting mood. When the idea of a continuous
reality intrudes, narrated in a third- or first-person voice, it sounds stilted and artificial. Thus Ingrid says, "Bauer asked Tomas to come at 6

P.M. tomorrow. And afterwards they would make a schedule for the work." Then Ingrid speaks in her normal voice to Tomas, telling him she loves him. They are two ex-students living in a typically messy sixties apartment. She puts on *Die Meistersinger*, which moves Tomas to ask: "Getting me in the mood for Bauer?" In Wagner's opera, Hans Sachs sees that his beloved Eva loves a younger man, and Hans decides to act as her go-between, furthering the interests of his rival—making him, in fact, a master singer so that he can become a husband worthy of Eva. Sontag twists this Wagnerian theme into a vision of life as a precarious round of power plays and politics. The aging, though still handsome, Bauer welcomes Tomas as a collaborator, encourages him to take care of his disaffected but attractive young wife, Francesa, and then turns on Tomas, accusing him of seducing his wife and thwarting Bauer's efforts to compose his memoirs and carry on his political work. Tomas is perplexed. Bauer keeps inviting him to become more intimate, and then Bauer accuses Tomas of betraying his trust. Tomas does fall in love with Francesca, but later the film reveals that Francesca has been playing Bauer's game—that is, pretending to be alienated from Bauer so as to draw Tomas's sympathy. This pleases Bauer, who likes to listen from a closet as his wife and Tomas make love. Ingrid, who has become increasingly upset that Tomas spends all his time with the Bauers, is seduced by Bauer in turn, and comes to work for him as cook and nurse to Francesca. Eventually, Bauer, Francesca, and Ingrid make a threesome in bed, and Tomas becomes the excluded one. When he tries to return to the fold, Bauer and Francesca stage an elaborate ruse that leaves Tomas thinking she has committed suicide, and Bauer, in front of Tomas, follows suit. Yet when Tomas leaves the Bauer residence with Ingrid, the Bauers stare down at him, looking impassive, remote behind a window, unreadable.

The inconclusive ending bothered reviewers. Sontag declared to Edwin Newman that she wanted the film to cause anxiety. She succeeds. It is impossible to say what Bauer's problem is because Sontag's script resists explication. Does he throw up his food because he fears it is poisoned, because it is poisoned, or because he suffers from an eating disorder in which he gorges himself and then regurgitates? This compulsive eating has its parallels in Tomas's heavy smoking. He cannot control it. He says, "I want to stop smoking." Ingrid says, "Then why don't you?" Tomas answers, "A question of stronger and weaker forces, isn't it?" The line might be applied to the whole film, to its reading of art and life: a question of stronger and weaker forces, of what prevails. Bauer lives for power, and for that reason his principles do not matter. He is utterly arbitrary: he can be charming or cruel and change moods abruptly. He can be ingratiating or seductive, menacing or pathetic. This bewildering range of behaviors is less bewildering if the viewer realizes—as Molly Haskell did in the best American review the film received—that what is always at stake is power and how to get it. It can be grabbed, it can be coaxed, it can be summoned in an incredible variety of poses or games. It all depends on how much one is a believer in what Ingrid calls the "power of the will," a phrase she employs as she hands Tomas a cigarette.

Put another way, this is a film about discipleship. Tomas wants to work for a great man who must test the disciple's loyalty on every level, from the trivial to the profound. Sontag, given her own participation in a variety of triangles, is rather adept at filming a power-mad world. Compared to the naïve politics of *Trip to Hanoi*, *Duet for Cannibals* is a cynical work. It idealizes and rationalizes nothing. The problem, of course, is that the film is thesis-ridden: since it is about the many different forms of domination—erotic, pornographic, political—Sontag deliberately, even perversely, refuses to give her audience any reason to care about Bauer or the other characters as individuals. Of course, this is her very point. Such identifications oversimplify the problem of human relationships, which is not just a matter of personality, of psychology, of sociology, and so on. Power has its own rhythm, which is a seesaw of emotions, an operatic scale that bursts the bounds of the decorum that most films observe.

With Bauer in the closet overhearing Tomas and Francesca making love, with Ingrid in the middle of the bed between Bauer and Francesca, the only missing couple is Bauer and Tomas in bed or in the closet, making love or watching Ingrid and Francesca make love. These are options in the world of this film, since an infinite variety of couplings are possible. Or as Sontag says in "The Pornographic Imagination": the "bisexuality, the disregard for the incest taboo, and other similar features common to pornographic narratives function to multiply the possibilities of exchange. Ideally, it should be possible for everyone to have a sexual connection with everyone else." Bauer is the father of these younger characters who idolize him. They also try to reject him, which accounts for his constant efforts to amuse them by varying the terms of their exchanges, by erotically intertwining all of them.

Sontag puts her own extraordinary experience as both master and disciple into this massive show of how power devours everything, just as Bauer devours his food, his friends, his lovers, his allies. Fixated on her theme, Sontag, no less than her characters, sees nothing else. Or as Ingrid puts it more obliquely: "How can one believe anything so long as something else is going on at the same time?" Bauer is a radical, opposed to the oppression of the status quo, yet his dissent is merely another act of coercion.

Although one reviewer identified Bauer as an example of a bad radical, it is hard to see how there could be such a thing as a good radical given the abuses of authority this film mercilessly exposes. Bauer is so bent on manipulation that he is comic, and many reviewers treated *Duet for Cannibals* as a black comedy. This reaction surprised Sontag, she told interviewer Mel Gussow, but she grew to rather like it—perhaps because it made her film more endurable, even enjoyable, without undermining her desire to remain inconclusive.

The quest for power is redundant and reductive: it turns all things into one thing; it transforms individuals into doubles of each other. Thus Bauer and Tomas face each other with identical guns—given to them by Francesca because, Bauer explains, "she wants us both to be safe."

Bauer has formed a brood akin to what Sontag experienced in the Taubes circles at Harvard and Columbia. Taubes cultivated an air of esoteric knowledge—intellectual and sexual—of the sort that emanates from Bauer. Drawn to these powerful characters, Sontag paid her tribute to them while simultaneously taking their measure.

Duet for Cannibals ends when it has become stifling, when both the Bauers and their young protégés realize that they are on the verge of suffocation. This is surely why the Bauers enact their mock deaths. Bauer lists the game's components for Tomas: a gun, a woman, a cause, Tomas's wish to destroy him, Tomas's wish to destroy himself. The men have become doubles of each other; the game has been played.

Sontag herself found the film claustrophobic, she told Mel Gussow. She wanted to do a second film with more locations, a third with as many as twenty-six characters, another that would be science fiction. She had exhausted the subject of power—or perhaps it is better to say that she wanted to loosen its grip.

In the spring of 1969, Susan Taubes, first novelist, instructor in religion at Columbia, ex-wife of Jacob Taubes, and a Susan Sontag intimate, drowned herself in the Hudson River. She had just published her first novel, _Divorcing_, a study of a woman's effort to break the power of her charismatic husband. Sontag would never get over the shock of that death, which seemed as willed as Sontag's desire to live. If she had ever been drawn to the idea of suicide, Taubes's death had shown her how impossible and terrible such an act of self-annihilation could be. Taubes had two children, and Sontag did her best to comfort them. She helped Taubes's son Ethan get settled in school. When Sontag returned to Europe to work on her second film, _Brother Carl_, the death of Susan Taubes haunted her—indeed, it would encroach on the film itself and on her fiction.

In her story "Debriefing," Sontag provides one of her rare, fully reported descriptions of a character, Julia, who has Susan Taubes's slight figure and sensuous, long reddish-brown hair. Her birdlike body gives her an ethereal air, as if she could take wing at any moment. It is an "absent body," remarks the story's narrator. Sontag was only nineteen when she met twenty-three-year-old Susan on the steps of Widener Library at Harvard, and these were also the conditions under which the characters meet in "Debriefing," a story about one woman's failed effort to save another.

Thwarted in her desire to make connections between things on every level—even between one leaf lying beside another in Central Park—Julia is starving herself and withdrawing from the world. The narrator thinks it unwise to ask questions that have no answers—or no answers that the questioner can be certain are right. But it is Julia's persistent search for a nexus that propels the narrator's own reverie about how, or why, people and events cohere. For if Julia's questions about connection cannot be answered, what is to prevent one from concluding that the world is random, that individual lives bear no relation to each other, that understanding one Doris (there are several in the story) does not lead to understanding the others. Of course, the obverse is equally disturbing: if one Doris does inevitably lead to another, and a deterministic pattern is established, then the concept of individuality itself is vitiated. The story is a debriefing in that affiliations are sought, as in _Duet for Cannibals_, but they are frustrated. The title is ironic, for we do not obtain the information that debriefings are supposed to yield. There is no sense of closure, no happy ending.

Julia has a psychiatrist father (like Susan Taubes, who had a psychiatrist father who shows up as a character in her novel, *Divorcing*). When he calls Julia, the narrator answers that Julia is not home. He is not fooled because he knows Julia goes nowhere. But she would have gone out, the narrator responds, "if she'd known you were going to call." This closed-in world, immune to therapeutic interventions, will appear in Sontag's second film, *Brother Carl*, in which the "childish" Julia of "Debriefing" is replaced by a mute child and by an adult, both of whom take refuge in a cellar reminiscent of Sontag's own childhood caves.

What binds the two Susans, and the "I" and Julia of "Debriefing," is a "pessimism of the intellect." But the "I" of the story, like Sontag, believes in self-preservation, in the "optimism of the will." The narrator imagines herself swooping down like a bird to pull her drowning friend out of the river. But Sontag, no less than the narrator of "Debriefing," lacked Julia's birdlike body and spirit.

When so many are absent from their lives, why does it have to be Julia who actually takes her own life? the narrator wonders. Sontag, more earthbound—sturdier than the other Susan—pictures herself, or her "I," as a Sisyphus, clinging to a rock and shouting "Stand back!" Susan Taubes's suicide left Susan Sontag feeling terribly alone but determined to persevere.

After the May 1969 premiere of *Duet for Cannibals*, Sontag spent a summer in Italy pondering what she had learned about film, and then she returned to New York in September to embark on her next shooting script. By December she had a draft ready, and by mid-January she was in Stockholm again assembling her crew and picking locations.

Just as the first film is a kind of parable about power, the second is an allegory about making art. Sontag calls Carl, a retired dancer, a "holy fool." Laurent Terzieff, who played Carl, was reminded of Nijinsky and his troubled relationship with Diaghilev. Carl's mentor/nemesis is the director Martin Ericsson, who has done something terrible (never divulged) to Carl, but who is determined to redeem himself and to rescue Carl from his silence (Carl speaks very few words in the film) and from his withdrawal from the world.

As Sontag suggests in "The Aesthetics of Silence," the only way for the artist to maintain integrity is to remain silent, for words are a potential betrayal, a misinterpretation, a distortion, and an exploitation of the artist by the artist—as Martin somehow misused Carl. Of course, to seek complete silence is to inhabit a kind of living death—or death itself, the course that Diddy and Susan Taubes and Julia choose.

Brother Carl dramatizes the fluctuating relationship between two women, Lena and Karen. At first Lena seems to be the strong one. She is a theater director taking Karen on a badly needed vacation, for Karen is involved in a tortured marriage that has produced an autistic child, Anna. But Lena is the truly vulnerable one. She brings Karen to her ex-husband, Martin, whom Lena still loves and to whom she tries to give herself once again. She wants to re-create her love for Martin by drawing on Karen's strength. She tells them: "How good we are together. I love you both so much." But Martin rejects Lena and gravitates toward the troubled but resilient Karen. Karen, Martin says approvingly, is unfinished and has a drive to complete herself. Karen herself says—as Sontag has—"I want to be what I admire." Consequently, Lena feels isolated and moves toward the silent Carl, who is ambivalent about her attentions and rejects her sexual advances. Feeling abandoned and suspecting that Martin and Karen are in love, Lena (like Susan Taubes) drowns herself.

Brother Carl presents, in the screenplay's words, the "very image of the person who is excluded." He walks into the water several times as though to drown himself; he plunges his head in the bath for an excruciatingly long interval as Martin bathes him; he withdraws into a cave/grave recess with Anna. Carl—everyone's brother, so to speak—is meant to alert us to the tragedy that we all sense is going to happen and yet feel powerless, like Lena, like one Susan with the other, to stop.

Karen's first reaction to Lena's death is the same as the narrator's reaction to Julia's suicide in "Debriefing": "How could she be so stupid!" Karen's anger, like that of the "I" in Sontag's story, gives way to grief and to a question, "Don't you think she'd see now what a stupid thing it was? She'd be sorry now. . . ." A remorseful film, *Brother Carl* desperately wants to relieve itself of guilt and the consciousness of death.

The childlike Carl, seemingly the most vulnerable character, survives—as Sontag did—drawing a blanket over himself like a tent, living in an earth cellar with old books, Indian blankets, and the kind of miscellany of objects that she surrounded herself with in her childhood retreat. Later he digs a hole, as though he were digging his own grave. But he does not lie in it. Rather, he seems an emblem (to use a Sontag word) of the artist, withdrawn into silence and yet eloquent on the subject of human isolation and mortality.

Ms. Sontag

1971–1973

The fusion of Susan Sontag, Women's Lib and *Vogue* magazine is one of those inevitable astrological conjunctions that outline the pattern of our culture in one bright electrical display—illuminating the coalition that now exists between intellectual personalities, chic radical issues and the fashion marketplace. —Robert Brustein, "If an Artist Wants to Be Serious and Respected and Rich, Famous and Popular, He Is Suffering from Cultural Schizophrenia," *New York Times Magazine*, September 26, 1971

After completing the editing of *Brother Carl* in January 1971, Sontag spent two months in Paris. She lived with Nicole Stéphane, whose address temporarily became her own. Sontag had secured the rights to do a film version of *L'Invitée*, Simone de Beauvoir's first novel, with Stéphane as producer. As Sontag told an interviewer in May 1972, she had become a part of the Parisian intellectual scene. Her first ten years (1958–68) of intermittent residence in the city had been as an outsider, an American among Americans, but now her circle became almost exclusively French. She had even secured Sartre's old apartment at 42 rue Bonaparte, where he had lived between 1942 and 1962. In back of the Place Saint-Germain-des-Prés, Sontag could see the Church of Saint-Germain-des-Prés and the Café Deux Magots, where Sartre and de Beauvoir had worked together, from her living room window.

De Beauvoir had signaled Sontag's new status by giving the film rights to her gratis. Sontag expected to make her filmmaking career in France, not knowing how to raise money as an independent director in the United States and not evincing any interest in making the compromises she supposed would be necessary if she were to seek American studio backing for her films. If France did not foster feminists or independent filmmakers, it nevertheless provided a narrow zone of opportunity that Sontag could capitalize on. France, like other European countries, had welcomed writers, like Alain Robbe-Grillet, who also became directors, and this was precisely the status that Sontag sought.

FSG promoted Sontag's reputation as a filmmaker by publishing her screenplays at home and abroad, and by planning a Susan-Sontag-on-cinema book, to be done in collaboration with another film critic/filmmaker. Sontag's first choice was the British writer Richard Roud, with whom she occasionally stayed on her visits to London. Later she opted for a Parisian colleague, the avant-garde filmmaker Noël Burch. But FSG found the screenplays a tough sell, the cinema book never jelled, and the film of de Beauvoir's novel never got made. Sontag accepted a $5,000 advance from a production company to produce an original screenplay, "The Year of the Ox." She later gave up her contract, and the head of production had to dun Sontag and FSG—even threatening legal action—to get back the advance, which Roger Straus doled out in $1,000 increments.

The film projects—not to mention the novel that Sontag always seemed on the verge of producing—her lecture appearances, and interviews, the mixed but gratifyingly widespread reviews of *Styles of Radical Will:* all sustained a sense of her seeming ubiquitousness. In fact, Sontag had, with regard to her writing, moved into a "quiet period," to borrow a phrase from Lila Karpf at FSG. This period would last from the summer of 1969 until the early summer of 1972, when Sontag wrote to Roger Straus, "I'm back in the race to become The Most Important Writer of My Generation and all that shit." She had returned to writing short fiction and to her groundbreaking essays on photography.

Sontag published a radical document, "The Third World of Women," in the spring 1973 issue of *Partisan Review*. The piece derived from her responses to a questionnaire submitted to her the year before by *Libre*, which was, in her words, a "Spanish-language, political and literary quarterly with a loosely Marxist orientation." The article's truculent tone is startling, rivaling only the stridency of "What's Happening in America."

While Sontag reaffirms her support for revolutionary socialism, she declares that no government purporting to adopt Marxist principles has ever liberated women—which in her lexicon would mean not merely establishing equality under the law but enforcing a power-sharing scheme between the sexes. Sontag regards women as threatened, vulnerable to attack on the street in virtually every part of the world. She scorns liberal panaceas. To simply work for equality under the law will always mean that women will lag behind men, for men have demonstrated their refusal to part with power. What ruling class has ever voluntarily reduced its own strength? Sontag asks. True change will only occur when women force men to change. The choice for change is just that stark, since the "very structure of society is founded on male privilege," Sontag declares.

How will women achieve power? They will have to labor for it. Every woman should work, Sontag insists: "It must be *expected* that most women will work." Until women have the means to support themselves, they will never be free. "Liberation means *power*," she reiterates.

Work also entails a psychosexual attack on the hegemony of "genital heterosexuality." A "nonrepressive" society, she explains, will be androgynous, for it will steadily subvert the differences between the sexes. This "depolarization" will lead to a redefinition of women's roles, so that they will no longer think of themselves first as "potential sexual partners." Instead sexuality will be "diffused." In "The Third World of Women," Sontag predicts that in a liberated society "homosexual choices will be as valid and respectable as heterosexual choices, both will grow out of a genuine bisexuality." She identifies the enemy: "machismo."

She then turns her article into a tactical manual. She enjoins women to take to the streets in protest. No marching men, please. Women should learn karate, whistle at men, attack beauty parlors, and organize campaigns against sexist toy companies. She endorses "militant lesbianism." Women should run their own abortion clinics—Sontag was one of several prominent women who revealed they had undergone abortions and

signed the *Ms.* "Abortion Law Repeal" petition in 1972. Women should
sue popular women's magazines, conduct male beauty contests, run feminist candidates for public office, deface billboards demeaning to
women, retain their own names, renounce alimony, and in general raise
hell wherever male privilege and female subordination are in evidence.
No matter how extreme, how rude, how shrill they are, women should
persist in a "guerrilla theater" that strikes at sexist standards. Reform
can only ameliorate, but radical agitation can fundamentally change the
terms that shape women's lives.

But that is not all. Women have to realize that the family by its very
nature holds women back. It incarcerates women in their homes, makes
them unfit to compete in society, and fosters a "guilt-producing factory,
and a school of selfishness." Sontag is even against every home having a
washing machine. Even if every family could afford domestic help, it
would not liberate women from an acquisitive consumer society bent on
devouring itself and everything else. The family is not a refuge but a
prison, where women are kept in line by the homogenized messages of
television sets now dominating living rooms everywhere.

Sontag had never linked her own success to a feminist agenda, or
even to a feminist reading of history. Surely some personal statement was
in order. What kind of example had Susan Sontag set? What drove her
sense of urgency? And where had that urgency been all along? How did
she view the choices she had made? How did she arrange her domestic
life? What kind of family did she have? Women awakened by feminism
in the late 1960s and early 1970s craved autobiography, examples of
lives they could learn from. Lillian Hellman made a new career for herself by her seeming candor about her own mixed-up, on-again, off-again
years with Dashiell Hammett. The title of her first memoir, *An
Unfinished Woman* (1969), boldly appealed to a new audience of feminist readers. Hellman was hard on herself for her failings, but also glorious in her feistiness. She had been vulnerable, but she was now
strong—admitting, bluntly, that she was unfinished, meaning not simply
incomplete but also ambitious to go on, to triumph.

Sontag was not alone in feeling the pressure of a feminist resurgence
that linked the personal and the political—that insisted the personal *was*
political. And like other women writers, she felt called upon to issue her
own manifesto. Indeed, what engaged woman would not want a statement
from Sontag about her level of engagement? Toward the end of "The

Third World of Women," Sontag turns to herself: "I would never describe myself as a liberated woman. Of course, things are never as simple as *that*. But I have always been a feminist." Then Sontag provides an auto-biographical précis: her dream of becoming a biochemist and winning the Nobel Prize, inspired, of course, by reading the biography of Marie Curie; then her desire to be a doctor, and then a writer—never dreaming that because she was born female she would be blocked from achieving her ambitions. Her family life is so "minimal" she calls it "subnuclear" and dismisses it in half a sentence. This unconscious feminist then ascends through the academic ranks, marrying at seventeen, keeping her own name, then divorcing her husband and rejecting her attorney's "automatic bid" for alimony, even though she was "broke, homeless, and jobless at that moment and I had a six-year-old child to support." She remembers feeling offended when people harped on her single-parent status and how hard it must be. After all, this was the life she had chosen. She did realize that her place and her position were exceptional. Indeed, becoming an exception gave her certain advantages that she "enjoyed as my right." But "I know better now," she concludes.

What did Sontag now know? That a woman with talent and drive had made it because she had "greater visibility," the "nigger in a room full of whites," as she told interviewer Victoria Schultz. The women's movement had taught her to view her own success in a political context. Her exception proved nothing. Indeed, she criticized other women (implicitly including herself) who had not seen that their success had actually confirmed the male prerogative to grant exceptions. Indeed, successful women, in her experience, had been misogynistic, actually preferring the company of men. She even went so far as to say that "most women who pass as being 'liberated' are shameless Uncle Toms, eager to flatter their men colleagues." The essay ended with a call for the successful woman not to maintain "good relations with men" at the cost of "betraying her sisters."

When Sontag was writing her manifesto, she was also writing her letter/reports to Roger Straus, her male champion, who was, she assured him, never far from her thoughts. She always missed him when she was away from New York, her letters say. But when she came home to FSG, the women, the underlings, felt her contempt. While she advised women to sue mass-circulation women's magazines, Sontag was publishing in them, trying to place, in fact, a piece called "A Movable Doom," a study of the "double standard of aging," which *McCall's* rejected as strangely impersonal and dated. Certainly by some feminist standards Sontag had shown enormous courage and resourcefulness, even if she had had the domestic help (during her marriage to Rieff) that she said society could do without. But she was not forthcoming about how she had played a male game. She stuck safely to generalities about women such as herself. Most important, her "visibility" was not merely a function of her being recognized as an "exception." Rather, she had *worked* to make herself visible, and that kind of work is not even hinted at in "The Third World of Women."

Feminism was not an issue Susan Sontag could afford to ignore, but she also did not want to address it personally. Jill Johnston could see as much. Johnston introduced Sontag to movement heavies: Gloria Steinem, Brenda Feigen-Fasteau, Phyllis Chesler, Kate Millet, and others. Johnston hoped Sontag would become involved: "She had us up to her penthouse at Riverside Drive where we sat around CR [consciousness-raising] style, discussing superficial feminist things."

CR intrudes in "The Third World of Women," but Sontag never went beyond this one fling. Indeed, her view of feminists, and her relationships with them, seemed to fluctuate with the fortunes of the movement. Feminist Vivian Gornick, who met Sontag almost a decade later, felt during her fleeting encounters with Sontag at various parties and other events that her reception depended on how well her own brand of feminist writing was faring in the New York literary stock exchange. When Gornick's shares rose, Sontag seemed welcoming; when the market dropped, so did Sontag's level of attention.

Jill Johnston is a fascinating figure to match against Sontag, for Johnston, at that time a militant lesbian feminist, was doing what Sontag could only urge others to do. Indeed, Johnston is like one of those doubles that Sontag plays with in her novels, stories, and films. An art and dance critic in the late fifties to mid-sixties, Johnston at one point had as a lover dancer Lucinda Childs; later, in the 1980s, Sontag would also become Childs's lover. But Johnston made the personal political, the private public. She was not afraid to look extreme. Sontag would not risk the marginalization that radical behavior virtually guaranteed. Sontag's mainstream allure—no matter that the literati knew she preferred women—was heterosexual.

Until the rise of the women's movement, Sontag's success had occurred in a vacuum; that is, neither she nor the culture was forced to think very hard about what her success as a woman meant. Sontag entered New York in 1959 at the end of the Old Left's period of dominance, consorting with New York intellectuals who had not taken feminism or most women writers very seriously. As late as the early 1960s, Lionel Trilling had dismissed Virginia Woolf as not deserving serious consideration as a canonical author. Except for Mary McCarthy, the thirties generation of women authors like Josephine Herbst and Zora Neal Hurston was largely forgotten. Women writers of Sontag's generation might receive good reviews and respectful treatment in the academy, but they simply did not function as exemplary figures—to borrow one of Sontag's favorite terms.

It was Sontag's exemplary quality that made her chary of acknowledging any identity that would make her a minority. It can even be argued that her combination of sexiness and braininess made it easier for a generation of men to cope with the increased intellectual assertiveness of women in the 1970s. It was in this context that she and Straus were so concerned about her sexual orientation becoming known to her mass audience—concerned perhaps that it would destroy the illusion of sexual availability to men that made her intellect acceptable.

As a writer, moreover, Sontag did not see why she must reveal more of her private life than she chose. She had matured in a period (the 1950s) when William Faulkner, for example, published a series of articles lamenting that the sanctity of privacy was an American virtue that the media and its consumers were rapidly destroying. Faulkner was deeply disturbed by the changes he saw occurring between the 1930s and 1950s. Now any writer of prominence was fair game, he felt, which is quite a different matter from the writer who seeks publicity. Sontag grew up in the Faulknerian tradition. She wanted her work to stand on its merits; she wanted to be admired for her style, not her lifestyle—a word she would surely reject as a vulgar coinage of a commercial culture. Yet her efforts to escape took the form of a denial that she was exemplary, that she was anything more than a writer, and thus to many observers she appeared disingenuous.

Sontag's dilemma was acute. If she had not recognized the importance of the women's movement, she would have limited her own ability to respond to a changing culture. How could she be exemplary without acknowledging the new wave of feminism? On the other hand, much about feminism was extraliterary, having little to do with her notion of the literary life. Her models had been Gide and Mann. Sontag could not be a movement person and remain true to her conception of a writer; movement politics would ultimately violate her sense of the decorum a writer had to maintain.

At Town Hall in Manhattan in the spring of 1971, Norman Mailer, fresh from baiting feminists in *The Prisoner of Sex*, confronted onstage a battery of formidable women: Germaine Greer, Diana Trilling, Jackie Ceballos (president of the National Organization for Women), and Johnston, then a columnist for the *Village Voice*. In the audience sat notables such as historian Arthur Schlesinger, Jr., Elizabeth Hardwick, and Susan Sontag. The evening turned raucous when Johnston was joined by two women (friends of hers) who ran onstage from the wings. The sight of these "three pretty solid women . . . hugging and kissing" provoked Mailer to scold Johnston: "Get up and act like a lady!" In cool contrast to the activists onstage, Sontag mildly reproved Mailer for using the word "lady."

In interviews during this period, Sontag recast her career in a feminist light. For example, she described *Brother Carl* as a film about a working woman (Lena) enslaved to a bastard of an ex-lover, and a married woman (Karen) trapped in a boring middle-class marriage. But *Brother Carl* makes nothing of these issues.

Where men come in for it is in "The Double Standard of Aging" (*Saturday Review*, September 23, 1972), a revision of "A Movable Doom," an unremarkable boilerplate piece, mainly useful to gauge Sontag's take on the world of male privilege. What strikes her is how long men can hold on to power, and how they can attract much younger women. Age and physical appearance matter little to men in authority. They can go on and on whereas age is a "movable doom" for women, who repeatedly anticipate catastrophe when they reach twenty-one or thirty or forty or fifty. Sontag described (without naming names) her friend Harriet's crisis at twenty-one: "The best part of my life is over. I'm not young any more," wailed Harriet to a befuddled sixteen-year-old Susan, who was "too young to have noticed." Harriet was beautiful then; now past forty, she was still an attractive, charming, vital, and "striking-looking" woman, Sontag assured her readers.

Women compensated for the double standard of aging by pretending to be younger, lying about their age, using makeup and all the skills of the actress. Women decorated and costumed themselves. They had to be acutely conscious of style. But Sontag said nothing about her own style-consciousness, and *McCall's* rejected the article.

Sontag got angry when women stopped her in the street and said they admired her but admitted they had not read her work. What an insult to a writer! Sontag said to friends like Richard Tristman. But many of these women had formed their idea of Sontag from photographs in *Vogue* and other mass-circulation magazines, or from her book jackets. To them, Sontag *was* her image, her striking poses and her provocative blurbs on the backs of other people's books; she was the glamorous figure whose epigrams columnists loved to repeat.

Of course, many young women did read Sontag, and many, like Camille Paglia, aspired to emulate her "celebrity, her positioning in the media world at the border of the high arts and popular culture," as Paglia puts it. In the spring of 1973, Paglia was working in her first academic job at Bennington College. She was in her mid-twenties, a militant feminist and an open lesbian. She thought of Sontag as a radical who had challenged male dominance. Like Sontag, Paglia had forsaken academic narrowness for a broadly based, interdisciplinary approach, although Paglia's earliest models were explicitly feminist icons like Mary McCarthy and Simone de Beauvoir. Paglia was working on a dissertation, *Sexual Personae,* which would later become a controversial, best-selling book.

Sontag had, in Paglia's words, produced a kind of public theater in *Against Interpretation,* dramatizing the role of an "*au courant* woman intellectual" and reviving and modernizing the conception of the woman of letters. Paglia hoped, however, that Sontag would go much further: "One of my primary gripes against Sontag from the very start," she wrote to Sontag's biographers, was "her cowardice about her sex life after Stonewall." Paglia had been the only openly gay student at Yale graduate school in 1968. Sontag, on the other hand, had, in Paglia's words, "marketed herself as a 'personality' in the media and in that superficial Manhattan party scene and yet tried to invoke the precedent of the reclusive, retiring pure writer, the transcendent artiste, in deflecting questions about her private life."

Paglia had first seen Sontag in person on October 15, 1969. Paglia can be precise because it was Vietnam Moratorium Day, and Paglia, then a graduate student at Yale, was visiting a friend enrolled at Princeton. "She was at the height of her fame. She was a very impressive presence," Paglia remembers.

Paglia drove to a Sontag appearance at Dartmouth in the spring of 1973, hoping to persuade her to come to speak at Bennington. The Sontag she saw at Dartmouth reminded her of the publicity shots on her Swedish film set: Sontag had a "very stylish lean look—boots, trousers, turtleneck sweaters, big belts, flowing scarves. Neither Mary McCarthy nor Simone de Beauvoir had such a persona or would have been able to carry it off." For sheer theatricality, Sontag could not be beat.

Paglia struggled to scrape together Sontag's speaking fee. It was agreed that Sontag would talk about contemporary issues. The college could only afford to pay $700—about half Sontag's usual fee and twice what the college usually offered speakers. She relied on help from Richard Tristman, a friend of Sontag's from her teaching days at Columbia, to persuade her to come. The Bennington faculty, mostly male, did not share Paglia's enthusiasm. Indeed, Paglia realized only much later that because they had paid double, the faculty expected Sontag to be twice as good. Paglia raised the stakes with her poster campaign, urging her students to bring their friends to this "extraordinary experience" during which Sontag would impart her valuable insights on contemporary culture.

On the "great day," late in the afternoon of October 4, 1973, two hours behind schedule, Sontag arrived sleeping in a car. Looking haggard and puffy, she explained to Paglia that she had been writing all night. She wrote in spurts, when the spirit moved her. She was quite "lazy," she told her, and had to take stimulants to get her through two-week writing jags. Sontag skipped a scheduled meeting at the college president's home, and Paglia escorted the college's guest to a restaurant, where a representative group of faculty and students met her. Sontag, with a "sonorous flourish . . . ordered steak *au poivre*, which seemed suitably grand and exotic." After the dinner Sontag ignored her host's reminders that they were behind schedule and "drank wine on and on and on as couriers kept arriving," Paglia recalls.

When Paglia finally got Sontag to the Bennington Carriage Barn, the site of her performance, an angry full house had been waiting for over an hour. Breaking the tension, Paglia gave a baroque introduction, comparing Sontag to the savants of the ancien régime. In the evening's only humorous moment, Sontag "stepped up to the podium and said good-naturedly, 'That was the most . . . *unusual* introduction I have ever received!' This brought down the house."

But then Sontag began reading one of her short stories—boring and bleak, according to Paglia—in the style of a French New Novel piece about "nothing." The faculty felt betrayed since "she had agreed to come to Bennington to give a non-fiction talk about cultural/political issues." The crowd glared at the mortified Paglia, then seemed to drift off into sleep. A seemingly oblivious Sontag read on . . . and on . . . and on. After the reading Sontag got upset at Bernard Malamud's house. Bennington's star novelist, Malamud was also known as a "general pain in the ass," says Paglia. Her friends felt Malamud had made a fool of himself, although no one seemed to know what Malamud had done to provoke Sontag. Sontag and Malamud had never met. "He invites me to his house to insult me!" Sontag fumed to Paglia as the two rode away from the Malamud party.

Energized with indignation, Sontag seemed fully awake and actually began to talk to Paglia as the two women chatted away for over an hour in the car. An amazed Paglia watched the erect public Sontag, "cool, detached, austere, and lofty," slouch down in the seat and become "'Susan,' warm, distinctly Jewish in speech and manner." To an interviewer, Sontag once said: "I really do like intimacy—intimacy of the Jewish kind, to put it in a code way. I like people who talk a lot about themselves, who are warm and physically demonstrative." Sontag appeared to welcome Paglia's rapid-fire delivery and her obvious wish for a personal connection.

Paglia liked what Sontag had made of herself: "Mazel tov! We need more women stars who can run their own studios," she wrote in her essay about Sontag in *Vamps and Tramps* (1994). With the pressure of public performance over, and alone with a responsive soul, Sontag decompressed. Paglia was surprised at how frank Sontag was in acknowledging the erotic allure of Nicole Stéphane. But they talked more about the sexy Adriana Asti, the beautiful Italian actress Sontag had used in *Duet for Cannibals*. Like two guys talking shop, they traded notes about hot women, Paglia recalls.

Paglia also tried to engage Sontag in discussion about her dissertation, *Sexual Personae*. Paglia, already beginning to have reservations about the "anti-intellectualism of feminist rhetoric," wanted to provoke Sontag's interest. But Sontag seemed "so slooooow" to Paglia, who saw her as a figure from another generation who had a bankable persona that she did not want to risk changing. When Paglia kept pushing, an irritated but also intrigued Sontag asked, "What is it you *want* from me?" A flustered Paglia said, "Just to talk to you." But Paglia admits that she also wanted Sontag's acknowledgment, if not her blessing. Later Paglia realized that she was playing out *All About Eve*, a film in which Margo Channing (Bette Davis) is stalked and supplanted by her younger protégé, Eve (Anne Baxter). Paglia says she saw herself as the "new girl." In retrospect, she remarks, "it's the stalking part that Sontag probably picked up on that night!"

Beginning with Sontag's Bennington appearance, Paglia became disenchanted with her role model, observing Sontag withdraw from a confrontation with the academic world. Instead of trying to change it, she settled for "snobbish scorn." Furthermore, Sontag's "mandarin disdain" of popular culture, especially of television, exhibited an elitism that betrayed her early work suggesting that culture—both the so-called high and low—reflected a new sensibility.

According to Sontag, Mary McCarthy once said to her, "You're the imitation me." In 1992, when Paglia went public with an attack on Sontag, she was in effect saying to her former role model, "I'm the next stage of you." A year later, Sontag was questioned about Paglia in *Istoe*, the Brazilian equivalent of *Time*. Sontag said Paglia should form a rock band.

1 9 7 1 – 1 9 7 4

In the spring of 1971, Susan Sontag was one of sixty signatories to a public letter to Fidel Castro protesting Cuba's treatment of the poet Heberto Padilla. The *New York Times* placed her photograph next to ones of Jean-Paul Sartre and Alberto Moravia. But she abandoned a book on the Cuban revolution.

She then planned a trip to China that would culminate in a book. *Ms.* assisted in paying the bill for China, contributing $1,000 for her "woman's eye view." In January 1973, Sontag took a three-week tour of the country. Except for "Project for a Trip to China," written before her voyage and published in the *Atlantic Monthly*, she never published another word about it.

In May 1973 British publisher Secker & Warburg, having sustained significant losses in publishing her work, dropped her. Sontag admitted that her visions of grandeur that yielded no books were "Thurberesque." Straus kept working on William Shawn at *The New Yorker*, but the magazine rejected most of Sontag's fiction, publishing instead her long essay "Approaching Artaud" on May 19, 1973. *Playboy* was more obliging, taking her short story "Baby" for $2,500.

The Yom Kippur War changed everything. Like her putative feminism, Sontag's Jewishness never seems to have been an issue for her until she suddenly made it one. Among her comrades on the Left, Israel no longer seemed the threatened entity of 1967, when the Arab world (as in 1948) seemed on the verge of annihilating it. Racism and imperialism were terms applied quite freely to the Jewish state.

For Sontag, in love with a Jewish woman who had been in peril in Paris during the war, and attracted to exiled peoples, the issue of Israelis and Palestinians was especially problematic. She and Stéphane decided to direct and to produce what became a remarkable documentary and one of Sontag's most honorable works.

"You are not going to believe this—hang on to your chair. Susan is in Israel right now in the Sinai desert filming a documentary with a whole team . . . !" Roger Straus wrote to FSG's London agent Deborah Rogers (October 31, 1973). A truce had not yet been called, still Sontag filmed in land-mined areas, determined to get close to the action. She would let the reality of what she witnessed script the film for her, allowing the accidental and even the unfortunate to intrude in ways that her tightly written and closeted Swedish films would not allow. There would be no voice-over narration; instead she would integrate layers of images and voices to suggest the complex reality of a land that had been promised to too many people.

The film opens with shots of Israel as a land of domes, crescents, crosses, and television aerials. Shots of an Arab herdsman in the desert give way to a scene in the Jerusalem War Cemetery. Heart-monitor beeps clash with battle sounds. Israel radio and Arab radio sounds are mixed with shots of battlefield corpses. There is a constant interplay of Israeli and Arab faces and places. The first of the film's two major voices, writer Yoram Kaniuk, begins to explain the origins of Israel as a response to the Holocaust, as a development of Zionism. There is Zionism's faith in socialism, its denial of tragedy; yet there is also Zionism's denial of Arab rights (earlier the film has a scene set in an Arab schoolroom showing the teaching of anti-Semitic texts). Kaniuk is a committed Israeli who nevertheless yearns for recognition of the Palestinians and for peace. But the country is changing, he notes, becoming more American, more consumer-oriented, and evolving away from its socialist past.

In shots emphasizing the country's growing commercialization, a second major voice is heard. Israeli physicist Yuval Ne'eman reports the

Arab view of Israel. It is an abscess that has to be lanced. The Israelis are intruders, like the Crusaders. Ne'eman refers to the Arabs' search for a "final solution"—the words reminiscent, of course, of the Nazis. He regards anti-Semitism as endemic to Arab society.

Kaniuk's and Ne'eman's voices constantly play off against one another. Reviewer Stanley Kauffmann called the film Hegelian, for it stressed "not a struggle between truth and falsehood but between two opposing, partial truths" (*The New Republic,* June 29, 1974). John Simon, praising the film's "fine eye for visual detail," said it also broke "new ground by allowing two main speakers to carry on an antiphonal debate that weaves its way through the entire fabric" (*Esquire,* October 1974). Of course, not every critic found the film so fascinating. One called it "stupefyingly tedious" (David Moran, *Boston Phoenix,* August 6, 1974), but then he was put off by the wailing tone, the constant grief that Sontag clearly wanted to emphasize.

There are no Arab voices to match Kaniuk's and Ne'eman's, and that alone might have exposed Sontag to charges of a pro-Israeli bias. But the film, beyond its ostensible setting in the aftermath of the Yom Kippur War and the broader Arab-Israeli conflict, is surely about the exploration of the Jewish conscience and consciousness. As Sontag said in her *Vogue* article about making *Promised Lands,* it is her most personal film.

It was during the making of the film that Sontag and Kaniuk became close friends. Born in Tel Aviv in 1930, Kaniuk had fought in Israel's 1948 war for independence. As a young man, he lived in New York for ten years painting and writing journalism. He returned to Israel in 1961 and began publishing prose in 1962. He gradually established an international reputation. It was his third novel, *Adam Resurrected* (1968), that attracted Sontag's attention. Praised as perhaps his greatest work, it tells the story of Adam Stein, who presides over a kind of demented kingdom in the desert, reenacting the comic routines that spared him from the gas chamber. Kaniuk's extraordinary range of tone—he was one of the first Israeli writers to deal with the Holocaust—shifting from the comic to the tragic, made him the perfect ambivalent voice to set the tone of *Promised Lands.* He speaks, off and on, for nearly half the film, almost writing the script for it as he speaks. His impact on Sontag was also extraordinary, for he stimulated in her an openness she has shared with few others in her life. In their most intimate period, she would introduce him as one of her three or four closest friends. She told him about Nicole, and even

about her parents. They had many heart-to-heart talks. She was quite
open about her sexuality. He met her son, David, and could not fathom
their odd connection: "She was not a mother, and he was not a son."

When Kaniuk first met Sontag, he felt overwhelmed. She told him she
had read *Adam Resurrected* in one night, and that it was a great novel. (She
would later provide a blurb for the Harper paperback.) He began to read
her work, attracted by her Middle-European mind, which reminded him so
much of Walter Benjamin and Karl Kraus. She used the same mixture of
philosophy and history, and she seemed to be carrying on a very long
German-Jewish tradition that no other American-born writer had mastered. Kaniuk doubts that she could have understood Benjamin so well if
she had not been Jewish. He thought of her as an "angel of reason."

Soon Kaniuk and Sontag were having long discussions about what
it meant to be Jewish. When she had first told him of her Jewish origins, he was shocked. There had been nothing about her that he associated with Jews. When Kaniuk visited Sontag later in New York, she
told him that first she was a Jew, second a writer, and third an
American. He thought it odd that she could be so emphatic, and he
questioned her several times about her Jewishness. He saw in Sontag
and in her close friend poet Joseph Brodsky the same pride in being a
Jew and the wish not to be burdened by all the history that came with
such an identity.

Kaniuk's visibility in America was low, and he hoped Sontag might
help him since she had promoted many writers she admired. He sent her
The Last Jew (1982), explaining that he had just been nominated for a
Nobel Prize. Later he realized it had been the wrong thing to say. She
seemed to withdraw from him. He had evidently asked her to do too
much. He badly wanted to be a success in America, which he thought of
as his second home. He thought Sontag would understand that and not
feel used by him. Once she had invited him to a Roger Straus party. He
had felt shy and awkward, but she took care of that, introducing him to
Straus: "This is Yoram Kaniuk, one of the world's greatest novelists."
Sontag spoke as a kind of ambassador, or as Kaniuk puts it, she had
become literature's world statesman.

Kaniuk related his feelings about 1973—the period of a nearly rap-
turous relationship with Sontag—and about the early 1980s, when she
backed away from him—in the same loving, respectful, and regretful
tones. He likened his experience with Sontag to her friendship with

Nobel Prize winner Joseph Brodsky. She was jealous of the poet, Kaniuk recalls. "She loved him and hated him at the same time." She could be petty about people. Kaniuk remembers her as discontented—but then that is what made her an artist, he believes.

Brodsky, a fiercely critical man, became an obsession with Sontag, who irritated people by calling him "our Joseph." He was hardly one to be patronized, however. If he could say quite wonderful things about Sontag, he often spoke critically of her as well, Kaniuk reports. "They saw in the other something he/she didn't have." Brodsky hurt Sontag, Kaniuk believes, for he was never one to give unqualified approval, which she craved. Sontag's eulogies of Brodsky address only the humorous side of his baiting. "Susan," he would say, "poetry is aviation; prose the infantry." Kaniuk remembers Sontag having had a similarly close yet troubled relationship with actor-director Joseph Chaikin.

Brodsky's Nobel Prize represented the world stage, where Sontag has always wanted to be. As Kaniuk says, "From a very young age she had, as we all do, conflicting ideals of what she wanted to be. She wanted to be very famous, very rich, very new, very innovative, and very avant-garde." She is one of the very few to succeed at balancing these conflicting desires. In America, Kaniuk observes, there is a special feeling about "making it," and "Susan wanted to make it." She has her intellectual recognition in Europe—as Kaniuk found out when a word from her did wonders for his career there. "I say this with great respect. Susan has used America better than anyone."

Kaniuk believes "there was a moment when Susan's ideals about herself—her self-theme—became a 'thought' to her. She managed to project an idea of herself into the world the way she wanted to." She wanted to be admired and loved. He remembers her walking like a queen in New York. She looked so grand in her appearance at the Cathedral of St. John the Divine (the largest Gothic cathedral in the world). Yet she was also so eager—a trembling queen, full of doubts, a person of great fears. "But she always managed to put on this strong thing," Kaniuk continues. She never gave in to fear, he says, obviously proud of her performance. "In *The Emperor Jones*, Eugene O'Neill says man is born broken and life is mending. The grace of God is glue. Susan is the only person I know who found the grace of God within herself. She glued herself from all these broken pieces."

In another sense, Kaniuk thinks that Sontag came

without history. I come full of history. Susan rejected her history. Even when she said she was a Jew, I can't say she meant it the way I would. She has to invent history. I didn't have to invent myself. I do it in books. Her writing and her being are one and the same. It's magic to be Susan Sontag in her writing and in her life. She is like a moving land, a moving country, a moving entity.

Her own promised land.

Old Complaints Revisited **15**

1975

> Dissent must be set off from dissent.
> I dissent differently.
> —*I, etcetera*

On February 6, 1975, the *New York Review of Books* published "Fascinating Fascism," Sontag's full-scale assault on the rehabilitation of Leni Riefenstahl, best known for her Nazi-era documentaries *Triumph of the Will* and *Olympiad*. As Sontag confided to Straus, she had written the piece to make a "splash"—which it did, provoking lavish praise and fierce criticism, as well as a high volume of letters that Sontag relished. Robert Silvers told her that that particular issue of *NYRB* had been one of their best sellers. Sontag began by evoking the beautiful—indeed ravishing—photographs in Riefenstahl's recent book, *The Last of the Nuba*. But then she meticulously set out to destroy the Riefenstahl persona, showing how the filmmaker had lied about her Nazi affiliations and how her publisher and film critics had collaborated to promote her elisions of history, which made her out to be an artist first and a propagandist second. Riefenstahl portrayed herself as a German Romantic who had had the misfortune of attracting Hitler's attention but who had been acquitted twice of any complicity in war crimes. The beautiful Riefenstahl—

Sontag made much of the way Riefenstahl had been photographed—this "character," as Sontag put it, "underwent a steady aggrandizement." It seemed to nettle Sontag that Riefenstahl billed herself as an independent filmmaker when, in fact, she had been bankrolled by Hitler, who had made his Nuremberg rallies into a movie set for her.

Had Sontag halted her blitzkrieg at this point, her essay would have kicked up a fuss mainly in the film world and among literary critics interested to find that she had reversed course. There had been that notorious passage in "Against Interpretation" in which Sontag had cautioned that merely to condemn Riefenstahl for her reprehensible Nazi content would be to diminish the vital experience of artistic form. Sontag knew quite well that "Fascinating Fascism" might be viewed as a repudiation of her earlier remarks, and she had her answer ready when Robert Boyers (a friend) gave her a forum in *Salmagundi* (Fall/Winter 1975–76) to explain that she had not contradicted herself so much as she had looked at the form/content distinction from a different angle. She had been concerned in the earlier essay to emphasize form because critics seemed obsessed with content. What mattered, Sontag argued, was context; it troubled her that *only* form had become the issue since Riefenstahl and her promoters ignored or excused her Nazi past. And what of Sontag's own role in shaping the taste for form that she now repudiated? "The hard truth is that what may be acceptable in elite culture may not be acceptable in mass culture, that taste which poses only innocuous ethical issues as the property of a minority becomes corrupting when they become more established," Sontag concluded.

Sontag had changed (she admitted in *Salmagundi*) insofar as she now had a "much denser notion of historical context," which led her to speculate on other reasons for Riefenstahl's rehabilitation. Surely the "fact that she is a woman" helped turn her into a "cultural monument." Here Sontag knew she had touched a nerve—one that she irritated further by claiming that feminists had embraced the beautiful Leni because of her status as one of the few world-class female filmmakers. To rile feminists even more, Sontag emphasized the demeaning nature of Riefenstahl's fascist aesthetic: it glorified submission to an all-powerful leader. Indeed, it was pornographic in its exultation in the triumph of the strong over the weak, turning people into things, celebrating the primitive, the virile, making a cult and a fetish of beauty. This fascist aesthetic had become fashionable, a part of the camp sensibility, Sontag said, echoing the essay that had first brought her fame. A liberal culture, she opined, revolved around cycles of taste; it was simply fascism's turn on the "cultural wheel."

Poet Adrienne Rich wrote *NYRB* (March 20, 1975) in shock. Was this the author of "The Third World of Women"? That essay had inspired Rich to expect more "lucid and beautifully reasoned" feminist insights. But "Fascinating Fascism" was full of "failed connections." It was so inimical to "The Third World of Women" that Rich wondered if that essay had been, "after all, more of an intellectual exercise than the expression of a felt reality—her own—interpreted by a keen mind." Why blame women for Riefenstahl's rehabilitation? Wasn't it mainly the work of cineasts? And why end the discussion of Riefenstahl with general comments about liberal society and its fads? Why not make the connection between "patriarchal history, sexuality, pornography, and power"? Why not explain how the passivity induced by ideologies such as fascism was always linked to female qualities? Not to demonstrate that the first people turned into things were always women, not to show that women's minds and bodies were always the first to be colonized, was to practice a "kind of dissociation of one kind of knowledge from another which reinforces cultism and aesthetic compromise with the representatives of oppression; precisely what Sontag herself was writing to deplore."

One Sontag friend remembers that Rich's letter devastated Sontag, and that it was an agony for her to compose a reply. In another mood, Sontag wrote a staff member at FSG: "I counterattacked. What else could I do?" Sontag attacked Rich as a commissar enforcing a party line— although Rich had stated she was "*not* looking for a 'line.'" Sontag scored against Rich for using terms like "male-identified 'successful' women" to compose an "ominous-sounding enemies list." Did Sontag have to mention feminism in everything she wrote? Was all history to be reduced to discussions of the patriarchy? "Like all capital moral truths, feminism is a bit simple-minded," she concluded. Most of history was, "alas, 'patriarchal history.'" But how to distinguish between one patriarch and another, one period of history and another? Rich's brand of feminism, in other words, was reductive in its demand for "unremitting rhetoric, with every argument arriving triumphantly at a militant conclusion."

Of course, that was the freight train of feminism Sontag rode in "The

Third World of Feminism." Why should she have been offended that Rich wanted to know where Sontag's apparently uncompromising feminism was headed? Instead Sontag turned the occasion of her reply into a diatribe against programmatic feminists and into a defense of Elizabeth Hardwick, whose book *Seduction and Betrayal* had been attacked by feminists. Sontag claimed that Hardwick's work had been dismissed because it had been regarded as too elitist, too taken with talent and genius, and insufficiently respectful of the movement's egalitarian ethics. In other words, Rich and her ilk were vulgarians, leftovers from the "infantile leftism of the 1960s." (There was no acknowledgment here of the Sontag who had contributed her share of Marxist platitudes to the period, and who had ended a piece on Cuban poster art by exclaiming "Viva Fidel.") For Rich history was no more than shallow psychology, Sontag suggested.

Sontag ended her rebuttal by refusing to take up Rich's personal challenge. In effect, Rich was asking Sontag: "Come on, what do you really *feel* about feminism?" Sontag sought the high ground: "Although I defy anyone to read what I wrote and miss its personal, even autobiographical character, I much prefer that the text be judged as an argument and not as an 'expression' of anything at all, my sincere feelings included."

But "Fascinating Fascism" is a fascinating study of Sontag. The parallels with Riefenstahl are obvious: both filmmakers, they know all about manipulating their images even as they vehemently deny that they do so. They are both promoted by powerful men. They both get caught up in revolutionary rhetoric and in the cult of the maximum leader. "Viva Fidel!" is the Communist version of "Heil Hitler!" Indeed, in "Fascinating Fascism" Sontag delineates a number of parallels between the aesthetics of fascism and those of Communism. In both, the "will is staged publicly." Castro's public, operatic theater—the idea of a whole society mobilized by his rhetoric— thrilled Sontag. Here is Sontag quoting Riefenstahl, but Sontag might as well be quoting herself: the "care for composition, the aspiration to form. . . Whatever is purely realistic, slice-of-life, which is average, quotidian, doesn't interest me."

Riefenstahl remains forever a Nazi in "Fascinating Fascism." Her pre-Nazi films, which emphasize the cult of the body, are treated as precursors of fascist aesthetics. Sontag ignores how Riefenstahl was using the pictorial devices of the German Romantics and the literary themes of

Novalis, Tieck, Goethe, von Eichendorff, and Hölderlin. By ignoring both form and context, Sontag denies Riefenstahl's development as an artist and the evolution of her ideology—a point several film critics have made about "Fascinating Fascism."

The animus between Riefenstahl and Sontag continues. In *Leni Riefenstahl: A Memoir* (1992), Riefenstahl attacks Sontag for her lack of objectivity, mentioning but not naming journalists who have disputed Sontag's statement of the facts. In the spring of 1995, Riefenstahl was invited to the San Francisco Film Festival, part of the highly successful City Arts & Lectures series, at which Sontag has often appeared. Riefenstahl, then ninety-two, wrote to say she could not come because— as columnist Herb Caen reported—the "tough old bird" had injured herself scuba diving. The trip would have been called off anyway, though, because the eight-member committee (mainly Jewish) responsible for inviting Riefenstahl included, according to Caen in the *San Francisco Chronicle* (March 30, 1995), one vociferous dissenter: "Susan Sontag, another tough bird."

It would be misleading, however, to simply equate Sontag and Riefenstahl. If Sontag has been attracted to power and to the powerful male, she has also been critical of both. Sontag was horrified at how much Riefenstahl's decades-long denial of her complicity in evil had degraded her ability to be an artist and had corrupted her. "Fascinating Fascism," then, has to be regarded as Sontag's first step in her public recantation of a politics that excused Communist tyranny and the cult, especially in Cuba, of the "maximum leader."

Becoming a Little Posthumous

1975-1978

Like his mother, David Rieff proved a restless traveler. He dropped out of Amherst. He worked in Mexico for educator Ivan Ilyich, one of Sontag's friends. He seemed to wander at will, meeting up with his mother from time to time in New York or Paris, where in the early 1970s he also became absorbed in French culture.

Concerning David, Sontag continued to alternate between periods of neglect and periods of attention. For example, in the mid-1970s, when David had resumed his education at Princeton, he was in New York visiting his mother. At a dinner party he had an allergic reaction to lobster bisque and began choking. One of his dinner companions, Carole Chazin, became alarmed. She looked over at his mother, who did not seem to notice David's distress. Chazin got up and took David out of the room and sat with him while he recovered, wondering when his mother would come to him. Sontag never came, never even mentioned the incident.

A few years later, at a theatrical event, an important contemporary novelist introduced a magazine editor to Sontag. The editor had commissioned a piece from David but had had to reject it. The editor began to praise David, explaining why the magazine could not run his article, but Sontag cut her off and began ranting about the rejection, giving the editor a full dressing-down in front of the aghast novelist, who was struck not only by Sontag's vehemence but by her complete disregard for the social conventions of such occasions.

Sontag conveyed to her son a sense of superiority. As one of his friends has said, "David can make anyone feel stupid, and he seems to enjoy doing it." Camille Paglia heard from a Princeton friend stories circulating about David's appearances there as the heir apparent. Dressed in velvet Edwardian garb at various dinner tables, he commanded attention with brilliant conversation. David certainly acted like royalty. In George Garrett's creative writing pass/fail class, David turned in no work and seemed to attend class only to brutalize everyone else's writing. In revolt, the class arrived as one at an ultimatum, which they delivered to their professor: If Rieff did not turn in a story to be discussed in class, they would protest to the school administration. The students knew their man, because Garrett admits that he probably would have passed Rieff on the strength of his attendance and class participation. So he told Rieff to bring in a story, and Rieff obliged, passing his work out in class rather than giving his fellow students several days to read it, as the course required. What they read were page proofs of a story of his about to be published in the *Paris Review*. Unimpressed, the class tore Rieff and his fiction to shreds. They were good critics, Garrett confirms, and knew how to do a hatchet job as well as Rieff did. Rieff did not seem too happy about the incident, Garrett recalls, but he did pass the course.

That *Paris Review* story had been submitted with the assistance of FSG, of course, with Susan Sontag carefully tracking her son's literary progress even as she gave him first look at everything she wrote. Indeed, in a few short years he would become her editor at FSG, and still later she would include one of his pieces in a *Best American Essays* collection she edited—without noting in her introduction that he was her son. Rieff's work was good, a reviewer noted, but shouldn't Sontag have at least told readers she was including her son's work?

In the fall of 1975, it was David who saved his forty-two-year-old mother's life. He said he would only take the physical exam for enrollment at Princeton if his mother also got a complete checkup. At the time,

Sontag felt well, but the examination and tests revealed that she had breast cancer. Not content with the first medical opinion she received, even though the positive biopsy dictated immediate surgery, Sontag spent ten days consulting doctors. She had more tests run and medical records checked, and even flew to the Cleveland Clinic to investigate modified radical mastectomy—then considered a very risky procedure because it might leave cancer cells in her chest muscles and other tissues. Sontag wanted to minimize her disfigurement, but she wanted even more to live, and she chose radical mastectomy as the best way to enhance her prospects of survival. In October 1975, Sontag underwent a radical surgery for breast cancer at Memorial-Sloan Kettering Institute Cancer Institute in Manhattan.

Sontag insisted on getting a candid assessment of her condition. Doctors told her there was only a 10 percent chance that she would still be alive in two years. One gave her six months to live. Another said, "Your cancer is very invasive." Her first reaction to the diagnosis was sheer terror. She thought of it as a death sentence, a curse, and wondered, "What did I do in my life that brought this on? . . . I never can tell when I'm feeling bad if it's physical as well as psychological, and my tendency is to think that it's always psychological, and therefore, ultimately, my fault." In the early weeks of her recovery from surgery, Sontag tortured herself with the idea that you could get cancer from holding in your grief. She condemned herself for leading the wrong kind of life. And now the grief overwhelmed her: the thought of leaving David and the writer's life she loved seemed unbearable.

It took Sontag a good month to work through these negative feelings, to realize how much she wanted to fight for her life. She became angry about the way ill people felt ashamed and humiliated, the way they blamed themselves for their diseases. They were frightened and acted as if what they had was obscene. Paralyzed with worry, they became incapable of coping with their illness. Cancer had a special stigma. It was not like having heart disease. Cancer patients were treated to a conspiracy of silence. Sontag became outraged when she noticed that the hospital sent her mail in unmarked envelopes as though the contents were pornographic.

Sontag began to read medical texts and foreign scientific journals, and it was months before she settled on a treatment program in Paris, an extreme experimental thirty-month course of chemotherapy, with massive doses of certain drugs that had not yet received FDA approval. Skeptical American doctors tried to dissuade her. Did she have any idea how agonizing and dangerous the treatment would be or how her hair loss would make her feel? She noticed that other patients were fixated on the image of their denuded heads. It deprived them of their dignity. One patient told her that she might wake up one morning to find her hair on the pillow. Then it came home to Sontag—this idea that her hair would come off, like a hat. Even at this moment of terror, though, she knew that losing her hair would not be the great tragedy of her life.

She began treatment in Paris, later persuading physicians at Sloan Kettering to follow the French plan, along with an immunotherapy treatment designed to boost her body's ability to resist the spread of cancerous cells. By the eighth month of therapy, Sontag's hair grew back, thicker and grayer than before.

This summary of what Sontag did and how she took charge of her treatment does not do justice to the courage and resourcefulness she exhibited in confronting and overcoming her own fears about cancer. Her reading of the medical literature led her to jettison psychological explanations of disease; people had to be shown that they were not responsible for causing their illnesses, but that they were obligated to resist them by seeking out the best available treatment. Here the idea for writing a useful book, *Illness as Metaphor*, arose as a counterattack on fatalism and fear, though it would be a good six months before Sontag felt well enough to write—and then she would have to complete her book on photography before attempting another full-scale assault on the rampant psychologizing that distorted so much thinking about disease and so many other matters as well.

The notion of resigning herself to death never occurred to Sontag. She wanted *more* of her life. She associated not fighting for life with her mother's passivity, and that association drove her wild. If Sontag had only a 10 percent chance of living two years, why couldn't she be part of that 10 percent? *"Somebody's* got to be that 10 percent," she thought.

Chemotherapy was agony. There were also follow-up and exploratory operations. As late as the spring of 1978, Sontag continued to be treated once or twice a week on an out-patient basis. "I am in some pain all the time," she said in an interview. "Right now, in this part of my left arm near my wrist, it hurts and that is because a nerve somewhere was affected by one operation."

But fighting cancer gave Sontag a sense of release. It also made her reflect on her career. Why was it that she kept delaying her return to fiction? Why did she begin novels and then abandon them? As always, she sought inspiration and insight in the careers of others. Even before the discovery of her cancer, she had written about the painter Francis Bacon, whom she called "falsely precocious" because he was "a late developer," a term she would begin to apply to herself.

Going to the hospital several times a week for thirty months obliged Sontag to deal with people in a new way. Patients were suffering and getting little support from their doctors. When Sontag asked one physician what he thought about the psychological causes of cancer, he replied: "Well, people say a lot of funny things about diseases." No help there. Sontag wanted to be useful, to write a book that would save lives simply by urging individuals not to feel embarrassed by their cancer, and to find doctors who would not treat it as something more than a disease. Cancer was no more a mystery than tuberculosis. Treatments and cures would be found.

Sontag became responsive to the psychology of ill people now that she herself had experienced it. Sick friends found in her not merely sympathy but a grasp of what it took to fight one's own fears. When Richard Tristman, diagnosed with cancer, had to undergo strenuous experimental treatments, she was a constant source of support. The doctors told Tristman that therapy would become so excruciating that he would have to stop. "When you reach that stage," Sontag told him, "take one more treatment, and then one more." Tristman did, knowing she had earned the right to offer advice.

Sontag called her life-threatening cancer a "watershed experience." She craved time with David and her friends, touching and cuddling and holding on to people. Ever since then, when she appears in public, when she appears to give a talk, she is almost always surrounded by friends, whom she kisses and hugs. With her entourage she looks like a movie star manifesting her power, but she is also a vulnerable woman who thinks of herself as a "little posthumous." She does not want to miss her moment. For thirty months she did not know if she would live or die. In one sense, she felt fortunate: "I'm lucky to have my own death." She felt she had that time to prepare for it, to say good-bye. In fact, as Yoram Kaniuk remembers, there was a good-bye party. He marveled at how calm—even stoic— Sontag seemed as her friends came to cheer her for perhaps the last time.

Within a week of Sontag's October 1975 operation, Joseph Chaikin had written to playwright Arthur Miller telling him about Sontag's condition and noting that she had enormous medical bills. Chaikin had spoken to poet Muriel Rukeyser, then president of PEN, about extending financial aid, which the organization had previously done for writers in distress. Arthur Miller addressed a PEN meeting, asking for $10,000 for "poor Susan who is dying of cancer in Paris and needs the money desperately." When PEN board member Thomas Lipscomb began asking for more details about Sontag's illness, Miller became indignant that anyone would question him about this dire dilemma. But as Lipscomb points out, the PEN fund for needy writers gave small grants—on the order of $300. Ten thousand dollars seemed impossible, more than the budget could stand. And what about all the other needy writers? Lipscomb asked. Miller walked out in a huff.

Robert Silvers got together the $150,000 to pay for medical bills since Sontag had no medical insurance. Martin Peretz, publisher of *The New Republic*, contributed $15,000. An appeal on Sontag's behalf was distributed and signed by Donald Barthelme, Joseph Chaikin, Barbara Epstein, Maxine Groffsky, Elizabeth Hardwick, Arthur Miller, William Phillips, Robert Silvers, Roger Straus, and Diana Trilling.

Even with the help of friends and fellow writers, Sontag had to work hard to pay her medical bills. She found the perfect way to deal with her stress: working on *Illness as Metaphor*. When she typed the words "death," "agony," "cancer," she laughed and said, "I've won." She wrote in a sort of controlled rage. The demon of recovery had dispossessed the demon of disease that had undone those she had seen succumb irrationally to the mystery of their maladies.

Recovery

1 9 7 6 – 1 9 7 7

During the summer of 1976, Sontag stayed in Paris with Nicole Stéphane, to whom her next book, *On Photography* (1977), would be dedicated. She still felt fragile and worried about any illness that might weaken her constitution. But she changed few of her habits—she still smoked, and she continued to write her first laborious drafts stretched out in bed before sitting up in a wooden chair and typing later ones.

Sontag was rewriting her *New York Review of Books* essays on photography, which began appearing in 1973. She recast the separate pieces as a continuous, overlapping, back-and-forth dialogue with herself about the nature of photography. She was quite right in thinking that nothing like this treatment of the subject had ever been published. Of course, Sontag drew on books by photographers, and she paid homage to critics such as Walter Benjamin and John Berger, but her precursors, she rightly maintained, had not provided the extended meditation that she was essaying, especially not from the perspective of a thinker who was not a photographer and who insisted, in fact, on treating photography not as a practitioner but as a consumer.

Part history, part philosophical speculation, part disguised autobiography, *On Photography* is a towering achievement, an essay with the nuances of a novel. The book begins with a grand flourish, the kind of authoritative sweeping up of history that makes Sontag so quotable: "Humankind lingers unregenerately in Plato's cave, still reveling, its age-old habit, in mere images of the truth." Here is the Puritan's call to reform, the epicure's pursuit of pure pleasure, and the philosopher's quest for truth existing in the tension that makes Sontag at her best so provocative, possessed of a voice that simply cannot be ignored.

For Sontag, the impulse to write about photography dated from the Museum of Modern Art's (MoMA) big retrospective of Diane Arbus in December 1972. Arbus had taken that melancholy, tender two-shot of Susan and David for *Esquire,* and Sontag had visited her studio. But Sontag had not previously seen the range of Arbus's photographs that the retrospective provided, and like many of the attendees, she was "knocked out" by them.

To Sontag, the show represented a "watershed in the consciousness of photography." The power of the images was such that day after day spectators lined up for blocks on Fifty-third Street to get into the exhibition. No photography show had ever attracted that kind of attendance, with the possible exception, Sontag thought, of Edward Steichen's "Family of Man" in 1955—also at MoMA. Indeed, Steichen's leadership of MoMA's department of photography had fostered the contemporary craving for camera art, but "Family of Man"—the "quintessential group show" in Sontag's estimation—had been organized around an "acceptable . . . that is innocuous theme," celebrating the human togetherness ballyhooed by the press during its worldwide tour.

The Arbus show, on the other hand, featured the "eccentric and strong personal vision" of an artist known mostly to those who took a special interest in photography. That tens of thousands would come to see the work of just one photographer fundamentally changed, in Sontag's view, the audience for photography. Suddenly the camera's peculiar possibilities, as filtered through a unique intelligence, were given a primacy previously unacknowledged by museums and the world of art.

Sontag kept returning to the Arbus show to watch the audience, to overhear what they said. She discovered that, like herself, many of these people were repeaters, who had come back again and again to these images. A few months later Sontag had lunch with Barbara Epstein, coeditor of the *New York Review of Books,* and recommended the show to her: "It's not just a body of work, it's an amazing cultural event." Epstein said, "Why don't you write about it?" Sontag said, "Oh, I don't have anything to say." A persistent Epstein got Sontag started on writing what seemed then, to Sontag, a very difficult assignment: how to do justice to the show and to explain its unusual reception. It seemed in order, however, to make some "speculative remarks" about photography before attempting to gauge the significance of the Arbus show. A few paragraphs is what Sontag had in mind. To her surprise, she wrote more than five thousand words about the phenomenon of photography and how it had been disseminated in the culture. How was it that photography had come to be taken as a particular form of knowledge? What was it that people believed they knew through photography? Why had the medium so captured the public imagination? These questions began to open up the subject of photography in ways that Sontag had not envisioned.

In a call to Barbara Epstein, Sontag explained that it now seemed as though she had a two-part article, the prolegomenon followed by an account of the Arbus show. Epstein approved and Sontag turned in the first part. But then there were just a few more thoughts that seemed necessary. Each paragraph began to turn into an essay in itself that would take between six and nine months to complete. The photography book took shape over the course of nearly five years, a protracted composition that accounts in part for its lapidary style; each idea in the book is a gem that has been repeatedly cut and polished. No book of Sontag's has shone with more facets than *On Photography*, a fact that has irritated some reviewers and readers who like a straightforward style, and exhilarated others who rejoice in viewing the same ideas from different angles. *On Photography* is a difficult masterpiece conscious of itself, of its image—so to speak—and as such is the perfect representation of its image-conscious author. *On Photography* is also a tour de force that advances opinions that need not find acceptance; indeed one could take issue with virtually every statement in the book and still find oneself mesmerized by Sontag's profound inquiry into the issues that make photography itself endlessly fascinating.

The subject seemed so full that Sontag realized, "To write about photography is nothing less than to write about the world." Photography led to a discussion of what it means to be modern, to explore the nature of consciousness and the nexus between knowing and acting. She could not possibly do justice to all the issues *On Photography* raised, and she had a sense that it would be possible to continue writing the book forever. She did stop, though, when she concluded that she had produced an original work. She was buoyed by the knowledge that she could make a contribution to the literature on photography which was not possible with regard to other arts that had already attracted a considerable body of theoretical and speculative work.

More than any of Sontag's other essays, *On Photography* is about the tension between opposing ideas, about the negative capability that Keats described. It is about the dialectic that Hegel identified, in which ideas turn into their opposites, in which one idea taken to its extreme contradicts itself, in which there is always a search for a synthesis of conflicting ideas. *On Photography* explores the very process of idea-making, the tension of cerebration. Sontag reinforces her dialectical point by including a final section, an anthology of quotations in homage to Walter Benjamin, who aspired to produce a book that would be composed entirely of quotations, a fitting tribute to the divergences inherent in any argument.

From her first sentence, Sontag makes clear that image-making is a form of deceit. She reminds us of Plato's dictum that the artist is a liar. If photography requires special censure, it is because it has been taken to be so real, a piece of the true cross—as Sontag put it to her Detroit Institute of Arts audience. If she is hard on humankind for accepting the photograph as a verity, her chastening purpose is directed at herself as well.

Few have reveled more in pictures than Sontag or become more absorbed in the lives of picture-makers. A year before publication of *On Photography*, she wrote a preface for Peter Hujar's book of photographs. Later she wrote a preface for one of Robert Mapplethorpe's books. In addition to her friendships with Peter Hujar and Robert Mapplethorpe, and to her liaison with Nicole Stéphane, Sontag would become close to photographer Annie Leibovitz.

Like Hujar and Mapplethorpe, Leibovitz would shoot Sontag in flattering poses—most conspicuously in the erotic jacket photograph for *The Volcano Lover*. Sontag would attend many Leibovitz exhibitions, traveling with her to Poland and Mexico, for example. Leibovitz would often be photographed by Sontag's side during Sontag's numerous appearances in New York for readings, lectures, and other events. Indeed, they were pictured together in the *New York Observer* and other

2409 East Drachman, Tucson (1943): In 1943 Mildred moved her two daughters to a neat, compact four-room stucco bungalow at 2409 East Drachman, then a dirt road. Sontag called her early years in Tucson "my desert childhood." *(Courtesy Arizona Historical Society)*

Sue Sontag, Editor, *Arcade* W'49: North Hollywood High School Yearbook *(Courtesy Jamake Highwater)*

Philip Rieff: About her first and only husband, Sontag later wrote that after reading *Middlemarch*, she "burst into sobs," realizing "not only that *I* was Dorothea but that, a few months earlier, I had married Mr. Casaubon." *(Courtesy University of Pennsylvania Archives)*

In 1958 Sontag contacted Harriet Sohmers, her closest companion at Berkeley, then working for the *Herald Tribune* in Paris. They became a couple again and traveled through Europe. Photographs of them in Paris, Spain, and Greece show Sontag at twenty-five, but looking eighteen. In Paris, her smile is almost broad— a girl on a field trip to the museum, admiring a Picasso. Harriet and Susan leaning on a brick wall in Spain present a picture of camaraderie— but with the darker Susan smiling less. In Greece, the pose seems yet more solemn. Leaning against a pillar, she begins to resemble the later dramatic, classical Sontag. *(Courtesy Harriet Sohmers)*

The Sorbonne: In Paris, Sontag attended the Sorbonne. Her friend Irv Jaffe remembered that they went to hear Simone de Beauvoir lecture there. They were impressed. They were critical. *(Authors' collection)*

In Paris, Harriet Sohmers introduced Susan to thirty-year-old Alfred Chester. He was ascending into the "hanging gardens of literary celebrity," to use Cynthia Ozick's evocative phrase. *(Courtesy University of Delaware Library Special Collections)*

Right from the beginning of her career in New York, Sontag did what many aspiring writers do: she cruised "all parties, bad parties." On occasion Richard Howard accompanied her. He is a devotee of French literature, a translator, poet, critic, and literary politician extraordinaire. *(Courtesy UPI/Corbis-Bettmann)*

Sontag met Cuban-American playwright María Irene Fornés at a party in early 1959. They began a relationship that would mark Sontag for life. The petite Fornés "could use four-letter words at a tea party . . . without ever being accused of not being a lady." *(Credit Photofest)*

"Roger and Me": Roger Straus, Sontag's one and only publisher, and one of her biographers attend the same event at the National Arts Club. Straus's partner, Robert Giroux, has praised his "publishing flair." Straus recognized Sontag's uniqueness— indeed he encouraged her to regard herself as a special case. *(Courtesy photographer Ted Klein)*

Sontag met actress Nicole Stéphane in the late 1960s. With Stéphane, hailed for her brilliant performance in *Les Enfants Terribles* (1950), Sontag was "very attentive, affectionate." *(Courtesy Corbis/John Springer)*

Irving Penn shoots Sontag and son as fashion idols with a head-on look that accentuates their very dark, large-eyed, wide-open Sumerian stares. *(Courtesy* Vogue. *Copyright 1966, renewed by the Condé Nast Publications, Inc.)*

Professor George Goldsmith invited Sontag to attend his class on photography at Boston University. Her book was able to "turn my students inward to see themselves as photographers," Goldsmith comments. His class did not view Sontag's essay "charitably," for they regarded themselves as "victims of Ms. S's penetrating eye." *(Courtesy George Goldsmith)*

Sontag and Nobel Prize–winning poet Joseph Brodsky became friends in the mid-1970s, a few years after the Soviet Union had expelled him. Their obsessive personalities were expressed in their smoking. Brodsky would not quit, even after heart disease and surgery mandated that he stop. Sontag continued smoking even after her bout with cancer. *(Reuters/Peter Skingley/Archive Photos)*

In the late 1970s and early 1980s, recovering triumphantly from her cancer, and with a flurry of publications culminating in *On Photography, Illness as Metaphor,* and *Under the Sign of Saturn,* Sontag seemed to open up, sitting for an engaging series of photographs with Dominique Nabokov. *(Photographer: Dominique Nabokov. Courtesy Liaison Agency)*

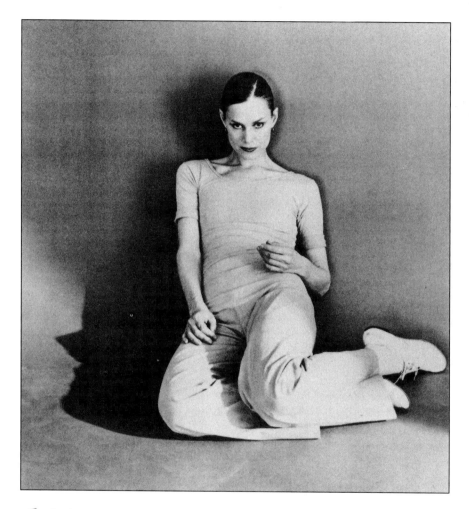

In the late 1970s Sontag was attracted to the dancer Lucinda Childs, who had an alluring inaccessibility: "I'm a beautiful catatonic," Childs told writer Edmund White, who empathized with Sontag's feeling for dance and the female form, a subject she would explore with increasing intensity in her later work. *(Copyright Lois Greenfield)*

By the 1980s Sontag and photographer Annie Leibovitz had become a much gossiped-about item in New York, occasionally breaking into print in published photographs and in news stories that mentioned their "friendship." Looking at one of Leibovitz's photographs in a gallery, Sontag turned to Leibovitz and said, "Well, you may turn out to be a photographer, after all." *(Courtesy Corbis)*

Helen Benedict, one of the few journalists invited to visit the inner sanctum of Sontag's study, remarked, "getting to meet her is a bit like trying to meet Joan of Arc on her day off." *(Courtesy Archive Photos)*

Sontag, one of the first writers to speak out against the death sentence pronounced on Salman Rushdie, commented: "We feel superior, in our imagination, to those Germans who in 1933 and 1934 didn't protest when their Jewish colleagues were being fired or dragged off in the middle of the night to camps. It's clear that the threat of violence by people perceived as fanatics is very terrifying. . . . But we have to be brave." *(Courtesy Archive Photos)*

In 1994 Sontag began researching the life of actress Helena Modjeska for a novel, *In America*. "I am myself an actress, a closet actress," Sontag told a Polish interviewer. *(Copyright Archive Photos)*

Still recovering from the effects of chemotherapy occasioned by her second bout with cancer, Sontag appeared at the 92nd Street Y in Manhattan to celebrate the twenty-fifth anniversary of the *New York Review of Books*. Pictured standing (l. to r.) are Robert Silvers, Susan Sontag, Joan Didion, Darryl Pinckney, Jonathan Miller, James Fenton, publisher Rea Hederman, and Alma Guillermoprieto; seated are Elizabeth Hardwick and Jason Epstein. *(Nancy Crampton)*

"Well, it works for Susan Sontag."

(Courtesy The Cartoon Bank)

Sontag seems once again—as she claimed after the success of *The Volcano Lover*—to be just beginning. Here she reads from *In America* at the Unterberg Poetry Center of the 92nd Street Y. *(Nancy Crampton)*

popular publications. Leibovitz's coworkers would often hear about Sontag's doings from Leibovitz, whose own vision of photography often seemed to echo Sontag's. If Sontag has not held a camera in a professional manner, she has certainly become its professional and personal subject.

Yet for Sontag, photography is problematic because it negates narrative. Photographs freeze time. They convey the illusion that we can stop history and encompass the world "as an anthology of images." What fascinates her is that collecting photographs is tantamount to collecting the world. She says as much in the first sentence of her second paragraph, promoting an imperialistic, aggrandizing notion that she will explore in the life of that consummate collector, the Cavaliere in *The Volcano Lover*. Photography—more than any other art—speaks to the human desire to acquire, to take command of the world, to exercise power over it. This is the quest, of course, that has propelled Sontag. In this respect, every sentence of *On Photography* is a way for Sontag to recover her sense of herself.

There is no author photograph on the jacket of *On Photography*, and the same is true of *Illness as Metaphor*. It is as if this time Sontag did not want her image to be confused with her work. Yet the books are unmistakably personal—a fact that was intuitively clear to students in an introductory writing course who knew virtually nothing about Sontag and had never read her work. As one student essay, "Susan's Addiction," put it:

> From the book's foreword in which Sontag admits to an "obsession" with photography to the final pages where the camera can inspire something "akin to lust," the author reveals her insatiable need for the photograph. In an attempt to separate herself from the addiction she attacks photography. The book is her admission of this lust and a means of self-cleansing.

Professor George Goldsmith, teaching a course on photography at Boston University in the early 1970s, found Sontag's air of authority appealing. When the first of five essays appeared in the autumn 1973 issue of the *New York Review of Books*, it was as if he had "specified its content. It transcended all of the other commentaries and interpretations of photography that I had been able to find in its ability to set down clearly just about all the many ways in which photography impinges on our consciousness." For a teacher, the book did something even more important: "It was able to turn my students inward to see themselves as photographers." Goldsmith's class did not view Sontag's essay "charitably," for they regarded themselves as "victims of Ms. S's penetrating eye." Goldsmith assigned that first essay year after year and never tired of rereading it, always finding it as "fresh and stimulating as it was the first time." He asked Sontag to come to his class during a visit to campus, and though she did a little grumbling beforehand, she fulfilled her role of guest interlocutor admirably.

The first essay in *On Photography* is a précis of the book, with subsequent chapters exploring tangents of her first rebuking sentence about humankind lingering "unregenerately in Plato's cave," a sentence that has provoked the ire of some readers. Equally hard for them to accept is her juxtaposition of Whitman and Arbus in the second essay, "America, Seen Through Photographs Darkly." The title evokes St. Paul and Taubes's teaching of the Gnostic idea that truth is esoteric. It is not to be had by just anyone—and certainly not through a collection of photographs. Whereas Whitman wanted to say yes to American culture, to embrace it in all its variety, Arbus's photographs say no—that much of America cannot be absorbed so easily. Sontag views Arbus as a segue to surrealism, which emphasizes the grotesque and the radical juxtaposition of unassimilable elements. Photographs can create the illusion that any two elements are next to each other, and as such photography is surrealistic. For Sontag, America is the "quintessential Surrealist country." Although she rejects "cut-rate pessimism" and a facile view of America as a "freak show, a wasteland," she can offer no other vision than Arbus's. Unlike her earlier, strident anti-Americanism, here she favors the more neutral tones of the cultural observer, noting that the "American partiality to myths of redemption and damnation remains one of the most energizing, most seductive aspects of our national culture."

Her third essay, "Melancholy Objects," pursues her surrealist line that photography turns the world into found objects, souvenirs of a life that is always escaping. Photography emphasizes found objects because this is a world of loss, of death, of grief, and of melancholy. This mourning over mortality is, certainly, Sontag's own.

The fourth essay, "The Heroism of Vision," is a contrapuntal movement, aiming to show how photographers have tried to acquire, to capture, a fleeting world, transforming it into an article of consumption. This argument is extended in the fifth essay, "Photographic Evangels," to photographers themselves, who have made aggrandizing but contradictory claims for their art, emphasizing on the one hand its objectivity (its direct connection to reality) and on the other its subjectivity (the skill, the guiding hand and focus of the photographer/artist). She deftly juxtaposes the conflicting views of the photographer as projector and as recorder, effacing or magnifying his art.

In the fifth and final essay, "The Image World," she returns to Plato and others who have tried to wean us from our addiction to images. Plato's fear is that images of this world will blind humankind to eternal truths. The image, the photograph, is too available, too widespread for Sontag, even as she concedes its narcissistic uses. Her sentences rock back and forth, imitating the counterindications of photography: "Cameras are the antidote and the disease, a means of appropriating reality and a means of making it obsolete." She worries that photography has "de-Platonized our understanding of reality, making it less and less plausible to reflect upon our experience according to the distinction between images and things, between copies and originals."

Sontag ends *On Photography* with a call for recovery, for a therapy that will somehow bridge the gap between life and art: "If there can be a better way for the real world to include the one of images, it will require an ecology not only of real things but of images as well."

The November 1977 publication of *On Photography* created a sensation. Roger Straus liked the "controversial and interesting" reviews. After an initial printing of 12,000 copies, FSG had gone back to press for another 3,000. Then two small book clubs took orders, and Straus approved a printing of another 6,500 copies. Ready to OK a fourth printing, an ebullient Straus declared that the book was beginning to perform like a bestseller.

Twenty-five years ago, when there were more independent publishers and bookstores, and when books like Sontag's got more review space, serious nonfiction was a success if it began to generate sales in the five figures soon after publication. Straus juiced sales with an ad campaign in early January timed to coincide with Sontag's return to the United States from Paris.

On January 19, 1978, *On Photography* won the National Book Critics Circle Award for Criticism. The day before, Sontag had delivered to FSG the book version of *Illness as Metaphor*, first published as a series of articles that had received a great reception from readers of the *New York Review of Books*. (*NYRB* had published an additional 10,000 copies of her third installment.) Four days later Straus made what he grandly called a "command decision," postponing the publication of Sontag's story collection, *I, etcetera,* from spring or summer to November 1978 in order to create space for *Illness as Metaphor,* scheduled to be released in late June. Suddenly he had enough Sontag product to do some strategic planning, and he obviously relished her deployment. By the end of January, he had 37,500 copies of *On Photography* in print with another 5,000 on order. The book had made the *Washington Post* best-seller list. And Sontag had agreed to make publicity appearances and sit for interviews until April, when she would return to Paris. On February 5 he sold paperback rights to Dell for $49,500.

This flurry of publication in the late 1970s and early 1980s, with *I, etcetera* (1978), *Under the Sign of Saturn* (1980), and *A Susan Sontag Reader* (1982), heightened the literary stature she had held in the late 1960s. *On Photography* and *Illness as Metaphor* will remain fixtures in the college curriculum and the American canon. *Illness as Metaphor* is often assigned to students in health care; it turns up again and again in Web searches of medical literature.

Nothing else Sontag has written is quite so straightforward. *Illness as Metaphor* is a clean book, a cleansing read, free of the kinks that irritate some readers of *On Photography.* Like all of her best essays and books, *Illness as Metaphor* begins with a powerful, resonant first sentence: "Illness is the night-side of life, a more onerous citizenship." More than any other subject Sontag has essayed, illness is a phenomenon that engages every reader. The word conspicuously absent from her first paragraph is disease, even though her book is mainly about tuberculosis and cancer. Occasionally readers misremember her book title, calling it "Disease as Metaphor." But it is part of Sontag's cunning that she doesn't use that word until the third page. We all become ill; we do not all become diseased—at least that is not how many of us would wish to put it. Physical illness—the term Sontag uses on her first page—affects us all in time. Even the healthy may dream of or dread illness, "the night-side of life," and remember what it is like, even for a day, suddenly to be removed from our place in the world by an illness. In other words, Sontag crafts an opening that manages to speak as swiftly and directly to all readers as does illness itself.

The ending of her first sentence is arresting. Citizenship? Well, yes, it makes sense when in her second sentence she speaks of the "kingdom

of the well" and the "kingdom of the sick." The term "citizenship" suggests both rights and responsibilities. There is a nobility in the word—
so different from the British use of the term "subject." There should be
nothing abject about feeling ill, even if one is cut off from the kingdom
of the healthy. Since Sontag's point is that our metaphorical use of language demeans the ill, her own prose has to exemplify—straightaway—
a therapeutic linguistic comportment.

Sontag first presents the history of diseases like tuberculosis, which
in the nineteenth century were thought to be connected with certain
kinds of artistic and sensitive personalities. When scientists discovered
the true, physical cause of the disease and developed an effective treatment, psychological explanations disappeared. So it will be with the
many different manifestations of cancer, she contends.

Illness as Metaphor is also a work of literary criticism in that Sontag
attacks writers, including herself, who have used cancer as a metaphor.
To call the white race the cancer of history is to demean people who have
real diseases and to use language not to reveal reality but to distort it.
Such metaphors, Sontag notes, further an understanding neither of cancer nor of the issues to which cancer is compared.

Thus Sontag cautions against using disease to define personality. To
suppose that a certain personality type is susceptible to cancer or other
diseases is to take away from the individual his or her ability to fight that
disease. Sontag is against fatalistic interpretations and believes that with
most diseases people can intelligently use medical advice to ameliorate,
if not always to cure, their illnesses.

Sontag acknowledges that people cannot do without metaphors;
they are the staple of language, and they establish human identity. But
to use metaphors without understanding their consequences can actually inhibit rather than extend the individual's control over his or her
life. She is no more against metaphor, per se, than she is against interpretation.

There is a pure, unadorned logic to Sontag's essay that seduces most
readers. Of course, reviewers took issue with her; what was Susan Sontag
good for if not to start an argument? Reviewer Edwin J. Kennedy, Jr.,
wrote in *The New Republic* (July 8 and 15, 1978): "Susan Sontag is a
combative person who feels more intensely alive when she is against
something, or things in general." Like many reviewers, Kennedy wondered why—if the etiology of cancer was not yet understood—it could

not have multiple causes that included the psychological. Why would the "actual dynamics" of tuberculosis and cancer be eventually proven to be the same? In her "noble desire" to alleviate psychological trauma, she had opted for a "heroically clear and strong" view. In *Commentary* (October 1978), Dan Jacobson criticized Sontag for refusing to impute anything but a physical meaning to disease while making "far-reaching diagnoses about the moral and psychological conditions of society as a whole on the basis of her partial readings of the most dubious or ambiguous symptoms." He thought her saturation in literature gave her no warrant for saying what society as a whole thought of tuberculosis. Literature was only one measure of society, and certainly not a scientific one. "Intellectual boldness should not be confused with intellectual self-indulgence. Miss Sontag seems to have some trouble in telling them apart," Jacobson sternly concluded. In *Soundings* (Spring 1989), Albert Howard Carter argued that just as it is impossible to purge language itself of metaphor, it is futile to root out metaphor from discussions of disease. Sontag could no more ban metaphor than Plato could successfully ban poets from his ideal republic. Her book was the product, in sum, of utopian thinking.

But what if Sontag had qualified her argument as her critics advised? Peter Brooks in *Partisan Review* (Summer 1979), expressing reservations about her arguments, nonetheless noted that to pin down Sontag's prose with the baggage of second thoughts would be to deprive her of "polemical vigor." She clearly did not want a thicker, denser argument. She had succumbed to her "ethical sensibility" rather than to her job as cultural critic, Brooks concluded.

Sontag wanted to change people's minds—not just to give those minds a workout. In 1992 the Women's National Book Association listed *Illness as Metaphor* as one of seventy-five books by "women whose words have changed the world." Sontag's short book was really a polemical pamphlet. As Maggie Scarf put it in *Psychology Today* (July 1978), "I have obviously stopped to take exception, to argue, to quarrel with some of her points. But I found her book unfailingly exciting, like nothing else on the subject I have ever read." Sontag has always rejected such terms as theorist, critic, and philosopher. The one term she finds truly acceptable is writer, and that is the term Scarf and so many readers of *Illness as Metaphor* honor. Writers move people. With her book Susan Sontag saved lives.

Illness had driven Sontag to reexamine the sources of her own thinking, to consider how she had used metaphor and how she had interpreted her own life. During her illness she had also begun to reappraise her politics. In the Summer 1978 issue of the French journal *Tel Quel,* she adverted to a Western tendency to "'excuse' what is happening in the East. To want to believe the *best* about everything that happens under the flag of communism or Marxism." The West in general? Sontag and the left? Who? She went on to say, "One hears disagreeable things about the camps, the prisons, the psychiatric hospitals. Right away one tries to find an interpretation that will excuse that." One? Not I? She was addressing an audience of French intellectuals busily revising their own sycophantic support of the Soviet Union, Mao, and other Communist regimes. She even touched on the long history of "our side" (again: the West? French intellectuals? the left?) rationalizing Communist atrocities. She cited the case of André Gide—at first a Soviet dupe and then a Soviet scourge. She said that the "binary reasoning" equating anti-Communists with fascists and pro-Communists with antifascists had to be rejected.

Finally, she admitted: "It's the intellectuals themselves who, in order not to lose hope, refuse to recognize the truth." She concluded, "I was also guilty in that regard." She and her cohort had all too willingly swallowed a line: "We believed things, coming from the East, that we wouldn't have believed for a second in our own countries." Why? It had to do with the "shame at being a bourgeois intellectual." Guilt made intellectuals condemn their own society and seek a better, more just, more equal world in the Soviet Union. It was time to stop blaming bourgeois society because it was so adept at absorbing dissent. Intellectuals should face it: they were part of the ruling class; they should do the hard work of campaigning for "real issues" like health and justice. The idea of revolutionary projects (such as those she had endorsed in Cuba and North Vietnam) was now passé. You could not change everything; when you tried, you were forced to "oppress." Sontag counseled against cynicism; there was still political work to do. She even wanted to remain a Marxist—whatever that meant. She did not spell it out, although her references to the contradictions of capitalism and its exploitative aspects have never wavered.

The shift in Sontag's political thinking came as a result of the influx into the West of Eastern European dissidents. They were distinguished intellectuals who simply could not be ignored. Even old-line Stalinists like Lillian Hellman had to acknowledge that the game was up. For Sontag, the key figure was Joseph Brodsky, who set her straight when she complained, for example, about Aleksandr Solzhenitsyn's "reactionary" politics. "Think what you want of him on the political level, but what he testified to, what he describes, those are *facts*."

Sontag and Brodsky became friends in the mid-1970s, a few years after the Soviet Union expelled him as a social parasite. When asked his profession at his trial, he answered poet. On whose authority did Brodsky call himself a poet? the judge wanted to know. On whose authority had he been included in the human race? Brodsky replied. Uncompromising, Brodsky had spent eighteen months in a Soviet labor camp, chopping wood, breaking stones, and shoveling shit. But through the intervention of W. H. Auden and other distinguished writers, his captors released him. He was passionately grateful to America, which gave him a home and teaching positions at the University of Michigan, Columbia, and other colleges.

Both Brodsky and Sontag were great stoics, capable of absorbing immense suffering without complaint. Sontag liked to mention Brodsky's claim that he had enjoyed his internal exile and farmwork. It was honest work, and all of Russia was "mired in shit" anyway. And their obsessive personalities were expressed in their smoking. Brodsky would not quit, even after heart disease and surgery mandated that he stop. It was not worth getting up in the morning, he said, if he could not light up. Sontag proved just as compulsive. She did try to quit, but more often she was unapologetic about her habit—even when her French physician told her to stop. She did try to behave herself for a few months, but it was smoking that got her through the writing of *On Photography*. One of her friends declared that if Sontag did not stop smoking, she would no longer see her. But denying herself the pleasure of smoking and feeling puritanical about it only made Sontag crave cigarettes more.

Hardly a timid person himself, Brodsky could be startled at Sontag's boldness and tenacity. During the Venice Biennale on Dissent (1977), Sontag invited Brodsky to join her on a visit to see Olga Rudge, companion of the great modernist poet Ezra Pound during his last years of exile in Italy. Sontag explained that she really did not want to go alone. Brodsky agreed to accompany Sontag and encountered in Rudge a powerful personality, who confidently explained why she did not think that Pound was really a fascist. Naturally, Brodsky had his own ideas, but in the presence of this persuasive talker, he let down his guard and entered into the spirit of her defense, feeling, for the moment, quite willing to forgive Pound. It all seemed wrapped up until Sontag suddenly said, "Don't think that Americans were so dismayed by Pound because of his radio broadcasts, Olga. Had it only been a matter of radio broadcasts, he would just have been one more Tokyo Rose." Brodsky "nearly fell out of my chair!"—as he later put it. He could not believe that Sontag had compared a "major eminence to Tokyo Rose!" (Sontag knew that Brodsky had, in her words, an "exalted, exacting sense of the poet's authority.") Rudge took the Sontag salvo well, only asking: "So then what did Americans find so repugnant in Ezra?" Sontag said, "Well, it's quite simple. It was Ezra's anti-Semitism." Of course, this set Rudge off on another effort at exculpation. But what impressed Brodsky was Sontag's wish to start the conversation all over again. No one was more persistent than Susan; no one was less likely to let a difficult issue alone.

Susan Sontag could not do without Joseph Brodsky. He did much, much more than reorient her politics. He was a fellow Jew, and he spoke to Sontag's sense of exile and her desire to wander. Brodsky was no more a religious Jew than Sontag was, but both, in Yoram Kaniuk's view, shared an uneasy sense of place. As Sontag wrote in a tribute to him, he was the type of the modern artist who lived, mentally, "in two places at once." She had in mind van Gogh's letter to his brother Theo about painting in the South of France while writing that he felt he was "really" in Japan. Sontag had spent her childhood—indeed, most of her life—living in one place and dreaming of another. She still felt (in 1979) a sense of claustrophobia in Manhattan, even though the ocean was, so to speak, down at the end of the street. She had never been comfortable in America; she preferred, she told a French journal, "ma condition d'Américaine avec une grande distance." For his part, Brodsky resisted all calls to visit his native Leningrad even after the collapse of the Soviet Union. He remembered everything, he said, but he did not want to return to Russia any more than Joyce had wanted to resume a life in Dublin.

This acute sense of displacement drives writers like Joyce, Brodsky, and Sontag to make a life out of literature, and to find physical places that at least approximate their idea of a literary kingdom. For years it had been Paris for Sontag: "Pour moi, c'était le symbole de l'intensité de la vie et de la pensée." Even in New York, she could not find the all-encompassing engagement in the life of the mind; people lived such private lives in New York that when together they seemed only able to exchange banalities, she complained. But now her Paris idyll was nearing an end, and she could not think of a single great writer under fifty, she told her *Nouvel Observateur* interviewer: "La culture française actuelle est presque nulle." This included French cinema; it now seemed moribund to her. Perhaps it deserved its moment of repose, she considered, but she had to move on.

With Brodsky, one of her most intimate friends, Sontag shifted the center of her intellectual world from Paris to New York. Left-wing political and literary romance—the Sartre/de Beauvoir years—had played itself out. The French influence would cease with thinkers such as Roland Barthes, and the next generation would interest her hardly at all, though she read them so as to remain au courant. She would bring the best of France to New York. She would create a kind of salon. She already had her power base at FSG, but she needed a vehicle and a venue, someplace to perch that was without the permanent academic ties that she considered stifling. She found her berth and an ally in the sociologist Richard Sennett, just then establishing himself at New York University with the mission of forming an Institute for the Humanities.

Sennett had come to NYU from Harvard in the mid-1970s. No one had a clear idea, then, of exactly what an Institute for the Humanities might do, but the notion was to bring the various intellectual, artistic, and academic worlds of New York City together. New to New York and shaped by the academic setting of Cambridge, Sennett looked to close friends like the writer Donald Barthelme—then teaching at City College—to make contacts and forge connections with "town and gown," as the institute's five-year report put it. Barthelme introduced Sennett to Sontag, who had taught at City College and made friends with Barthelme and his colleague, novelist Frederic Tuten. Intrigued by the idea of an institute, Sontag asked Sennett to call her when he got funding and was prepared to plan a program.

In 1977, the first year of the institute, Sontag, already a fellow, introduced Sennett to the nonacademic, intellectual side of New York. The first person she brought along was Joseph Brodsky. The two writers worked together and used the institute as a way of creating a literary community—ignoring a good part of other institute interests such as the seminars in urban studies. The institute reached out to European culture. When Roland Barthes came to America, he made the institute his first stop. German and Middle-European thinkers visited often. Sennett watched Sontag reconstitute her life abroad in New York.

Twenty years ago many of the Europeans who have since come to dominate American intellectual culture were unknown here. Brodsky brought in many exiles and dissidents. Derek Walcott, a Caribbean poet and later a Nobel laureate, joined the institute, becoming enamored of Sontag and Brodsky. He had been trying to write hit plays for many years, and he reveled in the culture of intellectual celebrity. Indeed, these three exiles in Manhattan, all FSG authors, became a sort of institution, carrying on a conversation that largely excluded others.

In the fall of 1980, Brodsky and Walcott jointly taught a weekly poetry course at New York University. In a class of vocal New Yorkers one woman, with a striking white streak in her hair (usually in the front row) dominated discussions. Most classes consisted of her conversations with Brodsky. Annoyed, the students wondered why Brodsky put up with this intrusive woman. She was obviously very taken with herself, and Brodsky treated her respectfully. Picking up a copy of the *Village Voice,* one student saw Sontag's picture and realized that the course had in effect been a Brodsky-Sontag performance. Walcott said little. At the final exam, only six students showed up; the others had come only to watch Brodsky and Sontag go at it.

People would come to lecture at the institute and remain for a few weeks in a loose ebb and flow that suited nonacademics but unsettled some professors who lived by schedules: "They like to know that from four to six-thirty they are going to think," Sennett observes. When Sontag had an idea, she would organize something at the institute—like a retrospective on Simone de Beauvoir that took place in September 1979.

Dennis Altman, a visiting Australian scholar, likened attendance at the institute to lunching with the *New York Review of Books* (editor Robert Silvers was also a fellow). Altman witnessed "ferocious seminars" featuring Sontag, sitting with "legs splayed across the long seminar table, munching with gusto at sandwiches and ideas alike. At one point Susan took great offense at something I had said and turned on me in full force, itself a majestic if rather terrifying experience." But the outburst, Altman discovered, was a "rite of passage" that others had undergone as well. Sontag, he realized, could be terrifying or charming. You never knew what side of an issue she might come down on, the institute's associate director, Jocelyn Carlson, told a friend. It depended on her mood that day, and her unpredictability gave her tremendous power to intimidate and to manipulate others. Sontag quickly forgave Altman's offense at a dinner in Chinatown. She laid out her life to him, explaining what it meant to be a freelance intellectual and telling him about the "advantages of living, metaphorically, on the streets."

All the institute's parts did not fit together; it was not a community held together by shared values but rather an anarchic collection of communities, with Sontag spearheading one cohort. One group might contest the work of another: why do we have to do that? Why this exhibition? Brodsky claimed that architecture was a degraded art. Why include discussions of it in the institute? Whatever its shortcomings, the institute served Sontag's purpose of maintaining an institutional connection without the burden of routine or responsibility. She could get the plane fare from the institute for Barthes or Borges to come to New York.

The institute was the main—but not the only—place where Sontag could try out ideas. She occasionally taught in the late 1970s and early 1980s at the New School for Social Research. She was unwilling to share much with students, pontificating in one autobiography course on the development of the ego from Jean-Jacques Rousseau to Norman Mailer—the one led inevitably to the other, she thought. Novelist Edmund White, one of her closest friends during this period and an executive director of the institute, attended her New School seminar on Nietzsche and was shocked at her lack of preparation and at such gushing asides as "Isn't Nietzsche great?"

Nonetheless, Sontag was also "a very courageous person. She is an intellectual who stayed out of the academy. She's the last of that kind of non-affiliated thinker," Sennett observes. Something is lost, he believes, when intellectual work is bureaucratized into teaching. Risk-taking gives way to teachable thoughts. "Explaining things to postadolescents restricts the things you can explain." Even the independent Brodsky had his academic commitments. Sontag "really held out," Sennett says, remembering a long talk with Lionel Trilling: "He felt a terrible sense of guilt that he hadn't followed that route of the freelance intellectual." In this context, Sontag was the last of a breed, its ultimate representative figure.

Sennett recalls the early years of the institute—from 1977 to the early 1980s—as a brief, golden moment, but he is certainly wary of nostalgia. Now New York seems to him taken with the notion of "intellectual display," rather than with the idea of a continuing process of work that is slow, sometimes erratic, tentative. The sense that intellectuals should be entertaining now pervades the culture, he thinks. But the intellectual as star has always been a component of Sontag's persona. If contemporary culture has turned too much of intellectual life into entertainment, it seems fair to suggest that Susan Sontag has contributed to the show.

From its beginning, the Institute for the Humanities was a family concern. Roger Straus served on the board of trustees and was a financial donor (1977–82), although Sontag and other fellows drew no salary or stipend. David Rieff had his own part to play, becoming general editor of *Humanities in Review*, a journal of writing commissioned by the institute that would serve as a record of its noteworthy activity. "What David and I really wanted to do was buy *Partisan Review*," Sennett explains, and keep it in New York City rather than see it move from Rutgers to Boston. *Humanities in Review* was just a kind of "holding station." Sennett and Rieff had NYU backing, but "we couldn't get Phillips [*PR*'s founding editor] to retire" so that Rieff could take over. (An aghast Phillips cannot remember ever entertaining such a proposal.) "David was born to be editor of *Partisan Review*," Sennett says, acknowledging exactly the sense of entitlement that Sontag and son have always shared.

Mother and son formed a "partnership," although David had his own separate life as someone of a different generation. Still, Sontag's appeal stretched across generations, with David often serving as her intermediary. Writer Edmund White (born in 1940) had hero-worshipped her. Starting out in New York in the 1960s, there were two people he had wanted to meet: Paul Goodman and Susan Sontag. They were, he emphasizes, "transference figures" whom he wanted to play a role in his life. Meeting Sontag and son at Richard Sennett's house fulfilled White's dreams, and Sontag reciprocated his respect and affection, writing a blurb for *A Boy's Own Story* and recommending the book for an award he received in 1982 from the American Academy of Arts and Letters. This official recognition and support (the award came with a $7,500 check) provided him with a superb launch for his literary career.

In the Age Before AIDS, an openly gay writer rarely secured such highly visible advocates. Gay fiction as an "over-the-counter, consciously named" phenomenon dated back only to the late 1970s, White points out. For Sontag, a closeted figure, to endorse White enthusiastically and openly seemed like a big gesture, he thought. She reread everything he had written, and White considered her blurb a very deliberate, calculated decision, treating *A Boy's Own Story* as the culminating achievement of his early career. When White later drew on her and David for characters in his novel *Caracole* (1985), Sontag, according to White, requested that her blurb be removed from all subsequent editions of his earlier book.

Treating Sontag as his patron, White hosted many parties for her at his apartment on Lafayette Street across from Joe Papp's Public Theater. White enjoyed introducing her to amusing people, such as writer Fran Lebowitz, who became a Sontag intimate. White remembers Lebowitz and Sontag making the gossip columns at the time, because Fran would take Susan to fashion shows where she had never been seen before. Meanwhile, Rieff and White became close friends, with Rieff treating White like another of the gay "uncles"—including painter Jasper Johns and poet Richard Howard—who had watched over his growing up. Composer Ned Rorem, another gay uncle, had been a little uneasy during one of Sontag's visits to his apartment when a preadolescent David sat next to his mother while Rorem taught her dirty French verbs. Rorem's memory of the boy David had been triggered, in fact, at one of White's parties, when one of Sontag's close friends, Stephen Koch, told Rorem that Sontag was in Europe. "Then what's she doing here?" Rorem asked, pointing out a figure in a "white jumpsuit, shoulder-length tresses of sombre hue, and a slouch." Koch replied, "That's not Susan, that's her son, David."

White observed a curious contradiction in both mother and son that other gay observers have also commented on. White said to Sontag, "If I ever wrote a book about you, I'd call it 'The Rabbi and the Dandy.'" Sontag wanted to know why. "Well, because there are two sides to your personality. If you are with people who are too dandified, then you become very rabbinical, and if you are with people who are too serious and moral, then you become very frivolous and dandified." Then he reminded her of her famous essay on camp, in which she expressed similarly divided feelings. Sontag liked the flattering analysis, except for the use of the term "rabbi." "I think you better call it 'The Priest and the Dandy.'" Susan and David were strange about their Jewishness, White felt. "They seemed to know nothing about it, really. And to take almost no interest in it."

White's experience was replicated with journalist Andrew Kopkind, who had accompanied Sontag to Hanoi. In the late 1970s, he took her on a tour of the gay disco scene. It was one of her flirtations with coming out. Kopkind and his lover, filmmaker Jack Scagliotti, watched with mounting irritation as Sontag played the scholar of the scene, never unbending, never just enjoying herself, but needing always to feel in control. The same was true of David, Scagliotti recalls.

It intrigued White that Sontag did not come out. Having lived now in France for many years, White feels he understands the origins of her reticence. Even French writers who are openly gay reject the label "gay writer." Identity politics, in France, seems to imply a loss of human dignity. In the French universalist tradition, one is first and foremost a citizen, and to put any finer point on it is to lose the freedom to define oneself. Of course, American writers have often rejected labels such as "black writer"—or, in William Faulkner's case, even "regionalist writer." White remembers Sontag saying she could not bear the idea of being called a "woman writer," to say nothing of "lesbian writer" (the latter being a term the two never discussed). Indeed, Sontag wanted to know why White was willing to settle for something so "crummy" as the title "gay writer." When White gave a paper on Ronald Firbank at the institute, Sontag encouraged him to publish it, and he said that perhaps he would give it to the *Advocate*, a gay publication. An astonished Sontag again wondered why White would be content to publish in such a marginalized magazine. But White felt a political commitment to gay politics. He viewed Sontag as political, too, but wishing to remove herself as far as possible from the arena of identity politics, which she deemed provincial.

In the early 1980s White witnessed Sontag's efforts to reshape her politics. Incensed at books like Paul Hollander's *Political Pilgrims* (1981), which had excoriated Western intellectuals for their abject submission to the Soviet line, she was organizing a reply, she told conservative critic Hilton Kramer at a party. Hollander's sin, in her view, was his lack of sympathy for those he criticized. David Rieff put his mother's view, as well as his own, best in *The New Republic* (July 28, 1986), where he referred to the "love affair between successive generations of *bien pensant* Western intellectuals and the revolutionary communist regimes that have come to power since the storming of the Winter Palace." Rieff called the love affair a "tragic," not a "pathetic," story because it "entails a stubborn refusal to despair of that hope" of a better world. It was a noble story. "The decent feeling of mourning for a great human hope is what is missing from neoconservativism; though its anti-communism is correct, its way with ideas is coarse and vulgar when compared with the tradition it criticizes." For Rieff, anyone outside the tradition of fellow traveling has no standing since they have never loved and lost.

Sontag outlined to White the case for a book she never wrote. Its title would have been something like "The Trip" or "The Voyage." She would provide a kind of guided tour to the pilgrimage Western intellectuals had made to the Soviet Union, to China, to the various Communist utopias. These were people who knew nothing about factories, Sontag explained to White, and now were being shown the modern triumphs of Communism. They usually did not know the country's language; everything was being filtered through interpreters; the intellectuals were stunned by the unfamiliarity of the industrial landscape; they were determined to like everything. To Sontag, it seemed entirely forgivable, for example, that English Fabian socialists like Sidney and Beatrice Webb should come back to Britain with a favorable report on the Soviet Union even as Stalin's Moscow purge trials were under way. But her real heroes were Emma Goldman and André Gide—both true believers who had recanted. "Susan had such a persuasive way of making you adopt her views," White recalls.

For instance, instead of saying in 1978, "Have you entirely broken with the left?" she would say, "When did you first become wise that the left was a total cheat?" So you'd gulp, and you'd say, "Oh, I guess when I read Mandelstam's *Hope Against Hope* [1970]." Then she'd say, "Ah, I see, that late."

Sontag also wanted to rethink her idea of camp, she told White. She began exploring the role of the dandy, a figure she saw as wanting to telescope different levels of culture and to make himself into the ultimate arbiter of the world. In our time, dandies are confused with gays, but she thought the concept of the dandy—dating back to at least the eighteenth century—had no necessary homosexual component. When did the idea of the dandy and the homosexual come together? she wondered. But to explore such ideas by referring to her own sexuality threatened her, White thought, because she suspected this new approach would lessen her credibility and importance. At any rate, the new line on camp never got very far.

Sontag wanted nothing like a reference to her sexuality to get in the way of seducing her readers, and "Susan could be a very seductive person," White recalls. After his break with her over *Caracole*, he remembers a visit from Marina Warner, a very attractive British writer, who told White: "You're completely wrong about Susan. She is simply enchanting. We had a wonderful time. You've just had a bad experience." White said:

> Okay, I'll describe to you your day with Susan Sontag. She invited you to a Chinese restaurant, told you everything to order, paid the bill, then walked around the Village with you, went into three or four different bookshops, was outraged that you didn't know certain titles, bought them for you, insisting you read them. She talked about her unhappiness and her love life. She asked you about yours. She confided other womanly things about her breast cancer.

Warner's jaw dropped. "This is the day one spends with Susan," White notes. "It is always the same day. It is always the same kind of rapid cycle of intimacy. And she knows how to lay it on."

Writer Philippe Sollers, one of the founders of the influential French journal *Tel Quel*, echoes White's account of Sontag's seductiveness. In his novel *Women*, Sollers presents a jaundiced view of her egotism, calling her a writer named Helen, "one of the system's real stars," a part of New York's "official, organized homosexual countersociety." Coming from a Paris where there is no closeted homosexual literary scene, Sollers skewers what he sees as Sontag's self-importance and her predatorial, insincere intimacies. As Helen, she greets the narrator of his novel with a "pleasant smile in which I easily discern intense hostility." Helen tells him her life story and describes her love affairs, concentrating on Jane (Irene Fornés) and explaining how hard it was to "become just good friends again." Helen presses her collected works on her

French visitor, telling him that since he is in New York on vacation, he will have time to read them "thoroughly" and then they will be able to talk to each other "intelligently." Making his escape, the narrator throws all ten kilos of Helen's collected works into the Hudson River.

White speculates that Sontag learned her charm offensives from Richard Howard, who is always picking up the check and buying recherché titles for his companions. To watch the erudite Howard work the large table of biographers at a recent dinner in Manhattan (after a talk about biography) is to learn from a political master. In *Caracole*, White portrays Howard as Mateo, putting on the "high-culture hustle." "Both Susan and Richard are those kind of old-fashioned intellectuals who know everything and think you should know everything," White comments. It is a "wonderful, admirable trait."

Yet Sontag in person could prove unimpressive, White observes. She once told White, "You know my essays are much more intelligent than I am. Do you know why? It's because I rewrite them so many times, and slowly, slowly, I nudge them up the hill from my natural state of medium intelligence to a high state of intelligence." White never regarded Sontag's conversation, even in seminars, as particularly enlightening. She had no ready wit or cleverness. She did not think on her feet especially well. She prized humor, but White saw little of it in her, even though she criticized others for their humorlessness. She thought herself easily capable of a French kind of frivolousness and lightness (*légèreté française*). But her idea of a joke might be to say, "Oh, Roland Barthes, he was so egotistical that when he'd see me coming across the room and he hadn't seen me in a few years, he would say, 'Susan, *toujours fidèle*.'"

Considering all the famous people Sontag knew, White never considered her a name-dropper. But her personality had been shaped by her early fame. At the movies people in line would be looking back over their shoulders at her and buzzing—though New Yorkers, true to form, rarely went up to her. It was like going about with royalty to public places, and of course she knew it. "By and large, she handled it well," although she did like to throw her weight around capriciously, abusing people she saw as boring or stupid or not talented enough. White did not always agree with her assessments.

"The sad end of it all," White confesses, came when he moved to Paris and began writing his novel *Caracole*. "It was a bit like the worm turning," he admits. "I had been too obliging to Susan—more than I really wanted to be. If there was part of me that was sort of cringing and servile to her, there was another part of me that was taking revenge against her, I suppose." By the early 1980s Sontag seemed cross with White, suspecting he was no longer a disciple. He believes the trouble stemmed from his review in the *New York Times Book Review* of a Roland Barthes book, *The Empire of Signs,* and of *A Barthes Reader,* which Sontag had edited. White realized that she regarded her introductions as important work, but he did not like her take on Barthes, which made Barthes out to be too much of a dandy and too little of a serious thinker. White preferred Gérard Genette, who had written much more convincingly on Barthes, although he praised both Sontag and Barthes's translator, Richard Howard—"but not enough to satisfy either of them," White recalls ruefully. Both phoned to express their displeasure. Susan said, "How could you talk about Gérard Genette? He's nothing, he's nothing! He is nobody, and I've written this great essay. How could you not have given it more attention?" White replied, "Well, I think people know about our friendship, and I think it would have looked almost too servile to have gone on about how great it was. But I don't agree with you. I think Genette is brilliant." Finally, at a concert in Paris, Sontag said, "You knew I was here, and you could have made an effort to get in touch with me, and you didn't." White said, "I didn't know where you were staying. You could have found me." They parted, feeling mutually aggrieved.

When literary friends and allies part—as in the case of Paul Theroux and V. S. Naipaul—a memoir or novel is often the result. *Caracole* became White's "recap of my New York Life, with the Chat Box becoming a version of the institute." The main character, Mateo, White says, was based on both himself and Richard Howard, although Howard took the character to be exclusively a send-up of himself. White regarded the character as "self-satirical but not particularly unflattering to anybody." Howard evidently took his revenge by sending out messages asking that White's novel not be reviewed (White saw one Howard letter on a bulletin board at a gay newspaper in Boston). Richard Sennett also became a character in the novel, but he took it in stride, saying only, with a laugh, that it was "wicked."

White says that in creating the character Mathilda in *Caracole* he had in mind both Sontag and writer Madame de Staël, Napoleon's archopponent. Both women traded on their reputations as a "rebel against the state." Sontag is Mathilda, a *monstre sacré* who "presented herself as a withdrawn, morose intellectual," but who actually led a very social life and had an "infallible sense of theater." Although White does not make Mathilda, an opera devotee, into a lesbian, she is undeniably giving a gay performance. He captures the Sontag for whom role-playing is identity-making. Such roles are a style, a way of becoming a self, manifestations of an evolving sensibility.

White portrays an operatic Sontag: "She was such a literary creature that most of her experience had been lived through characters in books or on stage, tragic vivid beings whose strong emotions she'd avoided out of fear of plagiarism." Mathilda, like Sontag, plays the aesthete among moralists and the moralist among aesthetes. The moralist sulked, the aesthete partied.

In Mathilda, White embodies Sontag's wonderful sense of timing and manipulation of her audience, her imperious aura:

Before she braved death, deficits, the law,
The press, free trade, lace cuffs, the cooked, the raw.

The last line, with its amusing allusion to anthropologist Lévi-Strauss's book *The Raw and the Cooked,* suggests just what an appetizing stew Sontag could make of her far-flung interests.

Sontag's voracious sensibility would seem to indicate incredible energy and confidence. But this too is, in part, a role. Like White's Mathilda, she has to dare herself to action, overcoming fits of morbidity (the state Sontag said she was in while writing her famous essay on camp). What pulls her through is her innate sense of drama and what White terms the "brute fact of an entrance or a speech, now rather than sooner or later."

Daniel (David's fictional parallel) looks like Mathilda's brother. Daniel loves his mother and loves to malign her, saying she had "less insight into herself than anyone else he knew." Mathilda refers to Daniel as "the darling," as though he were her pet. Mother and son quarrel fiercely but present a united front to the world. Like a lioness and her cub, Mathilda and Daniel relish the kill—the sport of turning on their company and demolishing their arguments, devouring "bloody sacrifices" heaped on the "altar of their love." Even Mateo feels bound to protest "how many ways" Mathilda was "being insulting."

Daniel bridles at Mathilda's constant references to him as her son, while at the same time promoting his connection to her. Although dressed like a dandy and behaving like an intellectual, Daniel, like his mother, has his eye on the marketplace and the main chance. She uses him to "test the waters of new salons," to take up new follies, and to squire her about.

Sontag/Mathilda treats her female admirers shabbily even as they take her contemptuous behavior as a sign of her integrity. There is only room for one woman in her universe and that is herself, yet she does not want anyone to say her power has anything to do with her being female.

Mathilda is a spent force: "She no longer had a politics (not even an aesthetics) of innovation." Still, she craves power and position. She attends events out of a "historian's curiosity." A connoisseur, she grills strangers until she discovers and extracts their expertise on music, restaurants—whatever comes to hand. She is always on to the next thing. There is no tow-line to the past, and discussions of family life bore her. She wanders her apartment, alone, frozen, at a loss when she is not involved in a controversy and does not have the public's attention. Her salvation comes from picking up a book in her huge library and getting lost in it—or in writing a new book. For "in spite of her celebrity, she was deeply unsure of herself and felt obliged to know everything." Otherwise, she would wither, vegetate, stew, become melancholy, worry. Scandal was better for her metabolism. She changes friends and travels often.

Rumor had it that Sontag threatened to sue White, but he emphasizes that he heard nothing about any legal action. Novelist David Leavitt had Sontag in mind when he spoke at an Authors Guild forum, "Whose Life Is It, Anyway?": "Writers who are famous advocates of freedom of expression are the first ones to pounce, the first ones to sue, the first ones to scream when something is written about them." (Leavitt himself had been sued by Stephen Spender, who objected to Leavitt's use of Spender's autobiography in a novel.) Leavitt continued: "Often writers are incredible hypocrites when the tables are turned, and the writer who would go to bat for his or her own freedom of expression has no qualms whatsoever about trying to quash in one way or another someone else's." When Cynthia Ozick asked Leavitt to be specific, Leavitt reported the gossip that Sontag and "several other writers on whom characters" in *Caracole* were based "tried to stop the book from being reviewed and tried to stop bookstores from stocking it. I was kind of shocked, not because I didn't understand their anger but because they had elected to express it by trying to stop the book from being known."

Rumor also had it that White had to make changes to appease Sontag and son, but White says he never heard from David or Susan. However, Bill Whitehead, White's editor at Dutton, gave a big masked ball to celebrate the publication of *Caracole*—an event in the spirit of the book itself—and David Rieff tried to crash the party. Whitehead told White that Rieff, dressed like a Regency rake, had a bullwhip with him, and announced he had arrived to give White a thrashing. But he never made it past the bouncers.

White feels that Sontag and son would not have been so upset about *Caracole* if they had not received advance word from a writer who had seen White's manuscript and who, though sworn to secrecy, immediately told them about it, suggesting it was a very negative portrait. White thinks Mathilda's combination of passion and intelligence makes her a great character. He regrets the estrangement the novel caused. Roger Straus, now friendly with White, seems to have forgiven his trespass. White wishes Sontag had taken the portrait as a tribute to her epic, operatic personality, and he adds: "I just hope I don't come out in your book as someone who hates her." He finds her endearing and maddening and "really rather piggy." He has this image of her as a Roman empress picking her teeth waiting for the crowds to amuse her. She has the rude manners of a monarch, White says. But he misses her. He has mentioned her name favorably in print several times since *Caracole* appeared. He wishes they could be friends. But they have never spoken again. "It is impossible," he sighs.

Richard Avedon once said to White, "Fame is like a valley. Once you get to the other side of it, and you're very famous, you can never be less famous." "We're all there," White concludes.

19

I, etcetera

1979

I, etcetera, the first book of fiction by Susan Sontag to appear in more than a decade, was a major publishing event. Writing to Peter Mayer at Penguin in the spring of 1979, Roger Straus crowed about the volume's "spectacular" sales, which were approaching 20,000 copies. The Sontag persona reemerged on *I, etcetera*'s back cover 1960s-style, cloaked in black sweater, pants, and boots, lounging in a window niche—in the background the foliage of Central Park and the surrounding apartment-house towers just visible in the shadowy gray of the black-and-white photograph. Tom Victor had taken one of the quintessential Sontag poses. Then in her mid-forties, she looked very youthful. The complex geometry of her pose—half reclining, her upper torso canted so that her left arm is planted on a pile of books and papers, and her left hand grasping her right—makes for her most intricately put-together "I," with all the etcetera very carefully choreographed. She appears to be very thin, though her face is beginning to show the first hint of the fuller, heavier jawline that will emerge in the next few years. Gray filaments grace the hair on each side of her part, a subtle version of the streak that first appeared in the early 1970s. In the 1980s the streak would become more pronounced—not through nature but through art. After her hair had fallen out in the course of chemotherapy, it had grown back with heavy gray flecks; dye jobs restored the patterned streaking that made Susan Sontag feel more like Susan Sontag.

Max Beerbohm believed that all artists and writers, including himself, strove to "make an effect" of themselves. One painter who was also a writer, the litigious James Abbott McNeill Whistler, captured Beerbohm's attention because he cunningly fashioned himself into a striking visual object. An American aesthete and dandy living abroad, much of the time in Paris, Whistler was combative, with a "strange lock of white hair," notes biographer N. John Hall—a sort of "white plume" Beerbohm called it. In Beerbohm's caricatures of this artist, the white plume sticks out of his top hat like a lance, a weapon of personality and also a mark of honor. In the Victor photograph, Sontag sits in her aerie at the peak of her power, just a few years away from her first lawsuit, the gray strands her mark of distinction, self-awarded.

Although there had been commentary on the stylization of Sontag's book jackets—and of course much discussion of her as a writer who both set and followed intellectual fashions—no interviewer (at least not one on the record) had yet asked her about her image-making—what might be called the Beerbohm effect. However, Paul Brennan, in a *London Magazine* interview (April/May 1979) came dangerously close:

> Looking back on your fifteen years of writing do you feel satisfied with the way you have been treated by publishers, reviewers and readers? If you were to manage yourself again in the same market would you do it any differently?

Sontag bridled:

> You always use these words that come from a realm of discourse that is so alien to me. I don't *manage* myself. I don't think of myself as being in a *market*. These are the ways people are talked about in the world of media and of the consumer survey. That is a language which doesn't do anything for me.

Brennan reported that he "felt accused. . . . Yes, yes, I had been vulgarizing the writer's role." The published interview ended shortly afterward.

What had Brennan done? He had overstepped the bounds Sontag imposed on interviews, which most interviewers respected without questioning her right to impose them. Many interviewers, like portrait photographers, see their role as one confined to presenting their subjects in the best available light. They feel privileged to gain access to the likes of Susan Sontag. Brennan had been carefully screened by FSG and was allowed no direct contact with Sontag before the interview—in his experience this was one of the most tightly controlled situations he had encountered.

During this period, Sontag had Roger Straus suppress an interview Suzanne Gordon had conducted on behalf of *Vogue*, a magazine friendly to Sontag and one that had published her articles. Sontag insisted she had prior approval—that is, that she could censor anything she liked in the interview, but Gordon, through her agent, Georges Borchardt, disputed this claim.

On French television, near the end of 1979, Jean-Louis Servan-Schreiber had another go at the Sontag persona:

> As for yourself, I have a feeling that, when we read articles about you, whether they're written in the United States or in France, finally what you say holds people's attention, but the fact that it's accompanied by your personal looks and not someone else's counts in the impression that people get. Isn't that something that seems evident in your experience?

> S. SONTAG: I never think about that. I can't tell you really.

End of discussion.

Interviewer Peter York found Sontag testy; she seemed contemptuous of his vulgar journalistic questions and denied him the company of a photographer. She became amicable when they hit on a topic of mutual interest and Sontag warmed to her current project: readjusting her sense of the relationship between the aesthetic and the ethical. Sontag had run this game before, sparring in the early rounds, feeling out her interlocutor, testing for strengths and weaknesses. This is not just her habit with journalists. Edmund White saw her do it dozens of times with anyone new she met.

Of course, Sontag is hardly alone among prominent public figures who are careful about the way they appear in print. And she was certainly not unique in wanting to dominate interviews. She understood that the nature of the questions can distort the impression she conveys. But her claim that she has never considered how her "market," her "image," and her physical attractiveness have shaped her career seems disingenuous or self-deceiving.

Sontag confronted an apparently insoluble problem: if she acknowledged the power of her beauty, she feared she would not be taken seriously. Yet she was taken seriously, in part, precisely because of her striking presence and her ability to court the public glance. Virtually everyone interviewed for this biography prefaced their remarks with some comment about her handsomeness. She transformed the image of the female intellectual from tweeds and flats to one of flowing scarves and high black boots. Her hip, sexy, and somehow fashionable aura enticed both men and women whether or not they had read her work.

In private, Sontag proved less guarded, complaining to one of her friends that "as a beautiful woman" she constantly had to deflect an obsession with her appearance. She knew the power of her looks, and she knew how to use it, but she also recognized the dangers of relying on her image to promote her work, an image that had the potential to subvert her goal to become one of the century's leading intellectuals. To a remarkable degree, she has managed to maintain this delicate balance of beauty and brains, and she has done so, as in the Servan-Schreiber interview, by compartmentalizing her life, separating herself from her public performance.

This is a time-honored technique employed by many public figures. Successful politicians are particularly adept at such compartmentalization, but Sontag has often shown signs of the strain associated with such difficult work. Rather than deal with the substance of questions about her public persona, she has simply dismissed them. She has enjoyed a luxury accorded few in public life. What politician or indeed movie star could afford to be so dismissive? And yet, Sontag's assumption of superiority has often enhanced her mystique. In every sense of the term, she became the dark lady of American letters.

I, etcetera is all about the composing of selves. Miss Flatface in "American Spirits" jettisons her Ozzie and Harriet family for a life of prostitution and pornography, egged on by the spirits of American self-aggrandizement like Benjamin Franklin and Tom Paine. The narrator of "The Dummy," bored with his bourgeois existence, finds a double, a second self to lead his routine life so that the narrator can withdraw from family and societal obligations. The anonymous narrator of "Old Complaints Revisited" wishes she (he?) could separate from the group (never named) that claims the self's allegiance. Like the book's title, Miss Flatface wants to deny a fixed identity, saying "Nor am I I." These characters, like the Sontag whom interviewers quiz about her beliefs, refuse to be bound by their own statements or by the record of their actions. The past can always be shed—though Sontag's most powerful stories, such as "Debriefing," expose with considerable irony, grief, and even humor the inability to transcend one's past. In that sense, *I, etcetera* is a species of autocriticism, giving the lie to that self-contained author's jacket photograph. As reviewer Benjamin Taylor put it, Sontag's volume of short fiction demonstrated the "impossibility of autonomous selfhood." (*Georgia Review*, Winter 1980). Yet the quest for independence is indefatigable: "In Sontag's work the self is always a will," Taylor notes, the world of will as Poe presented it to her in childhood. There is a sort of hep, modernist-fairy-tale twist to Sontag's stories, which are part Donald Barthelme (think of *Snow White*) and part Alfred Chester at his raunchiest. In Chester's *The Exquisite Corpse*, for example, characters' bodies are constantly invaded and sealed—stuffed with tampons and sewn up. Miss Flatface enjoys reading scandal papers screaming with headlines: "My In-Laws Drove Four Nails Into My Skull." Her Prince Charming is named Mr. Obscenity.

I, etcetera received respectful, rather guarded reviews. Writing in *The New Republic* (November 25, 1978), novelist Anne Tyler offered this representative evaluation: "*I, etcetera* is not always an easy book to read; it's not always a rewarding book, even. But it does possess its own kind of spirit and nerve, and it takes some magnificent chances." Tyler detected a lack of finish, the want of another page that would pull Sontag's experimental prose together, and suggested that Sontag had not been critical enough of her own fiction: "Even the freest internal voice, listened to with the utmost lack of criticism, must in the final step be screened for readability." Tyler never used the word "solipsistic," but it seems to apply to her reading of Sontag's fiction.

But the sheer variety of fictional forms and points of view in *I, etcetera* is impressive—from the autobiographical "Project for a Trip to China" and "Debriefing," to the sexually ambiguous narrator of "Old Complaints Revisited," to the collective voice of the parents in "Baby," to "Dr. Jekyll," a rewriting of Stevenson's classic tale. Sontag's last story, "Unguided Tour," sums up her own restless quest and that of her characters, traveling to see the world, to find themselves, to stave off the death, doom, and melancholy that the young Susan had found so compelling in Poe. *I, etcetera* ends with the black thoughts of a writer resisting her black mood: *"The end of the world. This is not the end of the world."*

Quite another Susan Sontag spoke at the University of Hawaii on May 8, 1979, on her way back from a three-week lecture tour in Japan. A genial writer responded well to her introduction, which presented her as "someone on whom nothing is lost." She read "The Dummy" and "Unguided Tour" and took questions for a good half hour. She was gracious—even sending a charming thank-you note to Mark Wilson, chair of the University of Hawaii English department in Honolulu. Wilson had made the arrangements, and he recalled her visit with great pleasure, commenting especially on her direct style and courteous manners.

Sontag was visiting her mother and stepfather, who had moved to Honolulu from California in the early 1970s. Nat Sontag had an advertising business. Wilson remembers speaking with him on the phone. Nat was proud of Susan, telling Wilson about her huge library of books and adding, "She's read every one of them." And then there were her friends. Nat was impressed and spoke of her life as something far removed from his own. Nat and Mildred Sontag were not intellectuals but their daughter's success gratified them. Reporter Cobey Black had the same impression: "very sweet people, not intellectual but very devoted."

On her Hawaii visits, Sontag always seemed relaxed. In the summer of 1977, for example, she visited her parents and talked to Cobey Black, then a *Honolulu Star-Bulletin* journalist, who described "a down-to-earth beauty, tousled and dark as a gypsy," barefoot and in blue jeans after a swim.

After the flurry of interviews and traveling to promote *I, etcetera,* Sontag headed for Italy. There, in the late summer of 1979, she went into six weeks of rehearsals for Pirandello's play *As You Desire Me* (1931), which she would direct as a modern feminist parable with operatic over-tones. The play starred Adriana Asti as "the Strange Lady," a woman whose identity is contested by a writer, Carl Salter, and by her family, who claim she is the lost Cia, who was abducted and apparently raped and assaulted during the war and has been gone from her home (a villa near Udine) for ten years. What was done to Cia is purposely left vague. It has made her, so to say, strange, the very embodiment of the decen-tered selves that people *I, etcetera.*

Indeed, the personal, professional, and political reasons for Sontag's decision to direct *As You Desire Me* are manifold. She told Edmund White that Asti, who had played Francesca, the female pivot between Bauer and Tomas in *Duet for Cannibals*, was the "love of her life." As Sontag described Asti to White, the actress was alternately passionate and inaccessible, and White's impression was that Sontag had chosen to direct the play to please Asti. A figure of desire in both the film and the play, a femme fatale, the two characters Asti played were each, Sontag says, a "woman whom everyone wants to possess." Her motivations are ambiguous. Is Francesca's allegiance to Bauer or Tomas? Will the Strange Lady stay with Salter in Berlin, or return to her putative husband in Italy? Salter says to her, "I know you better than you know yourself." She bows to him and says, "That is no great feat! It has been so long now since I wanted to know myself!" An aggrieved Salter shoots back: "Very convenient, when you don't care to be called to account for what you do!"

In performance, Sontag decided to give the play, in reviewer Alan Bullock's words, a *"ferocement feminista"* interpretation. Leonardo Sciascia, a Pirandello expert, seconded her approach, noting that ten years earlier he would have said the "central problem" in *As You Desire Me* "was one of identity. Today it seems to me that the problem is about women's identity." Sontag wanted to emphasize the excessive, the emo-tional, the world of desires that had cut a woman loose from her home— or from a sense of home as the ground of her reality. To her, it was a play about "desperation, about the desperation of a particular woman." By making her interpretation so biographical, Sontag was, it seems, acting out of her own volatile, restless quest.

Bullock disliked Sontag's direction, faulting her "crude dramatic effects" and an "indulgent theatricality reminiscent of Victorian melodrama." He also disapproved of the way Sontag shifted attention away from the self-destructive Salter to Cia, who became a more sexually ambiguous figure—even overtly lesbian in her scene with Salter's daughter, Mop. No better were Asti's "posturings and cavortings," or her solipsistic "fixed contemplation of her image in the symbolic mirror at the front of the stage." But what bothered the reviewer appealed to the director. Pirandello wrote a denouement that Sontag would choose for herself—like the Strange Lady, who goes to Berlin to create a life for herself as a dancer, Sontag was also attracted to dance, and especially to the dancer Lucinda Childs, who shared some of Asti's alluring inaccessibility. "I'm a beautiful catatonic," Childs told Edmund White, who empathized with Sontag's feeling for dance and the female form, a subject she would explore with increasing intensity in the next decade.

A Wandering Jew

20

1980

In the spring of 1980, Susan Sontag joined a group of writers, including Joyce Carol Oates and John Ashbery, for a tour of Eastern Europe sponsored by the United States Information Agency. Sontag performed flawlessly at a literary conference in Jadwisin, outside of Warsaw. Oates has captured Sontag in her story "My Warszawa: 1980," in which "formidable Judith Horne, enviable, much-photographed . . . striking to the eye, aggressively casual," with a "slightly Slavic?" face, "olive-dark skin . . . clean of makeup," addresses her Polish public in a voice that is "clear and dauntless as a bell."

Sontag relished her time in Poland, telling one interviewer about her family's Polish roots: "I must admit I had not given it much thought before, but once I am here I realized that I could have actually been a Pole, living in Poland." She called herself a "wandering Jew whose grandparents came to America from Poland. And then I wander all over the world. . . ."

Professor James McClintock of Michigan State University, who served on a panel with Sontag in Jadwisin, remembers hoping he would not be humiliated by her. He was sure she would hate what he had to say about contemporary fiction. But to the contrary, she was extraordinarily welcoming and good humored. She appeared to be having the time of her life and was genuinely touched by Polish hospitality. She seemed surprised by the liveliness of Polish intellectuals in general, students in particular.

That's all I remember—she was beaming; I was relieved.

To Joyce Carol Oates, Sontag proved quite a study. They had not begun the trip as friends. Indeed, Sontag had been quoted as observing that Oates's relationship to her characters was "vampiristic," and a *Newsweek* article—referring to Sontag as "one big female literary name"—had her dismissing Oates as "not our sort." Yet Sontag has a way of befriending writers whom she has trounced in print (Arthur Miller is a good example) and even developing rather chummy relationships with them. And in the case of Oates, it happened that she was not so different from Sontag after all. They had both vied for the title "the dark lady of American letters." More important, they both had ambivalent feelings about their respective ethnic ties. Until the trip to Poland, Oates had not cared to inspect her Hungarian heritage any more than Sontag identified with her Polish Jewish background. Rather, both women had an all-consuming, precocious commitment to writing that had emerged by their early teenage years. Both began as aspiring academics, good students who had discovered Nietzsche early and proceeded to latch onto supermen who were powerful father figures. Sontag and Oates were great admirers—even hero-worshippers (Sontag was about to publish *Under the Sign of Saturn*, whose alternative title could have been "Heroes and Hero Worship"). Their reclusive qualities came out in their devotion to reading, which both regarded as one of the greatest pleasures of civilization. Both had an innate puritanism and disliked any sort of vulgarity. In physical terms, Oates could be taken as Sontag's slighter sister. After Poland, Oates would dine in New York with Sontag and son, which put the seal on their sisterhood.

Greg Johnson, Oates's biographer, suggests that Judith Horne in Oates's story "My Warszawa: 1980" is a composite of Oates and Sontag. It is a likely equation. "My Warszawa" begins, in fact, rather like *Trip to Hanoi*, with Horne's "hazy but stubborn ideas about the 'people' and their integrity." She regrets her "penchant for noticing details, for being struck in the face by details . . . a symptom of her Western frame of mind—a hyperesthesia of the soul." Horne carries an enormous burden. She is a woman in a world where men bitterly resent her even as they court her. Life is easier for her in Poland because she is delightedly surprised to find that men have read her work. Here Oates might have gone further. Polish male intellectuals are courtiers. They kiss a woman's hand unaffectedly, as though it were her due. This old-world charm goes a long way, even with a woman who professes not to care about such things and writes articles and grants interviews in which she describes a future world in which the sexes will be depolarized. The level of both intellectual discussion and flirtation in Poland is very high, and Sontag's curiosity, her skepticism, and even her blunt questions (all of which Oates attributes to Horne in her story) were handled with panache by a fair number of Poles. In 1980, the Polish intellectual appetite for visiting Americans was insatiable. Americans represented power, news from abroad, and a network of connections that Sontag epitomized.

If Poland brought out Sontag's sunny side, it is because more than any other Eastern Europeans, the Poles pursued Americans with affection and enthusiasm. Poland is one of the few places in the world where a figure like Susan Sontag could be adopted and not resent the co-optation. This was not just another stop on the junket. As she told Monika Beyer, her Polish interviewer, "I want to come here again, this time alone, not with a group of writers."

Sontag began to form plans to help Polish writers. And her Polish audiences took a particular interest in her. As Oates recounts the parallel scene in her story: "The Poles are listening intently, hungrily. It is the first time they have looked at Judith Horne as she is accustomed to being looked at in her own sphere—as if she had significance, as if she possessed power." Oates captures how exotic Sontag seemed to the Poles. "*Is* she female in the classic sense of the word?" The much coveted Judith has had both male and female lovers. She is distinguished-looking—not beautiful precisely, but rather (Oates resorts more than once to that inevitable adjective) "striking." And what about the cast of her features. Is it Slavic? Jewish? She is a New Yorker, yet Horne keeps her "background to herself"—perhaps because she thinks of herself as only "obliquely Jewish." In her interviews in Poland, Sontag steered clear of any specific reference to her roots.

Sontag and Oates visited Poland less than six months before the first

Solidarity strikes, and Oates's story carries with it a foreboding of trouble. Anyone in Poland then could have sensed that some kind of eruption was about to occur. It is what made Poland so exhilarating: the sense that some kind of historical turning point was near. Pope John Paul II's trip to Poland the previous summer had sparked mass unrest and a yearning that had to find expression in some kind of definitive event, and Sontag (always wanting to hover over the action) was immensely gratified to come so close to witnessing it.

There was a darker side to Poland, of course—the anti-Semitism and the dreary Stalinist architecture, all of which Oates records in her story, as well as Horne's sense of vulnerability, her identification with Jewish victimhood in a solidly Catholic country, the overwhelming sense of history that shocks an American: "And in our country, Judith thinks, history is something that happened only a few weeks ago—or didn't happen." Sontag's interviews just before and after her trip to Poland indicate a major shift in her thinking: the need to treat the aesthetic/moral debate of her criticism in a broader historical context.

Five months later John Leonard, reviewing *Under the Sign of Saturn* for the *New York Times* (October 13, 1980), discovered a Susan Sontag "better acquainted with love and irony." Compared to *Against Interpretation* and *Styles of Radical Will*, the new book seemed less au courant and more attracted to the idea of "'historical perspective.'" Similarly, Leo Braudy in *The New Republic* (November 29, 1980) announced that Sontag "finds the aesthetic pose to be colored with self-indulgence and edged with fascism." He accounted for the change by noting that she had become a part of the critical establishment. In the *Village Voice* (October 15–21, 1980), Walter Kendrick went even further, calling Sontag an "eminent Victorian," and noting that although considered a swinger, she was always examining modernism as though it were a new phenomenon, as if she were coming at it from from the nineteenth century in a calm, rational, classical style. Even when writing about pornography and other perversions, she never used argot. Estranged from contemporary concerns, she took refuge in a "transcultural isolation." Sontag was really an "elitist," Kendrick like many others argued, for she had written about "enthusiasms of her own clique in the correct expectation that what her friends had already embraced the general public would eventually latch onto." *Under the Sign of Saturn* revealed a retreat from engagement with popular culture. Her retreat, Kendrick supposed, might just be that of a coterie intellectual: "She's been hanging out too much at *The New York Review* and hence has grown a bit skittish." Kendrick compared *Under the Sign of Saturn* to Samuel Johnson's *Lives of the Poets*. She had wrought old-fashioned literary portraits. She resembled, he concluded, that Victorian cultural arbiter Matthew Arnold, one of the bêtes noirs of *Against Interpretation*.

In the interviews she gave in the wake of *Under the Sign of Saturn*, Sontag made no secret of the fact that the book was a disguised autobiography. Every essay, she implied, constituted a version of Susan Sontag. Whether her subject was Benjamin or Elias Canetti, she realized she had left out of her essays many aspects of these writers that made them different from her. She had fastened, in other words, on just those aspects of their lives and work that spoke directly to her own sensibility. What she said of them was true, but it was not the whole truth. As Kendrick suggested, she was using the essay form to be creative and critical. To Sontag, at any rate, the criticism that she had not done full justice to her subjects was beside the point.

The title essay on Benjamin, "Under the Sign of Saturn," which is at the center of her book, is Sontag's *apologia pro vita sua*. Or as she says in regard to Benjamin: "One cannot use the life to interpret the work. But one can use the work to interpret the life." The first four paragraphs dwell on photographs of the writer, the entrancing effigy of the writer. Unwilling to comment on her own iconic charms, she nevertheless exposes how important the writer's likeness is to her. Benjamin's self-composure appeals to her, for it mirrors her own. She quotes his friend Gershom Scholem, who recalled that Benjamin spoke in a style "ready for print."

Benjamin, already a genius in childhood, has the "longing to be superior—on one's own terms." He sees himself as a text, a project, that is always under construction. He drops friends "brutally," he shamelessly flatters people, and treats others not on his level contemptuously, so that he is "faithless to people." He is a collector and a book hunter with a shrewd tactical sense. She even makes him out to be "against interpretation wherever it is obvious." He likes to allegorize reality because, like photographs, allegories miniaturize the world and are a form of controlling it. Because he is subject to melancholic fits, the will becomes a paramount subject. For him as for all melancholics, the challenge is to become, as in Poe, a "hero of will." Of course, he jettisons family ties, which deplete the will. But the demands of maintaining the will are such that he finds it difficult to write anything other than essays, whose form is naturally suited to the melancholic's intensive and exhaustive personality. Melancholics do not have staying power.

Virtually every sentence about Benjamin might be read as a Sontag self-portrait—including her remark that his sentences read like both beginnings and endings. (The first sentence of *On Photography* is both Sontag's conclusion and the premise she must begin with and explicate. Many of Poe's stories are similarly constructed.)

Sontag saves Benjamin's most appealing aspect for the end of her essay, concluding that he was a man of many positions: surrealist, aesthetic, communist. "One position corrects another; he needed them all." He soldiered on, defending the autonomous life of the mind in a capitalist society busily making the freelance intellectual obsolete.

In the next essay, "Syberberg's Hitler," Sontag shows how the director's seven-hour epic treats Hitler as a much photographed and filmed figure—as indeed a creation of cinema. *Hitler: A Film from Germany* is a mixed-media creation, a grandiose Wagnerian epic of the kind Sontag finds seductive. In "Syberberg's Hitler," she mourns the "lost paradise" of cinema that she now deems to have fallen into a period of mediocrity. His masterpiece is "noble," she emphasizes, and it asks for and compels our "fealty"—a curious choice of words that Sontag will use again in *Under the Sign of Saturn* and that will at last reveal her almost medieval sense of mastery and discipleship.

Sontag treats Syberberg as an oppositional figure. Similarly, her next essay, on Roland Barthes, describes an immensely engaging man who, like herself, resisted "received ideas," thought "an idea was always in competition with another idea," wrote with polemical vigor but also struck a celebratory note, and was eager to share his intellectual passions and keen to attract an audience. Again, Sontag focuses on a thinker whose characteristic form is the essay—with a creative, playful bent.

Sontag's concluding essay begins by observing that Elias Canetti's tribute to fellow writer Hermann Broch "creates the terms of a succession." Finally, she has given the reader a clue: in *Under the Sign of Saturn* she is placing herself in her heroes' line of succession. Canetti's desire for longevity and his intellectual insatiability are, of course, her own. Like her, he desired "strong, even overpowering models." He is "extremely self-involved in a characteristically impersonal way." He fears not being "insolent or ambitious enough."

Sontag's reprise of Canetti's biography selects those details reminiscent of her own life: a childhood full of displacements, a search for status in a world of exiles, cultivation of the self as polymath and collector, creator of a novel whose main character is driven to suicide by the "world in his head." Then there is Canetti's "acquisitive relations to knowledge and truth" and his "wistful, prudent fantasies of disburdenment." Although Sontag had nothing like Canetti's close relationship with his mother, who became his "primal admirer" and a "passionate merciless promoter," she replicates this mother-son bond with David.

Indeed, Canetti offers Sontag something more than her other allegorical figures of the self: an all-consuming fascination with power, which refuses to accept tragedy and death. What Canetti feels he owes to his formidable mentors is "fealty"—that word again, which evokes the master-disciple continuum of Sontag's life. But Canetti is the final surrogate in *Under the Sign of Saturn* because he is, in Sontag's words, not just another "hero of the will." He is a survivor. In his masterpiece *Crowds and Power* (1960), he shows that power is not enough. Neither is careerism or the accumulation of knowledge. Rather, one must take in the world—Sontag calls it breathing—which means to "go beyond avidity; to identify with something beyond achievement, beyond the gathering of power."

With these words, *Under the Sign of Saturn* ceases—as it must since Sontag herself was still in process. Frank Kermode remarked at the end of his review that perhaps Sontag would, in time, heed Canetti's advice: "learn to breathe, seek something beyond the gathering of power." Leo Braudy, a shrewd scholar of fame and power, had his doubts. He set her debunking essays, "Fascinating Fascism" and "Syberberg's Hitler," against her five tracts in hero worship:

> In essence, I think it is difficult for Sontag to maintain an argument that attacks one side of Romantic individualism (that led to political megalomania) in order to accept another (that leads to artistic self-

aggrandizement). I hardly want to equate the two myself: strutting artists do much less harm than strutting dictators. But the paradox of the grandly assertive work of art that attacks the grandly assertive gesture in the public world of politics is a delicate one indeed, and Sontag is unconvincing about the terms of the competition, perhaps because she is so caught up in it herself.

Susan the Apostate

1982

On February 1, 1982, Sontag joined Polish dissident poet Stanislaw Baranczak and Joseph Brodsky in a discussion of the writer's role in Poland, an event sponsored by the American Center of PEN. Richard Grenier watched Sontag the entire evening at Manhattan's Public Theater and later described a posture toward Brodsky and Baranczak that was "unremittingly hostile: arrogant, abrasive, patronizing, contemptuous." Grenier witnessed her declare, "apropos of nothing in particular," that she had been accused of "errors of perception" about certain Communist countries. She indignantly asserted that she had never been deceived about the Soviet Union's evil—only about certain later regimes that she mistakenly thought valued the artist. Grenier marveled at her tone of "instant self-exoneration." She seemed to absolve herself because, whatever her errors, her sentiments were commendable.

Jaroslav Anders, Sontag's Polish friend and a Solidarity member, protested Grenier's article in a letter to *The New Republic* (May 26, 1982). There was no hostility on either side, just differences of opinion. Yet Anders sidestepped Grenier's main point about Sontag's "mercurial nature." Five days later, at Town Hall (February 6), she would take the

Baranczak-Brodsky line, yet on February 1 she resisted it at every point, Grenier reports, until, tension mounting, she exploded: "We understand tyranny! We read!" Her air of certainty and superiority astonished Grenier—as it did friends of ours when years earlier (circa late 1960s) she condescendingly lectured Polish poet Czeslaw Milosz (later a Nobel Prize winner) on politics and literature at a public event in Berkeley. As Grenier said of the February 1 debate: "For ten solid minutes there, it seemed to her that she understood, and has always understood, everything."

Less than a week later, the context had changed for Sontag. The Town Hall gathering was not a panel discussion of writers. It had been orchestrated by Ralph Schoenman (last seen trying to get Sontag to join the Socialist Workers Party) as a news event—indeed a rally to support Solidarity, which martial law had banned in Poland. The rally was to be like a Solidarity rally because it included not only writers and intellectuals but a singer on the left (Pete Seeger) and union representatives from PATCO (the air-traffic controllers Reagan fired) and the UAW. Novelists Gore Vidal, E. L. Doctorow, and Kurt Vonnegut were there, and so was Joseph Brodsky. Town Hall is a favorite venue for the left, and fifteen hundred people had assembled to hear the left not only assert its support for Solidarity but condemn the Reagan administration, which could not be sincere in supporting Solidarity since it had fired unionized workers and was supporting repression in El Salvador.

Sontag and Brodsky watched in disgust as speaker after speaker tried to equate the suffering in Poland with the plight of PATCO and U.S. policy in El Salvador—the "typical therapy session of the *Weltschmertz*-ridden downtown left," as Brodsky later dismissed it in a letter to *The New Republic* (May 26, 1982). Sontag carefully scripted her speech so that it began on a communal note of Reagan-bashing and the need to "distinguish ourselves from others in the chorus of virtuous indignation." By her third paragraph (no more than a few minutes into her speech), she began to suggest that this very effort to "distinguish ourselves" could "lead *us* into certain hypocrisies and untruths." Suddenly the air of self-congratulation vanished, and the audience became restive. Although Sontag kept including herself in her bill of indictment, she did not look at her audience, and she was no longer "with" her listeners. By paragraph four she baldly said the left had told a lot of lies about Communism. By paragraph six, Communism itself had been denounced as an "utter villainy." There were boos and catcalls—but also a few bravos (among them, D. Keith Mano, a regular contributor to the conservative weekly *National Review*). Sontag explained that she did not want to believe Milosz's *The Captive Mind*, when it was published in 1953, preferring to think of it as an "instrument of Cold War propaganda." But now she had reread it, and she thought that perhaps Milosz had not been hard enough on Communism.

At this point Sontag's words took on a deeply familiar refrain—the accents of the apostate, of the former Communist or fellow traveler. It was a form familiar to her audience—indeed, so familiar that E. L. Doctorow and Ralph Schoenman, among others, were perplexed. Why would Susan Sontag, born in 1933, too young to have engaged in the debates of the 1930s, act like an earlier generation of leftie apologizing for having been philo-Soviet? Her "error" had been in thinking that societies like Cuba and North Vietnam would at last redeem Communism, but she had never been a Stalinist. The older members of the audience were irritated because they had heard all this before. Not only was it old news, but it was delivered by someone who had not herself been a part of it. No one in Town Hall that night believed any longer in the Soviet utopia.

But according to Sontag's logic, Communism was uniform. Whenever Communists took power—no matter where—they became tyrants, or, as she put it, fascists. Like many on the left, she had thought she could make distinctions between Leninism and Stalinism, for example. But now she realized that the *Reader's Digest* had been right and *The Nation* had been wrong: all Communists were bad.

Sontag's public penance angered the audience, but it moved Joseph Brodsky, who gallantly defended her afterward, praising her commitment to world literature and her writing about the "philosophy of perception and the way it evolves" (*The New Republic*, May 26, 1982). And indeed, her speech is about how she and the left looked at the world as devoted antifascists who could not bring themselves to admit that their antidote to fascism (Communism) had itself become the disease. She even attacked the smugness of the left: "We were so sure who our enemies were (among them, the professional anti-Communists) so sure who were the virtuous and who the benighted. . . . We thought we loved justice; many of us did. But we did not love the truth enough." Echoing Alexander Dubček, who thought he could reform Communism and give it a human face, Sontag concluded that Communism was simply a variant of fascism, with a "human face." She implied that in order to be in sincere solidarity with Solidarity, the left had to abandon its complacent view of itself as progressive and on the right side. Its rhetoric over many decades had excused enormous crimes and had rationalized the very regimes that had crushed movements like Solidarity.

With Town Hall in an uproar, Sontag got up and left. "Given the intellectual eating habits of her audience, it had been a brave endeavor. I felt both impressed and grateful," Mano reported in the *National Review* (April 16, 1982). The attacks on Sontag were fierce and often contemptuous. It was said, for example, that she was merely parroting the line of the new philosophers in Paris, who had rejected Sartre and his support for Stalinism, and who had branded much of the French intelligentsia with collective guilt for having excused the Gulag and so much more about the Soviet Union and its Cold War satellites. Sontag had "come out" as an anti-Communist four years earlier in the French journal *Tel Quel*, presided over by "new philosophers" such as Philippe Sollers, who, judging by his novel *Women*, regarded Sontag as a sort of hanger-on and trendy apostle.

Sontag was treated to a going-over in *The Nation* (February 27, 1982), which reprinted her speech and then gave several writers—some their regular contributors—a shot at her. No one, it seemed, had ever believed in Soviet Communism. Andrew Kopkind reminisced about his trip with Sontag to Hanoi a few months after Tet, 1968, and scorned her failure of nerve in not sticking with North Vietnam, which was "proceeding (dialectically, dare I say the word?) in its development according to the forces and furies of the real world." Some of the nastiness that would rile Sontag came out in book editor Philip Pochoda's reference to her as a "minor celebrity" who had simplified the "enormously heterogenous experience of Communism." Two Sontag friends, human rights advocate Aryeh Neier and Christopher Hitchens, were easy on her, generally welcoming her remarks without much cavil. Hitchens, who had in fact served as the go-between in setting up the *Nation* symposium, praised her for criticizing the left's record on Stalinism, although he chided her for "ill-tempered and ahistorical remarks." Acknowledging her penchant for the polemical, he concluded: "Let us be charitable and assume that she was trying to galvanize an audience by deliberate exaggeration."

Sontag's reply in *The Nation* was scornful. She rejected Aryeh Neier's sanctimonious anti-Communism. She dismissed Andrew Kopkind as that "noted disco expert of the 1970s." And what heterogeneous experience of Communism did Pochoda et al. have in mind? Every country with a ruling Communist party had become a tyranny, she emphasized. She was at her shrewdest dismissing those lefties who believed that Solidarity was somehow a product of a failed Communist system or that it would replace that system with a better communism: "What is brewing in Eastern Europe is not democratic socialism," she predicted. It had been proven that Communism was a failure. "We were wrong. It is the people who live in those countries who tell us that," she insisted.

Sontag's rebuttal to her critics was accompanied by the printed version of her Town Hall speech. For publication in *The Nation,* she toned down her remarks comparing *The Nation* and *Reader's Digest* and changed the wording of her comments on Milosz's *The Captive Mind*—whereas before she had implied that she had not believed him, now she said she had been "troubled" by his book. In her *Nation* reply to her critics, she amplified her way of dealing with his vexing testimony (he had served in a Communist government) by saying she had "bracketed what Milosz and other émigrés were saying." In other words, Sontag was an anti-Stalinist without ever acknowledging the *"essentially* despotic nature of the Communist system."

But had Sontag really liberated herself from doublethink? She rejected Diana Trilling's welcome into "her new difficult life as an anti-Communist." Sontag said "thanks but no thanks." As if to reaffirm her leftist credentials, she ended her *Nation* reply by expressing her support for the "democratic movement in El Salvador, whose struggle to overthrow the tyranny backed by the American government I passionately support." Yet as Leon Wieseltier observed in *Partisan Review* (Summer 1982), opposition parties in El Salvador ranged from reformist to revolutionary, but none seemed so pure or perfect as a "democratic movement." Sontag's comments revealed a person "innocent of the practice of politics. She is taking positions, that's all." Her words, Wieseltier implied, were those of the aesthete: "Politics is not pretty. Taking positions is."

In the *Soho News* (March 2, 1982), Marshall Berman, one of several intellectuals responding to Sontag's Town Hall speech, wondered, like

Wieseltier, at Sontag's penchant for making extreme, even absurd statements. Did she really believe that interpretation depleted and impoverished the world? Or that the "white race is the cancer of history"? Berman conceded that we all make exaggerated statements, but Sontag seemed to say things "*because* they are absurd." She was acting out, he hypothesized, her vicarious identification with the alienated writer who provides, as she put it in her essay on Camus, "excitement, an infusion of intense feeling," opening up "rare emotions and dangerous sensations." Sontag's "extravagant political mendacities, early and late," were, Berman supposed, part of what she regarded as her "spiritual adventure," a "modernist *liaison dangereuse*, the ultimate trip for an intellectual who has been everywhere else." Finally, Berman recalled the Sontag who reveled in jettisoning old positions like old skins, and who declared in "Project for a Trip to China" that "one must be simpler. . . simple, as in a great forgetting."

Although conservatives such as William F. Buckley saluted Sontag's courage, almost immediately the right and the left began to rethink what she had said. Was Communism the same as fascism? And why fascism with a "human face"? What was human about an ideology that had killed millions more than fascism? Martin Peretz, publisher of *The New Republic*, found Sontag's speech so confusing that he declared: "People like Susan Sontag, they should really have no political standing in the world." D. Keith Mano, after his initial enthusiasm, found the speech "nothing more than a semantic swindle." Just as Grenier observed several Sontags in the week of her Public Theater and Town Hall appearances, other commentators fretted over her very mixed message. Christopher Hitchens argued in *The Spectator* (March 6, 1982) that Sontag had "not really abandoned her old allegiances." Her speech was more like a therapeutic exercise. James Lardner characterized the nature of her speech and the reaction to it succinctly: "There is intense disagreement still about how communism should be viewed and about how—and in whose company—it should be opposed" ("Susan Sontag into the Fray," *Washington Post*, March 16, 1982).

Whatever might baffle Sontag critics about her speech, she had, "to her everlasting credit," chosen to "denounce the Left's refusal to acknowledge Communism's failure *as a system* at a forum where her views were guaranteed to meet with considerable hostility," as Arch Puddington put it in the *American Spectator* ("The Polish Example,"

April 1982). What is more, she had shattered the Cold War identity of a left that had clung to the "view of a world menaced in equal degrees by the Soviet Union and the United States." She had taken the trouble to go to Poland when "few Americans of any political stripe" had done the same, Puddington pointed out. She had listened carefully to what Solidarity activists had told her, and she was not about to have it all turned around to suit the sentiments of the American left. Sontag had broken leftist discipline, in which "criticizing the aims of individual Communist regimes is permissible; criticizing Communism as a system is not."

Sontag saw the power that was available to her in seizing the dramatic moment; she had found her aphoristic opportunity in "communism is fascism with a human face." This turn of phrase condemns and honors at the same time. Of course, it can be logically taken apart, but that is almost beside the point. Her formulation ensured extended debate. William Phillips, always her gallant defender, deemed her aphorism an expression of "authentic indignation and honesty" (*Partisan Review*, Summer 1982). But he suggested "it might have served her purpose just as well simply to say that both fascism and communism were the totalitarian evils of our time." But you don't become Susan Sontag by uttering such dull sentences.

Sontag made her role in the Town Hall rally more problematic when she sued the *Soho News* in U.S. District Court in New York for reprinting her Town Hall speech without her permission. She asked for $50,000 in damages, noting that the paper had lopped off two paragraphs at the end of her speech, thus distorting her meaning. Her attorney, Leon Friedman (FSG's attorney and also a legal advisor to PEN), also claimed that the *Soho News* had preempted Sontag's efforts to get her speech published in the *New York Times*, thereby depriving her not only of her chosen venue of publication but of the right to profit from what she had written. "I'm not a litigious person," Sontag claimed. "This is the first lawsuit I've ever brought in my life and I hope to God the last one." She conceded the paper's right to print a substantial part of her speech, but took issue with its methods, claiming that the paper had "kidnapped my speech and presented it outside of its context."

Sontag's statements reflect considerable defensiveness—in part because she was under attack in the *Village Voice*. Columnist Nat Hentoff, a widely recognized champion of the First Amendment, was

aghast that Sontag would resort to the law, and he regarded her position
as damaging to the cause of freedom of speech and indicative of an imperious attitude: "Susan Sontag, no matter what you may have thought, is
not of the royal family." To enlist the apparatus of the state against a
small newspaper seemed unworthy, an action he deemed no better than
Jane Fonda's threats to resort to the law to ban an unauthorized biography of her. Indeed, Sontag came off worse, because Fonda at least had
not actually filed a suit. When Sontag claimed that the *Soho News* had
misappropriated her "performance rights," thus violating a New York
law of unfair competition, Hentoff commented: "What a crabbed view of
political discourse." The Town Hall meeting was not a literary reading;
rather, it was a political event meant to influence public opinion. Sure,
Sontag had a right to be angry about a paper garbling her speech—
Hentoff had had many of his public talks distorted by the press—but
such was the price of engaging in the "hurly-burly of public discourse.
If you want to be politically perfect, like Mary Poppins, then stay home
and correct your galleys," Hentoff advised Sontag.

What Sontag really wanted was control over history's view of herself,
Hentoff argued. Why had she doctored her speech for publication in *The
Nation*? "Isn't this like the rewriting of public history that's practiced in
some countries? he asked. *Nation* editor Victor Navasky had restored
one of the censored passages in the periodical's introduction to Sontag's
speech, Hentoff noted, so as not to collaborate in Sontag's "purge."

Then Hentoff took up Leon Friedman's allegation that publication
in the *Soho News* had made Sontag's speech unmarketable to the *Times*.
A skeptical Hentoff asked why the *Times* would worry about the impact
of the small-circulation *Soho News*? Following up on Hentoff's suspicion,
another *Voice* columnist, Alexander Cockburn, spoke with the editor of
the *Times* op-ed page, Charlotte Curtis, who told him the paper had
turned down Sontag's speech because it did not say anything new or
newsworthy, not because it had appeared in the *Soho News*.

The mistake the *Soho News* made, Hentoff contended, was asking
Sontag's permission to reprint her speech. As a news event, he did not
think the speech fell under the copyright law. Hentoff conceded that
there were "conflicting analyses." He had spoken with attorneys who
held that Sontag had a case. The point about public debate is that it
should be free and open and heard by "as many people as possible."
Instead Sontag practiced the politics of constriction: "how unnatural it

is, how narcissistic, how solipsistic," Hentoff observed. Lawsuits like Sontag's would have a "chilling effect" on the reporting of public events. "What a lousy thing to do to James Madison," Hentoff lamented.

Hentoff's two columns hurt. They were answered in *The Nation* (May 8, 1982) by Sontag confidant Aryeh Neier, then chairman of the Americas Watch and Helsinki Watch committees. *The Nation*'s editors prefaced Neier's opinion piece with the comment that it opposed Sontag's lawsuit. Indeed, editor-in-chief Victor Navasky later said that although Sontag had granted permission for *The Nation* to print her Town Hall speech, he did not feel the magazine needed it. In an editorial (March 13, 1982), *The Nation* condemned her lawsuit as "inimical to freedom of the press, harmful to the writing and publishing community generally and, if successful . . . a dangerous and sticky precedent."

Neier took the *Voice* columnists, Hentoff and Cockburn, to task for not recognizing Sontag's right to control the manner in which her writing was disseminated. He made a powerful case. Taking Hentoff's open-ended view, no author could deliver a lecture, reading, or performance without having it immediately published in the press. Newsworthiness was not the issue. If Sontag had not spoken her written words but simply published them in *The Nation*, the *Soho News* would have had to obtain permission to reprint. In short, Hentoff's argument would ultimately destroy the very idea of copyright protection. In fact, Neier could have made his argument even stronger by pointing out that Sontag is a writer and that she had fixed her speech in writing before delivering it. She had a good case.

But neither Neier nor Hentoff was dealing only with the law. "As it happens, I regret that Sontag filed suit against the *Soho News*," Neier added. His first reason, he admitted, was identical to Hentoff's: he feared that a "court might hand down a more sweeping decision than is war-ranted by the circumstances." Second, Sontag could get nothing from the suit worth the attacks she had incurred for bringing it. Better to withdraw the suit, he counseled, in what amounted to a public letter to her. "Sontag is not entitled to escape criticism," Neier concluded, but she did not deserve the "mean-spiritedness and prosecutorial fervor of some of the attacks upon her."

This gallant and well-reasoned defense, however, would not end the acrimony. Sontag had behaved rather like Lillian Hellman, who brought suit in 1980 against Mary McCarthy for calling her a liar on network television. Indeed, the parallels between the suits are noteworthy. Hellman had the strong backing of Ephraim London—like Friedman, a renowned First Amendment champion—who not only had agreed to pursue McCarthy to the bitter end but who had done so without charging Hellman. Sontag had Friedman: same deal, or nearly the same deal, since Friedman did double—nay, triple—duty, as FSG's and PEN's lawyer as well.

The resort to law is meant to be intimidating and punitive. Like Hellman, Sontag was serving notice. Anyone reading the FSG files at the New York Public Library will see how meticulous the firm was in safeguarding Sontag's copyrights, in suppressing interviews she deemed counter to her interests, and in general by enforcing a regime of control over her writing that, if not unprecedented, is certainly remarkable when compared to the attention most authors—even the most successful—can expect from a publisher.

The *Soho News* went out of business on March 15, 1982, and somewhat later Sontag dropped her suit. But the ruckus caused by the Town Hall incident and its aftermath would poison the reception of Sontag's next publication, *A Susan Sontag Reader*. David Rieff and Roger Straus would feel obliged to defend the honor of a lady who had become derisively known in some New York circles as "La Sontag."

Retrospection

1 9 8 2 – 1 9 8 3

In the fall of 1982, FSG published *A Susan Sontag Reader.* When Roger Straus first proposed the project, Sontag demurred. As she told interviewer Charles Ruas (*New York Times,* October 24, 1982): "I felt what I imagine a painter feels. I'd like to have another show, but I don't think I'd like to have a retrospective. The convention of a 'Reader' is, after all, for writers whose work is finished." But she changed her mind, noting that she had been publishing for twenty years. Not only had she achieved a body of work, she could now re-present it with David's help, for he was now her editor and, in many vital respects, the caretaker of her reputation.

Reviewing *A Susan Sontag Reader* in *The Nation* (October 23, 1982), Walter Kendrick called her "our unofficial hostess of letters," a mediator between America and Europe: "She stands midway between the two continents, in what one might call the Sargasso Sea of thought. Her stance there is unique, but always a little shaky." To Kendrick, *A Susan Sontag Reader* presented her as a "fully established American fig-ure . . . ready for the archive"—especially so because of Elizabeth Hardwick's "elegiac introduction, which croons of 'unique talent' and

'profound authority' till you can fairly smell the formaldehyde."
Kendrick found little development in Sontag's thought—and certainly
none in her fiction, which (except for certain short stories) excited in him
no enthusiasm. Even her critical work seemed dated to Kendrick. Her
"eminence in American letters is disproportionate to the quality of her
thought," he suggested. What once might have looked avant-garde now
seemed in the "tradition of genteel literary discourse." Kendrick concluded on a note of personal testimony:

> I must confess, I don't know anyone who looks to Sontag for aesthet-
> ic guidance. But she takes herself so seriously, and her publisher
> treats her with such awe, that I can only presume the existence of a
> vast, anonymous readership, hungry for Sontag's pearls. If these
> readers exist, their reverence is Sontag's only real achievement, a
> notable achievement, to be sure, but a far more trenchant criticism
> of the world of American letters than any essay she ever wrote.

David Rieff wrote to *Nation* editor Victor Navasky accusing him of
addressing "unfinished business" with Sontag: "You really ought to be
ashamed of yourselves." Rieff was referring, of course, to Sontag's politics and the Town Hall uproar. Navasky replied that the magazine's literary department was autonomous and reviews were not used to settle
scores. So Rieff ought to retract his "nasty thought." Rieff had complained to Navasky about Katha Pollitt, then literary editor, who wrote to
Rieff that she had disagreed with parts of Kendrick's review, but that he
had "stuck to his guns" and she had printed his piece—"one of the best
manuscripts" she had received. Rieff's tactics troubled her: "Naturally,
I wish you had written to me rather than to Victor—Victor has absolutely no say over the book section, and it's a bit depressing to think that not
everyone knows this." Rieff then replied to both Navasky and Pollitt,
reiterating that he suspected *The Nation* of taking revenge, and that
Kendrick was motivated by personal animus when he wrote that no one
looked to Sontag for "aesthetic guidance." He still believed that Pollitt
as an editor should have had such a sentence removed. But Rieff accepted their good faith, and he retracted his nasty thought.

Neither David Rieff nor his mother saw anything untoward in his
editing her work. She reported to interviewer Charles Ruas: "Someone
said to David, 'Don't you think you're mixing church and state?' But I'm

very pleased with the arrangement. I have great confidence in Mr. Rieff's judgment." In fact, she told Ruas in another interview (in the *Soho News,* November 12–18, 1980) that David was her screen. He would read reviews of her work and tell her what she had to know. He had informed her, for example, about a terrible review of *Under the Sign of Saturn.* The reviewer said he had never read her creative work. And who was the unnamed reviewer? Walter Kendrick.

Kendrick's review of *A Susan Sontag Reader* was no anomaly. Similar responses came from Ann Morrissett Davidson in the *Philadelphia Inquirer* (December 26, 1982), from Stanley Aronowitz in the *Voice Literary Supplement* (November 1982), from Greil Marcus in *California* magazine (reprinted in his collection *The Dustbin of History*), from Hilton Kramer in the *Atlantic* (September 1982), and from the late Marvin Mudrick, who titled his *Harper's* review "Susie Creamcheese Makes Love, Not War." That little ditty provoked Roger Straus's wrath. *Harper's* sent him the galleys, which he called an "editorial obscenity." Like David Rieff, Straus went straight to the head man, the magazine's editor, Michael Kinsley, and to the magazine's editorial board, which included diplomat George Ball and Bard College president Leon Botstein. The vulgarity of the diatribe against Sontag "does dishonor to a magazine that has had a history of quality," Straus fumed.

What was so obscene? Well, FSG's publicity director, Helene Atwan, remembered a dirty line from school days: "Susie Creamcheese, she's so spreadable it's incredible." At *Harper's* they could only think of Susie Creamcheese as the "amiable groupie" in a Frank Zappa song from the 1960s. Helen Rogan, an associate editor at *Harper's*, acknowledged that the headline knocked Sontag "off her pedestal without any specific sexual allusion." Mudrick denied any pornographic intent, although he could not vouch for his unconscious.

In the *Washington Post*'s *Book World* ("Sticks and Stones," January 9, 1983), Michele Slung put the question: "Should Roger Straus have urged *Harper's*, as he did, 'to reconsider'?" When Slung questioned him, he reiterated that the title was "revolting and indecent," and said he "saw nothing untoward about the way he chose to protest to *Harper's* over their use of it." Slung asked Straus, then in Paris visiting Sontag, whether he had discussed the review with her. No, he had not mentioned it. Why not? It didn't "serve any useful purpose," a testy Straus replied. But shouldn't Sontag know what was being done on her behalf? the inquiring Slung wanted to know. Well, he did not have the article with him to show Sontag, Straus said. How strange, Slung thought, since the focus of Straus's outrage had been the title. Surely he had not forgotten it when he spoke to Sontag?

As in the Kendrick affair, the Mudrick fuss never involved Sontag herself. To this day, Pollitt does not know how Sontag felt. As Hilton Kramer, a former FSG author, notes, "Roger was always careful to keep Susan's fingerprints off everything."

Kramer is a well-known Sontag nemesis (see his devastating article "Anti-Communism and the Sontag Circle" [*The New Criterion*, September 1986]). In 1982, when he started *The New Criterion*, Roger Straus called him to say, "Did you have to start a magazine in order to attack Susan?" The left strafed her as well. Here is Alexander Cockburn's note:

FOREVER SUSAN

There's a forbidding picture of Susan Sontag, on the cover of *Vanity Fair*. She used to look so jolly in the early photographs—frolicsome yet brainy. I assume that Susan, no mean student of the icon, decided that the best presentation of self in 1983 was the grim visage she proffers to Irving Penn. I'm looking forward to the Susan Sontag Exercise Book all the same, with accompanying tape: "Now for the volte-face. . . ."

(*Village Voice*, October 11, 1983)

Negative notices did not injure Sontag. She prospered in the press. John Simon saluted her in *New York* magazine (December 24–31, 1984) as "The Light That Never Failed," lauding her "many-sidedness, curiosity, appetite, and stamina, with a willingness to pursue interesting new figures and ideas in many directions even risking the occasional dead end."

Sontag's appearance in Woody Allen's *Zelig* (1983) was but one validation of Simon's tribute. Sontag, together with Nobel Prize–winning novelist Saul Bellow, child psychiatrist Bruno Bettelheim, critic Irving Howe, and Professor John Morton Blum, were chosen, Allen said, to endow his film with the "patina of intellectual weight and seriousness." This group of notables provided commentary on the bizarre career of Leonard Zelig, who could change color, body shape, even ethnic and national identity, blending into whatever company he sought. In mock-documentary mode, with voice-over narration, expert testimony, and faked photographs, Allen superbly constructed an amalgam of *Citizen Kane* and *Reds*—with Zelig also acting as a kind of Jay Gatsby figure.

It is as if Allen were illustrating the thesis of *On Photography*, in which Sontag argued that photographs are not real but surreal precisely because they can fuse features that do not belong together into one credible image. Photographs, she contended, had become the standard measure of reality. Allen satirizes the authority of photographs as documents when he pictures Zelig on a medical table surrounded by nurses. Everyone in the photograph looks at the camera, and moviegoers look at Zelig, sitting up, his feet sticking out of his hospital gown and rotated so that his heels are up where his toes should be—in other words, he has somehow been able to twist his legs so that the back is now the front and vice versa. (The very difficulty of making this description emphasizes how quickly we can take in a photograph as "real," as making sense, even when it is patently false.)

Allen's elaborate joke addressed Sontag's de-Platonized world, in which we no longer refer the image to the idea; instead the image itself becomes the source of truth. Similarly, the efforts of psychiatrists to cure Zelig are a send-up of modern psychology, another one of Sontag's bêtes noires. Here she is assessing the role of Eudora Fletcher (Mia Farrow), who becomes not only Zelig's psychiatrist but his lover and wife:

> *As she talks to the offscreen interviewer, the caption* "SUSAN SONTAG, AUTHOR OF *Against Interpretation"* *pops on the screen.*

> SUSAN SONTAG: I don't know if you could call it a triumph of psychotherapy—it seems more like a triumph of aesthetic instincts. (*Gesturing*) Because Dr. Fletcher's techniques didn't owe anything to then current schools of therapy. But she sensed what was needed and she provided it, and that was, in its way, a remarkable creative accomplishment.

The "triumph of aesthetic instincts" is a quintessential Susan Sontag phrase—although she could not have known how the film mimicked her own work, since Allen did not give his intellectual stars scripts. They were not even told what the film was about; rather, they were part of the process of intellectualizing that Allen was satirizing. Perhaps that is why Saul Bellow later complained that he felt he had been made to look foolish.

Allen's shrewdness is also revealed in his decision to have Sontag open the film. She is first heard in a voice-over: "He was *the* phenomenon of the . . ." Then there is a cut to

> *the present day, in living color. Susan Sontag is sitting at an outdoor cafe, a coffee cup in front of her. She faces the camera, still talking, as behind her an idyllic glimpse of Venice is seen: a bright blue sky, gondolas on the canal, seagulls flying by the slanted roofs. Her name pops on the bottom of the screen*: SUSAN SONTAG.
>
> SUSAN SONTAG (*Continuing, fingering her napkin*): . . . twenties. When you think that at that time he was as well known as Lindbergh, it's really quite astonishing.

Like the other intellectual stars—except perhaps Bellow—Sontag seems to be enjoying herself. She looks cheerful, as if she is about to break into a grin, as if she knows that you know that she knows this is all camp, and as if she is pleased to be one of the four featured intellectual luminaries.

Roger Straus told his friend agent Harriet Wasserman (as she reports in her memoir *Handsome Is*, 1997) that he negotiated $5,000 plus royalties for Sontag's brief appearance. Wasserman dismissed his bragging until she found out that her client, Saul Bellow, got a similar deal without telling her. And what of Sontag's reaction to her cameo? During an appearance on the West Coast for the Portland Arts and Lectures series (1985), an audience member asked her what it was like to work with Woody Allen. "Next question," Sontag responded. Backstage, she complained about American audiences. In Europe, she would never have been asked such a question.

In 1982, at the time that Allen was shooting *Zelig*, Sontag wrote and directed her fourth film, *Unguided Tour*, an adaptation of her short story with the same title. In the story, a "woman of culture" speaks to her lover, who could be male or female. In the film, the lover is a male

(Claudio Cassinelli), and the woman is Lucinda Childs, then Sontag's lover.

Unguided Tour's generic couple are bound up in a journey to Venice that is really an identity crisis. The couple seem to be breaking up in this "capital of melancholy," as reviewer Gary Indiana puts it. The film is another one of those Sontag mysteries in which the characters acquire and disburden themselves of each other. Again the why—the psychological reasons for their alienation—is beside the point. Rather, this is the Romantic quest that begins in America (as the story makes clear) and inevitably ends in the sinking city of Venice. The gloom is only alleviated by the daunted/undaunted woman of culture, who sounds most American when she announces: "I've been everywhere. I haven't been everywhere, but it's on my list."

Childs, that elusive, charming self-described catatonic, has expressed herself best through her body. And in the film, Sontag gives Childs her physical release in what Indiana calls "a cryptic, improvised dance outdoors. . . ." The Childs of the early 1980s was the erotic embodiment of Sontag's aesthetics of silence. More than the story, the film is about the artist and art, the striving for perfect articulation, which is best exemplified in the dancer and the dance, a theme Sontag would soon develop in an article and in a television essay.

And Childs shared many of Sontag's enthusiasms: "I connect more in terms of film," she told an interviewer, "things that play themselves out in time, recurrent elements that take place in time, flashbacks, revisions of action in time, things that you see and see again. I'm particularly fascinated with Bresson. . . ." Childs's looks, her elongated figure, pale skin, and the "chiseled bone structure of a high-fashion model," bring to mind the actresses favored by Ingmar Bergman. And her work has provoked some of the same objections leveled at Sontag's, with dance critics complaining that Childs's choreography is too willed, some calling it "too abstract and calculating."

Childs, who has performed under the direction of Robert Wilson (with whom Sontag would later collaborate) and to the accompaniment of Philip Glass's music (another Sontag enthusiasm), was part of the late 1960s and early 1970s New York City art scene. It was there that Robert Wilson began welding together painting, set design, music, ballet, and pantomime—an amalgam that paralleled the experiments in music and dance of John Cage (another obsession of the adolescent Sontag) and

Merce Cunningham. This avant-garde, cerebral, often ascetic style—so different from, say, Martha Graham's histrionic theater/dance productions—a style in which Childs became known as the "super-cool mistress of spin," gives way in *Unguided Tour* to a more tender, troubled dialogue between lovers. Indeed, the film, more than the story, heralds changes in both Sontag's and Childs's art. For her part, Sontag was already moving away from the aesthetics of silence that had constricted her earlier novels and toward a passionate conversation with a wider audience in her best-selling novel *The Volcano Lover: A Romance*.

1 9 8 6 – 1 9 8 9

In "Writers Talk Among Themselves" (*New York Times Book Review*, January 5, 1986), Sontag heralded the International PEN conference in New York, the first such gathering in the United States in twenty years. "With age and a certain volume of accomplishment" writers became public figures and service-minded." Even though they spoke "condescendingly of these meetings," they would be "displeased never to be invited," for organizations like PEN were a part of their "pious duty" and ratified their status as elders in the "Church of Writers." Also, "nobody hates a free trip," she admitted—or a "star turn."

Sontag thought this latest world congress deserving of attention since it had "bent custom a little by choosing as the theme 'The Writer's Imagination and the Imagination of the State.'" As a member of the PEN program committee, she found the topic "piquant" and "slightly original."

Norman Mailer had developed the conference theme. Elected to the PEN presidency in June 1985, he had rejuvenated a small organization of about two thousand members, giving it a new role as a highly visible player in Manhattan, and host to perhaps the largest gathering ever of foreign writers on American shores. Mailer had close to a million-dollar budget and free hotel rooms from Donald Trump and other wealthy benefactors. "We had been talking for three or four years about hosting that congress," one PEN board member said, "but we never knew where to raise the money. But Norman knew what to do and how to do it." Gay Talese, like Sontag a PEN vice president and longtime PEN member, declared that without Mailer and "his fund-raising efforts, we would not be having the International Congress."

In the fall of 1985, it had been Mailer's idea to stage on Broadway a series of literary evenings with sixteen major writers, pricing the tickets at $1,000 apiece for the series. Kurt Vonnegut, Arthur Miller, Tom Wolfe, Woody Allen, William Styron, Joan Didion, and Susan Sontag had all performed.

PEN had a distinguished history, dating back to 1921, when novelist John Galsworthy had founded the P.E.N. Club (poets, playwrights, essayists, editors, and novelists), contending that "if the writers of the world could learn to stretch out their hands to each other, the nations of the world could learn in time to do the same." He was speaking in the aftermath of World War I, when acrimony among writers of different nations remained a serious problem. Later PEN officials spoke of writers as "trustees for human nature" (such noble rhetoric fills PEN's official history). And indeed the organization, with more than eighty centers in fifty countries, has fostered the development of an international literary community, arranged for the publication of translations and for translation prizes, protested and sometimes obtained the release of persecuted writers, initiated writing programs in prisons, and in general spread the good word.

Sontag had joined American PEN in the fall of 1964, attracted mainly by the idea of those international conferences. But the nugatory PEN of that time perturbed her. At a PEN dinner on November 7, 1966, she stood up to second Arthur Miller's speech bemoaning the American Center's feeble identity. Miller, then PEN's international president, said the club was always helping writers abroad, but had no sense of itself as a literary community. American writers were entirely individualistic, whereas the Russians, for example, thought of all writers as "pushing one spoke of the wheel," contributing to the glory of literature itself.

Miller had candidly identified PEN's major flaw, which not even the energetic Mailer, and later Susan Sontag, could eliminate. Sontag told the assembly of the faithful:

PEN is not a very interesting place. Now, why? What can be done about that? That obviously has to do with what Arthur Miller said about making a cockpit of controversy, a place of confrontation. How could it be made more interesting?

Why did PEN hold parties in the Hotel Pierre? It should be meeting somewhere, say, on Seventeenth Street, in shabby lofts. (She was describing the area very close to FSG's own rather run-down offices.) Forget the cocktails and dinners. Let publishers handle such functions. A self-described "teetotaler," she got nothing out of such frivolous activities. PEN should be a serious organization for serious writers. It should be making an impact on the New York scene, and it should be doing something for itself, not just for writers in other parts of the world.

Some PEN members grumbled about Sontag's criticism, thinking it unfair to harp on the cocktail parties and dinners. And what was she prepared to do as a "working member"? asked Joy Chute, a PEN veteran. Sontag did not take up Chute's challenge at the time, although she later became a board member and stepped up her level of activity in the organization in the 1980s just before Mailer took PEN to Broadway.

In January 1986 the advance press for the International PEN meeting in New York was remarkable—but then PEN had hired a public relations firm, and besides Sontag's precongress article, there had been E. L. Doctorow's *New York Times* op-ed piece complaining that PEN should not have invited Secretary of State George Shultz to speak at the opening ceremony. Doctorow opposed Reagan administration policies in Nicaragua and South Africa. He condemned the State Department for continuing to enforce the McCarran-Walter Immigration and Nationality Act of 1952 barring certain writers deemed subversive from entering the United States. By inviting Shultz, PEN had "put itself in the position of a bunch of writers' union hacks in Eastern Europe who have gathered for a pat on the head by the minister of culture," Doctorow concluded. Yet a year earlier PEN members—Sontag and Mailer included—had gone to Paris on a junket paid for and organized by the French Minister of Culture. PEN had also invited Omar Cabezas, a Nicaraguan minister of state in charge of prisons, and a government censor. He was an author, to be sure, having published *Fire from the Mountain,* a memoir of his radical student and Sandinista days.

Conservative critic Roger Kimball deplored the "moral equivalence" between governments implied in Doctorow's editorial. Kimball suggested that the International PEN conference theme likewise implied moral equivalence by indicating that the writer's imagination was in "radical conflict" with the imagination of the state "all over the world." In other words, it was made to seem that the situation for writers in Moscow was the same as that for writers living in New York. In practice, however, PEN members like Sontag, Mailer, and Doctorow did make distinctions between governments, and they were not averse to seeking money and support from the state. Kimball pointed out that part of the funding for the International PEN conference had come from the National Endowment for the Arts.

Old PEN hands like Donald Barthelme and Richard Howard fell into line, promoting the piquant program theme, as did Karen Kennerly, the executive director and behind-the-scenes fixer. Mailer had erred in not consulting the PEN board before inviting Shultz. There was a petition signed by prominent PEN members (including Sontag) taking the Doctorow line and protesting Shultz's appearance. But the board members (including Vice President Sontag) did not rescind the invitation, and Kennerly pointed out to the press that it had been standard practice at International PEN meetings in other countries for a government official from the host country to make a speech of welcome.

Few accounts of the contentious days that followed were as sensible as writer Richard Stern's retrospective wrap-up: "That PEN is itself an organization and, therefore, falls into the same kind of official behavior and language its charter rejects would be another development of this New York week which amused and dismayed some of the participants." Until the blowup over Shultz, Mailer had been, in Stern's words, an "efficient, engaging, and diplomatic bureaucrat." What is more, Sontag and company had been quite willing to follow his lead. Yet each time Mailer was challenged at the congress, Sontag took the part of the opposition, although she never took the lead. Her tack suited the conflicted situation well. PEN was evolving into a big-time organization that would soon see the need to elect a woman as its president. That woman must be one perceived to have power and to have sided with the insurgents, but—unlike Grace Paley and the more vociferous protestors—must not have made a spectacle of herself. Sontag would sign their petitions, but she would also take the high ground, expressing the wish that writers would say less about politics and more about literature.

When writers were not blaming each other, they were lavishly praising each other. As Stern noticed, Sontag spread her favors "like a Commissar." To the press, Sontag declared: "I feel emotionally connected with writers everywhere." She did allow herself a peevish moment, though, when she heard John Updike say that "government money in the arts can only deflect artists from their responsibility to find an authentic market for their products." An easy opinion to have, Sontag said, "if you'd signed a contract in your twenties with *The New Yorker*."

Stern sat next to Sontag and watched her as they awaited Shultz's arrival to speak in the grand South Reading Room of the New York Public Library. She gestured toward two men who Stern could see "patrolling the book stacks above the dais." Sontag said, "Look at the goons." They were, of course, part of Shultz's security detail, the kind of protection typically attached to high government officials, but somehow they seemed especially sinister to Sontag.

The writers who booed and hissed Shultz were surely bothered by his administration's policies, but they were also angry at having been kept waiting outside in the cold while security arrangements were checked. And they were upset because someone like Shultz had the stage. After all, as Stern confessed, writers came to congresses "to be seen as well as to see each other, to make as well as take impressions."

In the event, Shultz gave a sensible speech appropriate to the occasion. Stern and many other commentators, including Mailer, agreed that the secretary of state had acquitted himself well. Shultz provoked laughter when he cited Mailer's invitation "as another shining example of that charitable spirit for which New York literary circles have long been famous." Mailer, in his turn, denounced the protestors as "puritanical leftists."

Shultz's gentle, good-humored gibe alluded to a vision of the New York literary life that others expressed with much more hostility. Novelist James Purdy, for example, had contemptuously rejected an invitation to become a PEN member, writing a letter (June 16, 1978) to the admissions committee denouncing the *New York Times* and the *New York Review of Books* for propagating a literary establishment rife with cronyism and time-servers. Such writers and editors, who also dominated PEN, constituted an "incestuous closeted perpetual cocktail party."

They abused their power, while at the same time wringing their hands about the persecution of foreign writers and injustice abroad. Purdy would no more join PEN than a "Southern Black would reconsider and join the Klan." The late Anthony Lukas, a president of the Authors Guild, once told a PEN board member that PEN could not be taken seriously: it had the air of the bogus about it.

A more measured but no less damning view of the membership who scorned Shultz comes from novelist George Garrett:

> Most of the writers (practically anybody you have ever heard of) are involved in a close symbiotic relationship, cozy you might say, with the publishing world. Without the acquiescence and tacit support of the writers (especially the most successful ones), the whole creaky system might collapse. They can fool you, though, the writers. Take PEN for example, forever using our dues to battle against some form of overt censorship here and there, against racial separation and segregation in South Africa if not, say, Kenya or Ghana, firmly committed against torture everywhere in the world except in certain Eastern Bloc nations, and mostly keeping their own mouths tight shut about the inequities and injustices, trivial and profound, perpetuated on the American public by the same folks who give writers their advances against royalties and publish their books. Whatever the price is, it doesn't include a vow of silence or even very much self-sacrifice.

PEN members have tried to reform this self-serving system. Protests against PEN's undemocratic nature have been launched, including critic Seymour Krim's statement to the *PEN Newsletter* (May 30, 1979) reporting "griping in the ranks by writers too shy to make waves. The consensus seems to be this: We have to find a more democratic way to elect Presidents." He castigated a PEN rife with elitism; the rank and file had no voice. Of course, changes in bylaws got made, there was a show of reform, but PEN still is run more like an autocracy than a democracy.

In any event, Israeli novelist Amos Oz and Peruvian novelist Mario Vargas Llosa later addressed Shultz's most important point, which was akin to Kimball's concern about moral equivalence: "To declare one's alienation without distinction is to abdicate judgement, analysis, differentiation, wisdom. It is to risk marginality and estrangement from the roots of traditional and community life that nourish the creative imagination. It can be a recipe for irrelevance." In blunter words, writers may have good reason to feel alienated from the state, from their society, but not all societies and states are the same, and to pretend otherwise leads to estrangement from the real world. Oz noted the "gulf" between the simplistic way writers were speaking at the congress and the complexity of their writing. "Some states are almost fair, some are bad, some are lethal," Oz stated. To think that the issue lay only between the writer and the state was bogus, he concluded:

> The tragedy of history is not the perpetual hopeless clash between saintly individuals and diabolical establishments but rather the perpetual clash between the relatively decent societies and the bloody ones. To be more precise: the perpetual cowardice of relatively decent societies whenever they confront the ruthlessness of the oppressive ones.

Oz's point here contrasts with Sontag's quasi-Carlylean hero worship of literary and political figures, which has shifted from Ho and Fidel and Che to leaders like Václav Havel.

Sontag said little as she threaded through the second major controversy of the New York congress: the excoriation of Norman Mailer for failing to invite enough women writers as panelists. Only 20 of 117 speakers were female. "We're absolutely amazed over the situation," Grace Paley told the press. Mailer, author of *The Prisoner of Sex* (a rebuttal of his feminist foes) did nothing to win his critics over by stating:

> Since the formulation of the panels is reasonably intellectual, there are not that many women, like Susan Sontag, who are intellectuals first, poets and novelists, second. More men are intellectuals first, so there was a certain natural tendency to pick more men than women.

Nadine Gordimer, Erica Jong, and Margaret Atwood, to mention three of the most prominent writers to take issue with such statements, lined up against Mailer. He countered by reading a list of 24 distinguished women writers who had decided not to attend the congress. He was not going to replace them with less distinguished women. Gay Talese defended Mailer, noting that women had been involved in the planning of the congress and had to share the blame for the imbalances. Paley confessed to having been inattentive. Joyce Carol Oates refused to sign the petition indicting Mailer. "I really agree with you," she told the protestors, "but it's very complicated, and Norman's having such a difficult time that he's been in a difficult state all week. He worked very hard on this Congress, and I just can't sign." Mailer was especially angry with Susan Sontag. She had been on the PEN program committee. Why hadn't she just picked up a phone earlier and voiced her complaints?

Women journalists watched her closely, aware that her appearance commanded as much attention as what she did. Rhoda Koenig tracked her in "tweed trousers and boots, wearing an unbuttoned shirt over a buttoned one or a turtleneck, and one day adding a quilted leather vest and an untied scarf." Leslie Hanscomb of *Newsday* marveled at the one moment she saw Sontag upstaged by Toni Morrison. Sontag, after all, seemed

most to have been formed by nature to attend cultural congresses. She is mistress of the art of saying nothing in particular, but saying it with such gravity that the listener feels like writing it down and taking it home for study. She is also a striking-looking woman with a head of black hair in which one dramatically placed lock frames the side of her face with a streak of stark white. When she sits on a speakers' panel, it is hard to look at anybody else.

But then Morrison showed up on a cold winter day, the "only other woman on the patriarchal panel," wearing a

Caribbean sunshade of woven straw with a brim as big as an umbrella. Late in the program, when she had milked full effect for this arresting lid, she took it off, disclosing a kerchief of many colors as eye-catching as the hat. For once, it was possible to look away from Susan Sontag.

Norman Mailer deemed the PEN congress a failure, but he served out his presidency quietly and remained on the board as a vice president when novelist Hortense Calisher became PEN's next president in June

1986. Choosing a woman seemed imperative after the congress ruckus.
But Calisher, like other PEN presidents, ruled through an inner circle.
When she tried to make her mark on the organization, she confronted the
entrenched executive director, Karen Kennerly. Calisher departed within the year, off to a "better date," as one former board member said,
becoming president of the prestigious American Academy of Arts and
Letters.

The identity of the next PEN president seemed a foregone conclusion. Her name had been on the list of possible presidents for years. Her
election occurred without notable opposition, her elevation virtually an
entitlement. Sontag's presidency has received positive reviews inside
and out of PEN, even from those who do not care for her style. Asked to
comment on Sontag's performance in office, Norman Mailer would only
say—through the telephonic filter of his faithful assistant, Judith
McNally—"Susan Sontag was a good president." One board member
complained that she hogged the microphone, constantly replying to
board members and restating what they had said. But as another board
member counters, what is unique about that? PEN is hard on its presidents, Sidney Offit, a longtime member, observes, and he is thinking not
only of Mailer. Another former PEN president, Muriel Rukeyser, found
the job unnerving. Writers found it easy to pick apart arguments, suggestions, initiatives. A writers' organization, a former PEN board member remarks, is a contradiction in terms—"It's like herding cats." A
president like Rukeyser could be reduced to tears. After all, presiding
over PEN does not add one cubit to a writer's stature qua writer.

The timing has to be right for a person like Susan Sontag to accept
the presidency, as Offit, who has seen many PEN presidents in action,
points out. The writer has to have finished a book, be between books, or
in some way be susceptible, just then, to taking the lead. In Sontag's
case, it was an unsettled period when she was writing prefaces for other
authors' books, directing plays, and fitfully working at novels that never
quite jelled.

Calisher, brought in to be a healer, proved unable to stem the con-
tentiousness stirred up by the New York congress. For one thing, the lib-
ertarian-egalitarian wing of PEN loathed the organization's new ties to its
big-money financial backers. Most writers, by definition, elect careers at
a distance from the moneyed world and the market economy that Mailer
had introduced to PEN. PEN had been a small organization precisely

because it drew money largely from writers who did not have that much to give. This was not perceived as a failing. Indeed, to the young Susan Sontag, shabbiness was the writer's badge of honor.

Still, Sontag respected money and its power. When she complained to Edmund White about a couple of nobodies he had had to dinner, he lied and told her they were quite rich. "Oh, I see," she said with an understanding nod. She enjoyed luxury—first-class air tickets and the like when she traveled—when others paid for it. It seemed her due precisely because she had chosen to live abstemiously and not grub in the muck for dollars. Offit wondered how the Sontag he first met—the one who wanted literary discussions to take place over kegs of beer—would adjust to a PEN that now had rich patrons like Saul and Gayfryd Steinberg. They had hosted one of the bigger PEN parties at the 1986 International Congress. The event was covered extensively in the press. Most accounts humorously noted that PEN members, thinking that they were in artist Saul Steinberg's apartment, wondered how he could afford such expensive furnishings, old-master paintings, and so on. By way of contrast, Offit watched as Sontag graciously cultivated the Steinbergs. She did it as a matter of course, Offit thought, as a way of paying the bills.

"It was very difficult for members to start moralizing in front of Susan Sontag," Offit observes. Even staunchly leftist writers such as E. L. Doctorow accorded Sontag great respect. "To know how to reach an accommodation without compromise is an art," says Offit, who describes a pragmatic, grounded person, one whom he could call on for sensible advice. What especially surprised him, though, was Sontag's unpredictability and independence: he never felt confident that he could gauge her opinion of individual PEN members. She had no line or position she was protecting. He remembered a Sontag who was quite willing to listen, not lecture—and in his experience (thirty-five years at PEN), writers had trouble doing the former. She had an "institutional sense of respect," hearing out individuals whom, Offit was certain, she had little use for as writers. Her opinions, he recalls, were delivered without didacticism.

Sontag did believe in strong leadership and in holding together a chaotic organization like PEN by supporting its administrators. At a February 18, 1987, board meeting during Hortense Calisher's regime, she "questioned the rights of committees to discuss the extent of power

of the executive director [Karen Kennerly]." In office, Sontag commanded not only respect but fealty. Offit, who admits he rarely sees the negative sides of people, thought Sontag and Karen Kennerly got along well.
"Karen was the force who really ran PEN," Offit points out. Other PEN
members saw considerable tension between these two women. Indeed,
even a casual visitor to PEN during Kennerly's long tenure would note
her birdlike flitting from one board member to another as she carefully
tended her brood. She outlasted personalities as diverse as Bernard
Malamud, Mailer, and Sontag.

As early as March 1987, the PEN board knew that Sontag would
be taking over as president, although European commitments prevented
her from assuming office until June. She attended monthly board meetings assiduously in the period leading up to her presidency. Two major
issues confronted the board: the impending international meeting in
Korea, and a movement to make PEN more democratic. At the meeting of
March 18, 1987, board member Ted Solotaroff, the renowned editor of
American Review, where Sontag had published some of her fiction, "worried that the current leadership increasingly has the look of a Politburo."
But little was done to address his concerns. In the previous fifteen years
PEN had become a much larger organization. It now held an "indispens-
able Benefit Dinner" each year to solicit funds from the moneyed class.
The first one Sontag would preside over would be at the Hotel Pierre.

Sontag supported PEN's campaign to recruit membership among
minorities, but apparently reserved comment in contentious discussions
about rotating board membership to alleviate the "perception of cronyism." She saved most of her energies at board meetings for the upcom-
ing PEN congress in Seoul, South Korea. The country had a poor human
rights record, had imprisoned writers, and was notorious for pirating
American books. At the September 16, 1987, board meeting, Sontag,
now president, called the Korean congress a "complicated issue." If
PEN could play a positive role—use its meeting as a form of leverage to
free writers in prison and to foment debate in the country— then, on balance, the American Center should send representatives. In addition, she
liked the idea of addressing the "whole spectrum of Korean literature,"
but she worried that there might not be time enough to acquire the expertise to do it.

At the November 2, 1987, board meeting, the American Center was still debating the appropriateness of attending the Korean congress (now set to run from August 28 to September 2, 1988). Sontag decided to postpone a decision on Korea until the December meeting. In the meantime, the November *PEN Newsletter* carried a boxed editorial headlined "Seoul: 1988" suggesting the original decision to hold an international congress there (taken in June 1986 at the forty-eighth congress in Hamburg) had been hastily approved. At the May meeting of International PEN in Lugano, the American Center fought to have the Korean venue changed. Only the Scandinavian centers, the Australian (Melbourne) Center, the Center of the German Democratic Republic, and the four Yugoslav centers joined the protest, which caused (although this was not reported in the board minutes or in the newsletter) considerable resentment within the ranks of International PEN.

The American Center singled out a Korean PEN delegate who had made disingenuous representations about censorship and the persecution of writers in that country. Nevertheless, American PEN decided to attend the Korean meeting in part because Seoul was hosting the Olympics just before the congress. PEN would have a world stage on which to perform its duty, which the newsletter editorial (written by Sontag) proclaimed "will not be in a passive spirit. We will plan receptions and meetings with writers who represent the whole spectrum of literary activity in Korea," and "express our support for the forces in South Korea struggling to defend the freedom of literary expression."

In carrying out this mission to Korea, Sontag would need help. She announced to the PEN board that she would be taking David with her. One board member questioned her decision. Why David? The Koreans had asked for him, she replied. Another board member wondered: Did Sontag actually believe this fantasy of hers? He could not see how else she could brazen it out. But there it was. David did go. He was mentioned in press reports, but he did not sign his name to the January 1989 *PEN Newsletter* account of the contentious Korean meeting. Instead he wrote an article about it and published his piece, in which he quotes his mother favorably, in the December 1988 issue of Andy Warhol's *Interview* magazine. D. D. Guttenplan of *Newsday* ("Interview with Andy," January 3, 1989) asked the magazine editor why she had not identified Rieff as Sontag's son. "You think he should have mentioned it," Shelly Wanger replied. "Well, it's my fault, because I thought people would know. But you're probably right."

Along with David, Sontag took Karen Kennerly, Faith Sale, cochairwoman of the freedom-to-write committee and executive editor at Putnam, and the distinguished poet Robert Hass. The group's first salvo was printed in the *New York Times* on August 24, 1988. In "PEN's Larger Purpose," Herbert Mitgang reported that American PEN would give their own party honoring jailed writers and publishers. "Our aim is to persuade the Government to free them as a good-will gesture toward the PEN congress," Kennerly explained. The *Times* carried an Associated Press dispatch on August 31 quoting Sontag at the party: "To be at this gathering while our colleagues sit in prison, some of them ill, all of them, ironically, deprived of pen and paper, is a profound disappointment and morally troubling to many of us." The party, attended by writers from seven other countries, "allows us to express our admiration and support for the courage of the democratic movements in Korea at the same time that we are deliberating over the problems and literary concerns of writers all around the globe," Sontag said. The dispatch did not ask why only seven countries were represented at the party.

The January 1989 *PEN Newsletter* reported "there was throughout the week bitter division inside P.E.N. about how to act." It was a classic dilemma, former PEN board member Victor Navasky pointed out later. Do you help persecuted writers by calling the world's attention to their plight, or do such actions merely antagonize their jailers, making it worse for the very people you want to help? It is a tough call. Francis King, International PEN president, opted for the language of diplomacy, thus angering the American PEN delegation, which objected to phrases like "*extraordinary* graciousness," which King had used to describe PEN's treatment by the Korean government. The Americans rejected what they considered King's submissiveness, and they were not swayed by his report that "we have been permitted historic visits inside Korean prisons. No outside organization has *ever* been allowed inside Korean prisons before."

The American delegation's report in the January 1989 *PEN Newsletter* ridiculed King's concerns about their statements to the press, especially his anger over Karen Kennerly's conduct: he thought it absurd that she had arrived two weeks early in order to "perform the heroic

task" of setting up that American Center party honoring persecuted writers and publishers. Sontag had a press conference as soon as she
reached Kimpo airport—"unanticipated" is the *PEN Newsletter*'s word
for it—but King and other International PEN leaders regarded her
entrance as part of an "American media blitz." Rejecting the idea of
diplomacy out of hand as only a type of hypocrisy, the American delegation intoned: "When P.E.N. officials started talking about the *honor* of
being allowed to visit writers in jail, something has gone very wrong."

In spite of its high moral tone, the American delegation conceded:
"No one, of course, knew with any certainly how much power P.E.N.
actually had either to embarrass or to persuade." King deplored Sontag's
bad manners and her hunger for publicity. She countered that she did not
"regard herself as a house guest but as a writer at an international con-
vocation of writers." Other PEN leaders tried to mediate, saying the
Americans "no doubt meant well." Finding the tide of the meeting
against them, the American delegation scorned arguments such as the
suggestion that the Koreans needed a little room to maneuver, and that
humiliating them would serve no purpose. Other PEN members simply
found the Americans insufferable and bullying. The PEN American
Center, on the other hand, felt bulldozed, taking comfort only in the
meetings about imprisoned writers and in an event attended by hundreds
of university students: "The atmosphere was pretty much that of an
American college at the height of the civil rights and antiwar movements," the American delegation reported in the January 1989 *PEN
Newsletter:* "There was a solemn and rather sweet sense of justice and
moral clarity in the air that, after a week at the Sheraton Walker Hill, was
more pleasant to bask in than it was easy to identify with."

The American delegation accused International PEN leaders of
behaving "like diplomats instead of writers," "tend[ing] to value the
organization more than its purpose." The purpose of PEN was to take
"principled stands," and the American Center would just have to "insist
on principle" and continue to "seem confrontational at Congresses,"
wrote Robert Hass and Faith Sale, the official delegates of the PEN
American Center.

Francis King found it impossible to take Susan Sontag seriously. She
sat in King's hotel room, treating him and other writers to accounts of her
precocious childhood, in which she had taught herself French at a tender age—her talk punctuated by David's frequent trips to King's mini-

bar, during which he took whatever he pleased without even a "May I?" Sontag's pontificating and grandstanding made a farce of PEN, King thought. Indeed, he put her and David into a novel, *Visiting Cards*. There she appears as Margaretta, proud of her childhood reading of Proust. She sweeps into the World Association of Authors (WAA) international conference complete with her own "little coterie" to bedevil Amos Kingsley, WAA's president. David becomes Margaretta's "dear little Helga," who ransacks Kingsley's minibar while Margaretta declaims how "obscene" it is to be having parties while there are writers starving in prison. Some of Margaretta's lines are virtually straight out of the January 1989 *PEN Newsletter:* "Where principles are concerned, courtesy is irrelevant." Her smug superiority is too much for Kingsley:

> You come here. You demand a first-class ticket for yourself, although every other delegate is content to have an economy one. You then demand a ticket for your daughter, who isn't even a member of WAA. You accept another bedroom for her. And then you deliberately set about doing precisely the opposite of what your hosts ask you to do. You and your friends are like—like a pack of stray dogs who leave their visiting cards on the doorstep of the family kind enough to take them in and feed them.

Catching the Sontag pitch perfectly, King has Margaretta call Amos's behavior "extremely vulgar."

Amos Kingsley, no paragon, includes himself in an indictment of WAA writers who show, at best, a "semi-honesty." They feel "genuine indignation and anger" at the degradation of other writers, Amos acknowledges, but "there is also far too much self-righteousness—and with it, far too much sense of moral superiority and far too much moral indignation. . . . It's very nice—very comforting to one's ego—very sustaining to one's *amour propre*—to pass resolutions condemning this or that outrage and demanding this or that action."

It is also easier to have these feelings abroad, where so much more seems to be at stake for writers. At home, PEN shied away from the internal debate and self-examination that Ted Solotaroff had urged. On December 3, 1987, for example, gay writer and activist Larry Kramer sent an angry letter to President Susan Sontag. PEN, he charged, had an "intolerable attitude to anything gay." It still had not said "boo about

AIDS." The *PEN Newsletter* had canvassed every cause except the disease that was devastating a whole generation of writers. PEN was not even as current as the conventional *New York Times*. No benefits, no protests, nothing really. "I'm ashamed of the whole lot of your membership—which contains not a few gay and lesbian writers, many openly so." Why did PEN with all its awards and campaigns refuse to acknowledge the suffering of its gay writers as well as their contributions to literature?

Sontag did not reply. Kramer asked that his letter be published in the *PEN Newsletter*. It was not. John Morrone, a PEN staff member, thought Kramer's charges "preposterous," but he realized that "Larry isn't someone who will go away if you ignore him." And Morrone had to admit that PEN had responded positively to angry voices such as June Jordan's concerning the lack of minority representation. Morrone outlined his concerns in a letter (December 10, 1987) to Gregory Kolovakos, a gay writer active in PEN. Perhaps Kolovakos could mollify Kramer by talking up plans that were in the works to benefit gay and lesbian writers.

On December 16 Kolovakos wrote Kramer as a member of the PEN AIDS benefit committee and as a gay man responding to a gay man. It seemed unfair to single out PEN, Kolovakos argued, when society at large had been slow to respond to AIDS. How could Kramer expect united action in an "atomized artistic world" in which writers were so highly individualistic? Kolovakos did not defend liberals or gays in power who refused to speak out. But PEN had included him as an openly gay writer at its public events, and the real enemy, anyway, was the federal government and institutions like the Catholic Church. Some gays who had remained silent were also the enemy. There is no record in the available PEN archives of a Kramer reply to Kolovakos. Clearly, however, Kramer expected a high standard of conduct from an organization that lectured governments here and abroad about censorship.

It was simply far easier to champion other important causes less close to home. Thus in the spring of 1988, Sontag, acting as president of PEN, filed a friend-of-the court brief supporting a motion for summary judgment brought by author Peter Matthiessen and his publisher, Viking. The former governor of South Dakota, William J. Janklow, was suing them for libeling him in *In the Spirit of Crazy Horse*. Sontag, along with Kurt Vonnegut, John Irving, Alfred Kazin, and William Styron, argued that the libel action should be dismissed because its true intent was to "squelch the writing of history and contemporary views." The group contended that the litigation posed a "threat to the intellectual growth of our society." Such costly lawsuits would force publishers to turn away books on controversial subjects. Sontag and the others went even further, promoting the kind of bold freedom to interpret that biographies and histories of contemporary individuals and events require if writers are to make their contribution to society:

> At some point, if an author is deprived of the right to delve into controversial and unknowable material and to repeat caustic and harsh opinions and to draw conclusions to which he is led by instinct rather than certainty, then the book the author envisions cannot be written and will not be written.
>
> As writers of thought and philosophy, we fear the possibility of being financially ruined or otherwise completely consumed in litigation for expressing impressions and insights into people and events.

If Matthiessen were to face several more years of litigation, then no author could "feel safe in writing nonfiction concerning his perspective on contemporary history and public figures," the writers' brief concluded.

Sontag's legacy to PEN has been her unwavering defense of the writer's right to speak out about controversial issues and personalities, a legacy that faced its greatest challenge on February 18, 1989, when the *Washington Post* reported: "Fear has swept the North American literary and publishing establishment in the wake of Ayatollah Ruhollah Khomeini's 'death sentence' on novelist Salman Rushdie, author of *The Satanic Verses.*" Canada had barred new imports of the novel. Barnes & Noble, B. Dalton, and Coles Books in Canada announced they would not display the book. Reporters Lloyd Grove and Charles Trueheart discovered that a "host of normally loquacious American writers have fallen uncharacteristically mum when asked in recent days to appear on television to defend Rushdie's right to publish." Susan Sontag headed their list of those willing publicly to condemn the *fatwa* pronounced on a writer who had a bounty of five million dollars on his head for having, in Khomeini's view, blasphemed Islam and its prophet Muhammad.

Leon Wieseltier, literary editor of *The New Republic*, and William Styron condemned the cowardly writers. John Updike remarked in a press interview: "If we can't stand up on this issue and be counted, is our blessed freedom of speech worth a pin?" Gay Talese stated that "the character of American writers is very much on the line at this moment, and it looks like many of them lack the courage of the convictions they so often and so loudly espouse." Karen Kennerly took a more charitable line: "I think it's because they were stunned and didn't know what would be good for Rushdie." ABC's "Good Morning America" could not get Norman Mailer and Arthur Miller to appear on the topic. "I'm astonished," Grove and Trueheart quoted Sontag as saying:

> I have to assume that people are really intimidated. This kind of intimidation has a very strong chance of being successful. We feel superior, in our imagination, to those Germans who in 1933 and 1934 didn't protest when their Jewish colleagues were being fired or dragged off in the middle of the night to camps. It's clear that the threat of violence by people perceived as fanatics is very terrifying. . . . But we have to be brave.

Sontag announced that PEN planned to run advertisements in major newspapers around the world protesting Rushdie's plight. It would be holding a mass meeting in Manhattan.

With Sontag in the lead, Talese, Wieseltier, Styron, and a few other writers continued speaking out. Soon Mailer and others came out more visibly against the *fatwa*. Bookstores restocked the novel and President Bush issued a rebuke (albeit quite mild) to Iran's leader. The sequence of events, Sontag said, had been "educational." Writers had admitted to her they were scared. She sympathized with their feelings, if not with their actions. "We're not talking about people picketing here. We're talking about assassination." She did not know, of course, what the consequences of the writers' protest might be, but she wondered: "What if the Iranians change the decree and add his defenders to the death sentence on Rushdie and his publishers?" Later two bookstores in Berkeley, California, were firebombed, Rushdie's Japanese translator was murdered, his Italian translator wounded in a knife attack, and his Norwegian publisher shot.

As PEN president, Sontag cabled President Bush urging him to "take the necessary steps to protect American citizens in the free and unintimidated exercise of their constitutional rights." She called Khomeini's action "censorship by terror, and a fear that it has engendered, strikes not only at writers, publishers and booksellers, but finally at libraries, schools and the entire basis of the U.S. as a literate, free country." On February 22 Sontag addressed an audience of several hundred in a SoHo loft who had come, in her words, "to show a little civic fortitude under intimidation."

Many in PEN thought Sontag's unhesitating support of Rushdie constituted her finest moment. She noted that Rushdie was her friend as well as a writer in need. Showing fear now would mean "all of our institutions are hijacked." This was not about one persecuted writer, she told the audience; "this is an act of terrorism against the life of the mind." Sontag's call for a wider protest was answered by writers' rallies in Boston, Washington, Chicago, Minneapolis, and San Francisco. A Boston bookstore pledged that it would give the profits from the sale of Rushdie's novel to PEN. Screen Actors Guild president Barry Gordon sent Sontag a letter applauding PEN. "Susan Sontag was ubiquitous" in the Rushdie defense campaign, reported Richard Cohen of the *St. Louis Post-Dispatch*.

Nearly a month later Sontag appeared before a U.S. Senate subcommittee on terrorism, testifying: "Incredibly, at no point in this affair has the president, the State Department or anyone in the government actually issued a formal statement. Every utterance on the Rushdie matter—and there have been few—has been made in the form of a response to questions from the news media." Yet the *fatwa* was sure to have a "chilling effect" on the publication of controversial books. What publisher would take the risk if the U.S. government did not "stand up to Iran." She added, "Please do what you can to further the awareness—in yourselves, in the Executive Branch, and in your constituents—that our integrity as a nation is as endangered by an attack on a writer as on an oil tanker." Senator Patrick Moynihan had a question for her: "How much violence are you prepared to countenance in response to violence?" In other words, what should be the practical effect of her fighting words? "If you are asking do I think we should go to war with Iran over this affair, I do not," Sontag replied.

Although Sontag continued to receive an admiring press, Charles

Krauthammer concluded: "Ah, courage. Thumbing your nose at the imam from a Soho loft is indeed a thrill. But only among the bored and vain can it pass for heroism." But Richard Cohen argued in response: "Contempt for intellectuals is as American as apple pie and a staple of conservative politics."

Organizations seek out figures who command public attention in their own right. How could PEN not be pleased with a leader who acted on the organization's principles and made them manifest to the world at large?

Pitching Susan Sontag 24

1986–1989

During her busy and high-profile PEN presidency, Susan Sontag continued to write. She worked intermittently on a book about Japan. She continued to publish articles and stories in the *London Review of Books* and *The New Yorker* which added little to her stature as a writer but which helped to pay the rent. She struggled with another novel, "The Western Half," concerned with Polish and Soviet émigrés. "It's not working," she told Margaria Fichtner (*Miami Herald*, February 19, 1989):

> I think maybe I worked on it too long without the right amount of concentration. I would work for a few months and break it off and do something else, and then I would go back to it six months later. I think you have to paint with a wet brush. You have to move forward and stay with it, and I haven't had that kind of time for the simple reason that I had to make a living. To take two years off and just write a novel, how am I going to support myself?

Eight months later Sontag told *Time* interviewer Richard Lacayo

(October 24, 1988) that the novel was almost completed, yet she later abandoned it. Sontag then began another novel, *The Volcano Lover*, set in eighteenth-century Naples. She kept pace with a hectic travel and lecture schedule.

In late 1986 Sontag served on the film festival jury at the East-West Center of the University of Hawaii. She had been invited by Jeanette Paulson, a film festival organizer, who wrote directly to Sontag's home address at the urging of a mutual friend, film critic Donald Ritchie, who had a high opinion of the festival. Paulson remembers how easy Sontag was to talk to. Sontag seemed so interested in other people and not at all egotistical. She was a refreshing change from some of the other jury members with big names. Paulson's impressions, she remembers, were shared by the jury (comprising a Filipino, a Japanese, an Australian, and an Indian judge), which enthusiastically elected Sontag chairman. Sontag proved to be not only well liked but a good organizer, a superb discussion leader, an articulate spokesman for the jury, and an energetic participant in public events. Paulson later received the most personal and gracious letters from Sontag, along with an autographed book. Sontag was very excited about new Asian film and would sometimes write to Paulson with recommendations for the festival. They shared a belief that film should be accessible to everyone, and Paulson believes Sontag liked the fact that the festival was free and open to the public.

In early December 1986 (the festival ran from November 30 to December 6), a distraught Sontag had to withdraw from the final events. Mildred Sontag had suddenly taken ill and died. Nat would die in another year.

On December 21, 1987, a little over a year after her mother's death, Sontag published "Pilgrimage," her only memoir, in *The New Yorker*. It is a dark portrait of her Southern California years that belittles her stepfather while making her mother seem aloof. The loving Susan Sontag who liked to speak fondly of her mother on her visits to Hawaii does not appear in "Pilgrimage." She keeps her more complicated feelings about her mother to herself, concentrating instead on her sense of isolation and on the few friends who shared her intellectual and aesthetic interests. In that respect, the memoir seems faithful to Sontag's experience.

As in Sontag's other brief reminiscences in interviews, her sister Judith seems almost not to exist. After "Pilgrimage," Sontag thought she might further explore autobiography. Thus far she has not, except for fleeting references to her life that appear in the preface to her new novel, *In America*.

"Pilgrimage" did not so much mark a change in Sontag's presentation of herself as it confirmed her familiar posture: she remained publicly visible and available, while at the same time stressing her aloofness and desire to be left alone. Journalist Helen Benedict, assigned to do a profile of Sontag in the summer of 1988, remarked that "getting to meet her is a bit like trying to meet Joan of Arc on her day off." FSG requested Benedict's press clips, and even after the screening she was told, "Oh, I don't know when we'll fit you in. . . . Oh, she'll never let you into her apartment." Put through her paces, Benedict felt tricked when she easily got Sontag on the phone and set up the interview. "I don't know what they think my life is like," an irritable Sontag said to Benedict. "All I do is sit in my hot apartment all day and write." Benedict worked hard to earn a wary Sontag's approval. "She really liked my Brodsky piece," said Benedict, who could tell Sontag was relieved that she had not "let an idiot into her house who would ask stupid questions and trivialize things. I'd never been tested like that before." But Sontag warmed to her, Benedict said. "One thing that I really appreciated was that unlike some of my other interviewees she was interested in who I was." While it was a serious interview, they had their share of giggles together. And to think, Benedict remembered, that "all the people at Farrar, Straus made her sound like a dragon."

The Benedict profile showcased Sontag's very public irritation about being treated like a public figure. "Some people are awkward with me," Sontag told Benedict. "When they come up to me and say, 'I admire your work, but you intimidate me,' I feel as if I've been slapped in the face. It's such an act of hostility." Yet later in the interview Benedict reports that Sharon DeLano, a New York editor close to both Sontag and her son, declared that "Susan is fierce."

Like a good many reporters, Benedict wanted to get some perspective on a Sontag who had spent nearly twenty-five years in the public eye. She saw a woman thicker around the hips who joked about too many trips to the refrigerator. Sontag looked pale and tired as well as tall and strong, her somber demeanor suddenly breaking into a big "goofy" smile. These lighter moments relieved Sontag of about twenty of her years, so that Benedict could glimpse the young woman writer Herbert Mitgang had once called a "literary pinup." But the notion of being in vogue brought a petulant response from Benedict's subject:

> I wrote about some things no one else was writing about. Then people came along and said what I'd done was trendy. And this accusation is one of the reasons I rarely write about contemporary things anymore. I thought I was performing a public service, sharing the pleasure of discovering things, but if I'm going to be accused of being trendy, to hell with it.

Yet Sontag could not gainsay her image, disclosing that she dyed her graying hair black except for her signature streak of white. Benedict had been terrified to ask Sontag that question about her hair, although her editors insisted she do so. Sontag laughed. "She thought it was a funny question, and it elicited this really very informative answer," Benedict said.

Sontag made another concession to the marketplace. She acquired high-flying agent Andrew Wylie, with Roger Straus's blessing. In his seventies then, Straus would soon sell his firm to Holtzbrinck, acknowledging the inevitable: the virtual demise of independent publishing in New York. Straus would remain in charge of FSG and as close as ever to Sontag, but he realized that sooner or later she would need a younger, well-placed champion. In a world where huge multinational conglomerates control publishing companies, and where editors move peripatetically from firm to firm, making it difficult to maintain an author-editor alliance, a superagent like Wylie has enormous leverage.

And of course Sontag had her own reasons for choosing Wylie, telling *Miami Herald* reporter Margaria Fichtner: "I've decided to pay a little more attention to what happens to my books. Really I think I was living on the moon or the 19th century." Before Wylie, Sontag felt like the "only writer in America who didn't have" an agent:

> I was really pretending as if I were some not-for-profit foundation, which is fine if you have a private income but not so fine if you have no money but what you earn yourself and no resources and no family

to help out. . . . I don't want to be this totally undefended person who just says, "Oh, just give me a contract; I'll sign it and not read it."

By the late 1980s Andrew Wylie had acquired a menacing moniker: "the Jackal." Agent Mort Janklow stated the case memorably: "Wylie is to the literary business what Roy Cohn was to the legal business." Agents accused him of stealing their clients. An angry Harriet Wasserman, who felt Wylie had poached on her twenty-five-year relationship with Saul Bellow, told Wylie: "You have more literary territory than Alexander the Great." Wylie lured novelist Martin Amis—up to then accustomed to modest advances—to his list and transformed a literary phenomenon into a hot commercial property. With an agent like Wylie, Sontag could secure a multibook contract and ensure a steady cash flow that would end her days of doing piecework. In the spring of 1988, just before becoming a Wylie author, she told an interviewer that she could not afford to travel much anymore: "The economy got way ahead of me. I'm not making any more money than I was making ten years ago, so I'm a lot poorer."

On February 24, 1989, Wylie announced in the press that he had arranged a lucrative four-book deal for Sontag with FSG and Anchor Books. Wylie had just begun a new phase of entrepreneurial activity. With a client inventory that included Salman Rushdie, Norman Mailer, Saul Bellow, Philip Roth, and many other mature as well as promising literary lights, he shifted from the expeditionary to the establishment mode. The press reported on Wylie's new position. Frank Bruni titled his article in the *New York Times Magazine* (August 11, 1996) "The Literary Agent as Zelig": "Andrew Wylie has turned a groupie's love of famous authors, an accountant's eye for the bottom line and a sprinter's sense of competition into a global enterprise." Even after factoring in magazine hyperbole, the match Straus made between Sontag and Wylie seems, in retrospect, inspired. The Zelig-like Wylie, an extravagant admirer of literary greatness, would become Sontag's marketplace alter ego. Wylie on Wylie sounds like the Susan Sontag of *Under the Sign of Saturn*, projecting herself into the lives of the writers she adores. For Rebecca Mead's profile, "Mister Pitch" (*New York*, August 5, 1996), Wylie obligingly stated:

I have a nature that is sort of adoptive. I don't have a very stable character of my own; I have a series of sort of borrowed personalities. So I think the reason why I can frequently represent someone successfully is, I am literally able not only to see the world from their perspective but actually to become them. So I know pretty accurately what they want because I have abandoned my former personality and climbed inside theirs. So if I spend a day and a half with Susan Sontag and you catch me at the end of the day, you'll swear it's Susan Sontag.

In late February 1989, just after Wylie had publicized Sontag's multibook contract, she made an appearance at Endicott Booksellers in Manhattan to speak about her new book, *AIDS and Its Metaphors*. Stuart Bernstein, in charge of the event, looked forward to meeting an author he had long admired. Bad weather delayed Sontag's appearance for about a half hour as the store filled up with an overflow crowd of about two hundred people, including three or four reporters and photographers. Bernstein was a little surprised at the presence of these journalists, who said someone had promised them front-row seats, because the store usually had trouble persuading the press to attend author talks. Jonathan Mandell of *Newsday* watched a testy Sontag field hostile questions. When a questioner doubted her contention that using metaphors to fight disease was so wrong, she snapped and said, "I don't understand what you're talking about."

After the talk, Bernstein escorted the author to a table near the front of the store to hold court and sign books for a long line of people. He stood by to monitor the supply of books and to make sure Sontag had no problems. In a very loud voice, she announced to Bernstein, "I considered canceling this reading because Endicott had canceled a reading by Salman Rushdie." Taken aback by Sontag's confrontational tone, Bernstein wondered why she had not called before and discussed her concern.

Bernstein recalls that Rushdie had been scheduled to read from *The Satanic Verses* well before the *fatwa*, and before the tremendous publicity over the threat to the First Amendment that his case exemplified— although there were already rumors of bomb threats at Viking Penguin, Rushdie's publisher. Endicott's owner, Encarnita V. Quinlan, had indeed decided that the independent bookstore, housed in a residential building, could not handle the security demands and the expense of such an event and presumed that the publisher would find a safer venue for its author.

Bernstein tried to be polite, feeling this was not the moment to engage in a debate, but Sontag went on, for perhaps ten minutes, making what seemed to him pompous statements, prefaced with, "As the president of PEN . . ." Interspersing this tirade were Sontag's repeated queries as to the commercial success of the event: "How many books do you think we sold? How many books do you think we sold?" Bernstein finally went to the back of the store to check sales figures, only to return to Sontag's table to find she had left without a word.

After Sontag left, Bernstein half expected to get some sort of apology or explanation from her—"I was having a bad night. . . ." Something. But there was nothing. He complained bitterly to FSG, and he remembers that the sales rep was not surprised at Sontag's actions. Bernstein was told that she had been sent to a coach to learn how to be an author on tour. Bernstein describes his encounter with her as a "life-changing experience," tempering his tendency to form idealized images of big cultural figures.

At just about this time, Brandon Larson began working at Susan Sontag's favorite bookstore, Books & Company. At their first meeting, he did not immediately recognize her. "May I help you?" he asked. She stared at him and asked in turn: "Who are you?" (She was used to dealing with Peter Philbrook, whose position Larson had just filled.) Taken aback, Larson suddenly realized he was addressing Susan Sontag. Her tone offended him. On subsequent visits to the bookstore Sontag seemed friendlier, and Larson concluded that her initial reaction to him reflected her way of coping with strangers who accosted her. Soon he began ordering books for her, and she enjoyed browsing the shelves and talking to him about authors. One book would lead her to another. It was like taking a course: "Have you read this? . . . And he was influenced by . . . You have to read this. . . ." The store lined its shelves with her enthusiasms, and the staff let her stay after closing time, still scanning the shelves.

Some mornings Sontag would come into the store cranky, in a rut. But Larson liked this aspect of her, this evidence of the drama of being a writer. Larson remembers Sontag coming into the store one morning saying, "God, I've been writing all night." It had been a hot summer. She would write and sweat, write and sweat, she declared. Writing had to be a "real physical thing for her," Larson believes. "It's not a cool word processing, you know, writing." Sontag made it seem a struggle, a physical, passionate affair.

The Way We Live 25 Now

1986-1995

On November 24, 1986, *The New Yorker* published Sontag's tour-de-force story "The Way We Live Now." It became an instant classic, reprinted at the beginning of *The Best American Short Stories, 1987,* selected by John Updike as one of the *Best American Short Stories of the Century* (1999), dramatized in performances across the country, and widely discussed in books and articles surveying the literary treatments of AIDS. Novelist David Leavitt found the story therapeutic, making him feel "less alone in my dread, and therefore brave enough to read more." The story "transcended horror and grief, and . . . was therefore redemptive, if not of AIDS itself, then at least of the processes by which people cope with it. . . . It offered a possibility of catharsis, and at that point catharsis was something we all badly needed."

Leavitt is referring to a time when contracting AIDS seemed an immediate death sentence, when artists such as Robert Mapplethorpe, suspecting they had AIDS, refused to be tested for the disease. Sontag saw that the stigma attached to AIDS made patients feel isolated and fearful, much as the cancer metaphor had earlier made society shun the ill and the ill shun society. (Mapplethorpe was finally diagnosed with

AIDS in the fall of 1986, about two months before Sontag published her story.)

Sontag wrote "The Way We Live Now" after receiving a phone call telling her that a close friend had AIDS. She started crying. She could not sleep. She took a bath. Then the first words of the story began to form. "It was given to me," she told interviewer Kenny Fries, "ready to be born. I got out of the bathtub and started writing standing up. I wrote the story very quickly, in two days, drawing on experience of my own cancer and a friend's stroke. Radical experiences are similar." She visited the friend, Joseph Chaikin, almost every day, as others had visited her in the hospital. Chaikin could not talk, and it may be that his inability to speak gave Sontag the key to constructing a story in which everyone except the sick person had a voice.

But as Sontag would later say about *AIDS and Its Metaphors*, "The Way We Live Now" is not just about AIDS, it is about extreme changes in society. The story's title, taken from Trollope's great novel, suggests that her overarching theme is, in critic Elaine Showalter's words, "a loss of community and ethical value." The word "AIDS" is never used in the story, which is, like so much of Sontag's fiction, generic and allegorical, moving away from the specifics of culture to the Platonic universals or first principles she has pursued so persistently. What makes "The Way We Live Now" compelling, however, is its grounding in the human voice, in the twenty-six narrators (one for each letter of the alphabet) who make up the society that is reacting to the AIDS phenomenon.

The story also concerns a society that is ill. Its complex layering of speeches and social and psychological observations is enhanced by long sentences that continually switch speakers so that a community of friends with varying viewpoints is evoked sentence by sentence. The story has an effect comparable to that of compressing the one hundred chapters of Trollope's great novel into one hundred sentences.

The speakers retain their individuality, yet they also become a chorus in a Greek tragedy. They do not speak the same thoughts at once, but the syntax of the sentences makes them seem bound to each other—as bound together by their community of feeling as by the clauses that make up Sontag's sentences. A given speaker's thought at the beginning of a sentence is carried on, refuted, modified, or adumbrated by speakers in successive parts of the sentence. Each sentence is a grammatical unit that links the speakers to one another. Whatever their attitudes toward the disease, they cannot escape the thought of it. Thinking of it is, as one of them says, the way they live now.

AIDS and Its Metaphors seems a less personal response to the disease than does "The Way We Live Now," for in the former Sontag aims to continue the argument of *Illness as Metaphor*, to "dedramatize illness." Yet Sontag dedicated the book to "Paul [Thek], August 10, 1988," who had succumbed to AIDS. Although there had been a period of estrangement between them, Sontag visited the dying Thek regularly and read Rilke's *Duino Elegies* at his bedside. Thek's friend Ann Wilson remembers how Thek cherished Sontag's devotion.

AIDS and Its Metaphors appeared in a politicized climate that subsumed almost anything she had to say into urgent calls for massive government action to cure the disease. Her attack on AIDS metaphors received a less than grateful reception, in part because some activists on behalf of AIDS research and treatment found they needed the metaphors for propaganda purposes. To call AIDS a plague, for example, might offend Sontag's sensibility, but what if it produced not just fear but more government help? (In a series of lectures on AIDS, she argued that alarmism was self-defeating. The public would soon tire of predictions of an apocalypse that never quite arrived, she conjectured, and would instead be immobilized by an atmosphere of "apocalypse from now on.")

Sontag's cool, reserved tone—so effective in demolishing the romanticism and dread surrounding diseases like tuberculosis and cancer—enraged many gays. Her language seemed to divorce her from the suffering of a whole community. She used words like "homosexual" and "sodomy." Never once did she use the word "gay." Her rhetoric was deemed conservative—even reactionary—when it was not attacked as evasive. Passage after passage of her work provoked querulous critics to demand a more forthright statement. Where exactly did she stand?

One passage seemed especially troubling:

Of course, between the perennial official hypocrisy and the fashionable libertinism of recent decades there is a vast gap. The view that sexually transmitted diseases are not serious reached its apogee in the 1970s, which was also when many male homosexuals reconstituted themselves as something like an ethnic group, one whose distinctive folkloric custom was sexual voracity, and the institutions of urban homosexual life became a sexual delivery system of unprecedented speed, efficiency, and volume. Fear of AIDS enforces a much more moderate exercise of appetite, and not just among homosexual men. In the United States sexual behavior pre-1981 now seems for the middle class part of a lost age of innocence—innocence in the guise of licentiousness, of course. After two decades of sexual spending, of sexual speculation, of sexual inflation, we are in the early stages of a sexual depression. Looking back on the sexual culture of the 1970s has been compared to looking back on the jazz age from the wrong side of the 1929 crash.

Words like "libertinism" and "licentiousness" have an antique flavor, and her use of such language seems extraordinary for the once hip Susan Sontag. This moralistic language is balanced by an almost clinical academic terminology dealing with the "sexual delivery system" of urban homosexual life. She is more direct when she asserts that "we are in the early stages of a sexual depression." But then where is Susan Sontag in the passage's last sentence? Who is looking back? We? Who is doing the comparing? Others? Susan Sontag? Both?

The stern yet evasive grammar of this passage contributed to a feeling among gays that Sontag was guilty of bad faith. She was using words with connotations that condemned gayness. She seemed immune to the gay aesthetic—indeed she did not acknowledge its existence, but rather retreated into some vague clichés about homosexuality. Her most vocal critics believed that she would gain more authority if she made an open declaration of her sexual orientation.

It is not as if Sontag's sexual orientation has never been acknowledged publicly. There are entries on Sontag in *Gay and Lesbian Biography* (1998) and *The Book of Gay and Lesbian Quotations* (1999), although no specific comment is made about her sexuality. She is also included in *The Gay and Lesbian Heritage* (1995), where mention is made of her "lesbian sexuality." In *We Must Love One Another or Die: The Life and Legacies of Larry Kramer* (1997), Larry Mass has referred to Sontag's "public (official) invisibility as lesbian" and cited her relationship with her "longtime companion, Annie Leibovitz." Mass, in fact, was acknowledging a relationship that is common knowledge not only among Sontag and Leibovitz's friends but also in the literary/artistic community of New York City.

Yet Sontag has been accorded a special status by some gays and lesbians. Witness the gay activist/writer Larry Kramer. He is famous for outing public figures who remain closeted gays or lesbians, feeling that their silence has injured the movement for gay and lesbian rights and the battle against AIDS. But when Mass pressed Kramer on the subject of Sontag, Kramer responded in *We Must Love One Another or Die:*

> Susan is . . . beyond being a lesbian. I know I'm probably saying something very politically incorrect, but, except for the fact that she has affairs with women, she doesn't really fit into that category. . . . What she is more than anything else is an Intellectual, with a capital I. . . . I look upon her as, I don't know, as Venus with Hera, some great goddess that is on Mount Olympus and beyond sexuality, beyond category.

The Hera to whom Kramer refers is the commanding Annie Leibovitz. He evokes an image—familiar to literary New Yorkers—of these two tall women striding into events, inevitably capturing public attention. *Women* (1999), a collection of photographs by Leibovitz, includes an appreciative essay by Sontag, who remarks: "Each of these pictures must stand on its own. But the ensemble says, So this is what women are now—as different, as varied, as heroic, as forlorn, as unconventional as this."

What Mass and other gay and lesbian critics of Sontag want is some acknowledgment that Sontag's own sexual orientation just might have something to do with the subjects she writes about or with the stance she chooses to adopt toward them. Instead, in their view, she has been deceptive, presenting a counterfeit of herself, so to speak, to the public.

To put it another way, the society of women among whom Sontag has nurtured herself is not irrelevant to cultural history. Yet even a cultural historian such as Harvey Teres, in *Renewing the Left: Politics, Imagination, and The New York Intellectual* (1996), explains how difficult it is to say *anything* about what amounts to a secretive elite:

> Relationships among women are often formed backstage, so to speak, away from the spotlight of public alliances and battles. This

is of course especially true of lesbians, whose lives and culture scholars are just beginning to explore. There are layers of mutual influence, sympathy, and animosity among women that the historian must search out. As yet, we have no accepted vocabulary for these kinds of connections beyond alluding to "traditions" of female experience, literary and otherwise, or to "communities" of women. Categories such as support group, affinity group, or even subculture hardly do justice to the actual scope of their experiences.

Naturally, certain gay and lesbian writers are distressed that the context in which Sontag lives is reflected nowhere in her writing, as if she inhabited a heterosexual world separate from "homosexuals." For them, the socially lesbian Sontag does not square with the heterosexual writer/clinician. As Eve Kosofsky Sedgwick points out in *Epistemology of the Closet* (1990), "Closetedness is itself a performance." By remaining silent about her sexual orientation, Sontag is indulging in her own form of the "aesthetics of silence."

For some members of the post-Stonewall generation, Sontag's silence has been especially difficult to accept. Michangelo Signorile, born in 1960, began a two-year campaign (1989–91) in the short-lived *Outweek* to expose public figures who pretended to be heterosexual. His main targets were politicians, movie stars, movie executives, high-profile businessmen, and other celebrities, as well as the gossip columnists who collaborated in constructing their heterosexual fictions. But he also fastened on Susan Sontag and Annie Leibovitz. And what set him off, he says, was *AIDS and Its Metaphors*.

The curious result of Signorile's attempt to out Sontag and Leibovitz is that it provoked no reaction—not even from the principals. There simply was no uproar. Admitting defeat, Signorile published the following item in the January 9, 1991, issue of *Outweek*:

Outings That Went Nowhere (or Outings That Just Didn't Sell): Susan Sontag, Annie Leibovitz, Mary Martin, Glenn Plaskin, Billy Norwich, and Kaye Ballard.

The major media ignored him (see Larry Gross's account of Signorile's career in *Contested Closets*). Sontag's confidante, Fran Lebowitz, said of *Outweek*: "It's damaging, it's immoral, it's McCarthyism, it's terrorism, it's cannibalism, it's beneath contempt. . . . To me this is a bunch of Jews lining up other Jews to go to a concentration camp." How does it help matters, however, to pretend that you are not, to use her example, a Jew? Larry Gross invokes Hannah Arendt's reflection on her experience as a Jew expelled from Germany: "The basically simple principle here is one that is particularly hard to understand in times of defamation and persecution: *the principle that one can resist only in terms of the identity that is under attack.*" These words would seem especially relevant to a personage like Sontag, who has always regarded herself as an oppositional writer, dedicated to challenging the status quo.

Signorile served his apprenticeship working for gossip columnists who made their living pretending to reveal gossip often planted by the agents of subjects who publicly protested that they wanted their privacy protected. Like other public figures, Sontag has projected an image of herself (ex-husband, one son, very private), and Signorile obviously felt justified in revealing the process of image-making. To one of his attackers, gossip columnist James Revson, Signorile replied: "You see, homosexuality seems to be the only area in which journalism in New York is mandated to pursue lies and cover-ups rather than the truth. If you write about a closeted gay man's woman friend as his 'lover,' that is applauded. If you print the truth you are deemed 'frightening and offensive.'"

Jack Scagliotti, a gay film producer and the lover of journalist Andrew Kopkind, remembers they both found Sontag's public reticence about her sexuality perplexing because she certainly did nothing to hide it from her friends—or even from casual acquaintances

In October 1992, in a speech delivered to the Publishing Triangle's Writers' Weekend, a young lesbian novelist, Sarah Schulman, renewed the appeal to Sontag to come out. In *My American History*, Schulman took aim at a *New York Times Magazine* cover story profile of Sontag (part of the campaign to sell *The Volcano Lover*), objecting to the way Sontag camouflaged her sexual orientation. Why hadn't Sontag explored the nature of her own homosexuality?

Why isn't she concerned about the contribution she is withholding from us when she refuses—as one of the most respected women in the world—to come out as the dyke that she is? Lesbians suffer a real brain drain because so many of our great artists, leaders, and social thinkers are closeted. What does Sontag have to say about the struggle to build an integrated homosexual life? And how to build activist movements? About how to strategize to end AIDS? She did write a book . . . but her closet kept her from addressing homophobia and its impact on the epidemic in precisely the way that her openness about having cancer *enhanced* her analysis of the stigmatization of disease. . . . Can anything other than the desire to be accepted by straight people be at the root of Sontag's closet?

In her novel *Rat Bohemia* (1995), Schulman brilliantly evokes a bereft world of young lesbians and gays disowned by their parents and shunned by society. Speaking of herself and her friends, Rita, *Rat Bohemia*'s narrator, remarks: "The problem is how to keep us out." Rita yearns for "someone to be on her side. Someone to defend her." Another character, Muriel Kay Starr, a high-profile writer, presents herself as a power broker, a master of the blurb, who complains that her gay writer friend David abuses her generosity by attacking her in print (Edmund White? *Caracole*?). She subjects Rita to a lecture on how hard she has worked for the ungrateful David. "You're leaving out some very important information," Rita counters. "Like what?" asks Starr. "He was mad at you for writing closeted novels. For not even being out in your author bio on the back of the book." Starr mentions a gay publication she has published in (the Sontag interview in *Out*?) and dismisses Rita, summing up David as just another jealous male writer, the kind who simply cannot stand women who are smarter.

Meeting Schulman at a party, Larry Mass commented on Starr's resemblance to Sontag, and he thought that Schulman tacitly acknowledged the identification, although she now denies she had Sontag in mind.

Asked about the repercussions of her statements and her novel, Schulman remembered that an *Outweek* editor had once tried to arrange for her to interview Sontag, but that Sontag had "backed out," the editor told Schulman. The magazine had called Schulman the "gay Susan Sontag, and that was supposed to be a joke," Schulman recalled. But what about Schulman's appeal to Sontag to come out? "I admire Susan Sontag a great deal," Schulman said; "that's all I can tell you. I assume that she's gay, but she never told me."

After this brief conversation, an upset Schulman called Larry Mass, who reported on her phone call in *lgny* (Lesbian & Gay) *Perspectives*

(July 2, 1998). According to Mass, Schulman did not deny so much as distance herself from her earlier outspoken remarks about Sontag. She frankly acknowledged, in Mass's words, her fears about "how much damage this could cause her if it becomes too public." She wanted Mass to write a letter disavowing what he had said about her criticism of Sontag in his book about Larry Kramer. Instead Mass published his open letter in *lgny*, quoting verbatim from Schulman's criticism of Sontag and regretting her effort to rewrite history. He also noted that Schulman, now a well-regarded novelist, had told him she is afraid of Sontag's power. Like Sontag, who never answered Schulman's criticism, Schulman never responded to Mass's open letter.

Camille Paglia explains that in a draft of her essay "Sontag Bloody Sontag," Random House lawyers "red-penciled" out about a third of it, including a passage in which Paglia, like Schulman, excoriated Sontag for being

> grossly hypocritical in giving selected photos to the *NYT*. She was always claiming that her personal record was irrelevant to her vocation of writer. Surrendering family photos is hardly consistent with that pose. To be publicizing her early relationship with a man [Philip Rieff] to the exclusion of all her subsequent relationships with women, including her current one with a famous media professional [Annie Leibovitz], was close to delusional—and the *NYT*'s own behavior, in allowing that kind of dictatorial editing by a subject, was unethical in the extreme.

Paglia "hated SS's silence about homosexual issues in the twenty years following Stonewall," but Random House lawyers warned Paglia that to say what she suspected about Sontag's sexuality might invite legal action. They specifically pointed to her threatened suit against *Soho News* for reprinting her Town Hall speech.

To Paglia, Sontag's silence on her sexual orientation is just part of her "royal insulation from reality." When Paglia started her feud with Sontag in 1992, she did it in the pages of publications such as the *New York Post*'s Page Six and in *Entertainment Weekly* (calling Sontag the "heavyweight who used to be the bully on the block"), consciously picking "vulgar" venues more likely to air her complaints. When *New York* magazine (August 10, 1992) ran an article, "The 1992 Literary

Olympics," which imagined Paglia and Sontag at fisticuffs, Paglia was inspired to go "whole hog" after Sontag that fall.

Paglia has been ridiculed and censured for her claim that "I'm the Sontag of the 1990s—there's no doubt about it!" Yet Paglia has maintained a tireless presence in magazines, newspapers, and journals all over the world, demonstrating, in her words, "what cultural criticism at the close of the twentieth century should look like." More is at stake, she stresses, than her "colorful personal pique." Serious intellectual and cultural issues are involved in "my disillusion with Sontag," Paglia writes. "Sontag has made fetishes of depressive male European writers such as Beckett, whom she is always promoting either in her writing or in person in those Manhattan literary events." Sontag's later essays reflect the search for a "lost father figure," a major male presence in her writing. Rather than participate in American culture, rather than fully engage adversaries such as Adrienne Rich in a major debate over feminism, Sontag has over the past twenty-one years acted like a "European émigré," Paglia concludes.

Paglia contrasts Sontag's emergence on the cultural scene with her effort to remain there:

> The glamorous dust-jacket photo imprinted Sontag's sexual persona as a new kind of woman writer so indelibly on the mind that the image still lingers, wraithlike, and makes criticism of her very difficult. She was the dream date of bookish men and the chic Deirdre-of-the-Sorrows alter ego of educated but genteel, white, middle-class women, the latter of whom emerged as and remain (surely not to her satisfaction) her primary audience.

Paglia wanted her own debut to be like Sontag's and took the *Against Interpretation* photograph, together with other celebrity shots (all of rock stars), with her when she consulted a photographer and a makeup artist. She wanted the "French intellectual look. . . . I wanted to look like I'm austere, haughty." Paglia sought to capture what Angela McRobbie ("The Modernist Style of Susan Sontag," *Feminist Review* [Summer 1991]) calls "an image which combines sinewy female strength with casual elegance."

Paglia's tactics are aimed at an adversary who pretends not to be in the game. Journalist Zoë Heller told Paglia that Sontag said to her: "I'm pretending I never heard of Camille Paglia, and the reason is I went to this party and I heard this guy say, 'Gertrude Stein, who is that?' and I loved that. So I'm using the same thing on Paglia." During a book tour for *The Volcano Lover*, Sontag did say to television interviewer Christopher Lydon on Boston's WGBH that she had never heard of Camille Paglia. Paglia rejoins that in James Wolcott's *Vanity Fair* profile of Paglia (September 1992), David Rieff is quoted as saying of her: "She is a useful counterirritant to a certain type of academic cant. But she's substituting her own brand of unpleasantly self-promoting cant." Like his mother, Paglia reports, Rieff then retreated, refusing to say another word to other reporters. Wolcott chose to end his article with Paglia's remark: "I've been chasing that bitch for 25 years and I've finally passed her!"

A Sontag comment on Paglia appears in John Dugdale's "Feuds Corner" (*Sunday Times*, April 16, 1995):

> She should go join a rock band. Are people impressed by this shamelessness? We used to think Norman Mailer was bad, but she makes Mailer look like Jane Austen. The vindictiveness, the vulgarity, the aggression—she is repulsive to me.

An unfazed Paglia counters with a comment on the media attention Sontag's visits to Sarajevo occasioned:

> On "Person-of-the-Week," I saw Diane Sawyer [ABC correspondent and anchorwoman] saying "and we salute her." Does Susan Sontag understand what it means to be canonized by Diane Sawyer? She talks about vulgar! I like Diana Sawyer, but she is at the center of the socialite elite in New York. This is a woman who has her skin and her hair done every other day.

To Sontag's biographers, Paglia expounded on the New York celebrity aspects of Sontag's career and her need to feel part of a "power elite." Sontag had become addicted to adulation. Paglia guffawed when she heard Roger Straus say on ABC News, apropos of Sontag's visits to Sarajevo, "Susan goes wherever there is suffering."

Curiously Sontag and Paglia had a mutual friend, the late Richard Tristman, who was mentored by Sontag at Columbia and was one of

Paglia's colleagues at Bennington. Paglia's fury at Sontag troubled him, for never at any stage of his friendship with Sontag had he sensed those qualities that rile Paglia. Of course Tristman was not a member of Sontag's intimate circle, and there were long periods when he did not see her at all. Yet she had taken an interest in him and his work and shown hers to him. Unlike Paglia, Tristman had made no study of Sontag and wanted nothing from her. He described a generous and serious person, and he did not make the slightest effort to rationalize the behavior that Paglia faulted or to criticize Paglia for not seeing another side of Sontag. He was caught between two friends he respected, and he was diplomatic. He did not want to offend them.

On only one issue did Tristman dissent from Paglia. He accepted Sontag's reticence about her sexuality and about her position as public figure as genuine. He had been there, after all, when she and María Fornés formed their first writing group. He saw not a hypocrite but a woman and writer attempting to maintain the standards of an earlier age, and he found her effort honorable.

What Tristman did not see, perhaps because he felt so honored by Sontag's attention, was that she had done her part to create a culture that made a Camille Paglia possible. In *The Repeal of Reticence: A History of American Cultural and Legal Struggles Over Free Speech, Obscenity, Sexual Liberation, and Modern Art* (1996), Rochelle Gurstein attacks Sontag for spreading a promiscuous and even pornographic sense of culture and art. Gurstein does not acknowledge the contradictions in Sontag, the very conservative and traditionalist strain that led her to back away from—while at the same time refusing to recant—her early positions. By the mid-1980s, Sontag was using interviews to deplore the lack of seriousness in culture, not for a moment conceding that her own arguments had contributed to that lack of seriousness.

Many gay and lesbian writers suggest that the issue of Sontag's sexuality would go away if she would just own up to it. But there have to be other considerations—well beyond Schulman's speculation that the only reason Sontag would stay closeted is to court acceptance. For example, Sedgwick observes that "there are remarkably few of even the most openly gay people who are not deliberately in the closet with someone personally or economically or institutionally important to them." Coming out, in other words, may require not one big revelation but a series of very difficult disclosures. Even close friends, Sedgwick reports, do not, in many instances, discuss their erotic lives. Two of Sedgwick's friends knew each other for a decade before "it seemed to either of these friends that permission had been given to the woman to refer to the man, in their conversation together, as *a gay man*."

Sontag enforces a *politesse* concerning her sexual orientation which has inevitably become an aspect of her biography. She has triumphed in a society that has traditionally defined homosexuality as an aberration. As Jamake Highwater, her high school classmate, observes in *The Mythology of Transgression: Homosexuality as Metaphor*:

> No matter how vigorously we have attempted to redefine the term "homosexuality," it still has the built-in pathological context as a distortion of heterosexuality. Homosexuality is not about being someone. It is, on the contrary, about *not* being what one should be, namely, a heterosexual. We speak of ourselves as homosexual only because our orientation has been given a name that doesn't designate what we are but what we have failed to be.

Sontag has reified the terms "homosexual" and "homosexuality" countless times in her writing. They are a kind of barrier she and her society have erected, one that excludes another kind of language, a different kind of aesthetic.

To search for a new language, to construct an image of herself that is neither homosexual or heterosexual, would be difficult. What label would satisfy? Why a label at all? Highwater's book is sensitive to the problem:

> Probably one of the many reasons some people are reluctant to reveal their homosexuality is because they are uncomfortable with an arbitrary definition of who and what they are and with whom they do or do not share their identity. For instance, the openly gay novelist Djuna Barnes deeply resented being called a lesbian, not apparently because of any moral proprieties or because of her social coyness, but because the categorical description of her sexuality seemed to her too loaded with unacceptable preconceptions.

In the early 1980s Sontag canvassed the possibilities of coming out, as became clear at Roger Straus's house during a party for James Lord, an FSG author who had just published a book on Alberto Giacometti. After dinner, guests gathered for coffee in the living room. Hilton Kramer remembers walking in, seeing Sontag sitting in a chair, a group gathered "literally sitting on the floor at her feet": Walter Clemons, a book critic at *Newsweek;* Fred Tuten, a novelist who taught with Sontag at City College; and Tuten's wife, then an FSG employee. "There was a discussion that evening," Kramer recalls, "whether gays benefited or lost something from coming out." Like Walter Clemons, James Lord is gay. Lord was adamant that it was better to be in the closet. "Sontag was all for coming out," Kramer reports, and Lord, no friend of Kramer's, seconds his recollection. Lord remembers Kramer violently disagreeing with her. Lord's position on coming out has since changed (see his memoir *Picasso and Dora,* for a graceful example of how he incorporates his gay sexuality into his experience with art and artists). Kramer, wondering about Sontag's own closeted life, concluded that she felt it was "the right thing for other péople to do. Curiously, whether through an assumed collective sense of delicacy or not, this was all about homosexual men and the issue of homosexual women never came into the discussion."

Over the years Richard Howard and other openly gay friends close to her have urged Sontag to come out, and they have been frustrated with her approach/avoidance behavior. At one point Howard put together a panel of gay and lesbian authors and expected that Sontag would lend her name to it—if not exactly coming out, then taking a step in that direction. But ultimately she declined the invitation.

Sedgwick shows that there is "a family of reasons" for not coming out. In Sontag's case, to come out is to risk losing control of her persona and to jeopardize her iconic power. To refuse categorization, Jack Scagliotti points out, is a neat way to deflect phobic reactions to one's sexuality. Coming out may cost one a segment of one's audience, if not one's family.

To come out is often not to settle questions of identity but to raise them, especially in the last decade as gays and lesbians—not to mention the culture at large—have debated the genetic and social origins of sexual identity. When the enterprising Zoë Heller ("Side by Side with Sontag, *Irish Times,* September 26, 1992) asked Sontag point-blank about her sexuality (after fortifying herself with testimony from friends who said all her love affairs had been with women), Heller reported:

Sontag refuses to be categorized as a lesbian, or to confirm the status of her relationship with her long-term companion, the photographer Annie Leibovitz: "Of course I think it's wonderful that a woman of 59 is assumed to have an active emotional life—which I have—but I don't talk about my erotic life any more than I talk about my spiritual life. It is . . . too complex and it always ends up sounding so banal."

Susan Sontag does not wish to sound banal.

With her iconic status assured, Sontag also confronted the dilemma of many stars: everyone wanted to use her for their own purposes, to shape her into their idea of the proper role model. Yet not to deal with her sexual orientation at all seems a harsh alternative, making Sontag's work more problematic and making her seem more withdrawn from her times than she really is.

26

The Volcano Lover

1990–1992

I have a volcano in my heart.
—Sontag in conversation with Marian Christy,
Chicago Tribune, September 27, 1992

On July 17, 1990, Susan Sontag won a "genius award," the John D. and Catherine T. MacArthur Foundation fellowship for "exceptionally gifted individuals." Sontag, then fifty-seven, was overheard to say, "It's about time." She had complained for years about not getting the grants she deserved. E. L. Doctorow, sympathetic to her plight, remembers how sore she was about it. Now she had a five-year $340,000 grant. The award would help pay the rent, she added, and she could cut back on lecturing.

In early 1991, in the Chelsea section of Manhattan, Sontag purchased a penthouse apartment situated in the sixteen-story London Terrace, a.k.a. "the fashion projects" because so many designers lived in its fourteen buildings, which take up an entire block between Twenty-third and Twenty-fourth streets and Ninth and Tenth avenues. Sontag's partner, Annie Leibovitz, also had an apartment there, and the two shared storage space. Beginning in the 1980s, Chelsea had begun to rival SoHo as a location for artists. It was an easy walk from London Terrace to Leibovitz's studio on Varick and Van Dam. Built between 1929 and 1931, London Terrace had originally functioned as a city within a city, promoting itself as the world's largest apartment complex, with every amenity and a full-service staff. No longer quite so all-encompassing, it remains an impressive prewar edifice, a blend of Gothic and Romanesque architecture that has, in the words of a *New York Times* article, an appeal for the "smart set" and for artists with a "higher developed sense of esthetics."

In decor and ambience, the penthouse did not differ that much from previous Sontag abodes: airy, all-white, wood floors, prints on the walls, shelves and shelves of books (twelve thousand to fifteen thousand of them)—"advancing like a crazed kudzu vine" (observed one interviewer), a fluffy, well-worn couch, a Mission chair. Sontag's apartment was spare, spacious, spartan, austere, monastic.

By the 1980s Sontag and Leibovitz had become a much gossiped-about item in New York. They appeared together at parties and were seen dancing at a late-night club. Leibovitz, a high-profile photographer of high-profile subjects (Bill Clinton, Jodie Foster, and virtually every important performer or politician who has been on the cover of *Vanity Fair*), has been named one of *Life*'s "50 most influential baby boomers," listed as number 2 (after Princess Di) in *American Photo*'s list of the "100 most important people in photography," cited as only the second living photographer (Irving Penn was the first) to have an exhibition devoted to her work by England's National Portrait Gallery. But in the late 1980s, when she felt her creativity had "stalled," Leibovitz looked to Sontag for reassurance. To David Van Biema of *Life*, Leibovitz explained: "I'd always had this edge. I was the bad girl coming from the rock and roll magazine [*Rolling Stone*, where she began her career], and the edge was sort of peeling away." She confessed that Sontag "told me she thought I could be good."

What a humble admission from a photographer who began working for *Rolling Stone* at twenty, soon becoming as visible in the culture as the subjects she depicted. Like Sontag, Leibovitz felt uncomfortable in her role as fashion plate and trendsetter, and she sought out the serious. Yet also like Sontag, Leibovitz celebrated sensuous surfaces. Leibovitz played with the forms of celebrity photography (this tendency became especially pronounced after she moved to *Vanity Fair* in 1983). As she told Biema, "Sometimes I enjoy just photographing the surface because I think it can be as revealing as going to the heart of the matter."

Sontag is seventeen years Leibovitz's senior, and there appears to be more than a little of the master-disciple dynamic in their relationship. Looking at one of Leibovitz's photographs in a gallery where she could easily be overheard by several people, Sontag turned to Leibovitz and said, "Well, you may turn out to be a photographer, after all." In the form of gossip, the judgment sounds especially cruel, but it does not differ all that much from Sontag's more formal assessment of Leibovitz's art broadcast on a radio interview. Asked about the romantic jacket photograph for *The Volcano Lover: A Romance*, for which Leibovitz shot her reclining, her right arm raised and her right hand resting atop what interviewer Paula Span called her gray "battle ribbon," Sontag replied that, with all apologies to Leibovitz, the original, the great, photograph of her reclining figure had been taken by Peter Hujar. Simple justice to Hujar? No doubt, but it also put Leibovitz and her homage in their place. Not that Sontag has not encouraged Leibovitz or responded generously, on other occasions, to her work: "I am charmed that at the age of fifty-nine, I can still, without looking ridiculous, pose in a sensuous way. Perhaps I would not have the courage to do it if the photographer hadn't encouraged me," Sontag said.

Leibovitz lecturing on photography sounded like Susan Sontag, suspicious of the very image-making that engrossed her and that gave meaning to her life. The hypercritical Sontag, wary of photography's imperialistic usurpation of the world, has been one of Leibovitz's touch-stones, a figure of authority whom it is never quite possible to please.

Anna-Lou Leibovitz, born on October 2, 1949, in Westbury, Connecticut, had something like Sontag's peripatetic childhood, moving frequently from one military base to another with her father Sam, an Air Force officer, and her mother, a dance instructor who had once performed with Martha Graham's company. But Leibovitz is one of six children and is close to her family. Even taller than Sontag, the six-foot photographer has been a stylish portraitist to the famous. As critic Richard Lacayo puts it, she can "twit propriety in the slickest possible style." Angela Lambert of *The Independent* reported: "She is very difficult, I was warned, she'll be rude, impatient, arrogant." But then, Lambert adds, these are "typical criticisms leveled at successful women."

In person, Leibovitz is very attractive and favors the Sontag uniform:

layers of simple black. Like Sontag, she frequently emphasizes that she lives alone: these women do not live with but beside each other. Both are third-generation Jews—Leibovitz's family having come from Russia—who feel at home everywhere. If anything, Leibovitz's apartment seems less lived in than Sontag's; Leibovitz's is a crash pad, whereas Sontag's is an inventory of her brain.

Like Sontag, Leibovitz rejects any attempt to categorize her or her work:

> When I was at *Rolling Stone*, people called me a rock photographer. When I was at *Vanity Fair*, people called me a celebrity photographer. And when I started doing the American Express campaign, people called me an advertising photographer. So I don't know what will come next. I'm just a photographer. I've always been a photographer.

Mark Stevens, perhaps Leibovitz's most sensitive critic, asserts that her celebrity portraits are her best work. Other efforts, like her series on Olympic athletes, seem "too much like other photographers." He identifies a "high-brow savvy" in her work that seems to tie her to Sontag:

> It can seem tawdry to take an interest in movie stars unless there is a strong measure of wit, surprise, or, especially, camp. Emma Thompson in armor (for she's also a bit of the frosty schoolmarm) is also Emma Thompson in drag. To put it differently, Whoopi goes better with a clever subtext. So Leibovitz photographs Goldberg's black body in a bathtub full of milk and does a comic riff on both minstrelsy and traditional Hollywood cheesecake.

Conceding that Leibovitz is not a "big or deep artist," Stevens compares her spirit, if not her style, to the "brilliant confections of the rococo." Sontag's own eighteenth-century spree, *The Volcano Lover*, a romance about fame and fortune, art, history, and politics, parallels Leibovitz's elegant evocations of stardom.

The origins of *The Volcano Lover* date from 1980, when Sontag visited a London book and print shop seeking eighteenth-century architectural prints (architecture has always been one of her passions). A series of hand-colored engravings of Mount Vesuvius attracted her, and the clerk told her that Sir William Hamilton, British ambassador to Naples, had commissioned them in 1776 for a privately printed book. Sontag bought five prints, then bought five more the next day, then another seven. They showed the volcano in various states of eruption and quiescence. Like Hamilton, Sontag confessed to a fascination with "images of disaster"—an impulse that had, of course, led to her landmark essay on science fiction, "The Imagination of Disaster."

Sontag put the prints on her walls, like so many frames of film, projecting them for a full decade before she began what she thought would be a novel about Hamilton, a man of the Enlightenment with wide-ranging interests in science, art, politics, and collecting. Hamilton was a man for the ages, a scholar-connoisseur like her beloved Walter Benjamin, although he had been unjustly demeaned by his involvement in the legendary ménage à trois with his wife, Lady Emma Hamilton, and England's greatest naval hero, Lord Nelson.

Sontag barely remembered who Hamilton was when the clerk first mentioned his name. She had to look him up in the *Dictionary of National Biography*. Vague memories stirred of a film, *That Hamilton Woman* (1941), of her sighing over Sir Laurence Olivier as Nelson and Vivien Leigh as Emma. Sontag had forgotten the name of the actor who played Hamilton (Alan Mowbray), as had most of the film's audience, she supposed. And Sontag soon discovered that for all the retellings of the romance that scandalized England, there was only one biography of Hamilton, published in 1969. By focusing on him, she could strip the story of its sentimental gloss.

Sontag carefully studied Brian Fothergill's meticulous biography. Offended by his hero's humiliating reputation as an elderly cuckold, Fothergill rehabilitates Sir William, depicting an aesthete of the first order, a robust gentleman concerned to "hasten the progress of the Arts, by discussing their true and first principles." Like Sontag, Hamilton was a patron and "would go to great lengths and take infinite trouble to help" artists. He treated his nephew and eventual heir, Charles Greville, as a young "*Conoscente*," educating him very much in the manner Sontag used in tutoring her own son. Delighted to find that the cerebral Hamilton was also ardent, Sontag took him to her bosom, telling interviewer Irene Borger: "I am not a person of equanimity. I am a person of passion." Tall for his day (he was, at five feet nine, exactly Sontag's height), and handsome with an aristocratic aquiline nose, Hamilton suited Sontag perfectly.

Or so she thought. The trouble with focusing on Hamilton is that his full human dimensions do not emerge absent Sir Horatio and Lady Emma. Fothergill's biography, in fact, founders because he cannot account for Hamilton's rapture for both his wife and her lover. Fothergill is powerless to explain how the cautious diplomat and shrewd collector remained so infatuated with the pair. Angry that his hero is attached to what he considers a vulgar woman, a commoner who had been a kept woman and a shameless self-promoter, Fothergill resorts to clichés about the besotted, aging, and enfeebled man.

In her novel, Sontag persuasively portrays a vigorous man who enjoyed physical exercise and admired not only Emma's great beauty but also her facility with languages and her aesthetic sensibility, which made her famous for her "attitudes," a kind of miming in which she impersonated famous figures from history and art. Sontag saw that Emma Hamilton did not derail but rather furthered Sir William's aesthetic and romantic projects. He relished her because she had been painted by Romney, and he put her on exhibit for other painters and had her perform for Goethe and other great artists. Emma, in fact, is a version of Sontag, concerned with the beauty of form and the possibilities of self-invention. Born with another name, Emily Lyon, then adopting the more aristocratic-sounding Emma Hart, and finally becoming Lady Emma Hamilton, she is a quintessential Sontag creation—even if her real-life counterpart actually existed. Extolling Emma in one of her interviews, Sontag called her "enormously talented, enormously energetic. She wasn't made by these people, she was helped by them." Sontag went on to quote Sir Joshua Reynolds on Emma: "She poses and essentially the picture is done. I can't think anymore without her contribution." With interviewer Samuel R. Delany, Sontag was more explicit: "I love self-made people. I feel rather self-made myself . . . going someplace that's completely different from where you come from—I think Emma fabulous. And the way that people sneered at her because she lost her looks, you know, is—it's the Beauty Police."

To Sontag, Hamilton is more than the neoclassical man, Emma more than a romantic object, and Nelson more than a naval hero. Each of them has a sense of greatness and grandeur, with Nelson serving as the apex of their hero worship even as he sees his heroism reflected in their unstinting devotion. Sontag understands that theirs is a combined quest for fame and glory.

· While Sontag seems to scorn Nelson at times—and certainly his reactionary politics revolt her—his self-abnegating attitude toward history parallels her attachment to literature. On countless occasions she has rejected the notion that she writes to express herself. No, she has corrected interviewers, she writes to be included in the body of literature, just as Nelson strives to take his place in history as a hero. Like Nelson, Sontag is on a quest for immortality. What could be more romantic than this individual quest? To such individuals, however, it seems not an exercise in egotism but a mark of humility, a surrendering of the self to the highest standards, a neoclassical ideal not of assertion but of submission.

Yet Nelson was a needy man. He required constant proofs of his greatness. Witness after witness reported that he never tired of compliments, and that Sir William and Lady Emma were only too happy to oblige him. Only through a ménage à trois does each character complete the other in *The Volcano Lover*. "The art of it is that these are real people, but I reinvented them giving parts of myself to each character. I felt very emotionally involved with them," Sontag confessed.

The importance of the threesome, however, was not apparent to the author in the early phases of writing the novel. She got stuck at the end of Part One. Emma, Sontag says, rescued her: "Emma kidnapped the book," as Sontag told interviewer Paula Span. Part One had ended with the melancholy Sir William brooding over the death of his first wife, Catherine, who had worshipped him and shared his aesthetic sense, but who had not thrilled him. Then, as Sontag later described it, she arrived at the book's four-part structure, which mimics the medieval division of the psyche into the melancholic, the saturnine (full of blood, the passion that Emma and Nelson evoke), the phlegmatic (Hamilton's dying soliloquy), and the choleric (the tour-de-force monologues of the feisty female characters).

Sontag has said *The Volcano Lover* is the only one of her books she has really liked, the only one that has fulfilled her ambitions as a writer. In it she finally fuses in brilliant fashion the techniques of her fiction and her nonfiction. It is also her most autobiographical work, finally releasing a pent-up Romanticism.

The desire to possess the beautiful that both Hamilton and Sontag express connects them to the world, but it also alienates them from it. *The Volcano Lover* is studded with parabolic passages that evoke the melancholy of being unable to collect the world, to hold its attention:

> Collections unite. Collections isolate.
>
> They unite those who love the same thing. (But no one loves the same as I do; enough.) They isolate from those who don't share the passion. (Alas, almost everyone).
>
> Then I'll try not to talk about what interests me most. I'll talk about what interests you.
>
> But this will remind me, often, of what I can't share with you.
>
> Oh, listen. Don't you see. Don't you see how beautiful it is.

The artist, the aesthete, the collector become estranged from the world by the very process of attempting to bring it together. This paradox results, in *The Volcano Lover*, in a narrator who speaks to herself as much as to her readers.

The Volcano Lover marks an extraordinary advance in Sontag's powers as a fiction writer, yet it has not managed to bring her reputation as a novelist into line with her status as a critical thinker. Perhaps one novel—save for some phenomenon like an *Invisible Man*—cannot canonize a novelist.

The Volcano Lover made the best-seller list, helped by FSG's $75,000 promotional budget and Sontag's agreement to do a fifteen-city publicity tour—for her an unprecedented commitment to selling one of her own works. The first printing was an unusually large 50,000 copies. A month later a fifth printing brought the total to over 105,000. The Book-of-the-Month Club made it an alternate selection for September 1992. Sontag said *The Volcano Lover* felt like a new beginning, as though she were just beginning to write.

27 Sarajevo

1993–1995

The problem is how not to avert one's glance.
How not to give way to the impulse to stop looking.
—Susan Sontag, "Looking at the Unbearable:
On Francisco Goya," *The Disasters of War, 1863*

In April 1993 Susan Sontag visited Sarajevo. David urged her to go. He was then writing a book, *Slaughterhouse: Bosnia and the Failure of the West* (1995), one of the essential sources on the war. Sarajevo had been under siege from Serb gunners for a year, and David found his friends bored with his analyses of the Balkans. "I can't stand any of my friends anymore," he told his mother. "They only want to listen to my Bosnia stories for 10 minutes." He spread out maps for her and said, "You know, people would be very pleased if you came."

Before her first trip, Sontag had reacted with "horror and indignation" to the violence, and to the West's failure to intervene. These were her people, Europeans; they belonged to her culture. But what could she do? She did not consider herself a journalist, and she did not fancy working for a humanitarian organization.

Two weeks in the city that April gave Sontag an idea of the role she might play. She saw people suffer, of course, but the Bosnian aspiration to be a country moved her. One day there seemed like a week in New York, a month "full of new and terrible impressions." Sarajevo excited her, with its atmosphere of intensity, of bravery, that brought out the best and the worst of humanity and carried with it historical echoes and repercussions. She ranked the massacre of Bosnians alongside what she saw as the century's European atrocities: the Armenian genocide of 1915 and the Holocaust of the 1930s and 1940s. Remembering the assassination of the archduke Franz Ferdinand by Gavrilo Princep (a Bosnian) in Sarajevo which led to World War I, Sontag declared that the city "began and will end the 20th century."

In a city of 350,000, ten or fifteen people died every day and perhaps twice as many were wounded. Sontag estimated her own risk at one in a thousand. She arrived wearing a flak jacket, then discarded it to lessen the distance between herself and her new friends. She drove in a dilapidated car, becoming an easy target for snipers. She befriended a Bosnian who helped distribute food in the besieged city, and who later became her driver when he immigrated to New York. In Sarajevo, he was endowed with a kind of sixth sense, and he looked out for Sontag. Once, as she approached a doorway, he told her to move on; seconds later a shell demolished the doorway. Such incidents became her war stories.

Sontag admired the sheer nerve of the Bosnians, their dogged efforts to live normally amid the shelling and other terrorist acts. Multicultural Sarajevo, in which Serbs, Muslims, and Croats had lived peaceably, and even happily, intermarrying and giving little thought to their religious or ethnic differences, embodied her internationalist ideal, which Europe and the rest of the West did not have the courage or the imagination to defend.

Sontag pronounced such judgments knowing some of the region's literature but not much of its history. She had visited a writers' conference in Dubrovnik, and friends she made there called her when the Serbs attacked Croatia and started shelling the city. In July 1993 she declared that the "worst is yet to come. I think that the Bosnians are going to be completely defeated, that Sarajevo will be occupied, divided and destroyed. . . . The war also presupposes that Europe will be totally discredited." In July 1995 she added: "The United Nations will never recover from its failure in Bosnia, and neither will NATO from its reluctance to act."

A long-standing critic of American military might—of the idea that one country should have such an arsenal—she called for American intervention: "My government should intervene because it sees itself as a superpower." She did not want to support a superpower even as she called for that power to be used.

Sontag also deplored the inaction of the left. Virtually no one had joined her in Sarajevo. "There isn't any Left now. It's a joke," she told interviewer Alfonso Armada of *El Pais*. The left had splintered once again over Bosnia, with some for intervention in Bosnia, others against. Victor Navasky of *The Nation* saw his own contributors divide on the issue. E. L. Doctorow spoke for many writers when he observed:

> I didn't take to the streets to protest our lack of support for lifting the embargo [the ban on weapons that made it difficult for the Bosnians to arm themselves]. There were so many commentators who sprang up with this expertise to explain why the Balkans were an absolutely insoluble situation, and everyone was wrong, and they were all beyond redemption, mired in an ancient animosity. People gave up on it.

Doctorow agreed with Sontag: the left should have done more. But, referring to Sontag's earlier Town Hall tirade, Doctorow suggested that the left had been chastised and dispersed so that there was "nobody there to march behind her."

In "A Lament for Bosnia" (*The Nation*, December 25, 1995), Sontag laid out her brief against the left. It had become complacent, comfortable, consumer-oriented, and health-conscious. People wondered how her son could spend so much time among smokers, she reported. "Oh, you're back; I was worried about you," friends would say, but Sontag took such comments to mean they did not want to hear about her experience. The Dayton Peace Accord of late 1995 displeased her because it provided for an unjust peace. Bosnia's dismemberment mattered because it was one of those "model events"—like the Spanish Civil War of the 1930s. She did not want to speak too well of intellectuals—they could be as conformist and cowardly as the rest of humanity—but at least some writers had gone to Spain and maintained the "standard of dissent." The poor showing in Bosnia could be attributed, she conceded, to the "bad reputation of the Balkans as a place of eternal conflict," to prejudice against Muslims, to the view that the left had been too gullible about Communism in the 1930s and the 1960s. But the alternative was worse: "morosely depoliticized intellectuals . . . with their cynicism always at the ready, their addiction to entertainment, their reluctance to inconvenience themselves for any cause, their devotion to personal safety." Finally, she lamented "a vertiginous decay of the very notion of international solidarity."

"A Lament for Bosnia" elided certain uncomfortable truths: many writers in Spain had been duped—or worse, like Hemingway and Josephine Herbst, they had actually lied about Communist atrocities. But Sontag found that she was unable to deal with such issues. As she told interviewers Eilenn Manin and Sherry Simon, she had abandoned her essay on the

> relationship between intellectuals and the idea of revolution or revolutionary power. . . . It's quicksand! This was the first time in my life that I was bothered by the question of audience . . . who am I writing for? I'm not interested in giving aid and comfort to the neo-Conservatives. It's a crucifying dilemma. I was finally defeated by it. I spent a year and a half writing hundreds of pages and gave up.

Sontag, and Leibovitz, who accompanied her to Sarajevo on one of her trips, thrilled to the adventure of Bosnia. "People have no walls, no skin," Leibovitz remarked. "Everyone knows exactly who they are. All veneer has been rubbed off and you see a microcosm of life. . . . You become very small. You sort of get swept away with it," she added. When Leibovitz saw a bombing victim (a boy who had been riding a bicycle) die in her car on the way to the hospital, she photographed the scene: the abandoned bike and the boy's blood on the street. Critic Andrew Palmer called such photographs a "trivialised tribute to the photographer's integrity." Another thought Leibovitz as "tender and ruthless as ever." With no electricity available, she relied on natural light and admitted: "I was trying to crawl back to where I started, the purity of the early work." The photographer understood that she had made little more than a preliminary effort. The next week she returned to Los Angeles to photograph Sylvester Stallone posing as "The Thinker."

So what to do besides bear witness, take photographs, and organize public opinion in favor of a Bosnian state? Sontag's impulse was to write a book, but she did not want to upstage her son, and the siege called for some other, more direct form of action. Even a film would take time and would not involve her with Sarajevans as directly and immediately as she would have liked. She wanted not only to do something for a Sarajevo audience but to focus the world's attention on the very act of her doing so. It was an ambition worthy of Victor Hugo, although unlike Hugo, Sontag denied that she was attempting to use her celebrity to create an international audience.

In "Godot Comes to Sarajevo" (*New York Review of Books,* October 21, 1993), Sontag explained her decision to stage Samuel Beckett's *Waiting for Godot* as an act of solidarity, a "small contribution" to a city that refused to capitulate to "Serb fascism." During a conversation in April 1993 with Harris Pasovic, a young Sarajevo-born theater director, she asked if he would welcome her coming again to the city to direct a play. "Of course," he replied. "What play will you do?" Sontag impulsively answered, *"Waiting for Godot,"* perhaps thinking of the opening line from the play, which prefaced her *NYRB* article: "Nothing to be done." The play seemed perfect for Sarajevo because Beckett's characters persisted despite their despair, just as Sarajevans waited and waited for deliverance—for their Godot, for the West, for the Americans to bomb the Serbs back to Belgrade. The play's minimal stage set reflected the state of a city stripped bare by siege. Sontag believed, moreover, that "there are more than a few people who feel strengthened and consoled by having their sense of reality affirmed and transfigured by art."

Sontag was criticized—even ridiculed—by the press and by other writers (her *NYRB* article is a tacit reply to the attacks on her). Noting that Sontag had at her disposal the publicity machinery of *Vanity Fair,* a *Guardian* writer asked: "Despite her intentions, is this really so different from Cher's mercy mission to Armenia on which she took her own special Armenian, the woman who waxes her bikini line?" Gordon Coales of *The Independent* suggested that Sontag had begun an "Ars Longa" cultural service: "A performance of one of the classics of 20th-century drama (selected by experts to be relevant to your war), staged in the heart of the war zone, would be an extraordinary event and a unique contribution to both military and civilian morale." Joanna Coles of *The Guardian* wrote: "We seem stuck in a round of Charity Challenge; the latest game where celebrities compete with rival acts of very public charity." A milder form of criticism came from Croatian journalist Slavenka Drakulic, author of

The Balkan Express: Fragments from the Other Side of War: "There is a growing business centered around Sarajevo and Bosnia, and, sadly, the limelight is too often on the participants, not the public." Drakulic did not doubt Sontag's good intentions: "All I say is that if attention and understanding alone could save Sarajevo, then it would have been saved long ago." Luke Clancy of the *Irish Times* reported that the production of *Godot* "deeply angered many within the city," and he quoted theater director Dubravko Bibanovi: "She did it for herself, and for nobody else. It said nothing about Bosnia or Bosnian culture."

Erika Munk, a Yale professor who would interview Sontag and watch her work in Sarajevo, discovered that not all artists and intellectuals believed

> cultural work essential to the city's defense. . . . Why, they ask, should we do anything that creates the illusion of normal life? Gather wood, haul water, feed the hungry, help the wounded, build shelter, join the army: don't pretend we still have a city or prop up the outside world's pretense that we do.

Sontag erupted in the face of this barrage of criticism, saying to Erika Munk:

> I don't know how anyone can be furious. I didn't receive a penny. I paid all my own expenses. I volunteered a month and a half of my life, the actors are working for nothing as is every person on the staff, the tickets are free, and it's Sarajevo. How can they object? This is a very extreme case of a not-for-profit production. I should think they'd be proud. I venture to say that there are more people in this besieged, mutilated city, who have heard of *Waiting for Godot* than there are in Paris and London and New York. I'm stopped by children in the street who say to me in Bosnian, "Waiting for Godot!"— it's become a legend in this city. It's to the glory of this play that it should be played here.

The war correspondents admired Sontag. They were grateful for her appearance; they were impressed by her courage and fortitude. Janine Di Giovanni of the London *Times* watched Sontag run the gauntlet of Serbian sniper fire on the way to a theater only a thousand feet from where mortars were pounding the city. The theater's walls and windows shook. The chain-smoking director sat in the candlelight calmly discussing the play, speculating on the prospects of Western intervention. Air strikes would mean she would have to move out of the Holiday Inn and live with one of the actors. In fact, as Christopher Hitchens reports, Sontag spent "some nights sleeping on the floor of the *Oslobodjenje*," the Bosnian newspaper which continued to publish even as its offices were reduced to rubble. The bombardment had become "so ghastly that it was unsafe to go 'home,'" Hitchens explains.

Di Giovanni recited Sontag's war credits: present at the U.S. bombing of Hanoi, present in the Sinai in 1973 dodging heavy shelling. Sontag came to the theater with breakfast rolls taken from the Holiday Inn, and fed her feeble actors, who took rehearsal breaks as an opportunity to stretch out on the stage and rest. One of her cast told a reporter: "There is fighting on the frontline and then there is another kind of fighting. We must tell the world that we are not animals, that we are cultured, that we have ideas and dreams." The actors watched Sontag intently, welcoming her judgment that their performances had improved. Quoting one of the lines from the play, an actor responded: "We should celebrate, but how?"

John Burns of the *New York Times* reported:

> To the people of Sarajevo, Ms. Sontag has become a symbol, interviewed frequently by the local newspapers and television, invited to speak at gatherings everywhere, asked for autographs on the street. After the opening performance of the play, the city's Mayor, Muhamed Kresevljakovic, came onstage to declare her an honorary citizen, the only foreigner other than the recently departed United Nations commander, Lieut. Gen. Phillipe Morillon, to be so named.

Proud of her status as honorary citizen, Sontag told television interviewer Charlie Rose, "It means a lot to people that an independent foreigner wants to come and work there part-time in the city." That she would spend a month producing the play and then return to Sarajevo nine more times proved to many Bosnians that she was not seeking publicity. She worked with elementary school children, broadcast on the radio, and appeared in documentaries shot by SAGA, Sarajevo's film production company.

Sontag's *NYRB* apologia answers many of her critics' charges. She points out that it was hardly pretentious or inappropriate to produce *Godot* in a city with a tradition of staging the classics in repertory. In 1993 two of Sarajevo's five theaters were still operating, offering plays such as *Alcestis* and *Ajax*. Of course, Sarajevans also craved comic relief, Sontag wrote, and plenty would have preferred seeing a Harrison Ford movie to a Beckett play. But that was true before the war. Sontag freely identified herself as an "eccentric American writer," but she did not see her choice of play as at all odd. Her account of the play's production reveals a dedicated, determined, and ingenious director. But purblindness to her status as media star provoked skepticism. As Erika Munk suggests: "When a cultural celebrity lands in a nest of war reporters, the result is between *commedia* and farce." What to make of a sixty-year-old woman who records having been "surprised by the amount of attention from the international press that *Godot* was getting." She was staying in the Holiday Inn, a "journalist's dormitory," she concedes, yet the dozen or so requests for interviews troubled her, she says, and she made herself available to the press only after the participants in her production assured her the attention would be "good for Sarajevo."

Wanting to employ as many good out-of-work actors as she could, Sontag opted for a "gender-blind" production, picking a robust older actress to play Pozzo (normally the play's dominating male) and then casting three sets of actors to play Vladimir and Estragon in "three variations on the theme of the couple"—a theme, she might have added, that pervades her other directorial efforts in the theater and film. The actors were from Muslim, Serb, and Croatian families. To tether the couples to her internationalist and universalist ethic, Sontag made one relationship a "buddy pair," another a mother-daughter duo, and another a contentious husband-wife partnership. Situated in clearly demarcated upstage and downstage areas, the couples implicitly commented on each other and sometimes functioned as "something of a Greek Chorus as well as an audience on the show put on by the master and the slave," Sontag explains.

Sontag realized it would try the stamina of her audience to expect them to sit through both acts of a play performed in a poorly lit theater not far from the line of fire. She rationalized that the "despair of Act I was enough for the Sarajevo audience." It might be unbearable to wait for Godot and have him not arrive a second time.

Sontag made the play a "collective enterprise," observes critic David Toole. Vladimir and Estragon no longer seem so isolated. The people of Sarajevo could see themselves represented onstage and the "lives of the individuals in the theater attained an aesthetic justification that the world itself did not," Toole concludes. Erika Munk, a sympathetic witness who honors Sontag's work, remarks that

> somehow *Godot* became too apt; the fit was too tight. Topicality and humorlessness combined to create pathos, and when the candles were carefully extinguished at the end, the moment and its meaning were so calculatedly clear I was left dry-eyed. Perhaps a week later I would not have been.

Munk's last sentence suggests that Sontag's *Godot* was ritualistic; that is, her version of the play was addressed to an audience that would return for several performances. Munk notes that a local academic "sniffed. 'After all, it wasn't Beckett.'" She would like to regard him as simply a pedant, but she concedes: "Perhaps the way *Godot*'s relevance was underlined in Sontag's reading made it seem like a prison-visitor's or humanitarian worker's gift, which he slightly resented having to accept, rather than a work of art offered on its own terms."

Certainly Samuel Beckett would have been outraged by Sontag's interpretation of his play. In 1984, through his attorney Martin Garbus, Beckett had tried to shut down a production of *Endgame* at Robert Brustein's American Repertory Theater because the play's setting and stage directions had been altered. Aidan Higgins, in a letter to the *Irish Times* (October 30, 1993) complained:

> With respect, may I ask who has given Susan Sontag carte blanche to reinterpret that most austere of modern classics . . . as she sees fit in Sarajevo, and moreover in a language she doesn't understand? Beckett had already refused permission for an all-female Dutch Godot and would surely have disapproved of this farrago.

As if to answer such objections, Sontag explained in her *NYRB* piece that she had copied a Serbo-Croatian translation of the play into her English text and copied the English text into the Bosnian script. It took her about ten days, she said, to "learn by heart the words of Beckett's play in the language in which my actors were speaking it." (She also had the services of a translator, and some of the actors knew English.) What she had done was not that unusual. Arthur Miller had directed *Death of a Salesman* in Chinese, she pointed out. "Look, I know these people," Sontag told journalist John Pomfret. "I've been to their houses and shared a part of their life. I can tell when they make a mistake. We're that close. I listen to the emotion in a line." Critics like Higgins would probably not find her account convincing. "Beckett himself detested stage business and presumably had his own good reasons for limiting the cast to five. He would surely not have approved the swinging changes in order 'to update' his way of thinking, forsooth!"

Waiting for Godot played four to five times a week, with two performances on some days. The actors became faster and more energetic. In the SAGA documentary *Sarajevo Ground Zero* (a compilation of films about the city under siege), Sontag appears briefly, acknowledging the audience after a performance. She bows her head, pulling back her hair in a characteristic gesture and looking almost embarrassed.

By April 1995 Sontag's attempt to bring primary schooling to large apartment houses in Sarajevo had collapsed, and in "heartbreak" she deemed her efforts a "huge failure." Yet she continued to visit Sarajevo, making eleven trips altogether, lasting from a few weeks to months, and making good on her commitment to keep returning as long as the siege lasted. In February 1994 she received the Montblanc de la Culture Award for her work in Sarajevo, a $25,000 prize that she presented to the Bosnian center of PEN, saying, "This is really an award to Sarajevo. I am only an instrument."

Sontag's desire to stage a play in Sarajevo reflected not merely her commitment to creating an event for the besieged city, but a serious involvement with the theater that had led to the writing of her first produced play, *Alice in Bed*, which premiered in September 1991 in Bonn, Germany.

Sontag had directed *Jacques and His Master*, Milan Kundera's adaptation of a Diderot play, at Harvard's American Repertory Theater in 1985. Jacques and his master are on a journey that is trisected by the love stories of Jacques, of his master, and of Madame de La Pommeraye. Each story is a variation on the others. The stories interrupt and repeat each other, anticipating Sontag's direction of three sets of Vladimirs and Estragons in her Sarajevo production of *Waiting for Godot*.

Jacques and His Master is about the quest for direction and the drive to locate a sense of identity in love. There is the will to go on; there is the sense of fatalism that paralyzes movement. These conflicting impulses unite and divide master and servant, master and disciple, lover and lover.

Alice in Bed is an autobiographical play, in spite of Sontag's disclaimer to a German reporter: "I don't want everyone to think that it's about me." Alice in bed is a stand-in for the asthmatic Susan, with a bossy nurse very like Rose McNulty, who urges her charge to get up and confront the world. And the apparent subject of the play, Alice James, the brilliant sister of William and Henry, had been diagnosed with breast cancer at forty-two, the same age Sontag was when she was handed what seemed a death sentence.

The idea of *Alice in Bed* originated with Sontag's direction of *As You Desire Me*. Her star actress, Adriana Asti, asked Sontag to write a play for her in which she would never leave the stage. Sontag joked that she would have to put the actress in bed. The comment reflected a feminist view that women have rarely been allowed to dominate the stage, except as victims and captives of the male imagination. *Alice in Bed* reflects an anger at men that Sontag has rarely expressed openly.

References to Virginia Woolf proliferate in Sontag's later interviews, and it is not surprising to learn from her author's note to *Alice in Bed* that she had in mind Woolf's provocative book, *A Room of One's Own*, while writing her play. In Woolf's classic feminist tract, she speculates that if Shakespeare had had a sister she would not have had the "inner authority" (Sontag's words) to write. Sontag continues: The "obligation to be physically attractive and patient and nurturing and docile and sensitive and deferential to fathers (to brothers, to husbands) contradicts and *must* collide with the egocentricity and aggressiveness and the indifference to self that a large creative gift requires in order to flourish." All the "and"s convey a clear sense that a woman's role for Sontag is impossibly demanding. As a girl, Sontag experienced the demands she enumerates above, but she found in herself the authority and the egocentricity and aggressiveness to reject them.

In Sontag's view, Alice is the "Victorian girl-child" who is allowed an active role only in fantasies like *Alice in Wonderland*. Lewis Carroll's work is yet another key text for Sontag, because reading it helped save her from a dull and demeaning childhood. *Alice in Bed*—like *Alice in Wonderland*—evolves into a kind of mad tea party, Sontag explains. It is a work she has been "preparing to write" all her life. It is a play about the "grief and anger of women; and, finally, a play about the imagination."

Alice in Bed invents dialogue for Alice James, treating her invalidism not only as a feminist issue but as one of the existential problems of humanity. What are we supposed to do when we get out of bed? Take the world by storm, like the nineteenth-century feminist Margaret Fuller? (Fuller is one of the characters who acts as an advisor to Alice in the play.) Or do we stay at home, creating adventure through the medium of language alone? Such was the course of another of Alice's advisors, the nineteenth-century poet Emily Dickinson.

In her play, Sontag ranges far afield: from what it means to be a woman in the distinguished James family, to the nature of language ("tenses are strangely potent aren't they"), the patterns of history, class structure (Alice has a talk with a Cockney burglar), and the paradox of Alice herself, a woman who does not get out of bed and yet declares: "My mind makes me feel strong." But as one reviewer noted, the play's dramatic structures are frail. Sontag's production of Kundera's adaptation of Diderot at Harvard confirms Robert Brustein's belief that "Susan's theatrical imagination was (like that of Jonathan Miller whom she resembles as theatre person in many ways) essentially visual." She lacked the gift for directing actors, for finding a language in which to communicate with them. An analogous weakness in writing dialogue resulted in stilted action in *Alice in Bed*. As another reviewer put it, the essayist "overwhelms the dramatist."

In 1994 Sontag began researching the life of actress Helena Modjeska at the Getty Institute in Malibu, California. The Polish actress immigrated to Anaheim, California, in 1876, settled on a farm among a small colony of Polish exiles, and studied English for her debut in the Shakespearean roles she longed to perform in their original language. Modjeska became a world-renowned actress and a rival to Sarah Bernhardt—whose voice Sontag herself provided in Edgardo Cozarinksy's documentary film *Sarah* (1988).

In California, Modjeska became pinioned between her husband, Karol Chłapowski, the product of an old Polish landed family, and the young writer Henryk Sienkiewicz, who would later win the Nobel Prize. This "trio"—to use the words from "Zero," the preface to her new novel, *In America*—reprises the dynamic of *The Volcano Lover*. The narrator is recognizably Sontag, discoursing not only on the nineteenth-century story but on her experiences in Sarajevo, her childhood and grandparents, her marriage to Philip Rieff, her fondness for Polish poet Czeslaw

Milosz, her affinity with Europe. The Poland of her novel, partitioned by Austria, Prussia, and Russia, was a precursor to her beloved Bosnia, dismembered by Serbs and Croats. The Poles the narrator hears talking in a room as she begins to formulate her narrative are utopians and idealists, bitterly disappointed in Europe and yet cherishing the illusion that their "martyred nation" will be redeemed. Sontag even refers to the "supreme heroine of my own earliest childhood, Marya Sklodowska, the future Madame Curie."

Men in vast numbers were drawn to Modjeska—and so it is in Sontag's novel, where they bow down before her protagonist, the actress Maryna, and her "commanding gaze." They follow her to California, where she starts her career over again. The narrator says Maryna's story is appealing to her because "I like the feeling of being reduced to my own resources. Of having to do nothing but cope. (Perhaps that's why I've felt so exhilarated, so numbingly at home as well as convulsed with dread, during the six stays in besieged Sarajevo.)"

Sontag clearly enjoyed the break from the circumscribed role of essayist, expected to comment on the phenomena of the day. Interviewed in January 1998 by Elzbieta Sawicka in Warsaw (where she had accompanied Annie Leibovitz, who had an exhibition of photographs), Sontag stipulated that she would not address any political questions; her orientation had clearly shifted. She had given herself over to the sheer delight of performance. "I am myself an actress, a closet actress," she told Sawicka, by way of explaining her novel about Modjeska. "I always wanted to write a novel about an actress. I understand what acting is all about and what goes on in the profession." She had acted in school, and she really loved performing, but she herself had concluded that "this is not a life I want to live." Sontag insisted the novel was not autobiographical: "I am interested in a novel about immigrants and an actress." As in *The Volcano Lover*, she avoided using the real names of historical figures, allowing herself a certain degree of latitude in the creation of fictional events.

Curious about the Polish connection, Sawicka wondered if Sontag's own ancestry figured in her feeling for Modjeska. Sontag said, "No, not at all." Sawicka countered: "The land of your ancestors doesn't have any meaning for you? Aren't you sentimental?" It was not a question of sentiment, Sontag insisted. "I'm not egocentric. I don't think about myself too much or about my roots." Sontag then reminisced about her first visit to Poland in 1980. A Polish film critic took her to a Jewish cemetery in Warsaw. They walked around that sad, neglected place, trying to read the names on the tombstones. Sontag observed that half of the names ended in *ski* or *icz,* and the other half had German-sounding names. "Isn't it interesting," Sontag commented, "that so many Polish Jews have German names." The Pole replied, "Exactly like you." A shocked Sontag realized she had never thought about her name.

Of course, the story that Sontag tells actually confirms the autobiographical element in *In America,* and her effort to deflect her interviewer becomes one of those dodges that writers employ when they fear that the autonomy of their work as literature is threatened. Maryna indulges in the "art of thinking about herself," and like Sontag, she addresses questions such as: "How could she represent the ideal of an artist?" Attracted to extreme situations, Maryna says, "I adore recklessness." Sontag has fun with her heroine, placing her in the very American venues where Susan Sontag felt sequestered. Ignorant Americans who do not know how to handle genius advise Maryna to cultivate the common touch, because theater audiences "don't want a steady diet of lady." The novel's theater manager, Angus Barton, worries about Maryna's intelligence and pride, neither of which is necessary to an actress, he assures her. Like Sontag, Maryna is accosted by adoring fans. "You're an actress. You understand everything. . . . You're beautiful. You're a star. Everyone loves you," gushes Minnie, owner of the Polka Saloon. When Maryna tells her that she has chosen to visit because of the saloon's name, Minnie replies, "No kiddin'. I thought it was 100 percent American."

With Maryna, Sontag reverses destinations, making the Polish actress crave a new life in America just as Sontag sought a new one in Europe. Maryna, moreover, is a diva, one of many Sontag has found fascinating. In the autobiographical preface to *In America,* Sontag recalls the "first time I ever saw a diva close up." Maria Callas sat lunching at Lutèce, lecturing the director of the Metropolitan Opera: "Mr. Bing. [Pause.] Either we do things the Callas way or we do not do them at all." Sontag's inserted pause, like a stage direction, reveals how dramatic she found the scene. Both Mr. Bing and Sontag (Sontag reports) were reduced to silence for several minutes.

The closest Sontag has come to confession of her fascination with divahood is her endorsement of Wayne Koestenbaum's book *The Queen's Throat: Opera, Homosexuality, and the Mystery of Desire* (1993):

A brilliant book—an ecstatic book—inevitably, an elegiac book. And one which—like some operas, certain voices—has the power to provoke—in this reader and opera-lover, anyway—admiration, rapture, identification.

Koestenbaum points out:

> Long ago in the diva's life, she is not herself; she tries to forget that alienated prehistory. . . . Her confidence that she will be a diva lifts her from an obscure, immobile, difficult childhood; the vocation of diva permits her to read her life backward and see clear meanings, hints of tremendousness, where there was once shame.

A solitary woman, Koestenbaum concludes, all the diva wants is "sovereignty over herself."

Absent from all of Sontag's literature is the mother. Yet Koestenbaum shrewdly observes: "A diva begins by imitating her mother, even if the mother's voice hurts." The diva, indeed, may be, in Koestenbaum's terms, "a lesbian looking within her own gender at the mother." In terms reminiscent of Sontag's descriptions of her own mother, Mildred Sontag, Koestenbaum evokes the diva's mother as one who "once floated by with serene, oceanic detachment. And so the diva herself assumes that posture."

Although first announced for publication in 1997, *In America* did not appear then or for the next two years. Sontag was in no hurry—she scorned, for example, the regimen of British writers who feel they must produce a book at least every other year.

In the 1990s Sontag pursued her usual peripatetic schedule, traveling to her favorite performance sites: the City Arts & Lectures series in San Francisco, summers at a Skidmore writing institute, the Miami Book Fair, lectures abroad, and dozens of appearances on the lecture platforms of Manhattan. No matter the event, Sontag's demeanor tended toward the solemn—but with lots of hair-tossing (her widening white streak had begun to encroach on both sides of her face). She read fluently and with immense care. Her audience could always hear her consonants; no soft *t* or *r* in "wri*ter*" for her. She had begun to make some concession to color, wearing a variety of coral, brown, and maroon scarves, blouses, and light jackets.

In September 1996, for the fiftieth anniversary of FSG, Sontag wore several strings of black beads, black velvet pants, a salmon-colored sweater, and a black jacket. She loped onstage in black shoes with flat heels, fooling with her hair. Once seated, she began working over a draft of what she would read, ignoring the other speakers, occasionally looking at the audience, smiling a moment too late when something funny was said—always a beat behind because she was concentrating so hard on correcting her own text. She seemed to be circling and crossing out passages, making notes, and then, when her turn came, she got up and read flawlessly from *In America*. Of all the writers onstage, Sontag was the only one Roger Straus stopped to greet after making his remarks.

As Sontag built her body of work, she found it increasingly difficult to maintain the purity of her quest. For the writer "experiences himself or herself as both Dr. Frankenstein and the monster," she confesses. By now Sontag reluctantly recognizes that she has a public persona—no matter how much she protests that "I'm not that . . . image." Unlike some writers—she cites the example of Borges—she refuses to take refuge in an ironic distance from herself, insisting, instead, on "singleness." The books and the person are not the same, she admits, yet "the writer is me . . . there's only one person here."

Retrospectives of Sontag's career have begun to appear, but no convincing assessment of Sontag's enduring value has yet emerged. Distinguished art critic and philosopher Arthur Danto's work contains brief but respectful references to Sontag which suggest he thinks of her as a kind of touchstone figure. Yet he cannot say what it is about her that might speak to posterity. He has known her for years, although he does not claim to know her well. He calls himself a "fence-sitter" with regard to her reputation: "Her genius is in her titles, whatever the content of what she has written, for each title beams a ray of light on something previously obscure. It is to her credit that she brought so much out of the shadows, which has come to define central aspects of our culture."

The difficulty with Sontag is that so much of her writing has its own built-in dialectic. Hers is work that argues with itself. Sontag dislikes the idea of being tied to her opinions, and they often trail after her like orphans she would rather not acknowledge. It is probable that she will be renowned for her style and form long after the specific content of her work falls into desuetude. As she observes in her introduction to the *Best American Essays 1992:* "The influential essayist is someone with an acute sense of what has not been (properly) talked about, what should be talked about (but differently)." Beyond that, she points out, the work survives as a "display of a complex mind and a distinctive prose voice."

In September 1998 Annie Leibovitz spent a frantic September visiting Sontag in the hospital. Sontag had suffered a recurrence of breast cancer. Chemotherapy caused nerve damage, and Sontag experienced "massive amounts of pain." At one point her suffering drove her to say "I'm finished." She lost weight and hair and yet continued to make appearances. A Humanities Institute colleague saw her at a colloquium on Gertrude Stein, and he thought Sontag looked ghastly, with a turban covering her head. But she remained intensely involved in the discussion, and was dismayed to learn the extent of Stein's connections with France's Nazi occupiers. He liked Sontag's plain, honest, direct expression of shock. A few days later, on October 19, 1998, she appeared, wearing a wig and looking almost like her old self, on the stage of the 92nd Street Y, helping to celebrate the thirty-fifth anniversary of the *New York Review of Books*.

On February 24, 1999, Sontag was scheduled to appear at Columbia's Miller Theatre on a program devoted to Eastern European writing. Would she show up? She had recently canceled—at the last moment—an appearance at the National Arts Club. The event was to celebrate the *Threepenny Review*, and the journal's editor, Wendy Lesser, announced that Sontag was ill, although not seriously. But Sontag kept her date at the Miller, and she seemed more vibrant and more engaged than ever. She sat comfortably in her seat but shifted often, almost bouncing in her enthusiasm for literature and life. She told photographer Nancy Crampton that she had regained much of her old strength. Indeed, this was the same Susan Sontag, only more so. Now an older woman with very short all-white hair, she seemed once again—as she claimed after the success of *The Volcano Lover*—to be just beginning. And in "Singleness," a recent autobiographical essay, Sontag repeated the sentiment, declaring: "My life has always felt like a becoming. . . . I enjoy beginning again. The beginner's mind is best."

Appendix

A BRIEF ANTHOLOGY OF QUOTATIONS

[HOMAGE TO S.S.]

A literary pinup.
　　　　　　—Herbert Mitgang, *New York Times*

The dark lady of American letters.
　　　　　　—Norman Podhoretz

Our unofficial hostess of letters.
　　　　　　—Walter Kendrick, *The Nation*

The bad girl of contemporary American letters.
　　　　　　—*Albany Times-Union*

The *belle dame sans merci* of the literary world.
　　　　　　—Zoë Heller, *Irish Times*

The Natalie Wood of the U.S. avant-garde.
　　　　　　—*Contemporary Biography*

The Kenny G of literature.
>　—PEN board member

The Mary Baker Eddy of intellectual chic.
>　—Leslie Hancome, *Newsday*

The Passionara of the Left.
>　—Susan Sontag

The sibyl of Manhattan.
>　—Boyd Tonkin, *The Guardian*

For many years, our culture has viewed Susan Sontag . . . as some sort of leftist vestal virgin.
>　—Deirdre Donahue, *USA Today*

The "with it" girl.
>　—Susan Sontag

The Beatnik Boadicea.
>　—Alan Brien, *The Spectator*

The Queen of Camp.
>　—Edward Field, *Boston Review*

Susan Sontag, no matter what you may have thought, is not of the royal family.
>　—Nat Hentoff, *Village Voice*

A new Chanel of the arts.
>　—Mary Ellmann, *Atlantic Monthly*

Our Erasmus.
>　—Carlos Fuentes

A brick.
>　—Bruce Chatwin

The Paganini of criticism.
>—James Sloan Allen, *Saturday Review*

The imitation me.
>—Mary McCarthy

The writer and thinker in many variations: as analyst, rhapsodist and roving eye, as public scold and portable conscience.
>—*Time*

"The novels of Susan Sontag are self-indulgent, overrated crap."
"I think Susan Sontag is brilliant."
>—*Bull Durham*

You've probably heard of Susan Sontag, the American critic who sometimes writes in English.
>—Richard Fuller, *Philadelphia Inquirer*

The niceties, the fine points, diplomacy, standards, tradition—that's what we're reaching toward. We may stumble along the way but, civilization, yes, the Geneva convention, chamber music, Susan Sontag, yes, civilization.
>—*Gremlins 2*

"God, I wish I were Susan Sontag or somebody like that so I could explain it all with brilliance and authority. Are you intimidated by her, too?"
>—George Garrett, *The King of Babylon Shall Not Come Against You*

Behind Ross was a magazine-size black-and-white picture of Susan Sontag which had been matted and framed; someone had drawn a black bar across her eyes, like the "disguise" bars on the faces in Fifties true-confession magazines. On the black mat beneath her face was written, in white ink, *Eat higher on the food chain. Filets de Susan Sontag.*
>—Blanche McCrary Boyd, *Terminal Velocity*

"Susan Sontag has a stranglehold on the intellectual press. Without her say-so nothing gets accepted."
"You don't really believe that, do you?"
                    —Vivian Gornick, *Approaching Eye Level*

Dear Susan Sontag,
    Would you please read my books and make me famous?
                    —Kathy Acker, *Great Expectations*

Number of times a year Susan Sontag says she cooks dinner at home:
2. What she cooks: pasta.
                    —*Carper's Index* http://jokes.webdevelop.com

Just as Athena, the ancient goddess of wisdom, sprang full-blown from the brow of Zeus, so Susan Sontag, the contemporary essayist-novelist-filmmaker, seems self-created by a sheer act of will, existing in an ecstasy of ideas.
                    —Maralyn Lois Polak, *Philadelphia Inquirer Magazine*

The lovely brave Minerva of a genuine new underground/*avant-garde* or the glib bootlegger of the latest wave of French modernism, East Village Pop, and other modes of the higher unseriousness.
                    —Theodore Solotaroff, *The Red Hot Vacuum and Other Pieces on the Writing of the Sixties*

Our glamorous camp follower of the French avant-garde.
                    —John Updike

I'm looking forward to the Susan Sontag Exercise Book . . . with accompanying tape: "Now for the volte-face. . . ."
                    —Alexander Cockburn, *Village Voice*

Compassion, to fashion, to passion when it's new
To Sontag, to Sondheim, to anything taboo.
                    —*Rent*

A publicist able to make brilliant quilts from grandmother's patches.
>—Irving Howe, "The New York Intellectuals"

A truly gifted innovator.
>—John Hawkes

How come Susan Sontag is never criticized for the strange sexual implications of her work? Is it because she's the darling of the Establishment and I'm not?
>—Ronald Sukenick, novelist

Even her nursery-rhyme name seems designed for dropping.
>—Mary Ellmann

Sontag is the kind of person about whom people like to speculate endlessly. . . .
>—Helen Benedict, *New York Woman*

The most curious person alive.
>—David Rieff

Notes and Comments

A number of people in New York agreed to talk to us only with the clear understanding that we would not use their names. Susan Sontag is not just an important writer, she is a New York institution, perceived to have enough power to injure as well as to enhance reputations. How much power Sontag actually has is disputable, but the pervasiveness of the view that she holds a certain sway in the publishing world is not. There were publishers who would not even look at the proposal for this book solely because Susan Sontag was its subject. As soon as Sontag realized that we were seriously investigating her life and career, she had her lawyers put our publisher on notice.

It is a canard that only hostile witnesses speak to unauthorized biographers. On the record or off, we have had ample testimony from close and long-range observers of our subject—many of whom admire her extravagantly.

In this section, we provide a chapter-by-chapter summary of sources and provide additional comments. We have eschewed both footnotes and citations keyed to page numbers in our text for the following reason: they make for tedious reading and are usually ignored except by a few scholars and reviewers.

One most important source is Leland Poague's magnificently edited collection, *Conversations with Susan Sontag* (Jackson: University Press of Mississippi, 1995), produced with the full cooperation of Susan Sontag. To compare our version of her life with her own, consult Poague. Unless otherwise noted, all citations of correspondence are to the Farrar, Straus & Giroux Collection at the New York Public Library.

ABBREVIATIONS

AC	Alfred Chester.
ACP	Alfred Chester Papers. Special Collections, University of Delaware Library.
AF	"Susan Sontag: The Art of Fiction." *Paris Review* 37 (Winter 1995).
BR	Barbara Rowes. "Author Susan Sontag Rallies from Dread Illness to Enjoy Her First Commercial Triumph." *People*, March 20, 1978.
CR	Carl Rollyson.
CSS	*Conversations with Susan Sontag.*
DR	David Rieff.
EF	Edward Field. "The Man Who Would Marry Susan Sontag." Unpublished essay, courtesy of Edward Field.
EH	Ellen Hopkins. "Susan Sontag Lightens Up." *Los Angeles Times Magazine.* August 16, 1992.
FSG	Farrar, Straus & Giroux.
HB	Helen Benedict. *Portraits in Print: A Collection of Profiles and the Stories Behind Them.* New York: Columbia University Press, 1991.
HSA	Alfred Chester. *Head of a Sad Angel: Stories 1953-1966,* edited by Edward Field. Santa Rosa, Calif.: Black Sparrow Press, 1990.
HSZ	Harriet Sohmers Zwerling.
Int.	Interview.
LG	Leslie Garis. "Susan Sontag Finds Romance." *New York Times Magazine,* August 2, 1992.
LK	Lila Karpf of FSG.
LP	Lisa Paddock.
MD	Michael D'Antonio. "Little David, Happy at Last." *Esquire,* March 1990.
NY	New York.
NYPL	New York Public Library.
NYRB	*New York Review of Books.*
PIL	Susan Sontag. "Pilgrimage." *The New Yorker,* December 21, 1987.
PR	*Partisan Review.*
RG	Robert Giroux.
RS	Roger Straus.
SS	Susan Sontag.
TO	Thelma O'Brien. "A Close-up Picture of Susan Sontag." *Los Angeles Times,* April 23, 1978.
ZH	Zoë Heller. "Side by Side with Sontag." *Irish Times,* September 26, 1992.

1 : MY DESERT CHILDHOOD (1933–1945)

SS's Earliest Memory and Her Nurse: See AF and ZH. **On SS's Childhood**: BR; see also SS's rendition of childhood memories in "Project for a Trip to China," included in her volume of short stories, *I, etcetera* (NY: FSG, 1978). **Jack Rosenblatt**: His company is listed in the New York City directory for 1933–34. **On SS's Residence with Relatives:** EH. According to TO, Mildred and Jack met at Grossinger's, the resort in the Catskills where Mildred had a waitressing job. **Jack and Mildred Rosenblatt:** Census records and SS's int. with Elzbieta Sawicka, "Ostatni Chorazy Oswiecenia," *Rzeczpospolita* [daily newspaper], January 24–25 and 31, 1998, and February 1, 1998. See also Paul Grondahl, "Sontag Laments on State of Literature, *Albany Times-Union*, July 25, 1990. **Details of Jack Rosenblatt's Death:** American Foreign Service death certificate and from Terry Gross's int. with SS on the radio program "Fresh Air." **SS's Development Of Asthma:** This is reminiscent of Kandinsky, who hated his mother, felt alone and friendless, and at thirteen developed asthma. Whether SS really had asthma is uncertain. Many cases of shortness of breath are misdiagnosed as asthma for lack of a better term to describe a wide variety of maladies brought on by environmental and psychological conditions. **The Move to Miami:** Margaria Fichtner, "Susan Sontag's Train of Thought Rolls into Town," *Miami Herald*, February 19, 1989. SS told her son that she had vague memories of "white stucco houses with pseudo-Moorish detailing." See DR, *Going to Miami: Exiles, Tourists, Refugees in the New America* (London: Bloomsbury, 1987). **SS's Hostility to Her Mother:** It is apparent in ZH. Jill Johnston alerted us to an article by Hans J. Kleinschmidt, "The Angry Act: The Role of Aggression in Creativity," *American Imago* (Spring/Summer 1967), in which Kleinschmidt describes creative artists who as children felt abandoned by their parents and consequently elaborated myths about their own self-sufficiency. Absent parents stimulate in such children an "excessive reliance on intellectual endowment" and "feelings of omnipotence or, in any case, of being different and superior." Thus the "artist creates his own emotional history through his personal myth." SS's more charitable—which is to say more complex—feelings about parents and children are expressed in Cott int., *CSS*. **Asthma and Stress:** Eva Naunton, "Gasping for Life," *Miami Herald*, June 12, 1989. **SS on Her Tucson Childhood:** William Porter, "Romancing the Novel, Susan Sontag Dumps Essay for Freedom of Fiction," *Arizona Republic*, November 24, 1992. For an imaginative re-creation of her childhood, see "Project for a Trip to China," in *I, etcetera* (NY: FSG, 1978). For contrast: *Arizona: A State Guide* (NY: Hastings House, 1951). Our evocation of Tucson is based on a winter visit and on descriptions in Barbara Kingsolver's novel *The Bean Trees* (NY: HarperCollins, 1988). For Priestley's reminiscence, see *Arizona Memories*, edited by Anne Hodges Morgan and Rennard Strickland (Tucson: University of Arizona Press, 1984). Details of the Tucson climate and culture are drawn from Patricia Peters Stephenson, *A Personal Journey Through* *the University Neighborhood,* self-published; a letter by Dorothy Livadas of Rochester, New York, to the *Arizona Daily Star,* reprinted in C. L. Sonnichsen, *Tucson: The Life and Times of an American City* (Norman: University of Oklahoma Press, 1982). **SS on Her Tucson Schooling:** BR; EH; Cott int., *CSS;* "Project for a Trip to China." The subjects studied in Arizona schools were supplied via E-mail from the Reference Desk, Arizona State Library. **SS on Her Childhood Reading:** Marian Christy, "Sontag Brought Personal Passion to Tale of Romance," *Chicago Tribune,* September 27, 1992; Larry Bograd, "An Interview with Susan Sontag," *Muse: An Arts Newspaper for Colorado,* June/July 1985; SS mentions reading her mother's copy of Hugo in Lynne Tillman, *Bookstore: The Life and Times of Jeanette Watson and Books & Co.* (New York: Harcourt Brace, 1999); see also PIL. **Mother and Daughter:** See "Project for a Trip to China." **On Fathers and Literary Mentors:** Nin and Dinesen are discussed in Elyce Wakerman, *Father Loss: Daughters Discuss the Man That Got Away* (Garden City, NY: Doubleday, 1984); see also SS's introduction to *Homo Poeticus: Essays and Interviews* (NY: FSG, 1995), a collection of writings by Danilo Kiš (who became her friend, and who was also preoccupied with his father and with the idea of fathers): "One can, in literature, choose one's parents"; SS is quoted in "The Books That Changed Their Lives," *Washington Post,* December 7, 1997. See AF for a photograph of SS lying on a cot, reading a book, with one foot on the floor. The photograph's caption is crucial: "Sarajevo, July 1993, in the sub-basement bombshelter/editorial office of the daily newspaper *Oslobodjenje.*" SS at sixty was still trying to re-create her refuge, her cell, her cave of the imagination. See "Zero," the preface to *In America.* **SS's Definition of the Writer:** *Susan Sontag,* a documentary distributed by Films for the Humanities; see also SS's conversation with Nadine Gordimer in *CSS.* **Early Literary Influences:** SS in AF cites Alcott, London, Dreiser, and states: "I got through my childhood in a delirium of literary exaltations." London describes Martin Eden's imagination as high-pitched and writes that his emotions leap like a "lambent flame." We have also drawn upon *SCETV Writers' Workshop, Susan Sontag,* South Carolina Educational Television, hosted by George Plimpton, SS talking with William Price Fox and students, in the archive of the Museum of Television and Radio, New York City; EH. See Sam Baskett's introduction to *Martin Eden* (NY: Holt, Rinehart, Winston, 1956). **On Male Influences:** Read especially the essays on Paul Goodman, Walter Benjamin, and Elias Canetti in *Under the Sign of Saturn* (NY: FSG, 1980).

2 · A WORLD ELSEWHERE (1945–1948)

Nathan Sontag's Furlough: TO and PIL. Ten years before publication of PIL, SS gave a more pleasant picture of her stepfather to TO: "I really think of my stepfather as my father. . . . He was very glamorous with all his medals." She called him a "heroic businessman" who "never really settled into anything."

Arizona During the War: C. L. Sonnichsen, *Tucson: The Life and Times of an American City* (Norman: University of Oklahoma Press, 1982). **Nat as Parent:** ZH; Wendy Perron, "Style and Radical Will: An Interview with Susan Sontag," *Soho Weekly News,* December 1, 1997; Nora Ephron int. with SS in *New York Post,* September 23, 1967; Alice M. Robinson, Vera Mowry Roberts, and Millsy S. Barranger, *Notable Women in the American Theatre* (NY: Greenwood Press, 1989). **The Move to California:** In PIL, SS mentions her home in Canoga Park, but the only Sontag residence we could find was in Sherman Oaks, where SS's classmate Mel Roseman remembers visiting her. He confirms many of the details in PIL which we rely on in this chapter. For a picture of postwar California, see Kevin Starr, *The Dream Endures: California Enters the 1940s* (NY: Oxford University Press, 1997). **Thomas Mann:** PIL. *The Magic Mountain* is the origin of *Illness as Metaphor,* which came at a time when SS's own cancer turned her again into an exile from the land of the healthy. We are indebted to Anthony Heilbut and Ronald Hayman for discussing their biographical research on Mann and their reactions to PIL. One of SS's high school friends, Mel Roseman, who is mentioned in PIL, says in an E-mail to us that he did not know about the visit to Mann, adding, however, "I wasn't the least bit surprised to read that she had visited him." Mann, an indefatigable diarist, never mentioned the SS visit. However, in June 1945, Mann became enamored of a sixteen-year-old American girl named Cynthia carrying a copy of *The Magic Mountain.* He asked her mother to introduce him. Cynthia had no idea how much the talks excited Mann, or how much he liked to admire young boys and girls. (See the scene with Cynthia in Ronald Hayman, *Thomas Mann: A Biography* [NY: Scribner, 1995].) Sometime in 1995, Laurence Goldstein, editor of the *Michigan Quarterly Review,* got a manuscript about SS's first meeting with Thomas Mann. Unfortunately, Goldstein cannot remember the author's name—only that she had been a reporter in Southern California and had done articles on famous people and their houses. She had spoken to Mann one afternoon, and he had permitted her to take photographs of his home. She also happened to be a friend of SS's mother. SS ignored her until SS learned that she had met Mann. SS then asked the woman to arrange a meeting. Not only did Mann and SS meet, they met again and again (according to the journalist)—so taken was the great man with the young girl who had read his work. When Goldstein passed on this reminiscence to us, he remarked that "this is the kind of biographical shard of information that maddens biographers . . . but you're likely to come across the woman in your researches" (Laurence Goldstein to CR, July 25, 1996). Alas, not so. **North Hollywood High School:** PIL, int. Gail Coyle, Joan Kurland, Mel Roseman, Fred Margolin, Robert Low, and Joan Garner Taylor; see also Robert Low's letter to *Los Angeles Times Magazine,* September 27, 1992. We are also grateful to Dr. Louise Teams, the librarian/archivist of North Hollywood High School. She supplied us with copies of the school newspaper and yearbooks. See also TO for SS's recollection of Sophia Leshing. **SS's Feelings About Ethnicity:** Newman, Scarpetta int., *CSS.* **Jamake**

Highwater: We are relying on Highwater's memoir *Shadow Show* (1986) and on an unpublished memoir he has shown us. *Shadow Show* parallels PIL when Highwater speaks of their passion for music, of how SS became an usher at the Wilshire-Ebell Theater in Los Angeles (it still exists) and let him slip into an empty seat next to her. There they indulged the passion for Schoenberg that she evokes in PIL. Indeed, the last concert they saw together was Alice Mock performing Schoenberg's *Pierrot Lunaire*, conducted by a very young Robert Craft.

3 : TOWARDS A BETTER LIFE (1949–1953)

Hutchins as Star: Mary Ann Dzuback, *Robert M. Hutchins: Portrait of an Educator* (Chicago: University of Chicago Press, 1991). **Mildred on the University of Chicago:** Ron Grossman, "At the C Shop with Susan Sontag," *Chicago Tribune*, December 1, 1992; see also Philip Rieff, "The Miracle of College Politics," *Harper's Magazine*, October 1961, 159; Armada int., *CSS.* **SS's Opinion of Chicago:** Sharon Cohen, "Nobel-ist of All: U. of Chicago," *Sun-Sentinel* (South Florida), September 29, 1991. **Hutchins on Chicago's European Ambience:** Harry S. Ashmore, *Unseasonable Truths: The Life of Robert Maynard Hutchins* (Boston: Little, Brown, 1989). We're grateful to Earl Shorris for discussing his years at Chicago, which overlapped with SS's. Riesman is quoted in Dzuback. **Berkeley:** Kevin Starr, *The Dream Endures: California Enters the 1940s* (NY: Oxford University Press, 1997); int. HSZ. For our descriptions of Harriet, we rely on EF. **Chicago:** Ned Rosenheim provided us with invaluable memories of SS's years at Chicago, of Joseph Schwab, and of other professors who meant much to her. Steiner's and SS's memories of Chicago appear in Molly McQuade, ed., *An Unsentimental Education: Writers and Chicago* (Chicago: University of Chicago Press, 1995). See the profile of McKeon by Scott McLemee, "Fear and Learning," *Lingua Franca*, January 1998, 24–25. We are indebted to several Chicago alumni, including Paul Ekman (E-mail to CR and LP, June 16, 1958). Ekman is now professor of psychology, University of California, San Francisco. **Strauss:** See George Steiner's review of Strauss texts, "Inscrutable and Tragic," *TLS*, November 14, 1997; Kenneth Minogue's review, "Friends and Foes," *TLS*, August 2, 1996; George Bruce Smith, "Who Was Leo Strauss?," *American Scholar*, Winter 1997. **Kenneth Burke:** See SS's comments in the McQuade int. in *CSS;* see also Burke to Stanley Edgar Hyman, August 13, 1963, Stanley Edgar Hyman Papers, Library of Congress, and AF. We are indebted to Scott McLemee for bringing this letter to our attention. See Christine Stansell for a useful evocation of Burke's urban, New York City mystique: "The Strangely Inspired Hermit of Andover," *London Review of Books*, June 5, 1997. **Philip Rieff:** Our descriptions are derived from interviews with his students and colleagues, especially Sam Heilman. We also drew on BR and Marshall Ledger, "The Master Teacher," *Pennsylvania Gazette*, March 1977. SS's awareness of gossip about her and Rieff is retailed in LG. One of Rieff's rare public comments on his marriage to SS can be found in MD. SS describes Rieff as Casaubon in "Zero," the prologue to *In America*, published in *Artes* 11 (1995). See also HB and Cott int. in *CSS*. It may be significant that SS read Simone de Beauvoir's *The Second Sex* the year after her marriage to Rieff. See also Schultz, Manion and Simon, and Servan-Schreiber int., *CSS;* and Leticia Kent, "Susan Sontag Speaks Up," *Vogue*, August 1971.

4 : THE LIFE AND THE PROJECT (1952–1957)

David Rieff: We have drawn on SS's autobiographical story "Baby," in *I, etcetera;* MD, ZH, and Cott int., *CSS*. We have found Carole Klein's *Mothers and Sons* (Boston: Houghton Mifflin, 1984) also indispensable. **SS at Connecticut:** Int. with Seymour Kleinberg. **SS at Brandeis and Harvard:** Int. with the late Irving Howe and John Simon. We also draw on a letter to us from Henny Wenkart, one of SS's study partners. For additional information on SS at Harvard, see chronology and McQuade int. in *CSS*. **Jacob Taubes:** Int. with Peter Tumarkin, Marshall Berman, the late Richard Tristman, and other Taubes students who described the impact of his charismatic personality and his teaching. See also Susan Taubes's novel, *Divorcing* (NY: Random House, 1969), which has become a kind of legend among Taubes devotees. The comparison of the two Susans is derived from *Divorcing* and from "Debriefing," SS's story about Susan Taubes, collected in *I, etcetera*. We have also consulted Susan Taubes, "The Absent God: A Study of Simone Weil," Ph.D. dissertation, Harvard University, 1956. **SS's Ph.D. Research:** *Idealism at Work: Eight Years of AAUW Fellowships,* a report by the American Association of University Women, 1967.

5 : QUEST (1957–1958)

SS at Cambridge: A. J. Ayer, a logical positivist, rejected philosophy's traditional interest in metaphysics, relying rather on empiricism and logic and demanding scientific verification of ethical and value-driven statements. His classic work, *Language, Truth, and Logic* (1936), which attacked the propositions of metaphysics and theology, had to be reckoned with by any student writing a dissertation on values and ethics.

Murdoch would have been a more congenial professor for SS. A philosopher, poet, and critic, Murdoch exemplified her pupil's own literary and intellectual bent. She had published *Sartre, Romantic Realist* in 1953. Her second book, *Under the Net* (1954), explicitly linked philosophy and fiction, observing how the Existentialists pursued the theme of the self seeking absolutes (goodness, love, morality) in an absurd universe. Whereas Ayer analyzed statements and employed logic, Murdoch engaged with narratives and symbolic actions.

Judith Grossman generously shared with us her impressions of SS. **On Paris and the Romance of Traveling to France:** Lorna Sage, "Bitter Fruit," *TLS*, April 19, 1996; Alice Kaplan, *French Lessons: A Memoir* (Chicago: University of Chicago Press, 1993); SS's foreword to *A Place in the World Called Paris*, ed. Steven Barclay (San Francisco: Chronicle Books, 1994). Compare SS's catalogue of a Paris day with HSZ's memoir of that same period when she and Susan resumed their relationship: "A Memoir of Alfred Chester," *Raritan* 12 (Winter 1993). For an evocation of Paris during the period of SS's first residence, see Herbert Lottman, *The Left Bank* (San Francisco: Halo Books, 1991), and Stanley Karnow, *Paris in the Fifties* (NY: Random House, 1997). Our accounts of SS's relationships with Irv Jaffe and Harriet Sohmers are based on interviews with Jaffe and HSZ. **Alfred Chester**: Harriet Sohmers Zwerling, "A Memoir of Alfred Chester," *Raritan* 12 (Winter 1993); EF; Cynthia Ozick, "Alfred Chester's Wig," in *Fame and Folly: Essays* (NY: Knopf, 1996). It is a great loss to this biography that Chester's unpublished story "Trois Corsages," about his literary harem, has disappeared. Chester's career repays study (as will be shown in Allen Hibbard's forthcoming biography); for our purposes, Chester provides a valuable means of exploring how Sontag became the phenomenon he so bitterly envied and reviled. See also Vidal's foreword to *HSA* and *Selections from the First Two Issues of The New York Review of Books*, edited by Robert Silvers and Barbara Epstein, n.d. (this is essentially a promotional booklet distributed gratis to magazine subscribers). Rechy's letter, titled "Complaint," is printed in the October 31, 1996, issue. The editor does not respond, but Rechy said he received an apology from the *Review*, which later published an announcement of the Pen West Life Achievement Award to Rechy. See Pamela Warrick, "Credit Where It's Overdue," *Los Angeles Times*, October 26, 1977. **André Breton:** Mark Polizzotti, *Revolution of the Mind: The Life of André Breton* (NY: FSG, 1995); Tony Judt, *Past Imperfect: French Intellectuals, 1944–1956* (Berkeley: University of California Press, 1992), provides an excellent background for understanding the origins of SS's aesthetics and politics. **SS's Decision to End Her Marriage:** SS's story "The Letter Scene," *The New Yorker*, August 18, 1986; see also BR; ZH.

6: MAKING IT (1959–1961)

SS/Rieff Breakup: SS's story "The Letter Scene," *The New Yorker*, August 18, 1986; see also BR; ZH. Professor Daniel Aaron of Harvard University also provided a brief but vivid picture of Rieff's grief. **New York:** We draw on Joan Didion's classic essay "Goodbye to All That," in *Slouching Toward Bethlehem* (NY: Noonday Press, 1990), for our evocation of a woman with literary ambitions exploring the city. For SS on her arrival in New York, see BR, ZH, and LG. **SS's**

Comments On Her Dissertation: *Idealism at Work: Eighty Years of AAUW Fellowships,* a report by the American Association of University Women, 1967. **Glimpses of SS at *Commentary:*** Int. Martin Greenberg and Hilton Kramer. SS has so seldom been seen out of uniform that Kramer's snapshot is intriguing. In England, she had already adopted her trademark all-black ensemble, yet there are a few photographs of her as late as 1966 that show some variation in dress, including short hair and skirts. Just as it took Marilyn Monroe about seven years (1946–53) to settle on an image, it took SS a comparable time (1959–66) to fashion her iconography. **Richard Howard:** We have relied on conversations with many writers, none of whom would care to be named here—except the fearless EF and Larry Mass. **AC on Finding One's Own Way:** ACP, January 14, 1958. **María Irene Fornés:** HSZ to CRLP, June 6, 1999; *The Feminist Companion to Literature in English,* ed. Virginia Blain, Isobel Grundy, and Patricia Clements (New Haven: Yale University Press, 1990); SS wrote a preface to *María Irene Fornés Plays* (NY: PAJ Publications, 1986); we have also drawn many of our impressions of Fornés from interviews with EF and HSZ, and from the clipping files of the Billy Rose Theatre Collection, NYPL for the Performing Arts. As Don Shewey observes in *The Advocate* (May 26, 1998): "Fornés's plays rarely feature overt lesbian content, yet they revel in the inner lives of women." Women seem especially appreciative of Fornés. Adele Mailer, *The Last Party: Scenes from My Life with Norman Mailer* (NY: Barricade Books, 1997), turned to Irene as a traveling companion during one of her husband's bellicose periods, and Harriet Sohmers—whatever grief Irene caused her—cannot focus on Irene without smiling. We base our impressions of Fornés's charisma partly on watching HSZ describe her; see also EF. We also rely on EF int. with HSZ (n.d.), ACP. **Susan and Irene:** ACP, August 8, 1959. **Custody Battle with Rieff:** ACP, August 18, 1959; int. Richard Tristman; see also MD. For SS's and DR's comments on his childhood and her motherhood, see MD; HB; BR; ZH; DR, *Going to Miami: Exiles, Tourists, Refugees in the New America* (London: Bloomsbury, 1987); and Margaria Fichtner, "The Outsider," *Miami Herald,* August 8, 1993. **SS and DR and Cubans:** Cinematographer Nestor Almendros, one of David's baby-sitters, is remembered in the dedication of David's book, *Going to Miami.* **Fornés on the Writing Group:** Stephanie Harrington, "Irene Fornés, Playwright: Alice and the Red Queen," an otherwise unidentified article in the clipping files of the NYPL for the Performing Arts; Fornés's memories coincide with those expressed by Richard Tristman in our interview with him. **SS as Teacher:** We also draw on Gerald Ginsburg's letter to us, May 6, 1998. **On Taubes's Writing:** See Marin Terpstra and Theo De Wit, "'No Spiritual Investment in the World As It Is': Jacob Taubes' Negative Political Theology," unpublished essay courtesy of Marin Terpstra. We are indebted to a number of Taubes's students at Columbia. Taubes has been deemed a "turbulent thinker" since his work contains such a swirling brew of conflicting positions. Like SS, he liked to create a tension between left and right, radical and conservative. **Roger Straus and the Acceptance of SS's First Novel:** We have relied on

Ted Morgan's profile of RG, "Feeding the Stream," *Saturday Review,* September 1, 1979, in the FSG files at NYPL. We have had the benefit of testimony from many FSG authors and editors. We also interviewed Nobile and examined his papers at Mugar Memorial Library, Special Collections, Boston University. Nobile's collection includes letters from SS, Epstein, and other SS friends. Nobile later expanded his article on *NYRB* into a book, *Intellectual Skywriting* (NY: Charterhouse, 1974).

7. MADE (1962–1963)

AC's Comments on RS and SS: AC to Paul Bowles, April 2, 1963, ACP; see also to EF, April 8, 1963. The testimony we heard of a sexual liaison between SS and AC is conflicting. **On RS:** Paul D. Colford, "Could This Be the End of an Era for Farrar, Straus?," *Newsday,* October 31, 1994; SS is quoted in James Reginato, "Nobel House," *New York,* November 9, 1987; Dorothea Straus, *Thresholds* (Boston: Houghton Mifflin, 1971); Carlin Romano, "Straus, a Prince Among Publishers," *Philadelphia Inquirer,* September 23, 1996; Scott Turow is quoted in Margo Rabb, "Publishing with Passion: Farrar, Straus and Giroux Celebrates 50," *Poets & Writers,* March/April 1997. **Edmund Wilson on SS:** Edmund Wilson, *The Sixties* (NY: FSG, 1993). **SS and PR:** William Phillips, *A Partisan View: Five Decades of the Literary Life* (NY: Stein & Day, 1983). We attempted to interview Phillips, who accused us of misleading him. We had written him a letter mentioning we had interviewed SS friends such as Richard Sennett. Phillips then assumed we were writing an authorized biography. Arriving at his apartment, we found a recalcitrant figure who, at first, could not be budged—until we hit upon the idea of asking him about his *PR* memoir. He agreed to comment, but he became increasingly upset as we focused on page references to SS. His companion, Edith Kurzweil, seemed more sympathetic. But Phillips had checked with SS and was on orders not to talk. As we were leaving, Kurzweil took a phone call and waved to us as we exited the apartment. The call was from SS, and we could tell she was checking up on us, for Kurzweil was running down the list of people we said we had interviewed. **AC and PR and SS**: AC to Paul Bowles, April 2, 1963; to HSZ, August 2, 1962; to EF, February 2, 1963, and March 13, 1963; ACP; see also *HSA* and AF. When we asked Phillips about Chester, he paused—apparently struggling to recall a writer who has faded—and said "Wasn't he a homosexual?" **RG's and RS's Reaction to *The Benefactor*:** Had they consulted the work of one of SS's teachers at Chicago, Kenneth Burke, Straus and Giroux would have understood how SS selected her unusual style and structure. Burke wrote only one novel, *Towards a Better Life* (1932; revised and republished by University of California Press in 1966). It is a monologue—or, as he would have it, a series of arias—in which his main character, John Neal, laments, rejoices, beseeches, admonishes, moralizes, and rages against the world, the status quo. Neal is a Hippolyte, a narcissist concerned with perfecting himself. As critic Merle Brown points out, Neal's language is "pure artifice"; that is, it does not arise out of character development or plot. Instead he is his arias as much as Hipployte is his dreams. If we can suppose—as many critics have supposed—that Hipployte is going mad at the end of the novel, just as Neal appears headed for insanity, both SS and Burke confound their readers by insisting on narrators who write the "same well-rounded, periodic sentences." Merle Brown applies this judgment only to Burke, but it holds for Burke's pupil as well; she, like he, remains a "verbaliz- er and analyst." In AF, SS suggests that she realized Burke's novel was a model for her own only years after *The Benefactor* was published. See *Towards a Better Life: Being a Series of Epistles, or Declamations* (NY: Harcourt, Brace, 1932) and Merle E. Brown, *Kenneth Burke* (Minneapolis: University of Minnesota Press, 1969); Kenneth Burke to SS, July 25, 1963; Kenneth Burke to Stanley Edgar Hyman, August 13, 1963, Library of Congress, copy courtesy of Scott McLemee; RG to SS, January 9, 1963; Walman to Murry Pollinger [foreign agent for FSG], May 31, 1963. **Reaction to *The Benefactor* and Its Characters:** Paula Diamond to Herbert Lottman [FSG's agent in Paris], May 31, 1963; EF quotes Michael Finegold on AC in "The Mystery of Alfred Chester," *Boston Review*, 1997; Bruce Bassoff, "Private Revolution: Sontag's *The Benefactor*," *Enclitic* 3 (1979); Sohnya Sayres, *Susan Sontag: The Elegiac Modernist* (NY: Routledge, 1990); John Barth is quoted by Judith Marshall of the FSG publicity department to Lillian Friedman, station WEVD; Frederick Morgan's and Hannah Arendt's endorsements, August 20, 1963, are in FSG files, NYPL; LK to Catharine Meyer, Ausust 28, 1963; John Bright Holmes to RS, August 30, 1963. **"Literary Criticism Today":** Carol Brightman, *Writing Dangerously: Mary McCarthy and Her World* (NY: Clarkson Potter, 1992). **SS and Trilling:** Liam Kennedy, *Mind as Passion* (Manchester: Manchester University Press, 1995). **RS's Efforts on SS's Behalf:** RS to Arthur Schlesinger, Jr., August 22, 1963; to Monique Nathan, September 18, 1963. **Rejections of *Benefactor* Excerpts:** Arnold Ehrlich of *Show* to Paula Diamond, August 23, 1963; John R. Mong of *Saturday Evening Post* to Paula Diamond. **Sales Figures for *The Benefactor*:** RS to Monique Nathan, September 2, 1963, observing that the novel's sales were "quite modest."

8 ∴ SUPREMACY (1963–1964)

AC on SS/Fornés Affair: Letters to EF in ACP; see also Glass's essay in *HSA* and AC to EF, November 27, 1963, ACP. **SS on *NYRB*:** Janny Scott's profile of Robert Silvers, "*New York Review*'s Guiding Light: One Mind, But What a Mind," *New York Times*, November 1, 1997; Eugene Goodheart, *Pieces of Resistance* (Cambridge: Cambridge University Press, 1987); Hilton Als, "A Singular Woman," *The New Yorker*, July 13, 1998. SS is eager to acknowledge her debt to Hardwick. We watched SS and Hardwick in public together; the younger woman embraces her senior with a familiarity and reverence that speaks of deep family ties. It is no exaggeration to say that Hardwick's style is graven on SS: "Her sentences are burned in my brain. I think she writes the most beautiful sentences, more beautiful sentences than any living American writer," SS told Hilton Als. See also Philip Nobile, *Intellectual Skywriting: Literary Politics and The New York Review of Books;* Harvey Teres, *Renewing the Left: Politics, Imagination, and New York Intellectuals* (NY: Oxford University Press, 1996); William Phillips, *A Partisan View*; Willie Morris, *New York Days* (NY: Little, Brown, 1993); Roger Kimball, "A Nostalgia for Molotovs: *The New York Review,*" *The New Criterion*, April 1998; Derek Walcott, *What the Twilight Says* (New York: FSG, 1998), 99–100. We were also able to interview Phillips about his memories of Silvers and the founding of *NYRB*. **Camp:** A notation in the FSG files (December 11, 1963) mentions SS's contacting *Show* about her camp essay. The literature since SS's essay on camp has been extensive. Perhaps the place to begin is with David Bergman's essay and bibliography in *The Gay and Lesbian Heritage,* ed. Claude J. Summers (NY: Henry Holt, 1995). See also Bergman's *Camp Grounds: Style and Homosexuality* (Amherst: University of Massachusetts Press, 1993). *The Origins of "Notes on 'Camp'"*: Ned Rorem, *Knowing When to Stop: A Memoir* (NY: Simon & Schuster, 1994).

9 · FAME (1965–1966)

SS's Fame in Britain: Alan Brien, reviewing SS's appearance on Jonathan Miller's BBC television program "Monitor," *The Spectator,* January 22, 1965. **David**: MD. In AF, SS mentions that Herman Melville's *Pierre* is one of those novels she read as a child which instilled in her the desire to be a writer. In fact, *Pierre* provides a model of the writer with one kind of family attachment (a mother) and without another (a father). SS may have seen herself in both Mary and Pierre, mother and child, parent and writer. She has said she sees herself as both parent and child in "Baby." As Simone de Beauvoir writes, the "child is a double, an *alter ego,* into whom the mother is sometimes tempted to project herself entirely." In a Diane Arbus photograph of young Susan and son, they appear almost as brother and sister—and he resembles, unmistakably, the young Marcel Proust. Many have said so. In their closeness, SS and son project a marriage of souls. As Carole Klein concludes in *Mothers and Sons* (Boston: Houghton Mifflin, 1984): "Whether the statement is made by Michelangelo, Renoir, or Picasso, whether we glimpse it on canvas or in stone, we immediately understand that even without father, mother and son are remarkably complete." **SS's Blurb for William Gass:** To William Gass, May 1, 1966, Special Collections, Washington University Libraries, courtesy of Anne Posega. **SS Forsakes Fame:** To RS [1966]. SS's statement on movie stars is from an unidentified clipping in the FSG files. Marcie Frank: "The Critic as Performance Artist: Susan Sontag's Writing and Gay Cultures," *Camp Grounds: Style and Homosexuality,* ed. David Berman (Amherst: University of Massachusetts Press, 1993). **Jill Johnston:** We are indebted to Jill Johnston for her letters analyzing SS's sexuality in the context of her life and work. Our account of Joseph Cornell and SS relies on Deborah Solomon, *Utopia Parkway: The Life and Work of Joseph Cornell* (NY: FSG, 1998). **Leo Strauss:** See CR's forthcoming essays on Leo Strauss in *World Philosophy,* revised edition (Englewood Cliffs, N.J.: Salem Press). **Eliot Freemont-Smith:** Quoted in Victor Navasky, "Notes on Cult; or, How to Join the Intellectual Establishment," *New York Times Magazine,* March 27, 1966; see also Ihab Hassan, "Negative Capability Reclaimed: Literature and Philosophy Contra Politics," *Philosophy and Literature* 20 (1996); Elizabeth Bruss, *Beautiful Theories* (Baltimore: Johns Hopkins University Press, 1982); Liam Kennedy, *Susan Sontag: Mind as Passion* (Manchester: Manchester University Press, 1995), argues that SS's attack on Matthew Arnold in her essay on the new sensibility is an implicit criticism of Lionel Trilling. Arnold is the subject of Trilling's dissertation and first book. Morris Dickstein, *Gates of Eden: American Culture in the Sixties* (NY: Basic Books, 1977), has a sensitive discussion of Howe and SS. J. Hoberman, *Vulgar Modernism: Writing on Movies and Other Media* (Philadelphia: Temple University Press, 1991), cuts down some of the distance Howe puts between SS and an earlier generation of New York intellectuals. **Statistics on SS's Sales:** A Subsidiary Rights memo, November 9, 1965, FSG files, NYPL. **SS at Columbia:** RG to Harry Ford of Atheneum Publishers, June 4, 1964. **SS Helping RS with His List:** RS memo of September 17, 1963, and SS to RS, June 28, 1966. **SS's New Preface to Against Interpretation:** "Thirty Years Later . . ." appeared in the *Threepenny Review* (Summer 1996).

10: PETER AND PAUL (1965–1967)

AC on SS: AC to EF, April 5, 1965; AC to EF, August 18, 1965. Dick Kluger to SS, January 30, 1967, mentions the fact that AC asked SS to write a letter for him. HSZ on AC and SS: Field int. with HSZ. **EF on SS in Tangier:** "The Man Who Would Marry Susan Sontag," unpublished essay. On AC's behavior during SS's stay, we are indebted to Allen Hibbard's interview with Ira Cohen, one of AC's friends; see also Gore Vidal's foreword to *HSA.* **AC Book Jacket Controversy:** We rely on the FSG files, which include the letters exchanged between Kluger and SS, and on interviews with Richard Kluger. AC began writing "The Foot" in early 1966. Portions of it were published in the *Provincetown Review* (Fall 1968) and in issue number 9 of the *New American Review* in 1970. The fullest version of "The Foot" appears in *HSA.* **Medusa:** See the *Oxford Classical Dictionary,* second edition. **SS on Gass:** SS to David Segal, January 25, 1966, Special Collections, Olin Library, Washington University. **Peter and**

Paul: Int. Jill Johnston, Ann Wilson, and other friends of Peter and Paul. See also Urs Stahel and Hripsime Visser, eds., *Peter Hujar: A Retrospective* (NY: Scalo Publishers, 1994), 22; Helen Gee, *Limelight: A Greenwich Village Photography Gallery and Coffeehouse in the Fifties: A Memoir* (Albuquerque: University of New Mexico Press, 1997); Thomas W. Sokolowski, ed., *Peter Hujar* (NY: Grey Art Gallery & Study Center, New York University, 1990). **Reaction to Hujar's Photograph of SS:** David Bonetti, "Salutes Traditional Photography, *San Francisco Examiner*, December 23, 1996. **Paul Thek**: See *The Wonderful World That Almost Was: Paul Thek* (Rotterdam: Witte de With, 1996); we also draw on interviews with Jill Johnston and Ann Wilson. **Death Kit:** SS discusses her plans for the novel in a letter to RG, June 17, 1965. For criticism of *Death Kit*, see Elizabeth Holdsworth, "Susan Sontag: Writer-Filmmaker," Ph.D. dissertation, Ohio University, 1981; Gore Vidal, *United States Essays* (NY: Random House, 1993); Cary Nelson, *The Incarnate Word: Literature as Verbal Space* (Urbana: University of Illinois Press, 1973).

11: NEORADICALISM (1967–1969)

RS/FSG Concerns About *Death Kit*: RS to Robert Adams, September 20, 1967; to F. R. Ruskin, March 11, 1966; to Maurice Temple Smith, May 8, 1967; Maurice Temple Smith to RS, May 11, 1967; LK to Candida Donadio, June 16, 1967; Gerald Pollinger to RS, April 28, 1967; LK to Douglas McKee of McKee & Mouche, 14 rue du Regard, Paris, September 5, 1969; RS to Monique Nathan of Editions du Seuil, September 19, 1967; to Maurice Temple Smith, September 7, 1967; to Candida Donadio, August 25, 1967; to Alberto Mondadori, March 27, 1967. **Candida Donadio:** Letter to CR and LP from Donadio. Donadio was never officially SS's agent, although Straus occasionally found her useful in promoting SS's career. **SS as News Item:** Laurence Pollinger to RS, April 17, 1968; SS to RS, August 8, 1966. **SS on Her Jacket Photo:** To RS, June 29, 1967, FSG files, FSG. **James Dickey:** Writer David Slavitt heard Dickey tell one version of the story. Our thanks to George Garrett for providing this account. **SS's Anti-Vietnam War Speech:** Quoted by Beatrice Berg, "Susan Sontag: Intellectuals' Darling," *Washington Post*, January 8, 1967. For a description of her war protest activities we have consulted RS to Maurice Temple Smith. **Dot Lane:** Our thanks to Dot Lane for supplying documents about the protest and for her letter to us (September 19, 1997) and phone conversation describing SS. **SS's Hanoi Visit:** See "From Hanoi with Love," included in Andrew Kopkind's collection, *The Thirty Years' Wars: Dispatches and Diversions of a Radical Journalist, 1965–1994* (NY: Verso, 1995). We also interviewed Kopkind's lover, Jack Scagliotti, and Perry Stieglitz; see also Stieglitz's book, *In a Little Kingdom* (Armonk, NY: M. E. Sharpe, 1990); Milton J. Bates, *The Wars We Took to Vietnam: Cultural Conflict and Storytelling* (Berkeley: University of California

Press, 1996); Leo Marx, *The Pilot and the Passenger: Essays on Literature, Technology, and Culture in the United States* (NY: Oxford University Press, 1988); David Caute, *The Fellow-Travellers: Intellectual Friends of Communism,* revised edition (New Haven: Yale University Press, 1988). **SS on Cuba:** David Horowitz, *Radical Son: A Generational Odyssey* (NY: Free Press, 1997), gives his version of SS's contribution to *Ramparts* when he was an editor. We have also interviewed Horowitz and his coeditor, Peter Collier; see also Paul Hollander, "Intellectuals, Estrangement, and Wish Fulfillment," *Society* 35 (January–February 1998). **SS on Che:** Marianne Alexandre, *Viva Che! Contributions in Tribute to Ernesto "Che" Guevara* (NY: Dutton, 1968). **SS and the Socialist Workers Party:** Alan Wald, *The New York Intellectuals* (Chapel Hill: University of North Carolina Press, 1987); Leslie Evans to Scott McLemee, August 13, 1988, courtesy of Scott McLemee. **SS in Mexico:** Maya Khankhoje to CR and LP, September 15, 1997; CR int. MK.

12: STYLES OF RADICAL WILL (1969–1971)

SS's Greenwich Village Apartment: James Toback, "Whatever You'd Like Susan Sontag to Think, She Doesn't," *Esquire,* July 1968. Beatrice Berg, "Susan Sontag: Intellectuals' Darling," *Washington Post,* January 8, 1967. **SS at Brown:** Laurence Goldstein, unpublished memoir, n.d., courtesy of Laurence Goldstein. **Gladys Carr:** SS to Gladys Carr, April 13, 1965, and Gladys Carr to SS, April 19, 1965. **SS's "Marriage" to Irene:** SS to JC, June 26, [1969], Joseph Chaikin Papers, Special Collections, Kent State University Library. **SS and Nicole Stéphane:** James Lord to CR, March 22, 1997, and January 1, 1997. Writer James Lord saw them together in Paris. Lord was no friend of SS's. Indeed, he found her "basically very calculating and arriviste, though clever." SS names Stéphane as her producer in the Schultz int., *CSS.* When Stéphane appeared in New York in 1996 at the Museum of Modern Art (MoMA) for a retrospective of Melville's films, which Susan Sontag helped to organize, she looked just as sturdy as her film persona, a monument to a great age in French film, still a beautiful woman, still intact and poised. Age had softened her, to be sure, so that she now appeared as a rounded, fluffy-haired, sweet-looking woman. Sontag, sixty-three at the time of this event, acted like an excited adolescent, ushering Stéphane into the MoMA theater. The third row of the MoMA theater had been reserved for her entourage, which included David, and she animatedly made the rounds, squatting beside Stéphane, sitting on the arm of a seat, smiling a lot. She was up and down, up and down, a jet of energy and enthusiasm.

Sontag introduced Stéphane as Nicole, a "colleague and dear friend." In fact, they were "old, very, very close friends. . . . We did all kinds of things together. . . . Nicole is my closest European friend," Sontag assured the audience. She mentioned that Nicole had been born in Paris in 1924 and that she had qualified as an equestrian for the 1936 Olympics in Hitler's Berlin but did not attend. Melville spotted Stéphane, then only nineteen, at an audition, and Cocteau chose her for the role of Elisabeth. Later Stéphane became a labor organizer, and she had produced *Promised Lands*, Sontag's documentary about Israel and the Palestinians. After this little tribute, Sontag beamed and Stéphane kissed her on both cheeks.

Sontag describes her love affair with Stéphane in her letters to Chaikin. SS to JC, June 26, [1969], Joseph Chaikin Papers, Special Collections, Kent State University Library. A parallel bond between two women is the focus of SS's essay on Ingmar Bergman's film *Persona* (included in *Styles of Radical Will*), of her own film *Brother Carl*, as well as of "Debriefing," her fraught story about the suicide in 1969 of Susan Taubes, who had remained one of SS's closest friends.

For an insightful discussion of *Les Enfants Terribles*, see *Magill's Survey of Cinema*, 1995; *Le Silence de la Mer, Magill's Survey of Cinema*, 1997. **SS's Desire to Make Films:** Newman int., *CSS;* see also Mel Gussow, "Susan Sontag Talks About Filmmaking, *New York Times*, October 3, 1969. **SS in Sweden:** Goran Lindgren to CR and LP, December 16, 1997; we also interviewed Peter Hald. SS told a Swedish interviewer: "I don't like to have long discussions. Many actors understand things without talking about them, and many actors who talk very well about their roles can't in the end do what they promise. The verbal communication that a director can have with an actor is often misleading." We are grateful to Goran Lindgren for sending us this interview with Stig Bjorkman in *Film in Sweden* (January 1971). **Discipleship:** SS has never ceased pursuing masters, even after she might be considered to have become one herself. Librarian Mike Unsworth reported to us that he met her in Colorado. He did not recognize her, and they talked about a concert Philip Glass was giving. SS told him that she had been traveling in Glass's wake, catching his talks and concerts. **Reviews of *Duet for Cannibals*:** Frederic Tuten, "Movies," *Vogue*, October 15, 1969. SS called her work on the film "pure pleasure" in an interview on Swedish television. For the most insightful discussion of *Duet for Cannibals*, see Molly Haskell, "Film: *Duet for Cannibals*," *Village Voice*, October 30, 1969; see also Sayres; Martin Tucker, "Please Don't Eat the Cannibals," *Commonweal*, December 5, 1969; Stanley Kauffmann, "Stanley Kauffmann on Films," *The New Republic*, November 15, 1969; Roy Armes, "Three Women Directors," *London Magazine*, February 9, 1970; Pauline Kael, "Films," *The New Yorker*, November 1, 1969. Many Swedish reviews were negative, though others were polite if not enthusiastic. Swedish scholar Karl-Erik Tallmo translated for us a small excerpt from a review by Daen Nyheter which praises the eloquence of her dialogue but which calls *Duet for Cannibals* "diffuse," a slow-moving black farce. The film's expressionism seemed antiquated, and SS seemed to have done little to give her actors a sense of the "purpose and direction of her story." **SS on Susan Taubes:** SS to Joseph Chaikin, December 29, 1969, Joseph Chaikin Papers, Special Collections, Kent State University Library. **SS on Gestation of *Brother Carl*:** SS to RG, July 6, 1972; see also her published screenplay, *Brother Carl* (NY: FSG, 1974).

13 : MS. SONTAG (1971–1973)

SS on the Parisian Scene: Schultz int., *CSS;* SS to RS, May 12, 1971, and July 5, 1972. **Promoting SS as Filmmaker:** T. G. Rosenthal of Secker & Warburg to RS, April 1, 1971; RS to TGR, April 8, 1971. **"The Year Of the Ox":** The correspondence concerning the $5,000 advance and the contract for the screenplay, dated April 22, 1972, are in the FSG files, NYPL. **SS's Quiet Period:** LK to Michelle Lapautre, October 4, 1972; SS to RS, July 5, 1972. **SS on Making It as a Woman:** Schultz int., *CSS.* **"A Moveable Doom":** SS to LK [n.d., but clearly in June 1972]; Barbara Blakemore of *McCall's* to LK, June 9, 1972, and LK to SS, June 15, 1972, pointing out that the essay was too long and needed work; int. Vivian Gornick. **Jill Johnston:** JJ to CR and LP, March 6, 1997. In a review of Johnston's *Marmalade Me* and *Admission Accomplished: The Lesbian Nation Years,* Liz Kotz (*Women's Review of Books,* July 1998) notes that the "art world was perhaps less than willing to deal with an openly gay artist, especially a lesbian one, who was now taking questions of sexuality and gender as overtly political issues." And not just the art world but the literary one as well. Kotz believes that Johnston's "effrontery and intense partisanship" has kept her from "major recognition." Johnston identified herself and Sontag as Lucinda Childs's lovers. **Town Hall:** See the account in CR, *The Lives of Norman Mailer: A Biography* (NY: Paragon House, 1991). **"The Double Standard of Aging":** We interviewed HSZ, who confirms the details in SS's article. **Camille Paglia:** Int. Camille Paglia and Richard Tristman; Paglia mailgram to SS, September 10, 1973; "Sontag Bloody Sontag," in *Vamps and Tramps* (NY: Random House, 1994); Paglia also sent us detailed letters (July 27 and September 15, 1999) from which we have quoted with her permission; see also Stewart Brand interview with Camille Paglia, *Wired* (on-line database); Bob Fernandes's interview with SS, "Suburbana America," *Istoe,* June 23, 1993, courtesy of Camille Paglia.

14 : PROMISED LANDS (1971–1974)

SS on Cuba: LK to SS, May 25, 1971. **The China Trip:** RS to Pat Carbine of *Ms.,* October 19, 1972. **Secker & Warburg:** T. G. Rosenthal of Secker & Warburg to Deborah Rogers (FSG's London agent), May 25, 1973; see also SS to RS, May 14, 1973. *The New Yorker:* Shawn to RS (March 30, 1973) rejects "Debriefing": "This didn't work out for us, in spite of some dazzling moments. I've told Susan." He also rejected "Baby" and "Project for a Trip to China"; see also RS letter of July 30, 1973, to Robie Macaulay of *Playboy* thanking him for the $2,500 for "Baby." ***Promised Lands:*** "Susan Sontag Tells How It Feels to Make a Movie," *Vogue,* July 1974; int. Yoram Kaniuk.

15 : OLD COMPLAINTS REVISITED (1975)

Fascinating Fascism: SS to RS, February 24, 1975; see also Robert von Dassanowsky, "'Wherever you may run, you cannot escape him': Leni Riefenstahl's Self-reflection and Romantic Transcendence of Nazism in Tiefland," *Camera Obscura* 35 (1995–96); also available on-line at http://pow-ernet.net/~hflippo/cineam/tiefland.html>; Ruth Starkman, "Mother of All Spectacles: Ray Müller's *The Wonderful, Horrible Life of Leni Riefenstahl,*" *Film Quarterly* 51 (Winter 1997); "An Interview with Ray Müller, Director of *The Wonderful, Horrible Life of Leni Riefenstahl,*" http:www.apocalypse.com/movies/document/riefenstahl/mueller.int.html>; David Elliott, "German's Film Vision Artfully Examined," *San Diego Tribune,* June 30, 1994, accessed at http://www.uniontribune.com/news/utarchives. **SS and Feminism**: SS continued, in a very minor key, to write a few feminist articles. See her essay "Beauty" (*Vogue,* May 1975) and "Can Rights Be Equal?" (*Vogue,* July 1976).

16 : BECOMING A LITTLE POSTHUMOUS (1975–1978)

David Rieff: Carlin Romano, "A Writer Who Feels Compelled to Bear Witness to Bosnia," *Philadelphia Inquirer,* June 13, 1995; Margaria Fichtner, "The Outsider," *Miami Herald,* August 8, 1993; MD; George Garrett to CR, n.d. We are also drawing on interviews with dozens of people who have seen SS and DR in action. FSG efforts on DR's behalf are documented in the FSG files. **SS's Cancer:** DR's physical exam: Henny Wenkart to CR and LP, May 5, 1998. See SS int. with Raddatz, Cott, Servan-Schreiber, Ruas, Costa, and Lopez in *CSS;* see also Ron Grossman, "At the C Shop with Susan Sontag," *Chicago Tribune,* December 1, 1992; Carol Kahn, "Alone Against Illness, *Family Health,* November 10, 1978; LG. Two interviews in French reveal a good deal about Sontag's personal struggle with cancer: Michel Braudeau, "Petit Déjeuner chez Sontag," *L'Express,* June 9, 1979; Catherine David, "Les Diagnostics de Susan Sontag," *Nouvel Observateur,* June 25, 1979; Joseph Chaikin to Arthur Miller, November 10, 1975, Joseph Chaikin Papers, Special Collections, Kent State University Library. We interviewed Richard Tristman, Yoram Kaniuk, Thomas Lipscomb, Sidney Offit, and Lionel Abel. We corresponded with Martin Peretz.

17 : RECOVERY (1976–1977)

On Photography: Our account of the origins of SS's interest in photography is based on her talk, "Susan Sontag on Photography," at the Detroit Institute of Arts, October 13, 1989, a tape of which the museum kindly sent us. "**Susan's Addiction**": Brian Rice, English 2150, Section 54A, essay dated September 25, 1997, for CR's class at Baruch College, City University of New York. **SS at**

Boston University: We are grateful to George Goldsmith for sharing his memories of SS (via E-mail and telephone) and a gracious letter she sent to him on November 6, 1974, replying to his interest in her photography essays—then still appearing in the *New York Review of Books*. **SS and Annie Leibovitz:** Int. James Vernon. See UPI photographs of SS and Leibovitz in the photo section of this book.

18 : THE SALONISTES (1977–1985)

Sales of *On Photography*: RS to Peter Carson at Penguin, December 6, 1977; to SS, December 6, 1977; to Michelle Lapautre, January 19, 1978; to Liz Calder, January 23, 1978; to Rollene Sael, Literary Guild, January 26, 1978; to Deborah Rogers, February 5, 1978. **Tel Quel:** See Scarpetta int. in *CSS*. **Paul Saevig:** E-mail to CR and LP, May 26, 1998. **Brodsky on Solzhenitsyn:** Scarpetta int., *CSS*. **SS and Brodsky:** See Solmon Volkov, *Conversations with Joseph Brodsky: A Poet's Journey Through the Twentieth Century* (NY: Free Press, 1998); we heard SS reminisce about Brodsky at Columbia University's Miller Theatre on October 29, 1996, as part of a program that included Tatyana Tolstaya, Mark Strand, Richard Locke, and Derek Walcott. The event is reported in the *Columbia University Record*, vol. 22, no. 9, which we accessed on-line. SS reminisces about Brodsky in her afterword to Mikhail Lemkhin, *Joseph Brodsky: Leningrad* (NY: FSG, 1998). See also William Robertson, "Exiled Soviet Poet Wins Nobel Prize, *Miami Herald*, October 23, 1987. **Brodsky's and Walcott's Poetry Class:** Penny Cagan, an NYU graduate student in the creative writing program, took the course and sent an E-mail to CR and LP, September 4, 1997, and was also interviewed. Cagan reports that the students thought of SS as just another SSP (Shameless Self-Promoter). **Dennis Altman:** We are grateful to Dennis Altman for sending us his reminiscence, printed in his book *Defying Gravity* (London: Allen & Unwin, 1979); we also rely on Jocelyn Carlson in conversation with Zane Berzins, as reported by Berzins to CR. **SS's New School Courses:** Int. with Monica Strauss, one of SS's students, and Edmund White. **Ned Rorem:** *The Nantucket Diary of Ned Rorem, 1973–1985* (San Francisco: North Point Press, 1987). **Kopkind and Scagliotti:** Int. Jack Scagliotti. **SS and Identity Politics:** She gave an interview to the gay magazine *Out* (April 1974) and made comments like "Everybody has the capacity for homosexual feelings and homosexual relations," but she said absolutely nothing about her own sexuality. Interviewer Chuck Ortleb begins his piece by referring to his own decision to "come out," but the issue is never put to Sontag in the published interview. We rely directly on our interview with Edmund White for the parallels we draw between the characters in *Caracole* and Sontag and David Rieff. **Phillipe Sollers:** *Women* (NY: Columbia University Press, 1990). **Richard Howard:** We are indebted to Marion Meade for a report on Richard Howard among the biographers. **David Leavitt:** He made his remarks in a recent symposium, "Whose Life Is It, Anyway?," reprinted in the *Authors Guild Bulletin* (Winter 1999).

19: I, ETCETERA (1979)

Sales of *I, Etcetera*: RS to Peter Mayer, May 22, 1979. **Beerbohm:** Quoted in N. John Hall, *Max Beerbohm Caricatures* (New Haven: Yale University Press, 1997). **SS Interview with Suzanne Gordon:** There is an exchange of letters between Borchardt (May 30, 1979) and RS (June 1, 1979) in the FSG papers, NYPL. We interviewed Suzanne Gordon, who believes SS was embarrassed by some of her statements, which may have seemed a little silly in print. **Servan-Schreiber Interview: CSS**; see also Peter York, *Style Wars* (London: Sidgwick & Jackson, 1980). **Hawaii:** Int. Cobey Black, Jeannette Paulson, Mark Wilson; see also Cobey Black, "High Priestess in Bluejeans," *Honolulu Star-Bulletin,* July 12, 1977. **SS in Italy:** RS to Fritz Raddatz of *Die Zeit,* August 7, 1979; int. Edmund White; SS-Sciascia interview, *CSS;* for Bullock's review, see "Pirandello in Florence, 1980–81," *Bulletin of the Society for Italian Studies* 14 (November 1981). In a documentary, *Susan Sontag,* available on videocassette from Films for the Humanities, SS speaks of Italy as the country where she would have liked to have been born.

20: A WANDERING JEW (1980)

SS in Poland: See Beyer int., *CSS,* 165–74; E-mail from James McClintock to CR and LP, November 4, 1997. **SS and Oates:** We have teased out details about Oates and SS from Greg Johnson's alternately informative and elliptical biography, *Invisible Writer: A Biography of Joyce Carol Oates* (NY: Dutton, 1998). His biography was written with Oates's cooperation and was edited by Oates's editor, William Abrahams. As an authorized biographer, Johnson perhaps is chary of inquiring too closely into matters like the SS-Oates relationship. Consequently, a certain strangeness pervades the text, with SS first appearing as a disparager of Oates and then suddenly as her confidante. **SS on a depolarized sexual world:** Servan-Schreiber int., *CSS. **Under the Sign of Saturn:*** Walter Kendrick was not alone in his judgments. In *Telos* (Summer 1981), David Craven called it a hackneyed effort to revive the "tired Renaissance conceit" of the melancholy artist explored by Rudolf and Margot Wittkower in *Born Under Saturn* (1963). Although he did not invoke Arnold, Craven accused Sontag of an Arnoldian ploy—namely, a Victorian wish to tame the subjects she wrote about, to make them seem more mainstream. She transformed the radical Walter Benjamin into a liberal humanist, a Victorian eccentric of the kind John Stuart Mill would have endorsed. Similarly, in the *New York Times Book Review* (November 23, 1980), David Bromwich pointed out that

Sontag's chapter on Artaud domesticated Gnosticism and made him "tamer than he sounds in his own words." But Frank Kermode, writing in that club publication the *New York Review of Books*, suggested that Sontag's "characteristic strength" in the Artaud piece was to "domesticate" Artaud, to "make him useful, to make it possible for his work to be understood as other literature is understood."

21 : SUSAN THE APOSTATE (1982)

For accounts of the Town Hall episode, see Alexander Cockburn and James Ridgeway, "The Poles, the Left, and the Tumbrils of '84," *Village Voice*, February 10–16, 1982; "Communism and the Left," *The Nation*, February 27, 1982, reprints SS's speech, commentary on the speech, and her rebuttal; William F. Buckley, Jr., "Why Leftists Booed Sontag's Speech," *Philadelphia Inquirer*, March 2, 1982; Ralph Schoenman, "Susan Sontag and the Left," *Village Voice*, March 2, 1982; Jacobo Timmerman, "Moral Symmetry," *The Nation*, March 6, 1982; Christopher Hitchens, "Poland and the US Left," *The Spectator*, March 6, 1982; "Setting the Record Straight," *The Nation*, March 13, 1982. See also the letters section of *The Nation*, March 27, 1982; James Lardner, "Susan Sontag into the Fray," *Washington Post*, March 16, 1982; Richard Grenier, "The Conversion of Susan Sontag," *The New Republic*, April 14, 1982; D. Keith Mano, "The Strange Agony of Susan Sontag," *National Review*, April 16, 1982; Arch Puddington, "The Polish Example," *American Spectator*, April 1982; "Sontag Slugfest" (letters from Joseph Brodsky, Jaroslav Anders, and Grenier's reply), *The New Republic,* May 26, 1982; "Susan Sontag Comes In out of the Left," *Forbes*, May 10, 1982; Walter Goodman, "Hard to Digest" (comparing *Reader's Digest* to *The Nation* on the handling of Communism), *Harper's*, June 1982; Seymour Martin Lipset, "The Thugs and Susan Sontag," *American Spectator*, June 1982; Leon Wieseltier, "Ideas in Season," *Partisan Review*, Summer 1982; William Phillips, "Neo-History," *Partisan Review*, Summer 1982; Peter Shaw and Seymour Martin Lipset, "Two Afterthoughts on Susan Sontag," *Encounter*, June–July 1982; Charles Ruas, "Susan Sontag: Past, Present, and Future," *New York Times Book Review*, October 24, 1982; SS and Robert Silvers sent letters to *Encounter*, November 1982, defending her position; Laura Kipnis, "Aesthetics and Foreign Policy," *Social Text*, Fall 1986; Robert J. Branham, "Speaking Itself: Susan Sontag's Town Hall Address," *Quarterly Journal of Speech*, August 1989. We are also grateful to Ralph Schoenman, E. L. Doctorow, and Victor Navasky—each of whom was at Town Hall and consented to be interviewed for this biography. **SS and Soho News:** Marshall Berman joined a group of commentators that included Noam Chomsky, Garry Wills, Diana Trilling, Nathan Glazer, Mary McCarthy, Seymour Martin Lipset, Jessica Mitford, James Weinstein, Bernard-Henri Lévy,

Michel Foucault, Ben J. Wattenberg, Félix Guattari, and Julia Kristeva. A good many of the responses ignored SS and maundered on about the complexities of Communism. See "Newsmakers," *Philadelphia Inquirer,* February 20, 1982; "Susan Sontag Provokes Debate on Communism," *New York Times,* February 27, 1982; Nat Hentoff, "The Authorized Sontag v. That 'Dreadful' Soho Rag" and "First Amendment Jane and the Unauthorized Jane," *Village Voice,* March 16 and April 13, 1982; Alexander Cockburn, "Press Clips," *Village Voice,* April 8, 1982; Aryeh Neier, "Dissenting Opinion," *The Nation,* May 8, 1982. See also Tom Zito, "Soho News Ends Publication," *Washington Post,* March 16, 1982. **Leon Friedman:** Friedman took *The Nation*'s side in a copyright battle with Harper & Row, which had sued the periodical for printing three hundred words from a Gerald Ford memoir without his permission. *The Nation* lost the case because the court found it had quoted the three hundred best words, thus depriving Ford of the right to profit from his writing.

22 : RETROSPECTION (1982–1983)

Walter Kendrick: The exchanges between Rieff, Navasky, and Pollitt can be found in the FSG archives, October 21, 22, 25, 28, 1982. We are indebted to Victor Navasky, Katha Pollitt, and the late Walter Kendrick for speaking to us about this incident. Pollitt, who has become one of SS's favorite columnists (according to *The Nation*'s Web site), and who has had a collection of essays blurbed by SS (as she mentioned to one of us), now utters no criticism of SS. Instead she kept referring us to Pochoda (who did not answer our letters). See also Ruas int. in *CSS,* where Kendrick is referred to indirectly. Int. Hilton Kramer. ***Rolling Stone***: Laura Berman, "Another Page Turns on 'The Age of Junk,'" *Detroit Free Press,* December 16, 1983. **Zelig:** *Woody Allen on Woody Allen: In Conversation with Stig Bjorkman* (NY: Grove Press, 1993). Bellow made his comment on feeling foolish to Allen's biographer, Marion Meade. See also Harriet Wasserman, *Handsome Is: Adventures with Saul Bellow* (NY: Fromm International, 1997). Woody Allen was not available to comment on how he liked working with Susan Sontag. **Lucinda Childs:** Jill Johnston correspondence, March 6, 1997, to CR and LP; see the interview with Childs in *Soho News,* November 3, 1977; Sally Banes, "Lucinda Childs: Simplicity Forces You to See," *Vogue,* May 1977; Allen Robertson, "Be Am Is Are Was Were Been," *Soho News,* March 25, 1981; *Current Biography,* April 1984; Iris Fanger, "The New Lucinda Childs," *Dance,* October 1989; Jorn Rohwer interview with Childs in *Ballet International,* October 1995. We consulted these articles in the clipping files of the Library for the Performing Arts, NYPL. For our portrait of Childs and her background we have also drawn on interviews with Edmund White as well as on Charles Spencer, "The Arts: Terminal Malady Cruelly Drawn Out to the Crack of Doom," *Daily Telegraph,* November 10, 1997; "Theatre: The Best of the Edinburgh Festival," *The Independent,* July 20, 1994; Sophie Constanti, "The 360-Degree Dancer," *The*

Independent, May 17, 1996; Tim Page, *"Einstein on the Beach* Is Back as Revolutionary as It Ever Was," *Newsday,* November 19, 1992; June Ducas, "The Arts: Robert Gets What He Wants: Cult theatre director Robert Wilson has little time for interviews. But with a new work soon to be seen on the London stage, he talks to June Ducas," *Sunday Telegraph,* October 12, 1997; Chris Pasles, "A Ballet That Turns on Weight of Emotion; Dance: Anne Tere Keersmaeker Alludes to Love Triangle in *Woud,"* *Los Angeles Times,* October 13, 1997; Paul Ben-Itzak, "Dance/Step by Step," *Newsday,* December 12, 1996; "Music, When It Sizzled," *Time,* June 3, 1985; Peter Goodman, "A Powerful, Exciting *Einstein* Revival," *Newsday,* November 23, 1992; Janice Berman, "Lucinda Childs Adds Fun to Lift the Spirit," *Newsday,* February 10, 1994; Peter Goodman, "As Soho Has Changed, So Has Philip Glass" *Newsday*, May 22, 1995; Judith Mackrell, "Dance: Does the Shoe Still Fit? Balanchine Is Gone," *The Independent,* February 25, 1994, 23; Paul Taylor, "Arts: Time and Time Again," *The Independent,* November 8, 1997; Gary Indiana, "Susan Sontag's *Unguided Tour,"* *Artforum* 22 (November 1983). **Television Essay:** After *Unguided Tour,* Sontag would continue to explore "couple relation"—the term she uses in "A Primer for Pina. Susan Sontag on Pina Bausch: A Television Essay," shown on Channel Four in Great Britain in 1984, and in her direction of *Jacques and His Master,* Milan Kundera's adaptation of a Diderot play, which premiered at the American Repertory Theater in 1985. By means of various detours and digressions, Sontag was making her way toward *The Volcano Lover* and its triangulated couple relations. **Reviews of "A Primer For Pina":** John J. O'Connor, "Britain's Channel 4 Where Commerce Serves Culture," *New York Times,* June 22, 1996; Jennifer Dunning, "Pina Bausch and Susan Sontag," *New York Times,* August 11, 1986.

23 : PRESIDENT SONTAG (1986–1989)

SS and PEN: Our account of SS and PEN is based on documents, letters, board minutes, interviews with PEN rank and file, PEN board members, and former board members, including presidents, such as Francis King, Victor Navasky, E. L. Doctorow, and Sidney Offit, the last of whom gave us the most genial view of the organization and its members. Much of the primary evidence is housed in the PEN archive at Firestone Library, Special Collections, Princeton University. George Garrett's shrewd comments on New York literary life are to be found in *My Silk Purse and Yours: The Publishing Scene and American Literary Art* (Columbia: University of Missouri Press, 1992). We have relied on Richard Stern's account of the 1986 congress in *One Person and Another: On Writers and Writing* (NY: Baskerville, 1993), on his letter to CR, and on CR's *The Lives of Norman Mailer: A Biography* (NY: Paragon House, 1991). **SS and Václav Havel:** A few years later Alfred Kazin would watch SS in action at a *New York Review of Books* party for Havel after his election to the presidency of Czechoslovakia: "Sontag's eyes were glistening after embracing the president—'an old friend,' she confessed as she exited the circle around him. 'I've been invited to the presidential palace next time I'm in Prague.'" See *A Lifetime Burning in Every Moment: From the Journals of Alfred Kazin* (NY: HarperCollins, 1966). Kazin does not give a specific date for this event, which took place at the Vivian Beaumont Theater at Lincoln Center. **The Steinbergs:** "Is PEN Mightier Than the Checkbook?," *San Jose Mercury News*, August 20, 1990. **SS and Karen Kennerly:** John Simon told us, "Whether Karen speaks with you may depend on how well she is getting on with Susan." When we told him Kennerly would not talk—would not make any sort of statement on SS's presidency—Simon reflected that Karen must be going through a "good period" with Susan. One of PEN's more outspoken critics and a veteran combatant in the organization's internal power struggles discounts Offit's views, terming him an organizational loyalist. **Ted Solotaroff:** His remarks appear in the PEN board minutes for March 18, 1987; we also draw on PEN board minutes of September 16, 1987.

We found the following newspaper and magazine accounts helpful and drew many of our quotations from Edwin McDowell, "Mailer Sparkplug for Writer's Congress," *Chicago Tribune*, January 2, 1986; John Blades, "PEN Authors Ready to Unsheathe Vocal Swords at Congress," *Chicago Tribune*, January 12, 1986; Stephen Salisbury, "World's Writers Address a Foe: Government," *Philadelphia Inquirer*, January 12, 1986; Thomas Collins, "Shultz Heckled at PEN Meeting," *Newsday*, January 13, 1986; Larry McShane, "Shultz Heckled by World Writers over Issue of Free Expression," *Detroit Free Press*, January 13, 1986; Edwin McDowell, "Grass vs. Bellow over U.S. at PEN," *New York Times*, January 15, 1986; David Remnick, "PEN's End: Accusations & Acrimony; Mailer and Feminists in a Raucous Final Session," January 17, 1986; Stephan Salisbury, "What Do Those Who Write Owe the World?," *Philadelphia Inquirer*, January 16, 1997; Carlin Romano, "A Pride of Literary Lions: Matters Both Deep and Shallow Take Center Stage at the PEN Congress," *Philadelphia Inquirer*, January 17, 1986; Stephan Salisbury, "It's Mailer vs. Women on PEN's Final Day," *Philadelphia Inquirer*, January 18, 1986; John Blades, "International Writers' Congress PENS No Peaceful Prose with Its Bad Blood," *Chicago Tribune*, January 19, 1986; William Robertson, "The Literary Leap from New York to Key West," *Miami Herald*, January 19, 1986; Rhoda Koenig, "At Play in the Fields of the Word: Alienation, Imagination, Feminism, and Foolishness at PEN," *New York*, February 3, 1986; Leslie Hanscom, "A Literary Shebang That Had Its Share of Guff," *Newsday*, February 9, 1986; Roger Kimball, "Politics, Politics, Politics—the PEN Congress in New York," *The New Criterion*, March 1986; see also Francis King, *Visiting Cards* (London: HarperCollins, 1990). **Peter Matthiessen:** See the description of the lawsuit in "Five Authors Aid Matthiessen, See Litigation as Censorship," *Publishers Weekly*, March 18, 1988. **SS's Senate Testimony on Rushdie:** Reprinted in *The Rushdie File*, ed. Lisa Appignanesi and Sara Maitland (London: Fourth Estate, 1989), 166–68. For the Rushdie affair, we drew on Lloyd Grove and Charles Trueheart, "Silence in the

Eye of the *Satanic* Storm; Authors, Bookstores Fear Reprisals," *Washington Post*, February 18, 1989; Edwin McDowell, "Furor Over *Satanic Verses* Rises as 2 More Book Chains Halt Sales," *New York Times*, February 18, 1989; D. D. Guttenplan, "Fear Chills Writers' Defense," *Newsday*, February 18, 1989; "Devil's Work: How to Foil Khomeini" (editorial), *Newsday*, February 21, 1989; Vivienne Walt and Scott Ladd, "The Storm over *Verses:* Rushdie Supporters Return Iran's Fire; Writers Call on Bush for Backing," *Newsday*, February 21, 1989; Vivienne Walt, "A Day of Demonstrations," *Newsday*, February 22, 1989; Paula Span, "The Writers' Bloc, Authors Rally for Freedom of Expression," *Washington Post*, February 23, 1989; Robert L. Koenig, "Khomeini Stands Firm, U.S. Writers Stage Protest, Authors Read Aloud from *Satanic Verses*," *St. Louis Post-Dispatch*, February 23, 1989; Richard Bernstein, "Passages in Defense of a Colleague: Writers Read and Speak for Rushdie," *New York Times*, February 23, 1989; Shauna Snow, "Morning Report," *Los Angeles Times*, February 27, 1989; Richard Cohen, "Writers Don't Merit Charge of Cowardice," *St. Louis Post-Dispatch*, March 4, 1989; Charles Trueheart, "Witnesses for *Verses:* Senate Panel Weighs U.S. Response to Iran," *Washington Post*, March 9, 1989; Charles Krauthammer, "Heroism Comes Cheap 6,000 Miles from Iran," *St. Louis Post-Dispatch*, March 13, 1989; David Sheff, "*Playboy* Interview: Salman Rushdie," *Playboy*, April 1996.

PEN's Iron Curtain by Carl Rollyson, May 18, 1999: In October 1996 I called PEN American Center to request board minutes for 1987–89 when SS was president. An office assistant said they would get back to me. I called a week later and was informed that PEN's attorney had advised that my request be denied because, while I was then a PEN member, I had not been one during SS's presidency. I replied that such reasoning seems disingenuous for an organization created to promote openness, freedom of expression, and understanding among writers.

In early November I wrote to Karen Kennerly, then PEN's executive director, and got no answer until January 3, when she wrote (replying to my second letter of December 16) that I would have my answer when the new board met later in January. Hearing nothing, I wrote again on February 24, 1997, pointing out that it had been easier for me to obtain Lillian Hellman's FBI file (for my 1988 biography of Hellman) than to get an answer out of PEN.

PEN has seemed—at least since the days when Ted Solotaroff tried to reform it—neither democratic nor open when it comes to examining its own practices. When former *PEN Newsletter* editor Lucy Komisar complained about the organization's oligarchy, she found little support among prominent PEN members. As one writer quipped, PEN "would be the first to defend Lucy Komisar if she were in Bosnia or Tiananmen Square." (See Ralph Blumenthal, "Hard Words by Those with a Gift for Them; Stung by Dissident, a Divided PEN Ponders Its Role," *New York Times*, March 12, 1987.)

Behind the scenes, I was told that no one wanted to offend SS (still a board member), and that things are said at board meetings about other PEN chapters that would prove embarrassing if they saw daylight. When I wrote to Komisar at PEN, her letter was opened before it was forwarded to her at her home address. When I interviewed E. L. Doctorow and told him that I had been denied board minutes, he thought the basis of the denial "ridiculous," and that I should write directly to PEN's new president, Michael Scammell. I did so on April 8, 1997.

On April 16, 1997, near the end of a long PEN meeting about openness and democratization—called specifically to address Komisar's concerns—I spoke briefly about the organization's stonewalling about my request for board minutes. Clearly angry that I had raised the issue at a public meeting, Michael Scammell asked me if I had Susan Sontag's permission to write her biography. I replied that I had every right to write her biography, just as she had every right to oppose it. His remark suggested that he felt he needed SS's permission to release the board minutes—a curious position for the unauthorized biographer of Aleksandr Solzhenitsyn to adopt. After the meeting, I asked him: "What if I were writing a history of PEN? Would you still refuse me the minutes?" Changing the subject, he replied that he did not appreciate my hijacking the meeting to vent my personal grievances. Actually, I was speaking to a motion to appoint an ombudsman for PEN, since the organization clearly could not deal with requests such as mine.

Several members of PEN's Freedom-to-Write Committee told me that they were aghast that I had not received the minutes. As one committee member put it: "Our committee was all for you. Only PEN staff members were against approving your request." In fact, at the Freedom-to-Write Committee there had been a vote, 13–1, in my favor, with the lone dissenter Leon Friedman, an attorney for FSG.

Eventually, from conversations with several eyewitnesses I was able to piece together what had happened in the Freedom-to-Write-Committee. Karen Kennerly addressed the committee, saying PEN had a very difficult problem on its hands. A writer named Carl Rollyson doing a biography of Susan Sontag wanted access to board minutes dating from the period when she was president of PEN, and SS was opposed to his request. Kennerly wanted to get a reading from the committee about what it thought. With an ex-president of PEN present, Kennerly suggested it was an especially good time to bring the issue up. Kennerly smiled at Tom Fleming, one of her old friends. She then pointed out an irony, which made some committee members think she was in favor of granting permission, especially since she said the irony made her feel "uncomfortable." PEN's records before SS became president had been sold to Princeton Library, where anybody could consult them, "including those about you, Tom," she said. In fact, as I discovered, the records for SS's first six months as president were available at Princeton. Fleming said he could not imagine anything that had happened while he was president that he would want to conceal. But even if he could, he did not see how he could say no. "We are an organization that stands for freedom-to-write and free access to information. And we're defenders of the First Amendment. We try to strike down censorship. The principle is so glaringly obvious."

Kennerly wanted to hear from other committee members. There were a few

SS friends in the room, and they expressed sympathy for her, having to deal with an unauthorized biographer. But the committee nevertheless supported Fleming, except for Leon Friedman. Kennerly said that under the bylaws the committee did not have the power to release the board minutes, but that she would take the strong sense of the meeting back to President Scammell.

One former board member I interviewed did believe board minutes should be kept secret. How else, he said, could business get done? How could PEN officials keep confidences or explore positions that would immediately be made public? But he overlooked the fact that I was requesting minutes now nearly ten years old. I was doing nothing that could possibly jeopardize a sitting president's effectiveness.

On June 17, 1997, Scammell sent me a letter stating that "it appears that legally, members of an organization in New York State have the right to inspect board minutes 'only for corporate purposes,' that is, to further the aim of the organization in question, but not for the purpose of obtaining information about an individual member of PEN." Of course, I was not attempting to secure only information about SS but to ascertain her effectiveness as PEN president in the light of its corporate purposes.

Scammell made a show of openness by airing my case in the November–December 1997 issue of the *PEN Newsletter*. He argued that the First Amendment had its limits. How could any organization simply throw itself open to members and nonmembers alike? He wondered, "When does the past become history?" He treated me like a firebrand and reserved for himself the role of philosopher of history.

My reply to Scammell appeared in the January–February *PEN Newsletter* and noted that Scammell had a "timid idea" of independent intellectual and biographical inquiry if he thought that one needs permission to deal with public figures—"no less the President of an organization." I ventured the observation that he had an "extraordinarily genteel view of the genre that I don't think the membership will support." In fact, the *Newsletter* never printed a single letter supporting his position.

I traded more letters with Scammell, pointing out that PEN had not done me the courtesy of even supplying information already in the public record, such as press releases dating from the SS presidency. He replied saying he was sure that this had been an oversight, and if I would write to Karen Kennerly again, I would have the material. Kennerly never answered my letters. I made one final try with Michael Roberts, the new executive director of PEN, writing to him on January 4, 1999.

Roberts has not answered my letter.

24.· PITCHING SUSAN SONTAG (1986–1989)

SS's Trip to Hawaii: Int. Jeanette Paulson, Cobey Black. **Helen Benedict:** Int. See also Benedict's profile, which was published in several newspapers, including the *Chicago Tribune* (December 11, 1988), and is collected in her volume *Portraits in Print* (NY: Columbia University Press, 1990). **Andrew Wylie**: Margaria Fichtner, "Susan Sontag's Train of Thought Rolls into Town," *Miami Herald*, February 19, 1989. Harriet Wasserman, *Handsome Is: Adventures with Saul Bellow: A Memoir* (NY: Fromm International, 1997). Janklow is quoted in Wasserman. See also Robert Enright, "Style and Radical Will: An Interview with Susan Sontag," *Border Crossings* 7 (April 1988); the "People" column in *Newsday*, February 24, 1989. **Endicott Booksellers:** Correspondence and interview with Stuart Bernstein. See also Jonathan Mandell, "Notes on Sontag, *Newsday*, February 7, 1989. **SS at Books & Company:** Int. Brandon Larson.

25: THE WAY WE LIVE NOW (1986–1995)

Critics on "The Way We Live Now": David Leavitt is quoted in Elaine Showalter, *Sexual Anarchy: Gender and Culture at the Fin de Siècle* (NY: Viking, 1990), 206. See also Joseph Cady, "Immersive and Counterimmersive Writing About AIDS: The Achievement of Paul Monette's *Love Alone*," in *Writing Aids: Gay Literature, Language, and Analysis*, ed. Timothy F. Murphy and Suzanne Poirier (NY: Columbia University Press, 1993), 244–64; Sylvie Drake, "Bearing the Pain of AIDS in 'The Way We Live Now,'" *Los Angeles Times*, February 24, 1989; Annie Dawid, "The Way We Teach Now: Three Approaches to AIDS Literature," in *AIDS: The Literary Response*, ed. Emmanuel S. Nelson (NY: Twayne, 1992); see also Patricia Morrisroe, *Mapplethorpe: A Biography* (NY: Random House, 1995); see also Fries int., *CSS*. **Reviews of *Aids and Its Metaphors*:** SS received excellent reviews in *Newsday* (January 8, 1989), where Dan Cryer judged that she displayed the same "precision, clarity, and wide-ranging learning" to be found in *Illness as Metaphor;* and in the *Washington Post* (January 15, 1989), where Dennis Drabelle commended her "erudition." More mixed to negative reviews appeared in the *New York Times*, January 16, 1989, where Christopher Lehmann-Haupt complained that "the trouble is it is sometimes hard to tell what Ms. Sontag's point of view is"; in the *Chicago Tribune* (January 22, 1989), where Charles Perrow found her too abstract and too little concerned with the "realities of education, social conditions, and politics"; in the *Wall Street Journal* (January 20, 1989), where Paul Klinghoffer lamented that her work "reads more like an oracle than an essay"; in the *San Francisco Chronicle* (January 29, 1989), where Randy Shilts regretted her "omission of analysis" and said she had written "only half of a good book"; and in the *Village Voice* (March 14, 1989), where Richard Goldstein deplored SS's squeamish tone and oblique language: "She never, never uses the word 'gay.'" Similarly, Gregory Kolovakos (the same Gregory Kolovakos whom John Morrone at PEN had delegated to mollify Larry Kramer when he attacked SS for not recognizing gay authors or doing enough about AIDS), in *The Nation* (May 1, 1989), chided SS for employing "value-laden nouns such as 'sodomy' without comment." He found her unexamined rhetoric disturbing. Scott McLemee, "On Demythologizing AIDS," *New Politics* 2 (Summer 1989), took a more even-handed, though still skeptical approach, concluding: "It seems very dubious, very mystified, to argue that medical 'facts' and ideological 'values' can be separated so cleanly as Sontag would want." Few reviewers, however critical, closely examined SS's ideology. Joseph Sobran, *National Review* (February 24, 1989), noted that SS "simply assumes that revulsion against homosexuality and its characteristic practices is wicked. Conservatives who see in AIDS a sort of retribution for those practices—which can be, at least, recklessly unsanitary— are a 'predictable . . . sector of bigots,' mighty loose language to come from a careful analyst of rhetoric. *She* can excommunicate and stigmatize when she wants to." D. A. Miller, "Sontag's Urbanity," *October*, provides the most devastating exploration of SS's premises and her language, taking issue with her insistence that *AIDS and its Metaphors* should be viewed as writing, not simply for what it says about a particular disease. SS, Miller argues, simply collapses the behaviors of all gay men into the psychopathology of "'the' homosexual," and she has been doing so since "Notes on 'Camp.'" She hides behind terms, treating them as received ideas, employing phrases such as "regarded, seen, viewed as." She never defines, in other words, her relation to her subject. Her "mandarin aloofness" and her language "continue to ratify the prejudice, oppression, and violence that gay people and people with AIDS daily encounter." In spite of this chorus of criticism, SS was honored for her contribution to "gay rights and awareness about AIDS" at the eleventh anniversary of National Gay Rights Advocates. See Jeannine Stein, "Trio Honored for AIDS Work," *Los Angeles Times*, April 17, 1989. **SS's Sexual Orientation:** Larry Gross, *Contested Closets: The Politics and Ethics of Outing* (Minneapolis: University of Minnesota Press, 1993). Signorile and Scagliotti were also interviewed for this biography. **Sarah Schulman:** Int. and *My American History: Lesbian and Gay Life During the Reagan/Bush Years* (1994). **Camille Paglia:** Int. and correspondence with Paglia; int. with Christopher Lydon. **The Party at RS's House:** Int. with Hilton Kramer; letter to CR from James Lord, March 22, 1997.

26: THE VOLCANO LOVER (1990–1992)

MacArthur Award: "4 Californians Among 36 Winners of MacArthur Foundation Grants," *Los Angeles Times*, July 17, 1980; "Sudden Wealth . . . Grant Lets a Writer Write, an Activist Act, and a Professor Buy a Rain Forest," *St. Louis Post-Dispatch*, July 18, 1990. SS has received the following honors:

1966	Receives a George Polk Memorial Award in criticism and a Guggenheim Fellowship
1967	Elected to executive board of the American Center of PEN International

1974	Receives a Rockefeller Foundation grant through PEN
1975	Receives a Guggenheim Fellowship
1976	Receives Arts and Letters Award of the American Academy and Institute of Arts and Letters; Brandeis University Creative Arts Award citation; Ingram Merrill Foundation Award in Literature in the field of American Letters
1978	*On Photography* receives the National Book Critics Circle Award for criticism
1979	Elected to American Academy and Institute of Arts and Letters; annual award of the Academy of Science and Literature in Mainz, Germany; New York City Mayor's Award of Honor for Arts and Culture
1987	Elected president of the PEN American Center
1990	Receives MacArthur Foundation Fellowship
1991	Receives Elmer Holmes Bobst Award
1992	Receives Harold Washington Literary Award in Chicago
1993	Receives an honorary degree from Harvard
1994	Receives the Montblanc de la Culture award in recognition of her work in Sarajevo
1995	Listed as one of 50 Great Living Americans by Marquis's *Who's Who;* number 61 on *Life*'s list of "Women Who Shook the World"; named Chevalier in the Order of Arts and Letters in Paris
1997	Included in Volume II of *The American Intellectual Tradition* (Oxford: Oxford University Press)
1999	"Notes on 'Camp'" is listed as number 72 on American Journalism's Top 100 works, compiled by thirty-six judges working under the aegis of New York University's journalism department

London Terrace: We are grateful to our friend and colleague Bert Hanson for taking us on a tour of London Terrace and for providing the following articles: "Where Seventh Avenue Goes to Sleep," *New York Times,* March 26, 1995; Christopher Gay, "Time Erodes Unity of a 1,665-Unit City Within a City," *New York Times,* October 30, 1988. See also Holland Cotter, "A Tour Through Chelsea, Art's New Center of Gravity," *New York Times,* May 15, 1998. **Annie Leibovitz:** For accounts of Leibovitz, with passing mentions of SS, see Richard Lacayo, "Photography: Shadows and Eye Candy: Major New Books from Annie Leibovitz and Irving Penn Frame Two Contrasting Angles on Celebrity," *Time,* September 30, 1991; Irene Lacher, "Annie Leibovitz Is a Camera," *Los Angeles Times,* October 30, 1991; John Robinson, "Photographs Fan the Flame of Fame," *Boston Globe,* June 18, 1992; "People," *Newsday,* February 15, 1993; Angela Lambert, "Talking Pictures with Annie Leibovitz," *The Independent,* March 3, 1994; David Van Biema, "Annie Leibovitz, *Face to Face: The Eye of Annie*

Leibovitz," *Life,* April 1, 1994; Mark Stevens, "Shining Stars," *New York,* September 23, 1996; Robert McHenry, ed., *Her Heritage: A Biographical Encyclopedia of Famous American Women* (NY: Merriam-Webster, 1994). There is an interview with Leibovitz at an exhibition of her work in Warsaw available at http://fotoapeta.art.pl/fti-ale.html. Mention of Leibovitz as one of *Life*'s top 50 baby boomers is on a Web site: http://www.pathfinder.com.Life/boomers/top50.html. Richard Johnson, "Page Six," *New York Post,* April 30, 1998, reports that Leibovitz has made *American Photo*'s top 100 list. SS expressed her feelings about Leibovitz and the jacket photograph to Scott Simon of National Public Radio. We interviewed James Vernon, one of Leibovitz's interns, and observed SS and Leibovitz together at numerous public events. **SS's opinion of *The Volcano Lover*:** SS, "Singleness," in *Who's Writing This?: Notations on the Authorial I with Self-Portraits,* ed. Daniel Halpern (Hopewell, N.J.: Ecco Press, 1995). For an arresting historical treatment of ménages à trois, with an excellent chapter on the Hamiltons, Nelson, and SS, see Barbara Foster, Michael Foster, and Letha Hadady, *Three in Love* (NY: HarperCollins, 1997). For SS's comments on *The Volcano Lover,* we drew on personal recordings of interviews conducted by Irene Borger, Scott Simon, and Eleanor Wachel, and printed interviews by Paula Span (see *CSS*); EH; Sara Mosle, "Talking with Susan Sontag," *Newsday,* August 30, 1992; Mary Ann Grossmann, "Shaking Loose," *St. Paul Pioneer Press,* September 10, 1992; Inga Saffron, "Sontag's Stuff," *Philadelphia Inquirer,* September 24, 1992; Samuel R. Delany, "Under the Volcano," *Reflex,* October 6, 1992; D. C. Denison, "The Interview: Susan Sontag," *UpFront,* November 1, 1992; Margaria Fichtner, "Sontag Basks in Success of Romantic Novel," *Miami Herald,* November 22, 1992.

The reviews of *The Volcano Lover* ran something like three to one in its favor. Sven Birkerts called the novel a "wonderful fusion of the concrete and the conceptual," and he paid SS an enormous compliment by claiming that her work reminded him of Marguerite Yourcenar's *Memoirs of Hadrian,* the standard by which modern historical novels are measured (*Newsday,* August 2, 1992). Novelist John Banville found SS's novel "impressive, at times enchanting, always interesting, always entertaining" (*New York Times,* August 9, 1992). Kevin Ray praised a "magnificent and generous novel, recalling Lampedusa's *The Leopard* in insight as well as in venue" (*St. Louis Post-Dispatch,* August 9, 1992).

Reviewers like Peter Kemp (*Sunday Times* [London], October 4, 1992) objected to SS's aggressive presence, both on her book tour and in her book. In *The New Republic* (September 7 and 14, 1992), Richard Jenkyns wrote: "What Sontag says of Hamilton could be applied to herself: 'He wanted to make sure that their amusement was as saturated with knowledge as his own. Wherever he was, the Cavaliere was prone to cast himself in the role of guide or mentor.'" See also John Simon (*National Review,* August 31, 1992); Adam Begley (*Miami Herald,* August 9, 1992); and Rhoda Koenig (*New York,* August 17, 1992).

27: SARAJEVO (1993–1995)

Epigraph: SS's short essay on Goya is in Edward Hirsch, ed., *Transforming Vision: Writers on Art* (NY: Art Institute of Chicago, 1994). **Sarajevo:** We found the following published accounts most helpful in documenting SS's stays in Sarajevo: Armada int., *CSS;* her interview with Charlie Rose (interview transcript, August 2, 1995); a taped interview on National Public Radio (n.d.); "Pass Notes: No. 206: Susan Sontag," *The Guardian,* July 28, 1993; "Moreover . . . ," *The Guardian,* July 30, 1993; Charlotte Eager, "Play Shapes Up amid Bomb Blasts," *Cleveland Plain Dealer,* August 2, 1993; Gordon Coales, "Coales' Notes: War Efforts," *The Independent,* August 2, 1993; Marcus Tanner, "A Long Wait for Godot," *The Independent,* August 2, 1993; Janine Di Giovanni, "Waiting for the Barbarians," *Sunday Times* (London), August 8, 1993; Neely Tucker, "In Sarajevo, the Backdrop Is War Still, Actors Are Fighting to Keep the Theater Alive," *Detroit Free Press,* August 8, 1993; John Pomfret, *"Godot* amid the Gunfire; In Bosnia, Sontag's Take on Beckett," *Washington Post,* August 19, 1993; Hilton Kramer, "In Sarajevo, False Echoes of Spain," *Wall Street Journal,* August 24, 1993 (see the letters criticizing Kramer, September 3, 1993); Jean Baudrillard, "No Reprieve for Sarajevo," *Libération,* January 8, 1994, translated by Patrice Riemens, <patrice@xs4all.nl>, Amsterdam; Slavenka Drakulic, "A Winter's Tale," *The New Republic,* January 10, 1994; Luke Clancy, "Rising Above the Rubble of War," *Irish Times,* January 22, 1994; Joanna Coles, "Commentary: When Sweet Charity Begins at Germaine's Own Home," *The Guardian,* February 4, 1994, 18; Tom Disch, "A Sestina for Susan Sontag," *Poetry* 167 (March 1996); Julie Lasky, "Art out of Rubble" *American Scholar* 66 (Spring 1997); George Spiro, *Dobardan: A Tragedy in 12 Scenes,* http://www.drames.org/plays/scripts/dobardan.txt; Caroline Bayard and Graham Knight, "Vivisecting the 90s: An Interview with Jean Baudrillard," http://www.ctheory.com/a24-vivisecting_90s.html (the French version appears in *Research in Semiotic Inquiry/Recherches Sémiotiques* 16 [Spring 1996]. SS's *El Pais* interview appears in *CSS.* We also had the benefit of interviews with Victor Navasky, E. L. Doctorow, and Erika Munk. See also Todd Gitlin's "The Culture Wars; Lost Cause: Why Intellectuals of the Left Miss Communism," *Los Angeles Times,* January 14, 1996: "Some, including myself, wanted the United States to bomb the Bosnia Serbs shelling Sarajevo; others said America had no business meddling. It couldn't have been any plainer that, on foreign matters at least, the left had broken up." **SS's Abandoned Essay on Intellectuals and Revolutionary Power:** Manion and Simon int., *CSS.* **Leibovitz in Bosnia:** David Van Biema, "Face to Face: The Eye of Annie Leibovitz," *Life,* April 1, 1994; Andrew Palmer, "Photography: A Ride on the Back of a Horse Called Fame," *The Independent,* March 9, 1994; Angela Lambert, "Talking Pictures with Annie Leibovitz: From Jagger to Trump," *The Independent,* March 3, 1994. **Erika Munk:** "Notes from a Trip to Sarajevo," *Theater* 24 (1994); "Only the Possible: An Interview with Susan Sontag," *Theater* 24 (1993); Thomas

Akstens, "Under Fire: Sontag, *Godot*, Sarajevo," *Assaph: Studies in the Theatre* 11 (1995); see also SS's article, "Being Translated," *RES* 32 (Autumn 1997). **Christopher Hitchens:** See his preface to Kemal Kurspahic's *As Long as Sarajevo Exists* (Stony Creek, Conn.: Pamphleteer's Press, 1997). **Endgame:** See the exchange of letters between Martin Garbus and Robert Brustein in the *New York Times Book Review*, February 21, 1999. **SS's Primary Schooling Project:** SS discusses her Sarajevo experience in Robert Vorlicky, ed., *Tony Kushner in Conversation* (Ann Arbor: University of Michigan Press, 1998). **The Montblanc Award:** See Nadine Broan, "Chronicle," *New York Times*, February 17, 1994, for a brief article on SS's award; see also Peter Goodman, "Writer's $25,000 Prize Will Go for Relief; Sontag's Bosnia Work Honored," *Newsday*, February 21, 1994. SS continued her commentary on the Balkans in "Why Are We in Kosovo?," *New York Times Magazine*, May 2, 1999, in which she expressed her support for the NATO bombing of Serbia, declaring, "There is such a thing as a just war."

28 ·· THE END AND THE BEGINNING (1991–1999)

Alice in Bed: The real Alice James was a bedfast recluse who died at age forty-three. **Robert Brustein:** E-mail to CR and LP, February 2, 1999. **Reviews Of Alice in Bed:** John O'Mahony, "Dramatically Seeking Susan," *The Guardian*, September 20, 1993; Marie Olesen Urbanski, "A Festering Rage: *Alice in Bed: A Play in Eight Scenes* by Susan Sontag," *Los Angeles Times*, October 10, 1993; Boyd Tonkin, "The Sleep of Grievance," *The Guardian*, September 6, 1994; Patti Hartigan, "Notes on the Bed: Susan Sontag, Woman of Ideas, Takes to the ART Stage to Dramatize Ideas of Women," *Boston Globe*, April 7, 1996; Terry Byrne, "Theater: Sontag in Wonderland," *Boston Herald*, April 10, 1996; Iris Fanger, "Alice James Faced Life in a Nightgown," *Christian Science Monitor*, April 24, 1996. **In America:** See "Zero" in *Artes* 11 (1995). **SS Publications in the 1990s:** *A Parsifal* appears in *Robert Wilson's Vision* (Boston: Museum of Fine Arts, 1991); "The Very Comical Laments of Pyramus and Thisbe" in *The New Yorker*, March 4, 1991; Sontag's "A View From the Ark" appears in Richard Misrach, *Violent Legacies: Three Cantos* (NY: Aperture, 1992); a scene from *The Lady from the Sea* in Robert Wilson, *RWWM* (Zurich: Memory/Cage Editions, 1997). SS continued to write the occasional essay, including a foreword to Machado de Assis, *Epitaph for a Small Winner* (NY: Noonday Press, 1990), and a provocative if minor effort, "The Decay of Cinema" for the *New York Times Magazine* (March 17, 1996). In response to her postmortem on the movies— which contended that the magic was gone, despite the occasional brilliant film—came over a hundred letters protesting that cinephilia, as she termed it, was not dead. She still had her knack, in other words, for touching a nerve. Her essay was reprinted in Geoffrey C. Ward, ed., *The Best American Essays 1996* (Boston: Houghton Mifflin, 1997). Dancer-choreographer Min Tanaka, an SS friend, toured the United States in what he called "The Poe Project," inspired by SS, he said, whom he credited with writing the "libretto"—a dubious term for a contribution of what Tanaka calls "woven images and sound ideas." SS, calling Tanaka "one of the greatest dancers and choreographers in the world today," said she had given him an "IV drip" of material from Poe's stories. Critics generally found the production a "pretty incoherent jumble." For reviews, see Karen Campbell, "Min Tanaka's Take on Poe Is Not Quite a Nightmare," *Boston Herald*, August 22, 1997; Tresca Weinstein, "'Poe Project' a Trip Back to Asylums," *Albany Times-Union*, August 23, 1997; Jennifer Dunning, "Quirky Passage to Poe's Haunted World," *New York Times*, August 25, 1997; Elizabeth Zimmer, "Sacred Monsters," *Village Voice*, September 9, 1997, 91; Jordan Levin, "Surreal Dance Captures Poe's Macabre Beauty," *Miami Herald*, September 13, 1997; Tobi Tobias, "Keeping It Real," *New York*, September 29, 1997; Chris Dohse, "The Poe Project," *Dance*, December 1997. **On SS's "Indifference to Self"**: See her essay "Singleness," in *Who's Writing This? Notations on the Authorial I with Self-Portraits*, ed. Daniel Halpern (Hopewell, N.J.: Ecco Press, 1995). **Retrospectives on SS:** Conservative Roger Kimball published a deft attack in *The New Criterion* (December 1997). Popular-culture critic Greil Marcus, *The Dustbin of History* (Cambridge: Harvard University Press, 1995), is equally contemptuous, berating her anti-Americanism and failure to connect with her culture. Far more positive assessments have appeared in scholarly books by Harvey Teres, *Renewing the Left: Politics, Imagination, and the New York Intellectuals* (1996), and James Seaton, *Cultural Conservatism, Political Liberalism* (1996). Teres suggests that Sontag, like McCarthy, has often been treated unfairly because she is a woman: "Women were often identified with the aggressive aspects of their work, whereas the men [Teres cites Edmund Wilson and Lionel Trilling] were identified with the more balanced, circumspect aspects." Seaton is especially good on showing how traditional SS was from the beginning, and how many of Matthew Arnold's ideas she borrowed even as she seemed to be attacking him. Sontag's comments on the recurrence of her cancer appear in Dale Peck, "The Big Idea: An Interview with Susan Sontag," *Book Forum* (Winter, 1999).

Acknowledgments

During the writing of this biography, we formed a fellowship with three friends also working on unauthorized biographies. Carole Klein, Marion Meade, and Ann Waldron shared with us their experiences researching the lives of Doris Lessing, Woody Allen, and Eudora Welty, respectively, even as we shared ours with them. Without their support and good humor, it would have been much more difficult to do this book. We also relied on many other members of the Biography Seminar, which meets at New York University. We do wish to thank Judy Feiffer for not only recommending people to interview but also supplying phone numbers. It was Judy, for example, who led us to Yoram Kaniuk.

Of a different order is our indebtedness to Samuel R. Delany, who made us ponder the problematic nature of biography, unauthorized and otherwise, in a series of probing letters. He kindly gave us a copy of his interview with Susan Sontag, but he also respected her wish that he not cooperate more closely with us.

In a similar vein, Scott McLemee shared with us a very impressive and far-reaching knowledge of Sontag, sending us many items and keeping up a steady E-mail correspondence about her life and work.

Special thanks have to be given to Joan Mellen, author of a superb biography of Kay Boyle published by FSG. Joan was a fount of information about Roger Straus and his firm. She made many important suggestions about whom to contact, and she helped set up our interview with Ralph Schoenman.

Sontag is such a presence in New York that we often found conversations with new acquaintances turning into interviews about their encounters with her. Although we conducted approximately 150 formal interviews, those who had something to say about Sontag probably numbered twice that.

For graciously consenting to interviews and sending E-mails and letters, we would like to thank: Daniel Aaron, Lionel Abel, Sigrid Bauschinger, Helen Benedict, Marshall Berman, Stuart Bernstein, Cobey Black, Irene Borger, Robert Brustein, Penny Cagan, Susan Chambre, Carole Chazin, Karen Chen, Kelly Cherry, Peter Collier, Gail Coyle, Arthur Danto, E. L. Doctorow, Candida Donadio, Terence Dougherty, Paul Ekman, Betty Falkenberg, Leslie Fiedler, Edward Field, Nina Finkelstein, Seth Fortin, George Garrett, George Goldsmith, Laurence Goldstein, Suzanne Gordon, Vivian Gornick, Judith Grossman, Joanne Gumbert, Peter Hald, Pete Hamill, Anthony Heilbut, Sam Heilman, Michele Herman, Jamake Highwater, Irv Jaffe, Jill Johnston, Yoram Kaniuk, the late Alfred Kazin, the late Walter Kendrick, Maya Khankhoje, Francis King, Seymour Kleinberg, Richard Kluger, Hilton Kramer, Edith Kurzweil, Brandon Larson, Goran Lindgren, James Lord, Robert Low, Christopher Lydon, Fleurie Mackie, Catherine Mackinnon, Norman Mailer, Irving Malin, Helen Marcus, Lawrence Mass, James McClintock, Celia McGee, Michael Millgate, Erika Munk, Victor Navasky, Philip Nobile, Sidney Offit, Michael Packenham, Camille Paglia, Donald Paglia, Jennette Paulson, Martin Peretz, William Phillips, Katha Pollitt, Nora Roberts, Mel Roseman, Ned Rosenheim, John Scagliotti, Richard Sennett, Sarah Schulman, David Shapiro, Earl Shorris, Michelangelo Signorile, John Simon, Harriet Sohmers-Zwerling, Richard Stern, Perry Stieglitz, Sunlight (Dot Lane), Joan Garner Taylor, Joseph Trigoboff, the late Richard Tristman, Peter Tumarkin, Mike Unsworth, James Vernon, Henny Wenkart, Edmund White, Reese Williams, Ann Wilson, and Mark Wilson.

Several people assisted our quests for interviews, providing names and numbers: John Blesso of the Authors Guild, and Zane Berzins, Andrea Dworkin, Bruce King, Norman Podhoretz, Sue Russell, and Sidney Stern.

Others provided important information about materials relevant to this biography: Nicholas Altenbernd of MIT; Dennis Altman, Axel

Claeges, and Mary Bolling of the New York Public Library; Maurice Crane of the Sound Library at Michigan State University; Tom Curwen of the *Los Angeles Times;* Betty J. Davis of the Detroit Institute of Arts; Mary Dearborn, Noel Riley Fitch, Robert Giard, Marek Grygiel, and Martin Hacket of the University of Pennsylvania; Bert Hansen, Allen Hibbard, and Fred Lenczycki of the Tucson Unified School District; Elaine Kauvar, Mark Lilla, Spencer Means, and Louisa Moy of the Newman Library, Baruch College, City University of New York; Dr. Louise Teems of North Hollywood High School; Donald Mengay, and Anne Posega of Washington University Libraries; Ned Rorem; Megan Rupnik of the Archives of American Art; Elzbieta Sawicka, James Seaton, and Thomas J. Travers of the Hotel Beacon; Ben Yagoda. A note of special thanks to the staff of Special Collections at the University of Delaware Library, which houses the Alfred Chester Collection, and to Tom and Bonnie Scott, our friends and hosts during our stay in Newark.

For their helpful comments on drafts of this biography we thank Edward Field, Allen Hibbard, Jamake Highwater, Jill Johnston, Francis King, Elizabeth Knappman, Camille Paglia, and Harriet Sohmers-Zwerling.

We were most fortunate to have research assistants, Melissa Bailey, Jyotsna Etikala, and Daniel Yiu, provided by Baruch College, and we are grateful to the City University of New York for awarding grants that helped to defray the considerable expense of travel and the acquisition of photographs and other materials. The Weissman School of Liberal Arts and Sciences, under the able leadership of Dean Alexandra Logue, made provision of reassigned time that reduced Carl Rollyson's teaching load and made possible long periods of concentration on this project.

We owe a great debt of gratitude to Gerald Howard, who acquired our book when he was at Norton. Not only was he a great champion of our efforts, he provided numerous contacts and took an active hand in shaping our vision of the biography. When he left Norton, he put us in the expert hands of Alane Mason, our editor.

At the beginning and end of all of our writing projects, we rely on our cheerful and always supportive agent, Elizabeth Frost Knappman of New England Publishing Associates. No writers could ask for a kinder, more understanding collaborator and friend.

Our "Notes and Comments" records the more specific debts we owe to the many generous people who answered our authors' queries for reminiscences of encounters with Susan Sontag.

Index

Page numbers beginning with 310 refer to "Notes and Comments."

Aaron, Daniel, 51, 317–18
ABC-TV, 253, 274
Abel, Lionel, 327
abortion rights, 148–49
Adam Resurrected (Kaniuk), 160, 161
Adams, Robert, 72, 75, 119, 323
Adler, Mortimer, 29
Advertisements for Myself (Mailer), 61
Advocate, 194
"Aesthetics of Silence, The" (Sontag), 130, 144
Against Interpretation (Sontag), 92, 94, 95, 96–104, 106, 107–8, 114, 131, 132, 154, 213
    dust jacket photograph for, 72, 97, 120, 273
    foreign editions of, 74, 120
    paperback edition of, 91, 102, 103
    reviews of, 96, 97–99
    sales of, 102, 103
"Against Interpretation" (Sontag), xii, 40, 96, 98–99, 107, 165
AIDS, 193, 251, 264–69
AIDS and Its Metaphors (Sontag), 261, 265–67, 269

Air Force, U.S., 15
Akstens, Thomas, 341–42
Albigensian Crusade, 89
Alcott, Louisa May, 12, 313
Aletti, Vince, 113
Alexandre, Marianne, 324
"Alfred Chester's Wig" (Ozick), 48
Alice in Bed (Sontag), 297–99
Alice in Wonderland (Carroll), 298
All About Eve, 157
Allen, Woody, 231–33, 237, 331
Almendros, Nestor, 318
Als, Hilton, 80, 321
Altman, Dennis, 190–91, 328
"America, Seen Through Photographs Darkly" (Sontag), 180
American Academy of Arts and Letters, 192, 244
American Association of University Women, 42, 51–52
American Communist Party, 122–23
American Council of Education, 27
American Indians, 8, 117, 123, 125
American Repertory Theater, 295, 297
American Review, 246

American Smelting & Refining, 65
American-Soviet Friendship Society, 122
American Spectator, 223–24
"American Spirits" (Sontag), 205–6
Americas Watch, 226
Amherst College, 169
Amis, Martin, 260
Anchor Books, 58, 80, 112, 131, 260
Anders, Jaroslav, 218, 330
anti-Americanism, 180
anti-Communism, 20, 99, 186, 218–24
"Anti-Communism and the Sontag Circle" (Kramer), 231
anti-intellectualism, 100, 157
anti-Semitism, 159, 160, 188, 213, 253
Appignanesi, Lisa, 333
"Approaching Artaud" (Sontag), 158
Arab-Israeli conflict, 159–60
Aragon, Louis, 50
Arbus, Diane, 89, 114, 176–77, 180, 321
Arcade, 19–21
Arendt, Hannah, 61, 66, 73, 270, 320
Aria da Capo (Millay), 13
Aristotle, 25, 99
Arizona, University of, 6, 8
Armada, Alfonso, 289
Armance (Stendhal), 75
Armenian genocide of 1915, 288
Armes, Roy, 325
Arnold, Matthew, 40, 100, 214, 322, 343
Aronowitz, Stanley, 230
Artaud, Antonin, 70, 330
Ashbery, John, 210
Ashmore, Harry S., 315
Associated Press, 248
Asti, Adriana, 156, 208–9, 298
Astor House Hotel (Tientsin), 4
As You Desire Me (Pirandello), 208–9, 298
Atlantic Monthly, 90, 158, 230
Atwan, Helene, 230
Atwood, Margaret, 242
Auden, W. H., xiii, 82, 83, 86, 187
Austen, Jane, 33
Authors Guild, 200, 241
Avedon, Richard, 201

Avon Books, 76
Ayer, A. J., 43, 316–17

"Baby" (Sontag), 42, 158, 207
Bacon, Francis, 173
Baldwin, James, 102
Balkan Express, The: Fragments from the Other Side of War (Drakulic), 292
Ball, George, 230
Balzac, Honoré de, 8, 80
Banes, Sally, 331
Banville, John, 340
Baranczak, Stanislaw, 218–19
Bard College, 230
Barnes, Djuna, 23, 27–28, 32, 59, 276
Barnes & Noble, 252
Barranger, Millsy S., 314
Barth, John, 72, 320
Barthelme, Donald, 174, 206, 239
Barthes, Roland, 104, 189, 190, 191, 197, 198
Barthes Reader, A (Sontag, ed.), 198
Baskett, Sam, 313
Bassoff, Bruce, 320
Bates, Milton J., 323–24
Batista, Fulgencio, 56
Baudelaire, Charles-Pierre, 39
Baudrillard, Jean, 341
Bausch, Pina, 332
Bauschinger, Sigrid, 72
Baxter, Anne, 157
Bayard, Caroline, 341
B. Dalton, 252
Beatles, 100
Beaton, Cecil, 113
Beatty, Warren, 89
Beckett, Samuel, 100, 116, 273, 291–97
Beerbohm, Max, 203, 329
Behar, Jack, 99, 100
Behold Goliath (Chester), 105
"Behold Goliath" (Chester), 105
Bellow, Saul, 231, 233, 260, 331
Benedict, Helen, 258–59, 318, 336–37
Benefactor, The (Sontag), 63–78, 115, 117, 319–20
   dedication of, 78
   dust jacket photograph for, 73–74,

89, 96, 97, 120
promotion of, 65, 73, 74, 75
publication of, 58–61, 63–65, 72
public reception and sales of, 64,
    68–69, 72–73, 75–76, 103
reviews of, 72–73, 75–76
SS's advance for, 64
story line and style of, 68, 69–72
writing of, 52, 55, 58, 63, 67, 68
Ben-Itzak, Paul, 332
Benjamin, Walter, 58, 103, 161, 175,
    178, 214–15, 283, 313, 329
Bennington College, 154–57, 275
Berek, Peter, 131
"Berenice" (Poe), 9
Berg, Beatrice, 323, 324
Berger, John, 175
Bergman, David, 321
Bergman, Ingmar, 135, 136, 234, 325
"Bergman's *Persona*" (Sontag), 130,
    135, 136
Berkeley, University of California at,
    18, 27–29, 46, 87, 219
Berkley, Miriam, 59
Berman, Laura, 331
Berman, Marshall, 222–23, 316, 330
Bernhardt, Sarah, 299
Bernstein, Richard, 334
Bernstein, Stuart, 261–62, 337
Berzins, Zane, 328
Best American Essays, 1992 (Atwan and
    Sontag, eds.), 170, 303–4
Best American Short Stories, 1987, 264
*Best American Short Stories of the
    Century* (Updike, ed.), 264
Bettelheim, Bruno, 231
Beyer, Monika, 212
Bibanovi, Dubravko, 292
Biema, David Van, 280–81
Bing, Rudolf, 301
Birkerts, Sven, 340
Bjorkman, Stig, 325
Black, Cobey, 207, 329
Black Mountain College, 27
Blades, John, 333
Blakemore, Barbara, 326
Blum, John Morton, 231
Blumenthal, Ralph, 334
Bobbsey Twins books, 16

Body in Pain, The (Scarry), 45
Bogart, Humphrey, 30
Bograd, Larry, 313
Bonetti, David, 323
*Book of Gay and Lesbian Quotations,
    The,* 267
Book-of-the-Month Club, 286
Books & Company, 262–63, 337
Borger, Irene, 283–84, 340
Borges, Jorge Luis, 68, 191, 303
Boston Phoenix, 160
Boston University, 179–80, 328
Botstein, Leon, 230
Bowles, Jane, 79
Bowles, Paul, 48, 64, 67, 79, 83, 106,
    107, 319
Boxer Rebellion, 89
Boyers, Robert, 165
Boy's Own Story, A (White), 192–93
Brand, Stewart, 326
Brandeis University, 36, 38
Branham, Robert J., 330
Braudeau, Michel, 327
Braudy, Leo, 91, 213, 216–17
Brecht, Bertolt, 138
Brennan, Paul, 203–4
Bresson, Robert, 107–8, 234
Breton, André, 49, 50, 317
Brien, Alan, 88, 321
Broan, Nadine, 342
Broch, Hermann, 215–16
Brodsky, Joseph, 64, 258, 328, 330
    Nobel Prize of, 162
    Soviet expulsion of, 187
    SS and, 161, 162, 187–90, 218–19,
        220
    SS's tribute to, 188
    teaching positions of, 187, 190, 191
Bromwich, David, 329–30
Brook, Peter, 134
Brooks, Peter, 99, 185
Brother Carl, 130, 142–46, 325
    scenario of, 143–45, 153
Browning, Robert, 80
Brown University, 132
Bruni, Frank, 260
Bruss, Elizabeth, 322
Brustein, Robert, 146, 295, 299, 342
Buckley, William F., 223, 330

Bullock, Alan, 208–9
Burch, Noël, 147
Burke, Kenneth, 31–32, 34, 47, 69, 74, 77, 315, 319–20
Burns, John, 293
Bush, George, 253–54
Byrne, Terry, 342

Cabalistic mysticism, 69
Cabezas, Omar, 238
Cady, Joseph, 337
Caen, Herb, 168
Cagan, Penny, 328
Cage, John, 234
Calder, Liz, 328
Caleb Conover, Railroader (Terhune), 6
California, 230
California, University of:
    at Berkeley, 18, 27–29, 46, 87, 219
    at Los Angeles (UCLA), 22, 24
Calisher, Hortense, 243–44, 245
Callas, Maria, 301
Cambridge, Mass., 38–42, 189
Campbell, Karen, 343
Camus, Albert, 223
Canada, 135, 252
Canetti, Elias, 104, 214, 215–16, 313
Cannes Film Festival, 138
Čapek, Karel, 13
capitalism, 123, 130
Capote, Truman, 52
Captive Mind, The (Milosz), 220, 222
Caracole (White), 193, 197–201, 271
    SS's displeasure with, 196, 200–201
Carbine, Pat, 326
Carlson, Jocelyn, 191, 328
Carr, Gladys, 133, 324
Carroll, Lewis, 298
Carson, Peter, 328
Carter, Albert Howard, 185
Cassinelli, Claudio, 234
Castro, Fidel, 56, 57, 58, 128, 158, 167, 168, 242
Catholic Church, 251
Caute, David, 324
Ceballos, Jackie, 153
Cela, Camilo José, 64
Chaikin, Joseph, 134, 162, 174, 265, 325, 327

Chazin, Carole, 169
Chekhov, Anton, 11
Cher, 291
Chesler, Phyllis, 151
Chester, Alfred, 64, 70–72, 82, 115, 320, 322
    character and personality of, 47–48, 79, 84, 105–7, 112, 113
    death of, 49
    gay lifestyle of, 47, 70, 74, 84, 106, 120
    literary career of, 47–49, 79, 84, 105, 106–11, 136, 206
    SS's relationship with, 47–49, 53–55, 67, 70–71, 78–79, 83, 105–11, 317, 319
Chicago, University of, 22–27, 47, 81
    SS at, 25–27, 29–36, 38, 49
Children's Hour, The (film), 93
Children's Hour, The (Hellman), 93
Childs, Lucinda, 151, 209, 234–35, 326, 331, 332
China, 3–4, 6, 8, 9
    SS's trip to, 158, 195, 293, 326
    Tiananmen Square massacre in, 129
Christianity, 40, 57–58, 69
Christy, Marian, 279, 313
Chute, Joy, 238
Cicero, vii
Cioran, E. M., 138
Citizen Kane, 232
City College of New York, 26, 52, 57, 189, 277
City of Night (Rechy), 48
City of Words (Tanner), 116
Civilization and Its Discontents (Freud), 34
Clancy, Luke, 292, 341
Clemons, Walter, 277
Cleveland Clinic, 171
Clift, Montgomery, 20
Coales, Gordon, 291, 341
Cockburn, Alexander, 225, 226, 231, 330, 331
Cocteau, Jean, 135
Cohen, Ira, 106, 322
Cohen, Richard, 254, 255, 334
Cohen, Sharon, 315
Cohn, Roy, 260

Cold War, 122–23, 220, 221, 224
Coleridge, Samuel Taylor, 51
Coles, Joanna, 291, 341
Coles Books, 252
Colford, Paul D., 319
Collier, Peter, 324
Collins, Thomas, 333
Collins publishers, 69
Columbia University, 26, 80, 121, 142,
    187
  Miller Theatre of, 304
  SS's teaching position at, 56–58,
    103, 141, 274
Commentary, 47, 52, 99, 185
Commonweal, 131
Communism, 21, 50
  American, 122–23
  Cuban, 127–28, 167, 168, 186, 220
  Soviet, 186–87, 194–95, 218–24
Compton's Encyclopedia, 16
Connecticut, University of, 38, 53
Conrad, Joseph, 32, 118
Constanti, Sophie, 331–32
Constitution, U.S., 23
Contested Closets (Gross), 269–70
Conversations with Susan Sontag
    (Poague, ed.), 310
Cornell, Joseph, 94–96, 322
Cotter, Holland, 339
Coyle, Gail, 314
Cozarinksy, Edgardo, 299
Crampton, Nancy, 304
Crane, Hart, 32
Craven, David, 329
Critter and Other Dogs, The (Terhune), 7
Croce, Benedetto, 33
Crowds and Power (Canetti), 216
Cryer, Dan, 337
Cuba, 53, 57–58, 126–29, 326
  Communism in, 127–28, 167, 168,
    186, 220
  repression in, 127–28, 158
  SS's trip to, 56, 129, 324
Cuban Revolution, 56, 123, 126–28,
    158, 186
Cunningham, Imogen, 112
Cunningham, Merce, 235
Curie, Eve, 10–11
Curie, Marie, 10–11, 150, 300

Curie, Pierre, 10–11
Curtis, Charlotte, 225
Czechoslovakia, 138

Danto, Arthur, 303
D'Antonio, Michael, 318
Dartmouth College, 155
David, Catherine, 327
Davidson, Ann Morrissett, 230
Davis, Bette, 157
Dawid, Annie, 337
Dayton Peace Accord, 289
Death Kit (Sontag), 115–22, 323
  dust jacket photograph for, 112,
    120–21
  foreign editions of, 120
  paperback edition of, 112
  promotion and sales of, 119–20
  reviews of, 116, 117–18, 119, 121
  structure and story line of, 115–18,
    136
Death of a Salesman (Miller), 296
de Beauvoir, Simone, 37, 46, 146–47,
    154, 155, 189, 190, 316, 321
"Debriefing" (Sontag), 142–43, 144,
    206, 207, 326
DeLano, Sharon, 258
Delany, Samuel R., 284, 340
Dell, 102, 183
Delta, 102
DeMott, Benjamin, 96, 97, 121
Denison, D. C., 340
Detroit Institute of Arts, 178
Dewey Commission, 128
De Wit, Theo, 318
Diaghilev, Sergei, 143
Diamond, Paula, 75, 320
Dickey, James, 121–22, 323
Dickinson, Emily, 299
Dickstein, Morris, 322
Dictionary of National Biography, 283
Dictionary of Slang (Partridge), 84–85
Diderot, Denis, 297, 299
Didion, Joan, 237, 318
Di Giovanni, Janine, 292–93, 341
Disch, Tom, 341
Divorcing (Taubes), 142, 143
Doctorow, E. L., 219, 220, 238–39, 245,
    279, 289, 330, 332, 335, 341

Dog Named Chips, A (Terhune), 6–7
Dohse, Chris, 343
Donadio, Candida, 109, 120, 323
Donoghue, Denis, 119
"Double Standard of Aging, The"
    (Sontag), 153–54
Drabelle, Dennis, 337
Drake, Sylvie, 337
Drakulic, Slavenka, 291–92, 341
"Dreams of Hippolyte," *see Benefactor,*
    The
"Dr. Jekyll" (Sontag), 207
Dubček, Alexander, 220–21
Ducas, June, 332
Duet for Cannibals, 130, 137–41, 143,
    156
  reviews of, 139, 140, 141, 325
  scenario of, 138–41, 142, 208
Dugdale, John, 274
"Dummy, The" (Sontag), 49, 206, 207
Duncan, Robert, 27
Dunning, Jennifer, 332, 343
Dustbin of History, The (Marcus), 230
Dutton, 201
Dzuback, Mary Ann, 315

Eager, Charlotte, 341
Editions du Seuil, 103
Ehrlich, Arnold, 84, 320
Einstein, Albert, 11
Eisenhower, Dwight D., 61
Eisenstein, Sergey, 122
Ekman, Paul, 315
Eliot, George, 8
Eliot, T. S., xiii, 23, 58, 99
Elizabeth I, Queen of England, 87
Elliott, David, 327
Ellipsian, The (Cornell), 96
Ellmann, Mary, 90
El Salvador, 219, 222
Emma (Austen), 33
Emperor Jones, The (O'Neill), 162
Empire of Signs, The (Barthes), 198
Endgame (Beckett), 295
Endicott Booksellers, 261–62, 337
Enfants Terribles, Les (Cocteau), 135
Enfants Terribles, Les (film), 135
English Speaking Union, xiii
Enlightenment, 69, 283

Enright, Robert, 337
Entertainment Weekly, 272
Ephron, Nora, 314
Epistemology of the Closet (Sedgwick),
    269
Epstein, Barbara, 80, 174, 176–77
Epstein, Jason, 58–59, 60, 67, 80–82
Erasmus, Desiderius, 60
Esquire, 60, 89, 90, 102, 160, 176
Evans, Leslie, 128, 324
existentialism, 49, 125
Exquisite Corpse, The (Chester), 107,
    108–10, 206
Eyre & Spottiswoode, 74, 120

Fabians, 195
"Family of Man" show, 114, 176
Fanger, Iris, 331, 342
Farrar, John, 66
Farrar, Straus and Giroux (FSG),
    58–61, 64–66, 102, 103,
    119–20, 131, 133, 135, 303
  David Rieff as editor at, 170,
    228–30
  founding of, 66
  prestigious authors list of, 58,
    64–65, 190
  promotion and marketing of SS by,
    63–65, 73, 74, 119–20, 147,
    158, 182–83, 286
  sale of, 259
  SS's screenplays published by, 147
  see also Giroux, Robert; Straus,
    Roger
Farrow, Mia, 232
"Fascinating Fascism" (Sontag),
    164–68, 216–17
fascism, 18, 164–68, 186, 188,
    220–21, 223–24
Faulkner, William, 152, 194
Feigen-Fasteau, Brenda, 151
Feingold, Michael, 70
Feminine Mystique, The (Friedan), 61
feminism, 61, 75, 89, 146, 147–53, 165
  anti-intellectualism and, 157
  consciousness–raising (CR) and, 151
  lesbianism and, 92–94, 151–57
  militant, 32, 77, 148–51, 153, 154
  patriarchal history and, 166

politics and, 149, 150, 151
prominent proponents of, 61, 75,
    151, 153, 154, 166–67
SS on, 147–51, 166–67, 298
SS's dilemma with, 152–53
women writers and, 61, 75, 151,
    152, 154–57, 166–67
Feminist Review, 273
Fernandes, Bob, 326
Fichtner, Margaria, 256, 259–60, 312,
    318, 327, 337, 340
Field, Edward, 28, 48, 53–54, 67,
    78–79, 105–7, 315, 317, 318,
    319, 320, 322
films:
    Asian, 257
    avant-garde, 94, 95, 97, 107–8, 137
    documentary, 159–60, 164–68, 296,
        299
    European New Wave, 97
    French, 107–8, 135, 136, 234
    Nazi-era documentary, 164–68
    science fiction, 97
    SS's appearances in, 231–33
    SS's interest in, 46, 49, 53, 61, 94,
        95, 97, 107–8, 122, 137, 257,
        325
    SS's Israeli documentary, 159–60
    SS's original screenplays for, 71,
        130, 136–47, 233–35
    SS's reviews and essays on, 61, 97,
        98, 107–8, 130, 131, 135, 136,
        164–68, 215, 342
    underground, 82, 98
Finegold, Michael, 320
Firbank, Ronald, 194
First, Elsa, 40
First Amendment, 224–25, 227, 261
Flamand, Paul, 103
Flaming Creatures, 98
Fleming, Tom, 335, 336
Flying Carpet, The (Halliburton), 7
Fonda, Jane, 89, 225
Food and Drug Administration (FDA),
    172
"Foot, The" (Chester), 48–49, 70–71,
    110–11
Ford, Harry, 322
Ford, Henry, 23

Fornés, María Irene, 53–54, 56, 78–79,
    134–35, 275, 318
    SS's relationship with, 53–54, 56,
        78–79, 134–35, 320, 324
Fothergill, Brian, 283–85
Fox, William Price, 313
Frakes, James B., 75–76
Francis, Kay, 89
Frank, Marcie, 91–92, 322
Franklin, Benjamin, 206
Franz Ferdinand, Archduke, 288
Fremont-Smith, Eliot, 97–98, 322
Frenzy of Renown, The (Braudy), 91
Freud, Sigmund, 34, 40–41, 51, 69
Freud: The Mind of the Moralist (Rieff),
    40–41, 46, 51
Friedan, Betty, 61, 75
Friedman, Leon, 224, 227, 331, 335
Friedman, Lillian, 320
Fries, Kenny, 265, 337
Frost, Robert, 75
Fulbright Fellowships, 55, 123
Fuller, Margaret, 299
Further Adventures of Lad (Terhune), 7

Gable, Clark, 136
Gaddis, William, 58
Galsworthy, John, 237
Garapedian, Seda, 20
Garbo, Greta, 95, 131
Garbus, Martin, 295, 342
Garis, Leslie, 318
Garner, Frances, 22
Garrett, George, 170, 241, 323, 327
Gass, William, 90, 321–23
Gay, Christopher, 339
Gay and Lesbian Biography, 267
Gay and Lesbian Heritage, The, 267
Gee, Helen, 112
Genet, Jean, 39, 70, 76, 107
Genette, Gérard, 198
Georgia Review, 206
German American Hospital (Tientsin), 4
German Democratic Republic, 46, 55,
    120, 247
Germany, Nazi, 31, 160, 164–66, 253,
    304
Getty Institute, 299
Ghostly Lover, The (Hardwick), 80

Giacometti, Alberto, 277
Gide, André, 17, 153, 186, 195
Ginsberg, Allen, 80, 122
Ginsburg, Gerald, 318
Girard, Robert, 52
Giroux, Robert, 58–60, 61–62, 68, 103, 319, 322, 323
Gitlin, Todd, 341
Glass, Norman, 79, 320
Glass, Philip, 234, 325, 332
Gnostics, 39, 40, 57, 180
Godard, Jean-Luc, 136, 137
"Godot Comes to Sarajevo" (Sontag), 291, 294, 295–96
Goethe, Johann Wolfgang von, 284
Goldin, Nan, 112
Goldman, Emma, 195
Goldsmith, George, 179–80, 328
Goldstein, Laurence, 132, 314, 324
Goldstein, Richard, 337
Goodheart, Eugene, 321
Goodman, Paul, 192, 313
Goodman, Peter, 332, 342
Goodman, Walter, 330
"Good Morning America," 253
Gordimer, Nadine, 65, 242, 313
Gordon, Barry, 254
Gordon, Suzanne, 204, 329
Gornick, Vivian, 151, 326
Gottlieb, Robert, 108, 109
Graham, Martha, 235, 281
Grammar of Motives, A (Burke), 31
Great Expectations (Acker), 308
Greeks, ancient, 40, 125
Greenberg, Clement, 66, 87, 99, 100
Greenberg, Martin, 52, 318
Greenblatt, Robert, 123
Greer, Germaine, 153
Gremlins 2, xi
Grenier, Richard, 218–19, 223, 330
Greville, Charles, 283
Groffsky, Maxine, 174
Grondahl, Paul, 312
Gross, Larry, 269–70, 338
Gross, Terry, 312
Grossinger's, 4
Grossman, Judith, 43–45, 317
Grossman, Mary Ann, 340
Grossman, Ron, 315, 327

Grotowski, Jerzy, 134
Grove, Lloyd, 252–53, 333
Guardian, 291
Guevara, Che, 128, 242, 324
Guggenheim family, 65, 66
Gurstein, Rochelle, 275
Gussow, Mel, 137, 138, 141, 325
Guttenplan, D. D., 247–48, 334

Hald, Peter, 137, 325
Hall, N. John, 203, 329
Halliburton, Richard, 7–8, 9, 10, 16
Halsman, Philippe, 120–21
Hamilton, Catherine, 285
Hamilton, Lady Emma, 283–85
Hamilton, Sir William, 283–86
Hamlet (film), 20
Hammett, Dashiell, 149
Handsome Is (Wasserman), 233
Hanscomb, Leslie, 243, 333
Hanson, Bert, 339
Happenings, 97, 98
Harcourt, Brace & World, 58
Hardwick, Elizabeth, 66, 73, 80–81, 82, 153, 167, 174, 228–29, 321
Harlequin Club, 21
Harper, 161
Harper's, 73, 80–81, 230
Harper's Bazaar, 86
Harrington, Stephanie, 318
Hartigan, Patti, 342
Harvard University, 26, 27, 51, 141, 189, 297, 299
  SS's postgraduate work at, 38–42, 141
  Widener Library at, 142
Hasidism, 69
Haskell, Molly, 140, 325
Hass, Robert, 248, 249
Hassan, Ihab, 98, 322
Havel, Václav, 242, 332–33
Hawaii, University of, 207
  East-West Center of, 257
Hawthorne, Nathaniel, 40
Hayden, Tom, 89
Hayes, Harold, 60
Hayman, Ronald, 314
Heaney, Seamus, 65

Hebrew University, 39
Hegel, G.W.F., 38, 160, 178
Heidegger, Martin, 31
Heilbrun, Carolyn, 73–74, 121
Heilbut, Anthony, 314
Heilman, Sam, 315
Heller, Zoë, 45, 55, 273–74, 277–78,
    312, 318
Hellman, Lillian, 93, 149, 187,
    226–27, 334
Helsinki Watch, 226
Hemenway, Robert, 75
Hemingway, Ernest, 290
Hennessee, Judith, 75
Hentoff, Nat, 224–26, 331
Hepburn, Katharine, 12
Herald Tribune (Paris), 46
Herbst, Josephine, 152, 290
Here Be Dragons (Chester), 47
"Heroism of Vision, The" (Sontag),
    180–81
Her Own Terms (Grossman), 43–44
Hess, Harry, 73, 97
Hibbard, Allen, 322
Hicks, Granville, 75
Higgins, Aidan, 295, 296
Highwater, Jamake, 22–24, 28, 276,
    314–15
Hijuelos, Oscar, 57
Hirst, Van, 20
History of Surrealism, The (Nadeau), 94
Hitchens, Christopher, 221, 223, 293,
    330, 342
Hitler, Adolf, 164–65, 167, 215
Hitler: A Film from Germany, 215
Hoberman, J., 322
Holdsworth, Elizabeth, 118, 323
Hollander, John, 80
Hollander, Paul, 127, 194, 324
Holmes, John Bright, 74, 120, 320
Holocaust, 31, 159, 160, 288
Holtzbrinck, 259
homosexuality:
    bisexuality and, 27, 134, 148
    "camp" sensibility and, 46, 83–87,
        91, 92, 95, 97, 194–96
    "coming out" and, 92–93, 193, 194,
        269–70
    dandyism and, 195–96

    homophobia and, 105
    militant, 148–49
    politics and, 92–93, 148, 194
Honolulu Star-Bulletin, 207
Hope Against Hope (Mandelstam), 195
Hopkins, Ellen, 312, 313, 340
Horowitz, David, 324
House Committee on Un-American
    Activities, 23
Howard, Gerald, 81
Howard, Richard, 52, 75, 109–10, 193,
    197, 198, 239, 318, 328
Howe, Irving, 99, 100–102, 231, 316,
    322
Hudson Review, 73, 76, 99
Hugo, Victor, 7, 291, 313
Hujar, Peter, 72, 97, 323
    character and personality of, 112–14
    photographic career of, 111–15, 117,
        178, 281
Humanities in Review, 192
Hume, David, 33
Hurston, Zora Neal, 152
Husserl, Edmund, 98
Hutchins, Robert, 25, 26, 29–31, 315
Hyman, Stanley Edgar, 31–32, 69, 315,
    320

"I, Etc." (Chester), 71
I, etcetera (Sontag), 71, 114–15, 164,
    183, 208, 329
    dust jacket photograph for, 202–3
    sales and reviews of, 202, 206
    stories in, 205–7
Illness as Metaphor (Sontag), xi, 172,
    174, 179, 182–85, 266
    content and style of, 183–84, 185
    reviews of, 184–85
Ilych, Ivan, 169
"Image World, The" (Sontag), 181
"Imagination of Disaster, The"
    (Sontag), 100, 283
imperialism, 123, 124, 159
In America (Sontag), 299–301, 302,
    303
Independent, 281, 291
Indiana, Gary, 234, 332
International War Crimes Tribunal, 128
Interview, 247–48

In the Spirit of Crazy Horse
(Matthiessen), 251–52
Invitée, L' (de Beauvoir), 146, 147
Irish Times, 277–78, 292, 295
Irving, John, 251–52
Isherwood, Christopher, 84
Islam, 253
Israel, 159–60
Istoe, 157
Italy, 143, 187–88, 208–9, 329

Jacobs, Jane, 122
Jacobson, Dan, 185
Jacobson, Dora Glasskovitz (grand-
mother), 4
Jacobson, Isaac (grandfather), 4
Jacques and His Master (Kundera), 297
Jaffe, Irv, 46, 317
James, Alice, 298–99, 342
James, Henry, 70, 298
James, William, 298
Jamie Is My Heart's Desire (Chester),
47
Janklow, Mort, 260, 337
Janklow, William J., 251–52
Jenkyns, Richard, 340
Jerusalem, 39, 159
Jesus Christ, 57
Jewish Theological Seminary, 39
Jews:
   anti-Semitism and, 159, 160, 188,
   213, 253
   conscience and consciousness of,
   159–61
   Hasidic, 69
   history and tradition of, 41, 57, 69
   Holocaust and, 31, 159, 160
   "Our Crowd" mentality of, 81
   see also Israel; Sontag, Susan, Jewish
   heritage of
John D. and Catherine T. MacArthur
   Foundation fellowship, xi, 279
John Paul II, Pope, 213
Johns, Jasper, 89, 92, 93, 193
Johnson, Greg, 211–12, 329
Johnson, Richard, 340
Johnson, Samuel, 214
Johnston, Jill, 92–94, 151, 153, 312,
   322, 323, 326, 331

Jones, James, 49
Jong, Erica, 242
Joyce, James, 99, 188

Kael, Pauline, 325
Kafka, Franz, 34, 68
Kahn, Carol, 327
Kaniuk, Yoram, 159–63, 173, 188,
   326, 327
Kaplan, Alice, 317
Karpf, Lila, 73, 120, 147, 320, 323,
   326
Kauffmann, Stanley, 160, 325
Kazin, Alfred, 82, 251–52, 332–33
Keats, John, 178
Kemp, Peter, 340
Kendrick, Walter, 213–14, 228–31,
   329, 331
Kennedy, Edwin J., 184–85
Kennedy, John F., 75, 138
Kennedy, Liam, 76, 102, 320, 322
Kennerly, Karen, 22, 239, 244, 246,
   248–49, 253, 333, 334–36
Kent, Leticia, 316
Kentucky, University of, 80
Kermode, Frank, 216, 330
Khankhoje, Maya, 324
Khomeini, Ayatollah Ruhollah, 252–54
Kimball, Roger, 239, 241–42, 321,
   333, 343
King, Francis, 248–50, 332, 333
King Kong, 85
Kingsley, Amos, 250
Kingsolver, Barbara, 312
Kinsley, Michael, 230
Kipnis, Laura, 330
Kiš, Danilo, 104, 313
Klee, Paul, 22
Kleinberg, Seymour, 53, 316
Kleinschmidt, Hans J., 312
Klinghoffer, Paul, 337
Kluger, Richard, 108–10, 322
Knight, Graham, 341
Koch, Stephen, 113, 193
Koenig, Rhoda, 243, 333, 340
Koenig, Robert L., 334
Koestenbaum, Wayne, 301–2
Kolovakos, Gregory, 251, 337
Komisar, Lucy, 334, 335

Kopkind, Andrew, 123, 124, 194, 221, 270, 323, 328
Korvettes, 119
Kotz, Liz, 326
Kramer, Hilton, 52, 194, 230–31, 277, 318, 331, 338, 341
Kramer, Larry, 250–51, 267–68, 272, 337
Kraus, Karl, 161
Krauthammer, Charles, 254–55, 334
Kresevljakovic, Muhamed, 293
Krim, Seymour, 109, 241
Kundera, Milan, 297, 299, 332
Kung Chen Fur Corporation, 3
Kurland, Joan, 20, 21, 314
Kurzweil, Edith, 319

Lacayo, Richard, 256–57, 281, 339
Lacher, Irene, 339
Ladd, Scott, 334
Ladies' Home Journal, 75
Lambert, Angela, 281, 339, 341
"Lament for Bosnia, A" (Sontag), 289–90
Lamont, Corliss, 122
Lane, Dot, 122, 323
Laos, 123–24, 126
Lapautre, Michelle, 326, 328
Lardner, James, 223, 330
La Rochefoucauld, François de, 79
Larson, Brandon, 262–63, 337
Lasky, Julie, 341
Last of the Nuba, The (Riefenstahl), 164
Laughlin, James, 65
Lawrence, D. H., 41
Leavitt, David, 200–201, 264, 328–29, 337
Lebowitz, Fran, 193, 269–70
Ledger, Marshall, 315
Lehmann-Haupt, Christopher, 337
Leibovitz, Annie, 341
    family background of, 281–82
    photographic career of, 178, 268, 280–82, 290, 300
    SS's relationship with, 178–79, 267–69, 278, 279–82, 290, 300, 304, 328, 339–40
Leigh, Vivien, 283
Lemkhin, Mikhail, 328

Lenin, V. I., 128, 220
Leningrad, 188
Leni Riefenstahl: A Memoir (Riefenstahl), 168
Lennon, John, 88
Leonard, John, 130–31, 213
Lesbian Nation (Johnston), 93–94
Leshing, Sophia, 22, 314
Lesser, Wendy, 304
Levin, Jordan, 343
Lévi-Strauss, Claude, 199
Libre, 148
Liebmann, Dorothea, *see* Straus, Dorothea
Life, xi, 98, 280
"Light That Never Failed, The" (Simon), 231
Lincoln, Abraham, 21
Lindbergh syndrome, 91
Lindgren, Goran, 136–37, 325
Lipscomb, Thomas, 174, 327
Lipset, Seymour Martin, 330
"Literary Agent as Zelig, The" (Bruni), 260
Literary Guild, 119
Little Women (Alcott), 10, 12
Little Women (film), 12
Lives of the Poets (Johnson), 214
Living Theater, 134
London, 88–89, 130, 147
London, Ephraim, 227
London, Jack, 13, 313
London Magazine, 203
London Review of Books, 256
"Looking at the Unbearable: On Francisco Goya" (Sontag), 287
Lorca, Federico García, 23
Lord, James, 135, 277, 324, 338
Los Angeles, University of California at (UCLA), 22, 24
Los Angeles Times, 23
Lottman, Herbert, 320
Low, Robert, 20, 21, 314
Lowell, Robert, 58, 80, 122
Lukas, Anthony, 241
Lydon, Christopher, 274, 338

Macaulay, Robie, 326
McCall's, 75, 151, 154

McCarran-Walter Immigration and Nationality Act, 238
McCarthy, Mary, 61, 63, 67, 76, 79, 152, 226–27
  anti-war stance of, 123–24
  feminism of, 154
  SS compared with, 61, 73, 90, 155, 157, 343
McClintock, James, 210–11, 329
Macdonald, Dwight, 66, 76, 87, 90, 99, 100
McDowell, Edwin, 333, 334
McHenry, Robert, 340
McKee, Douglas, 323
McKeon, Richard, 30–31, 34, 315
Mackrell, Judith, 332
McLemee, Scott, 315, 320, 324, 338
McNally, Judith, 244
McNulty, Rose, 3, 37, 41, 116, 298
McQuade, Molly, 30, 31, 315, 316
McRobbie, Angela, 273
McShane, Larry, 333
Madame Curie: A Biography (Curie), 10–11
Mademoiselle, 82–83, 84, 101, 121
Madison, James, 226
Magic Mountain, The (Mann), 18, 39
Mailer, Adele, 318
Mailer, Norman, 49, 75, 102, 122, 153, 246, 253, 260
  as PEN president, 236–44
  works of, 61, 120, 153, 242
Maitland, Sara, 333
Malamud, Bernard, 122, 156, 246
Maloff, Saul, 105
Malraux, André, 50
Mambo Kings Play Songs of Love, The (Hijuelos), 57
Mandell, Jonathan, 261, 337
Mandelstam, Osip, 195
Manin, Eilenn, 290
Mann, Thomas, 18–19, 28, 153
  SS's meeting with, 19, 32, 314
Mano, D. Keith, 220, 221, 223, 330
Mansfield, Jayne, 113
"Man Who Would Marry Susan Sontag, The" (Field), 48
Mao Tse-tung, 57, 186
Mapplethorpe, Robert, 112, 178, 264–65

Marcus, Greil, 230, 343
Marcuse, Herbert, 38
Margolin, Fred, 20–21, 314
Marilyn (Mailer), 120
Marshall, Judith, 320
Martin Eden (London), 12, 13
Marx, Karl, 40
Marx, Leo, 122, 324
Marxism, 23, 98, 99, 101, 124, 129, 148, 167, 186
Mason, Felicity, 112–13
Mass, Larry, 267–68, 271–72, 318
Matthiessen, Peter, 251–52, 333
Maximes (Rochefoucauld), 79
Mayer, Peter, 202, 329
Mazzocco, Robert, 98
Mead, Rebecca, 260–61
Meade, Marion, 328, 331
Meistersinger, Die (Wagner), 139
"Melancholy Objects" (Sontag), 180
Melville, Herman, 321
Melville, Jean-Pierre, 135–36, 324–25
Memorial-Sloan Kettering Cancer Institute, 171, 172
Merrill Foundation, 103
Metropolitan Opera, 301
Mexico, 129, 135, 169, 178
Mexico City, 129, 138
Meyer, Catharine, 73, 320
Miami Book Fair, 302
Miami Herald, 256, 259–60
Michelangelo, 37
Michigan, University of, 187
Michigan Quarterly Review, 132
Michigan State University, 210
Mid-Century Book Society, 102
Middlemarch (Eliot), 35
Millay, Edna St. Vincent, 13
Miller, Arthur, 174, 211, 237–38, 253, 296, 327
Miller, D. A., 338
Miller, Jonathan, 55, 299, 321
Millet, Kate, 151
Milosz, Czeslaw, 220, 222, 299–300
Minogue, Kenneth, 315
Misalliance (Shaw), 74
Misérables, Les (Hugo), 7
"Mister Pitch" (Mead), 260–61
Mitgang, Herbert, 248, 259

Mobray, Alan, 283
"Modernist Style of Susan Sontag, The"
    (McRobbie), 273
Modern Library, 25, 27
Modjeska, Helena, 299–300
Mondadori, Alberto, 323
Mong, John R., 320
Monroe, Marilyn, xiii, 75, 120, 121,
    132, 136
Monsieur Phot, 95
Montblanc de la Culture Award, xi, 296
Moran, David, 160
Moravia, Alberto, 158
Moreau, Jeanne, 95
Morgan, Frederick, 73, 320
Morillon, Phillipe, 293
Morocco, 79, 82, 105–8, 111
Morris, Willie, 321
Morrison, Toni, 243
Morrisroe, Patricia, 337
Morrone, John, 251, 337
Moscow Purge Trials, 128, 195
Moses and Monotheism (Freud), 34
Mosle, Sara, 340
"Movable Doom, A" (Sontag), 150–51,
    153
Moynihan, Daniel Patrick, 254
Mozart, Wolfgang Amadeus, 16
Ms., 158
    "Abortion Law Repeal" petition of,
        149
Mudrick, Marvin, 230–31
Müller, Ray, 327
Munk, Erika, 292, 294, 295, 341
Murdoch, Iris, 43, 316–17
Museum of Modern Art (MoMA):
    Arbus retrospective photography
        exhibit at, 176–77
    "Fame After Photography" exhibit
        at, 82
    "Family of Man" exhibit at, 114,
        176
My American History (Schulman),
    270–71
Mystery and Manners (O'Connor), 118
Mythology of Transgression, The
    (Highwater), 276
"My Warszawa: 1980" (Oates), 210,
    211–13

Nadeau, Maurice, 94
Naipaul, V. S., 198
Nairn, Tom, 98
Napoleon I, Emperor of France, 198
Narrative of Arthur Gordon Pym, The
    (Poe), 9
Nathan, Monique, 320, 323
Nation, 220, 221–22, 225, 226,
    228–29, 289
National Arts Club, 304
National Book Award, 67
National Book Critics Circle Award for
    Criticism, 182
National Endowment for the Arts, 239
National Mobilization Committee to
    End the War in Vietnam, 128
National Organization for Women
    (NOW), 153
National Review, 220, 221
National University (Mexico City), 129
Navasky, Victor, 225, 226, 229, 248,
    289, 322, 330, 331, 332, 341
Ne'eman, Yuval, 159–60
Neier, Aryeh, 221–22, 226, 331
Nelson, Cary, 118, 323
Nelson, Emmanuel S., 337
Nelson, Lord Horatio, 283–85
New Criterion, 231
New Criticism, 77
New Directions, 65
New Left, 77, 122, 126–27
Newman, Edwin, 136, 139
New Republic, 76, 119, 160, 184–85,
    194–95, 206, 213, 218, 219,
    220
New School for Social Research,
    191
Newsday, 23, 247–48
New Statesman, 98
Newsweek, 211, 277
New York, 231, 260–61, 272–73
New York, N.Y., 3–4, 16, 51–52,
    131–32
    Central Park, 142, 202
    Chelsea, 279–80
    gay life of, 52–54, 56, 92–93, 151,
        193
    Greenwich Village, 32, 53, 95, 131
    hotels of, 108, 110, 238, 246

New York, N.Y. (*continued*)
  publishing and literary world of,
    52–54, 58–67, 75–77, 79–87,
    105–6, 108–10, 133, 224–56
  Town Hall, 122, 153, 218–21, 223,
    330
  Upper West Side, 80, 131, 151
New Yorker, 75, 80, 101, 158, 240, 256,
    257–58, 264
New York Film Festival, 136, 138
New York Herald Tribune, 75–76, 94
  Book Week section of, 108
"New York Intellectuals, The" (Howe),
    99, 102
New York Observer, 178–79
New York Post, 272
New York Public Library, 64, 227, 240
New York Review of Books (*NYRB*), 47,
    48, 60, 67, 75, 79–82, 96, 98,
    101, 119, 176, 190, 214, 304
  inaugural issue of, 79, 82
  SS articles in, 79, 164–68, 175,
    179–80, 182–83, 236, 291, 294
New York Times, 81, 82, 97–98, 121,
    129, 158, 213, 224, 225,
    238–39, 248, 293
New York Times Book Review, 96, 97,
    105, 108, 109, 198
New York Times Magazine, 146, 260,
    270
New York University, xi, 48
  Institute for the Humanities at,
    189–92, 198, 304
Nicaragua, 238
Nichols, Mike, 30, 137
Nietzsche, Friedrich Wilhelm, 40, 41,
    191
Nightwood (Barnes), 27–28, 45
Nijinsky, Vaslav, 143
92nd Street Y, 304
Nobel Prize, 11, 18, 64–65, 150, 161,
    162, 190, 231, 299
Nobile, Philip, 60, 82, 319, 321
Noonday Press, 103
North Atlantic Treaty Organization
    (NATO), 288
North Hollywood High School, 17–24,
    25–26

North Vietnam, 122, 127, 130–31, 220
  SS's trip to, 123–26, 129, 130, 131,
    194, 221, 293, 323–24
  "Notes on 'Camp'" (Sontag), 67, 83–87,
    92, 95, 166, 193–94
  impact and influence of, xi, 71,
    86–87
  opening paragraphs of, 84–85
Nouvelle Revue Française (NRF), 74
Nouvel Observateur, 189
Novak, George, 128–29
Nyheter, Daen, 325

Oates, Joyce Carol, 210–13, 243, 329
O'Brien, Thelma, 312, 313
Occidental College, 24
O'Connor, Flannery, 58, 118
O'Connor, John J., 332
Offit, Sidney, 244, 245–46, 327, 332
"Old Complaints Revisited" (Sontag),
    206, 207
Old Left, 77, 82, 126–27, 152
Olivier, Laurence, 20, 283
Olson, Elder, 30
Olympiad, 164
Olympia Press, 47
Olympic Games, 138, 247
O'Mahoney, John, 342
Omensetter's Luck (Gass), 90
O'Neill, Eugene, 162
On Photography (Sontag), 114, 175–82,
    328
  content and style of, 177–81, 215,
    232
  reviews of, 182
  sales and success of, 182, 183
  writing of, 175–79, 187
"On Style" (Sontag), 67, 96, 98, 107
Order of Arts and Letters, xi
Ortleb, Chuck, 328
Orwell, George, 58
Oslobodjenje, 293
Ostriker, Alicia, 99
Outweek, 269–70, 271
Oxford University, 42–45
Oz, Amos, 241–42
Ozick, Cynthia, 47, 48–49, 79, 107,
    201, 317

Padilla, Heberto, 56, 127–28, 158
Page, Tim, 332
Paglia, Camille, 154–57, 170, 272–75, 326, 338
Paine, Tom, 206
Pais, El, 289
Paley, Grace, 122, 239, 242
Palmer, Andrew, 290, 341
Papp, Joe, 193
Paris, 10–11, 12, 29, 45–50, 60, 70, 80, 81, 130, 171–72, 175–76, 188–89, 326
  bisexual life in, 27, 53, 85
  Café Deux Magots, 147
  writers and artists in, 47–50, 53–54, 146–47
Paris Review, 3, 47, 170
Partisan Review (PR), 16, 47, 61, 75, 76, 80, 81–82, 98, 99–102, 185, 192, 222
  circulation of, 82, 84
  SS's articles and reviews for, xi, 66–68, 71, 83–87, 101, 102, 147–51
  "What's Happening in America" questionnaire in, 123, 124, 148
Partisan View, A (Phillips), 87
Partridge, Eric, 84–85
Pasles, Chris, 332
Pasovic, Harris, 291
PATCO, 219
Pater, Walter, 33, 49
Pathet Lao, 124
Paul, Saint, 39, 40, 57–58, 180
Paulson, Jeanette, 257, 329, 336
PEN, 22, 59, 66, 174, 224–56, 332–36
  American Center of, 218, 237, 246, 247, 249
  Bosnian Center of, 296
  distinguished history of, 237
  International Congress sponsored by, 236–37, 238–43, 244, 245
  literary evenings staged by, 237, 238
  Mailer as president of, 236–44
  Shultz's appearance before, 238–41
  South Korean congress of, 246–50
  SS as president of, 244–56, 262
Penguin Books, 202

Penn, Irving, 89, 121, 231
PEN Newsletter, 241, 247–51
Peretz, Martin, 174, 223, 327
Permanence and Change (Burke), 31
Perron, Wendy, 314
Perrow, Charles, 337
Persona, 130, 135, 136
Phelps, Robert, 98
Philadelphia Inquirer, 230
Philbrook, Peter, 262
philistinism, 99, 100, 123
Phillips, William, 66–67, 79, 81, 82, 84, 87, 101–2, 174, 192, 224, 319, 321, 330
Philosophy of Literary Form, The (Burke), 31
"Photographic Evangels" (Sontag), 181
Picasso, Pablo, 132
Picasso and Dora (Lord), 277
Pickwick bookstore, 16
"Pilgrimage" (Sontag), 13, 257–58
Pima Indians, 8, 117
Pirandello, Luigi, 208–9
Plath, Sylvia, 43
Plato, 31, 33, 99, 178, 181, 185
  cave image of, 176, 180
Playboy, 158
Plimpton, George, 47, 81, 313
PM, 122
Poague, Leland, 310
Pochoda, Philip, 221, 331
Poe, Edgar Allan, 9–10, 68, 70, 71, 117, 207, 215
Poland, xii, 10, 69, 178, 299–301, 329
  Solidarity movement in, 213, 218, 219, 221, 222, 224
  SS's trips to, 210–13, 224, 300–301
Political Pilgrims (Hollander) 127, 194
Pollinger, Gerald, 323
Pollinger, Laurence, 120, 323
Pollitt, Katha, 229, 331
Pomfret, John, 296, 341
"Pornographic Imagination, The" (Sontag), 130, 140
Porter, William, 312
Portraits in Life and Death (Hujar), 111–12
Pound, Ezra, 187–88

Prentice-Hall, 133
Priestley, J. B., 5–6, 312
Princep, Gavrilo, 288
Princeton University, 155, 169, 170
Prisoner of Sex, The (Mailer), 153, 242
"Project for a Trip to China" (Sontag),
    158, 207, 223
Promised Lands, 159–60
Psychology Today, 185
Public Theater, 193, 218–19, 223
Publishers Weekly, 59
Puddington, Arch, 223–24, 330
Purdy, James, 240–41
Puritanism, 176

Queen's Throat, The: Opera,
    Homosexuality, and the Mystery
    of Desire (Koestenbaum),
    301–2
Quinlan, Encarnita V., 261–62

Raban, Jonathan, 131
Rabb, Margo, 319
racism, 5, 138, 159
Radcliffe College, 38
Raddatz, Fritz, 329
radical chic, 146
Rahv, Philip, 76, 81, 101
Ramparts, 126–28
Random House, 58, 272
Rat Bohemia (Schulman), 271
Raw and the Cooked, The (Lévi-
    Strauss), 199
Ray, Kevin, 340
Reader's Digest, 19, 220, 222
"Read-in for Peace in Vietnam," 122
Reagan, Ronald, 219, 238
Rechy, John, 48, 317
Recognitions, The (Gaddis), 58
Red Hot Vacuum, The (Solotaroff), 116
Red River, 20
Reds, 232
Reginato, James, 319
Remnick, David, 333
Renewing the Left (Teres), 268–69
Repeal of Reticence, The (Gurstein), 275
Republic (Plato), 31
Revson, James, 270
Reynolds, Joshua, 284

Rheingold Beer, 65
Rhode Island School of Design, 132
Rice, Anne, 5
Rice, Brian, 327
Rich, Adrienne, 166–67, 273
Richard Halliburton's Complete Book of
    Marvels (Halliburton), 7
Ridgeway, James, 330
Riefenstahl, Leni, 164–68, 327
Rieff, David (son), 88, 89, 127, 128,
    170, 193, 201, 312, 321, 327,
    328, 331
  birth of, 37
  character and personality of, 55–56,
    89, 135, 170
  childhood and adolescence of,
    37–38, 40, 41–42, 44, 46, 51,
    52, 54–56, 88–90, 121, 135,
    150, 193
  custody struggle over, 55, 89–90,
    318
  editorial positions of, 170, 192,
    228–30
  education of, 88, 169, 170
  fictional works of, 135, 170
  journalism career of, 56, 169–70,
    194–95, 287
  Philip Rieff and, 54–55, 90
  SS's relationship with, 37–38, 44,
    46, 47, 52, 54–56, 88–90, 135,
    150, 169–70, 173, 192–94,
    199–200, 216, 247–48
  temporary jobs of, 169
  travel of, 90, 135, 169
Rieff, Philip (husband), 319
  character and personality of, 34–35,
    41, 46, 50, 51
  David Rieff's relationship with,
    54–55, 90
  educational and academic career of,
    34–36, 42, 52, 54–55
  literary works of, 40–41, 46, 51
  SS's relationship with, 29, 34–36,
    37–38, 40–42, 43–44, 46, 50,
    51, 52, 54–55, 89–90, 150,
    151, 272, 299, 315–16,
    317–18
Riesman, David, 26
Ritchie, Donald, 257

Robbe-Grillet, Alain, 147
Roberts, Michael, 336
Roberts, Vera Mowry, 314
Robertson, Allen, 331
Robertson, William, 328, 333
Robinson, Alice M., 314
Robinson, John, 339
Rogan, Helen, 230
Rogart-Roth, Patricia, 23
Rogers, Deborah, 159, 326, 328
Rohwer, Jorn, 331
Rolling Stone, 280, 281
Roman Empire, 40
Romano, Carlin, 319, 327, 333
Romney, George, 284
Room of One's Own, A (Woolf), 298
Roosevelt, Theodore, 65
Rorem, Ned, 85, 193, 328
Rose, Charlie, 293, 341
Roseman, Mel, 16, 20–22, 314
Rosenblatt, Aaron (uncle), 4
Rosenblatt, Gussie Kessler (grandmother), 4
Rosenblatt, Jasky "Jack" (father), 3–5, 312, 313
    early death of, 4, 5, 9, 18
    fur trading business of, 3, 4, 8
Rosenblatt, Mildred, *see* Sontag, Mildred Jacobson Rosenblatt
Rosenblatt, Samuel (grandfather), 4
Rosenheim, Ned, 25, 26, 33–34, 49, 315
Rosenthal, T. G., 326
Roth, Philip, 260
Rothschild family, 136
Roud, Richard, 147
Rousseau, Jean-Jacques, 191
Rowes, Barbara, 312, 313, 315, 318
Royal Road to Romance, The (Halliburton), 7
Ruas, Charles, 228, 229–30, 330, 331
Rudge, Olga, 187–88
Rukeyser, Muriel, 174, 244
R.U.R. (Čapek), 13
Rushdie, Salman, 252–54, 260, 261–62, 333–34
Ruskin, F. R., 323
Russell, Bertrand, 128

Sabbatian heresy, 69
Sael, Rollene, 328
Saevig, Paul, 328
Saffron, Inga, 340
SAGA, 293, 296
Sage, Lorna, 317
Sale, Faith, 248, 249
Sale, Roger, 76
Salisbury, Stephen, 333
Salmagundi, 165
Sandinistas, 238
Sandrews film company, 136–37
San Francisco Chronicle, 168
San Francisco City Arts & Lectures series, 168, 302
San Francisco Film Festival, 168
Sarah, 299
Sarah Lawrence College, 52
Sarajevo:
    multicultural population of, 288, 294
    Serbian siege of, 287–93
    SS's trips to, xi, 274, 287–97, 341, 342
Sarajevo Ground Zero, 296
Sartre, Jean-Paul, 49, 57, 146–47, 158, 189, 221
Satanic Verses, The (Rushdie), 252–54, 261–62
Saturday Review, 16, 75
Sawicka, Elzbieta, 300, 312
Sawyer, Diane, 274
Sayres, Sohnya, 70, 72, 320, 325
Scagliotti, Jack, 194, 270, 277, 323, 328, 338
Scammell, Michael, 335, 336
Scarf, Maggie, 185
Scarry, Elaine, 45
Schlesinger, Arthur, Jr., 75, 153, 320
Schoenman, Ralph, 128, 219, 220, 330
Scholem, Gershom, 214
Schorer, Mark, 27
Schulman, Sarah, 270–72, 275, 338
Schultz, Victoria, 150
Schwab, Joseph, 30, 315
Schwed, Peter, 109
Scott, Janny, 320–21
Screen Actors Guild, 254
Seaton, James, 343
Secker & Warburg, 120, 158

Second Sex, The (de Beauvoir), 37
Sedgwick, Eve Kosofsky, 269, 275–76, 277
Seduction and Betrayal (Hardwick), 167
Seeger, Pete, 219
Segal, David, 322
Selznick, David, 12
Senate, U.S., 254, 333–34
Sennett, Richard, 189–90, 191–92, 198, 319
"Sensational Susan Sontag, The" (Ellmann), 90
Servan-Schreiber, Jean-Louis, 204, 205, 329
sexism, 43, 44, 148
Sexual Personae (Paglia), 154, 156
Shakespeare, William, 58, 298, 299
Shaw, George Bernard, 74
Shaw, Peter, 330
Shawn, William, 158, 326
Sheff, David, 334
Shepro, Harry, 23
Shewey, Don, 318
Shilts, Randy, 337
Shorris, Earl, 26, 315
Show, 84
Showalter, Elaine, 265, 337
Shultz, George, 238–41
"Side by Side with Sontag" (Heller), 277–78
Signorile, Michangelo, 269–70, 338
Silence de la Mer, Le, 136
Silvers, Robert, 47, 67, 80, 81–82, 164, 174, 190, 330
Simon, John, 84, 86, 160, 231, 316, 333, 340
Simon, Scott, 340
Simon, Sherry, 290
Simon & Schuster, 108–10
Singer, Isaac Bashevis, 67–68, 69
"Singleness" (Sontag), 304
Skidmore College, 302
Slaughterhouse: Bosnia and the Failure of the West (Rieff), 287
Slave, The (Singer), 67–68
Slavitt, David, 323
Slung, Michele, 230–31
Smith, George Bruce, 315

Smith, Jack, 98
Smith, Maurice Temple, 120, 323
Snow, C. P., 100
Snow, Shauna, 334
Snow White (Barthelme), 206
Sobran, Joseph, 338
socialism, 7, 10, 32, 99, 127, 148, 159
Socialist Workers Party (SWP), 128, 219
Socrates, 30, 93
Sohmers, Harriet, 27–29, 79, 107, 315, 317, 318, 319, 322, 326
  SS's relationship with, 27–29, 46–47, 49, 53–54
Soho News, 222–27, 230, 330–31
  SS lawsuit against, 224–27, 272
Sokolowski, Thomas W., 323
Sol, Art, 20
Sollers, Philippe, 196–97, 221, 328
Solomon, Deborah, 94–96, 322
Solomon, Harold, 44, 45
Solotaroff, Theodore, 116, 117–18, 121, 246, 250, 333, 334
  Solzhenitsyn, Aleksandr, 187, 328, 335
"Some Thoughts on the Right Way (for us) to Love the Cuban Revolution" (Sontag), 126–27, 128
Sontag, Henriette, 96
Sontag, Judith (sister), 4, 8, 15, 116, 258
Sontag, Mildred Jacobson Rosenblatt (mother), 161, 313
  character and personality of, 5, 14, 18–19, 26, 172, 207, 302
  death of, 257–58
  remarriage of, 14–16
  SS's relationship with, 4–5, 8–9, 18, 22, 26, 27, 37, 41, 312
Sontag, Nathan "Nat" (stepfather), 14–16, 207
  death of, 257
  SS's relationship with, 15–16, 20, 33, 313–14
Sontag, Susan:
  abortion and, 148–49
  academic excellence of, 5, 6, 20, 24, 29, 30, 32, 38–39, 42

alimony and child support rejected by, 52, 150

androgynous appeal of, xii, 43, 44, 46

anthology of quotations about, 305–9

artistic and ideological synthesis sought by, 32

ascetic living environment of, 131

asthma attacks of, 4, 6, 18, 298, 312

birth of, 3–4, 117, 220

cancer diagnosis and treatment of, 171–74, 186, 196, 298, 304, 327, 343

in care of relatives and nannies, 3, 5, 37, 116, 298

censorship deplored by, 252–55

character and personality of, 3, 6, 9–10, 16–17, 27, 29, 35, 37, 40, 44, 55, 70, 72, 91, 100, 103, 108–10, 113, 115, 124, 132–35, 157, 161–62, 170–74, 187–88, 191, 196–97, 199–201, 204–5, 213–14, 218, 223, 252–55, 261–62

childhood and adolescence of, 3–24, 37, 55, 76, 93, 116–17, 143, 144–45, 188, 298, 312–13

colleagues' work supported by, 56–57, 79, 103–4, 105, 108, 161, 192–93

early intimations of a literary career for, 11–13, 16

early literary newsletter published by, 13

entourage of, 77, 173

fame and iconic status of, xi–xii, 16, 60–62, 74–75, 77, 83, 84–92, 93–98, 106, 110, 132–33, 154–55, 197

fascination of caves and tunnels for, 9, 27, 116, 118, 143, 144–45

father figures sought by, 72

feminist status of, 61, 147–53, 165–67

fictional characters based on, 43–44, 48–49, 110–11, 116–17, 196–97, 198–201, 210–13, 250

film appearance of, 231–33

financial concerns of, 131–32, 150

gossip and rumors about, 121–22, 193, 200–201, 280

hair and hair styles of, 22, 33, 38, 73, 82, 88, 89, 94, 120, 172, 190, 202–3, 302, 304

honors and public recognition of, xi, 42, 51–52, 82–83, 121, 132, 182, 185, 279, 293, 296, 338–39, 342

humanitarian work of, xi, 274, 287–97

image-makers attractive to, 111–12

imposing stature and size of, xii, 6, 18, 43–44, 88, 258–59

"intellectual as star" persona of, 133, 146, 151, 154, 157, 162, 192, 204–5

intellectual development and appeal of, xii, xiv, 3, 6–7, 17–24, 28–29, 38–42, 64, 66

interviews with, 3, 4–5, 38, 72, 100, 102, 121, 136, 137–38, 139, 141, 146, 147, 150, 153, 172, 189, 203–5, 212, 214, 228, 229–30, 256–57, 292, 293, 298, 300

Jewish heritage of, 4, 21, 77, 134, 156, 159–63, 188, 194, 210–11, 282, 300–301

lawsuits of, 203, 224–27

leftist leanings and activism of, 7, 56, 58, 77, 93, 122–29, 137, 147–52, 158, 168, 186

literary ambition of, xiii, 11–12, 13, 16, 50, 52, 55, 60–62, 66–67, 89, 90, 115, 147, 162, 211

literary community of, 189–92

literary influences on, 9–13, 17–19, 23, 27–28, 30–33, 47–50, 152–53, 313

mature friendships of, 134, 159–63, 178, 187–90

medical fund raised for, 174

medical reading and study of, 171–72

musical taste of, 16, 21, 315

mysterious and exotic air of, 33, 35, 46, 57, 90

Sontag, Susan (*continued*)
    personal style and clothing of, 21,
        33, 38, 39, 43–44, 45, 52, 77,
        83, 89, 94, 112, 155, 202, 243,
        302–3, 318
    philosophical training and approach
        of, 38–42, 49–50, 77, 84, 161
    photographic memory of, 28, 81
    photographs of, xii, 17, 72, 73–74,
        82–83, 88–89, 91, 94–95, 96,
        97, 112, 120–21, 154, 158,
        176, 178–79, 202–3, 231, 313,
        318, 321, 323, 328
    political awakening of, 7, 18, 19–20,
        23, 122
    political reorientation of, 168,
        186–89, 194–95, 218–27
    postgraduate education of, 38–45
    pregnancy and motherhood of,
        36–38, 41–42, 44, 47
    public persona disclaimed and
        avoided by, 90–92, 121,
        132–33, 152–53, 303
    public school education of, 5, 6–8,
        17–24
    public speaking and lectures of, 20,
        21, 87, 102, 129, 130, 131, 132,
        147, 154–57, 178, 207, 302–3
    reading habits and taste of, 6–8,
        9–13, 16–20, 23, 31–32, 33,
        35, 76, 117, 132, 207, 211, 298
    as role model, 154–57
    screen test of, 82
    self-assurance and poise of, 21, 30,
        38, 44, 60–61, 66, 74, 82, 87,
        162, 298
    self-created image of, xii, xiii, xiv,
        40, 59–60, 68, 162–63, 202–4
    self-promotion of, 11, 60–61, 71, 74,
        101
    Senate testimony of, 254, 333–34
    sexual orientation guarded by,
        152–54, 193, 194, 267–78,
        328, 338
    single-parent status of, 52, 55–56,
        88–90, 135, 150
    striking physical appearance of, xii,
        21, 22, 27, 28, 33, 35, 38, 40,
        43–44, 52, 66, 73–74, 77,
        88–89, 162, 204–5
    teachers and mentors of, 30–33,
        38–40, 42, 69, 80
    teaching positions of, 38, 52–53,
        56–58, 102–3, 189–92, 277
    television and public appearances
        of, 82, 88, 94, 102, 204
    theater experience of, 30, 137,
        208–9, 291–99, 300
    undergraduate college education of,
        11, 25–36, 77, 315
    unqualified approval craved by, 162
    war experiences of, 293
    writing group formed by, 54, 56–57,
        275
    writing habits of, 11, 64, 132, 155,
        175, 197, 256, 263
    youthful friends of, 17–24, 27–28,
        46–49
Sontag, Susan, works of:
    advances and earnings for, 64, 131
    "aesthetics of silence" as key con-
        cept in, 71, 144, 145, 234, 235
    on aging, 150–51, 153–54
    on American popular culture, 49,
        61, 77, 87, 85
    on art and artifice, 49–50, 61, 62,
        85, 98, 114, 131, 143–44
    best sellers among, 183, 235
    college curriculum use of, 183
    controversial and difficult style in,
        64, 65, 68, 177
    on disease, x, 9–10, 172, 174, 179,
        182–85, 261, 264–69
    dust-jacket photographs for, 72,
        73–74, 89, 96, 97, 120, 154,
        178, 202–3, 273
    early examples of, 13, 16, 17, 19–21
    first publishing contract for, 59–61,
        64
    landmark essays, xi, 40, 49, 61, 62,
        67, 71, 83–87, 92, 94, 96–104,
        112, 114, 115, 130–32, 135,
        136, 138, 140, 144, 147–51,
        153–54, 158, 164–68, 175–82,
        193–94, 197, 211, 213–16,
        223, 228–31, 283, 303–4
    "new sensibility" articulated in, 50,
        94, 96, 97, 100, 157

paperback editions of, 58, 76, 77, 80, 91, 102, 103, 112, 131, 183
on photography, xi, 71, 111–12, 114, 147, 172, 175–83, 232
on pornography, xi, 47, 127, 130–31, 140
on science fiction, xi, 97, 100, 283
short fiction, 13, 16, 42, 49, 71, 114–15, 136, 142–43, 147, 156, 158, 183, 205–7
synthesis of high arts and popular culture in, 100–101, 154, 157
theme of bifurcated self in, 136, 151
translation and foreign marketing of, xi, 63–64, 120, 137, 158
as "words that have changed the world," xi, 185
see also specific titles
"Sontag Bloody Sontag" (Paglia), 272
Sorbonne, 45–46, 57
Soundings (Carter), 185
South Carolina, University of, 13
Southern California, University of, 24
Souvanna Phouma, 123
Soviet Union:
  collapse of, 188
  Communist era in, 186–87, 194–95, 218–24
  invasion of Czechoslovakia by, 138
Soyinka, Wole, 64
Span, Paula, 281, 285, 334, 340
Spanish Civil War, 70, 289
"Speaking of Susan Sontag" (Heilbrun), 121
Spectator, 88, 131, 223
Spencer, Charles, 331
Spender, Stephen, 200–201
Spinoza, Baruch, 93
Spiro, George, 341
Spock, Benjamin, 12
Staël, Madame de, 198
Stahel, Urs, 323
Stalin, Joseph, 128, 187, 195, 213, 220
Stallone, Sylvester, 290
Stanford University, 52
  Center for Advanced Study in Behavioral Sciences at, 42
Stansell, Christine, 32, 315

Starkman, Ruth, 327
Starr, Kevin, 314, 315
State Department, U.S., 238, 254
Steichen, Edward, 176
Stein, Elliott, 85
Stein, Gertrude, 99, 274, 304
Stein, Jeannine, 338
Steinberg, Saul and Gayfryd, 245, 333
Steinem, Gloria, 151
Steiner, George, 29, 30, 32, 315
Stendhal (Marie-Henri Beyle), 75
Stéphane, Nicole, 156
  film career of, 135–36, 146, 159
  SS's relationship with, 135–36, 146, 159, 160, 175, 178, 324–25
Stern, Richard, 239–40, 332
Stevens, Elizabeth, 119
Stevens, Mark, 340
Stevenson, Robert Louis, 207
Stieglitz, Perry, 123–24, 126, 323
St. John the Divine Cathedral, 162
St. Louis Post-Dispatch, 254
St. Luke's Hospital, 53
Stonewall riot, 92–93, 154, 269
"Stop the Draft Week," 122
Strasberg, Lee, xiii
Straus, Dorothea, 65–66, 319
Straus, Oscar, 65
Straus, Roger, 58, 59, 64, 65, 68, 74–76, 106, 159, 161, 174, 192, 303, 315, 319, 322, 323, 326, 327, 328, 329, 338
  character and personality of, 64, 65–66
  FSG sold by, 259
  publishing philosophy and style of, 61, 63–66, 81
  SS's career nurtured by, 60–61, 63–66, 75–76, 92, 97, 103–4, 106, 108–10, 119–21, 131, 133, 147, 150, 153, 158, 182–83, 202, 204, 227, 230–31, 233, 259, 320
Strauss, Leo, 30, 31, 32, 93
Strauss, Monica, 328
Student Mobilization Committee, 128
Styles of Radical Will (Sontag), 123, 127, 138, 213
  reviews of, 130–31, 147

Styron, William, 102, 122, 237, 251–52, 253
Sullivan, Jane, 21
surrealism, 50, 94, 95, 108, 180
"Susan's Addiction," 179
Susan Sontag Reader, A (Sontag), 183, 227, 228–30
  reviews of, 228–29, 230
Swan Lake, 85, 95
Sweden, 71, 120, 136–37, 143
Swedish Film Institute, 137
Syberberg, Hans-Jurgen, 215
"Syberberg's Hitler" (Sontag), 215, 216–17

Talese, Gay, 237, 243, 253
Tallmo, Karl-Erik, 325
Talmud, 34
Tanaka, Min, 342–43
Tanner, Marcus, 341
Tanner, Tony, 116, 117
Taubes, Ethan, 142
Taubes, Jacob, 39–40, 47, 54, 56–58, 141, 142, 180, 316, 318–19
Taubes, Susan, 40, 56, 142, 143, 144, 316, 325
Taylor, Benjamin, 206
Taylor, Joan Garner, 22, 314
Taylor, Paul, 332
Teams, Louise, 314
Tel Quel, 186, 196, 221
Teres, Harvey, 268–69, 321, 343
Terhune, Alfred Payson, 6–7, 117
Terpstra, Marin, 58, 318
Terzieff, Laurent, 143
Thackeray, William Makepeace, 8
That Hamilton Woman, 283
Thek, Paul, 114–15, 266, 323
Theroux, Paul, 198
These Three, 93
"Third World of Women, The" (Sontag), 147–51, 166–67
Threepenny Review, 304
Three Sisters, The (Chekhov), 51
Thresholds (Straus), 65–66
Tiananmen Square massacre, 129
Tillich, Paul, 38, 42
Tillman, Lynne, 313
Time, 66, 86, 91, 157, 256–57
Times (London), 292–93

Timmerman, Jacobo, 330
Toback, James, 324
Tobias, Tobi, 343
Tokyo Rose, 188
Tonkin, Boyd, 342
Toole, David, 295
Towards a Better Life (Burke), 32
Trilling, Diana, 153, 174, 222
Trilling, Lionel, 23, 66, 76–77, 101, 152, 191, 320, 322, 343
Trip to Hanoi (Sontag), 122–26, 127, 128, 130–31, 137, 140, 211
Tristman, Richard, 56–57, 68, 89, 154, 173, 274–75, 316, 318, 326, 327
Triumph of Will, 164
Trollope, Anthony, 265
Trotsky, Leon, 128, 138
Trueheart, Charles, 252–53, 333, 334
Trump, Donald, 237
Tucker, Martin, 325
Tucker, Neely, 341
Tucson, Ariz., 5–16, 116–17
Tumarkin, Peter, 316
Turow, Scott, 65, 66, 319
Tuten, Frederic, 189, 277
Twain, Mark, xiii
Tyler, Anne, 206

UAW, 219
UCLA (University of California at Los Angeles), 22, 24
Under the Sign of Saturn (Sontag), 183, 211, 213–17, 260, 329–30
  essays in, 214–17
  reviews of, 213–14, 216–17, 230
"Under the Sign of Saturn" (Sontag), 214
Unfinished Woman, An (Hellman), 149
Unguided Tour (film), 233–35
"Unguided Tour" (Sontag), 207, 233
United Nations, 19, 288
United States Information Service (USIS), 123, 210
Unsworth, Mike, 325
Updike, John, 240, 253, 264
Urbanski, Marie Olesen, 342

Vamps and Tramps (Paglia), 156
Van Biema, David, 339–40, 341

van Gogh, Theo, 188
van Gogh, Vincent, 188
Vanity Fair, 231, 274, 280, 281, 291
Vargas Llosa, Mario, 241–42
Venice Biennale on Dissent, 187
Venice Film Festival, 136
Vernon, James, 340
Victor, Tom, 202, 203
Victory (Conrad), 32
Vidal, Gore, 48, 82, 102, 107, 108,
    117, 131, 219, 317, 322, 323
Viet Minh, 123–24
Vietnam, North, *see* North Vietnam
Vietnam Moratorium Day, 155
Vietnam War, 129
  opposition to, 122–26, 128
Viking, 251
Viking Penguin, 261
Village Voice, 70, 92, 190, 213, 224–25
Visiting Cards (King), 250
Visser, Hripsime, 323
Vogue, 74, 75, 101, 146, 204
  "People Are Talking About" column
    in, 86, 88–89, 90
  SS articles in, 168, 204
  SS photographed by, 121, 154
Voice Literary Supplement, 230
Volcano Lover, The (Sontag), 18,
    282–86, 299, 300, 304, 340
  as best seller, 235, 286
  dust jacket photograph for, 178, 281
  origins of, 282–83
  promotion of, 270, 274
  SS's ambitions as a writer fulfilled
    in, 285
  story line of, 72, 179, 235, 283–86
  writing of, 257
Volkov, Solmon, 328
von Dassanowsky, Robert, 327
Vonnegut, Kurt, 219, 237, 251–52
Vorlicky, Robert, 342
Vursell, Hal, 60

Wachel, Eleanor, 340
Wagner, 139, 215
Wain, John, 76
Waiting for Godot (Beckett), 53, 116
  SS's Sarajevo staging of, 291–97
Wakerman, Elyce, 313
Walcott, Derek, 65, 80, 190, 321, 328

Wald, Alan M., 128, 324
Wallace, Henry A., 18, 122
Walman, Milton, 69, 320
Walser, Robert, 104
Walt, Vivienne, 334
War and Peace (Tolstoy), 89
Warburg, Fred, 63
Warhol, Andy, 82, 89, 247
Warner, Marina, 196
Warrick, Pamela, 317
Washington Post, 121, 183, 223, 252
Wasserman, Harriet, 233, 260, 331,
    337
"Way We Live Now, The" (Sontag),
    264–66, 337
Webb, Sidney and Beatrice, 122, 195
Weil, Simone, 76
Weinstein, Tresca, 343
Wells, H. G., 134
We Must Love One Another or Die: The
    Life and Legacies of Larry
    Kramer (Mass), 267–68
Wenkart, Henny, 39, 316, 327
West, James, 124
West, Mae, 84
West, Nathanael, 59
"Western Half, The" (Sontag), 256–57
"What's Happening in America"
    (Sontag), 123, 124, 148
Whistler, James Abbott McNeill, 203
White, Edmund, 191–201, 271, 328,
    329, 331
  David Rieff and, 193, 199–201
  literary career of, 192–94, 196,
    197–201
  SS and, 192–201, 204, 208, 209,
    245
Whitehead, Bill, 201
White House, 18, 75
Whitman, Walt, 180
Who's Who in America, xi
"Why I Hate Susan Sontag" (website),
    112
Wieseltier, Leon, 222–23, 253, 330
Wilde, Oscar, 49, 55, 83–84, 86
Wilson, Ann, 323
Wilson, Edmund, 58, 63, 76, 319, 343
Wilson, Mark, 207, 329
Wilson, Robert, 234–35, 342
  SS's collaboration with, 234

Wolcott, James, 274
Wolfe, Tom, 237
Women (Leibovitz), 268
Women (Sollers), 196–97, 221
Women's Hospital, 3
Women's National Book Association, xi, 185
Wood, Natalie, 89
Woolf, Virginia, xiii, 152, 298
World Association of Authors (WAA), 250
World Friendship Oratorical Contest, 21
World in the Evening, The (Isherwood), 84
World War I, 11, 32, 237, 288
World War II, 13, 15, 66, 159
"Writers Talk Among Themselves" (Sontag), 236

Wyler, William, 93
Wylie, Andrew, 259–61, 337

Yale University, 154, 155, 292
"Year of the Ox, The," 147
Yeats, William Butler, 41
Yom Kippur War, 159, 160
York, Peter, 204, 329
Young Socialist Alliance (YSA), 128–29
Yourcenar, Marguerite, 340

Zappa, Frank, 230
Zelig, 231–33
Zimmer, Elizabeth, 343
Zionism, 159
Zito, Tom, 331